The Tragedy of the Vietnam War

The Tragedy of the Vietnam War

A South Vietnamese Officer's Analysis

VAN NGUYEN DUONG

McFarland & Company, Inc., Publishers
Jefferson, North Carolina, and London

Library of Congress Cataloguing-in-Publication Data

Duong Van Nguyen, 1934–
The tragedy of the Vietnam War :
a South Vietnamese officer's analysis / Van Nguyen Duong.
p.   cm.
Includes bibliographical references and index.

ISBN 978-0-7864-3285-1
softcover : 50# alkaline paper ∞

1. Vietnam War, 1961–1975 — Personal narratives, Vietnamese.
2. Duong Van Nguyen, 1934–   I. Title.
DS559.5.D853   2008   959.704'3 — dc22   2008024226

British Library cataloguing data are available

Cover photograph: A cross dangling from her neck,
a 12-year-old girl with multiple wounds uses a stick
to hobble through battle debris to an evacuation helicopter
in South Vietnam, June 19, 1965 (AP Photo/Horst Faas)

Manufactured in the United States of America

*McFarland & Company, Inc., Publishers
Box 611, Jefferson, North Carolina 28640
www.mcfarlandpub.com*

Acknowledgments

My father once said to me, "To become a dignified career soldier, you'd better not only look to fight your enemy but also stick with your colleagues in the army and devote yourselves to the service and care of unfortunate people who suffer physical and spiritual losses in this cruel and destructive war. Never associate with people who compete for power."

During the war in Vietnam I did my best to realize my father's instructions, but I failed, as we soldiers of the Republic of Vietnam Armed Forces were forced to give up our arms on a tragic day in April 1975.

Now, more than three decades after the end of the war, I still think of my old friends and colleagues among the millions in that valiant army, including those who sacrificed their lives on the battlefield, those who still endure a miserable existence in Vietnam under the cruel communist regime, and those who are in exile overseas. I am trying in another way to contribute by writing this book with the intent of making clear the nuances of our defeat and of amplifying the just and noble causes of South Vietnamese soldiers who fought against the Vietnamese communists in that critical war. We maintain our pride of having once served in our armed forces to pursue aspirations of independence, justice, and freedom for our people. An army may be disbanded but its spirit is eternal. Such is the case of the Republic of Vietnam Armed Forces.

RVNAF soldiers were trusted, admired, and loved by the people of South Vietnam. Their heroic images are engraved on my memory and inspired me to document their merits and glories as well as their sufferings. They fought for the people, but they were betrayed by their political leaders and their cunning allies, and then treated cruelly by their enemy. These events all made them suffer deeply. Any story of a South Vietnamese soldier and his family has the power to bring forth emotion and tears from virtuous and humane people.

First and foremost, I would like to thank all South Vietnamese soldiers and express my highest admiration and respect for their sacrifices and devotion to the country. I would like to also express my heartfelt gratitude to my parents for their clear-sighted instructions and profound love.

I am also grateful to four of my friends who helped me in the past ten years: Cung Tram Tuong, Do Ngoc Uyen, Sao Bien, and Nguyen Cau.

In addition, I would certainly like to express my gratitude for the advice and support of Professors Nguyen Xuan Vinh, Nguyen van Canh, and Pham van Phuc. Deep thanks are also conveyed to Todd and Kim Elvyn and Gordon Yamaguchi. Without their help I could not have realized and completed my work.

Finally, I would like to thank my lovely wife, who has endured her humble life while encouraging me, believing that I would satisfactorily finish my exhaustive work. She is the constant and profound source of love and assistance in my life.

Again, thank you all.

Table of Contents

Preface

Good policies and well planned strategies, as well as economic and military strengths, usually determine the outcome of conflicts between opposing forces. Paradoxically, the Vietnam War defied this established rule. Public opinion contended that the United States, after committing to the Vietnam War for almost a decade, might not want to subdue the underdog Democratic Republic of Vietnam (or the Communist North Vietnam) by military force due to several internal problems and international and diplomatic reasons. However, the realities of signing the 1973 Paris Peace Treaty with the Vietnamese Communists, withdrawing combat forces from Vietnam, abandoning a longtime ally — the Republic of Vietnam (or the Free South Vietnam) — and finally rescuing the remaining military personnel and diplomatic corps by "Operation Frequent Wing" (helicopters) on top of the U.S. Embassy building just hours prior to the final Communist attack on Saigon, led to the contradictory interpretation that the United States had lost the war in Vietnam. This was a paradox. And this paradox remains a mystery of American foreign policies toward Southeast Asia and Vietnam during that period and has kindled numerous debates, discussions, and symposiums for decades after the war's end. Historians, observers, politicians, and strategists have microscopically dissected American policies and strategies in Vietnam as carried out by several presidents. However, no satisfactory answer has emerged.

After suffering with shame and confusion day and night for thirteen years in different communist concentration camps after the fall of South Vietnam in April 1975, I became determined to penetrate to the heart of these matters to clarify the dark hints in my mind.

I was released from the communist concentration camps in April 1988 and came to America in September 1991. This was a blessed opportunity for me to realize my longing for clarity. After seven years of study and research, I began to write my book. First of all, I saw the United States as committed to the war, but without the will to win it. Thus, the "Vietnam War" seemed to be "illogical," and I call it an "Off-Design War." Then, for five continuous years, I put everything that I objectively knew about the war into my book.

In addition, I wanted to share some war experiences with younger Vietnamese generations in exile to elucidate important issues, such as the fighting competence of the South Vietnamese Armed Forces. In my opinion, the Republic of Vietnam Armed Forces (RVNAF) would have ultimately defeated the North Vietnamese Army (NVA) or the People's Army of Vietnam (PAVN) of Communist North Vietnam in this long and difficult war if only we had been continuously supported by the United States as the PAVN was supported by both the Soviet Union and China. Neither the French Expeditionary Forces nor the American forces could have done this, since this kind of war, in which time was the decisive factor, would not be suitable to any free-world nation. (Recently, the "war on terror" has been based on the sensitive factor of space. Yet, this has also proven to be a big problem for free-world nations, especially the United States and Britain.)

I had an intense desire to write a book on the war in Vietnam because I was one among millions of South Vietnamese soldiers who had endured it and suffered its destructions, both materially and spiritually. I would like to expose our lonely distress and resentment so the world can become more aware of the pains of those millions of anonymous South Vietnamese soldiers who had sworn to give their lives to protect their land, their democracy, and their national colors. Tens of thousands of RVNAF heroes fought and sacrificed on the battlefield to safeguard freedom for South Vietnam and prosperity for other nations in Southeast Asia.

Yet, after all our sacrifices, RVNAF soldiers suffered bitterly. Immediately after the war's end, 200,000 of us were sent to communist concentration camps for years and thousands died of exhaustion from hard labor, hunger, and illnesses, or were killed by torture and execution without any sound resonating from these camps. Also, more than 300,000 former disabled veterans and wounded soldiers were chased out of their military sanatoriums and hospitals when the communists victoriously came into the South. Moreover, a few months later, the graves of our heroes at the military cemeteries in Saigon, Bien Hoa, and throughout the South were dug up and the remains discarded so these plots could be used for the burial of communist soldiers. That vindictive behavior of the communists was cruel and inhuman. We suffered our pains in silence. This was tragic.

However, the outcome of the war would lead to greater tragedy for the Vietnamese people. In fact, after the reunification of the country under the dogmatic communist regime, people had to endure more misery and suffer more misfortunes, particularly in South Vietnam. Immediately after the war's end, millions of people lost their properties and were arrested or forced to resettle in hundreds of "new economic sites" in remote areas around the country. Millions of others tried to flee from their homeland and a third of them disappeared under the waves of the Pacific Ocean or in the forests of Indochina. Moreover, tens of millions of other citizens had to endure excessive poverty after the Vietnamese communist leaders sent their troops to invade Cambodia and to wage war against China in the late 1970s.

Most of these previously mentioned issues are traced and related in this book. I invite young American and Vietnamese readers to join me on the journey back to our interrelated history during the three decades since 1944. Perhaps many young American readers would desire to know why the United States committed to the war in this faraway country, Vietnam. Perhaps young Vietnamese in exile would like to better understand why South Vietnam lost that bitter war. To answer these questions requires us to review United States policies toward Southeast Asia under several administrations and to review the development of the Vietnam War since its beginning. It is my hope that the long journey will provide clarity for the reader as it has for me. I want to also mention that I restrained myself to a minimum from referencing Vietnamese communist documents, books, chronicles, records, and especially Hanoi leaders' and generals' speeches, writings, or memoirs, which I believe are rewritings of history, exaggerations, or lies.

However, before starting on the path to that sorrowful past, as a refugee among millions of South Vietnamese who are scattered around the world, I would like to express my deepest gratitude to the people and government of the United States and other nations of the free world. Despite the tumultuous past, these nations have given us great opportunities to reshape our lives.

Abbreviations

AFC	Armed Forces Council of South Vietnam
AID	U.S. Agency for International Development
ARVN	Army of the Republic of Vietnam (South Vietnam)
CBUs	Cluster Bomb Units
CCP	Chinese Communist Party
CENTO	Central Treaty Organization
CIA	Central Intelligence Agency (U.S.)
CIDG	Civilian Irregular Defense Group
CMAG	Chinese Military Advisory Group
COSVN	Central Office of South Vietnam (or the Communist High Command Headquarters of all Communist Forces in South Vietnam)
CP	Command Post
CPAG	Chinese Political Advisory Group
DAO	Defense Attaché Office (U.S.)
DOD	Department of Defense (U.S.)
DRVN, or DRV	Democratic Republic of Vietnam (North Vietnam)
FANK	Forces Armées Nationales Khmères, or Cambodian National Armed Forces
FRAC	First Regional Assistance Command in ARVN I Corps and Region (U.S.)
GI	A member of U.S. Armed Forces, especially an enlisted person (GIs: U.S. soldiers)
GVN	Government of Vietnam (South Vietnam)
FPJMT	Four-Party Joint Military Team
JGS, or RVNAF-JGS	Joint General Staff of the Republic of Vietnam Armed Forces (South Vietnam)
ICC	International Control Commission in South Vietnam
ICP	Indochinese Communist Party
MAAG-Vietnam	Military Assistance Advisory Group Vietnam (U.S.)
MACV	Military Assistance Command, Vietnam (U.S.)
MATA	Military Advisory Training Assistance (U.S.)
MEDTC	American Military Equipment Delivery Team, Cambodia (U.S.)
MIA/KIA	Missing in Action/Killed in Action
MIG	A Russian-Built Fighter Aircraft
M5-TEAM	Mission #5, French Intelligence Team in Kunming, China, in 1945
NATO	North Atlantic Treaty Organization
NCO	Non-Commissioned Officer

NLF	National Liberation Front, or the Communist Organization in South Vietnam
NSC	National Security Council (U.S.)
NVA, or PAVN	North Vietnamese Army, or the People's Army of Vietnam
OPLAN-34A	Operation Plan 34A (U.S.)
OPLAN-37–64	Operation Plan 37–64 A Bombing Scenario Against North Vietnam (U.S.)
OSS	Office of Strategic Services
PAVN	People's Army of Vietnam
PLA	People's Liberation Army
PRC	People's Republic of China
PRG, or PRGSV	Provisional Revolutionary Government of South Vietnam (Communist Government in South Vietnam)
PT-Boat	Patrol Torpedo Boat
PTF-Boat	Patrol Torpedo Fast Boat
POW	Prisoner of War
RVN	Republic of Vietnam (South Vietnam)
RVNAF	Republic of Vietnam Armed Forces
SAC	Strategic Air Command (U.S.)
SAM	Surface to Air Missile
SEATO	South East Asia Organization
SMM	Saigon Military Mission (U.S.)
SSPL	Sacred Sword Patriot's League
TAC	Tactical Air Command (U.S.)
374th-TAW	U.S. 374th Tactical Air Wing
TCK-TND	Tổng-Công-Kích/Tổng-Nổi-Dậy, or Communist Total Offensive and General Uprising Campaign
TRIM	Training Relation Instruction Mission (U.S.)
U.S., U.S.A.	The United States of America
USOM U.S.	Overseas Mission
USSR	Union of Soviet Socialist Republics
VC	Việt-Cộng, or the Communists in South Vietnam
VCI	Việt-Cộng Infrastructure
VNAF	Vietnam Air Force (South Vietnam)
VNN	Vietnam Navy (South Vietnam)
VNQDD	Việt Nam Quốc Dân Đảng or the Vietnam Nationalist Party

1

The Spirit of the Land

The ups and downs of nations and empires as well as the lives and deaths of humans are at the mercy of God. But this does not stop our tears in the face of heart-rending disaster, calamity, or death. Since the beginning of time, war has brought more tears to human eyes than any other catastrophe.

When I was a child, I witnessed firsthand the shedding of tears from war. I saw killing and burning and fear, and I will now tell the truth of that bitter war beginning with my dreary memories of disaster in my small town and the war's destruction of my country.

I was born on January 8, 1934, among the dark rice fields and virgin forests of a remote village in Camau District, the corner of the farthest peninsula in South Vietnam. My father was a farmer and my mother a homemaker. I have two elder brothers, an older sister, and a younger sister. My family belonged to the middle class; my father owned nearly one hundred hectares of fertile land — about four hundred U.S. acres. He had a modest education that enabled him to speak French and to write the difficult Chinese characters.

The war in Vietnam began in December of 1946. But it had been smoldering several years before that. At about the same time I first began to notice my own existence and I became aware of a world even larger than the love of my family.

THE FIRST LESSONS IN HISTORY

Before the summer of 1944, I spent my whole childhood on my family's rice field. I ran and played games with other children without thinking of much else. Then I and the other third-grade students in our village began our first lessons in history. Our teacher, an old but clear-headed man, taught us about love for other people, and about the "spirit of the land," the "foreign domination," "independence," and the "war." I had only a foggy notion of what my teacher was telling us. But one day, I suddenly felt that the rice field itself had been concealing a marvelous and passionate force. This force sounded in me on sunny days when I heard the wind fleeing on the blades of the rice plants, when the chants and riddles of the peasants trilled the air, and even on rainy nights with the raindrops falling on the foliage and the chirps of the crickets lulling from the plain. I began to love the rice field, not because it belonged to my father but because that land probably had its own means of pleasure and sadness. All lured me to come every day, sunny or rainy.

Day after day, I observed that the sun always rose in the east and set in the west. However, many days it did not appear. On those days when it rained, the sky was covered with dark clouds and the field was overcast, wet, and dreary. Night often fell with the heavy thunderstorms of the monsoon. On many days I spent hours waiting for the sun. In my little mind, I thought that it was still sleeping in the east because my teacher had once lamented, "Now the sun has set, but why in the East?"

One day in class I suddenly understood what his words meant. He taught us "You know, the elementary history book teaches us 'nos ancêtres sont des Gaulois.' But, I tell you the Gauls were the ancestors of the French, not of us. Our ancestors were the Lạc-Việt. We are in the East; the French are in the West. The men from the West came here to plunder the prosperity and the spirit of the land — our ancestors' land. They took away our independence." This was my awakening; and then I began to understand more things.

After many rainy monsoon days, the sun reappeared and brought its brightest light to the rice field. I admired its colored radiance, but I felt something was missing. The sunlight was there. The rice field was the same, except that the young rice stems grew taller and turned into a darker shade of green. There was nothing tangible missing, but something was indeed gone. I guessed that was the spirit of the land — perhaps our independence — but the feeling was still vague to me. One thing I knew. I became fonder of the rice field, every stem of rice, every piece of land, and every bank of earth. I loved all people, all the buffaloes, the birds, and every living thing around me. On windy mornings I often contemplated the beautiful waves of paddies running far to the horizon and at sunset I watched the herons flying in the shape of a reverse V with the leader pointed ahead, fluttering and disappearing in the skyline. My emotions were in flux, but I had a growing compulsion to know things beyond my sight. I did not realize that I had a "thirsty soul." I often asked the elders what was beyond the horizon. Many told me: "It is just like here!" My father laughed and said: "Heaven or Hell!" Only my teacher complained: "War and more war; war from the ancient times. They still fight now for their reasons, in Europe and in the Pacific. One day you are going to grow bigger, you might fight for your reasons." I did not know exactly where Europe and the Pacific were, or what the war was or why it was being fought.

A decade later, I began to fathom the scope and the dimension of the Second World War from the West to the East, perceive the causes and effects of this massive conflict, and differentiate the reasons why the worldwide powers had to fight. I realized and ascertained that my old teacher at my home village's school was a compatriot.

In the summer of 1944, my family moved to our town house, newly built, in Camau City. My mother opened a business and my older sister and I continued our education at the city's primary school. One morning in September of 1945, we heard a commotion coming from the soccer field across the street from our classroom. Our teacher went out to look, and came back moments later shouting: "Independence! Independence! Vietnam independence!" and "Out! Out! All of you out to join them. We have independence!" Immediately, all students from our class and other classes poured out. We crowded the street and most of us ran to the soccer field shouting, "Independence! Independence! Long live Vietnam! Long live independence!" We were deeply moved. Most of us were crying. My eyes were blurry with tears.

We joined hundreds of people who had been in the soccer field. We continued to shout and celebrate with them. How lovely and precious was the word "independence" that I had heard from my teacher! At that very moment, I thought I could see it, touch it and grasp it. Was my feeling wrong? A meeting was held to celebrate our independence led by a group of people unknown to me. Some came up to a newly made podium to talk to the crowd and lead it in shouting hurrah. We did not know who they were and what they were talking about, but we did not mind. We cheered with joyful emotion. We cried and we laughed. By afternoon, the meeting exploded into a massive parade that lasted until midnight. It seemed that thousands of people left their homes in town and happily joined in. We marched through the streets carrying a forest of flags, banners, slogans, lamps, and torches. Our small city radiated with light and color, joy, excitement, and animation. No one could say how many times we marched around the city and how many times we exclaimed, "Long live Vietnam! Long live independence!" This sudden display of enthusiasm and elation by the masses in our small town illustrated how much we loved our country and wanted independence.

Unfortunately, we were not to enjoy independence very long. Two weeks later the communists — the group who had led the last meeting and parade of independence — began to turn victory into tragedy. Two months later the French returned and plundered it from us again.

After that exhilarating day of independence, the communists began to form committees to rule the city, to censure every family, and to monitor each individual suspected of having had close relations with the French and the Japanese. Communist guerrillas began to arrest, torture, and execute suspected collaborators (called "Việt-gian"). Some executions were performed by shooting but most people were drowned alive (called "Mò-Tôm"). The first victim was the district chief of police, a martial arts master, who had had close relations with the Japanese when they came to town in March. He was executed by gunfire under the city bridge one morning in mid–September. In the following days, many former employees of the colonial government were arrested and tortured or executed. I learned that my old village teacher was also arrested and executed. I profoundly mourned his death. This patriot and moral master who had devoted his whole life to teaching history and sowing seeds of knowledge and love for our country was unjustly killed by the communist butchers.

Only two days after the independence parade, my father disappeared. In 1921, he married my mother in Saigon. In 1922, the couple moved to the Mekong Delta to become farmers and owners of a small parcel of cultivated land at Thai Binh Village. There, they lived quietly and happily until the summer of 1944. Because my mother moved to Camau City, my father had to commute from the countryside into town. He retained our beautiful house and our productive land in my natal village. In the summer of 1945, feeling that he could not peacefully live with the communists, my father slipped out of their clutches and fled. I did not know the reason.

I also did not understand why the communists hated the indigenous Cambodian monks so violently. Many were arrested and executed by "Mò-Tôm" in bundles of three, four, or five at a time. Several days later, the bundles of corpses emerged from the bottom of the river and drifted along the waters.

The communists were expert not only in the art of killing, but they also excelled in propaganda and in the collection of money. With the slogan of "A Week for Gold to Save the Country in Danger," the communists in Camau District collected a fabulous fortune of gold and money from the city residents through this so-called "Voluntary Donation." Under the rules of the communists, independence apparently meant killing and extortion.

Besides suffering the malevolence of the communists, the residents of our small city faced another fear. The French returned to Saigon in mid–October and their pacification forces had launched southward of the peninsula. They reoccupied its lowlands from Tan-An, My-Tho, Ben-Tre, and Vinh-Long to Can-Tho Province. Panic spread over Camau District as we heard gruesome news. The French forces, when coming down to Soc-Trang and Bac-Lieu Provinces, brought with them hundreds of indigenous Cambodians formed into "partisan units," which then massacred innocent Vietnamese, included women and children as they marched through city and countryside. These cruel wholesale slaughters — called "Cáp-Duôn" — were considered to be acts of revenge for the killing by the communists of their respected Buddhist leaders. Indeed, as the Vietnamese communists sowed the wind, the Vietnamese innocents reaped the whirlwind.

WAR, EVACUATION, AND DESTRUCTION

In the midst of these fearsome circumstances people around the city prepared to evacuate to the countryside. The communist "Administrative Committee" of Camau District changed its name to the "Committee for Resistance and Administration." The new committee ordered all residents of the town to evacuate and everything to be burned by the guerrillas in a "scorched earth policy" to fight against the French (Sách-lược Tiêu-Thổ Kháng-Chiến, chống Pháp).

At the end of November 1945, my family — composed of my mother, my two sisters, and me — was forced to flee to the coast in a small boat. The night we left our home the city was torched. After traveling several miles on the waterway, I looked back to see a large column of bright flame tearing the dark sky over the city. We knew that the town and our house were burning. We cried in silence. Only my mother spoke: "We lost our house in town, but we still have our village house and you will meet your father and your brothers. God bless them."

My two elder brothers, who had been attending the second cycle of education at Phan Thanh Gian College in Can-Tho, became stuck at Bac-Lieu provincial city on their way home and could not join us. They and some of their classmates joined with the communist "Committee for Resistance and Administration" of Bac-Lieu Province and ran with its members to some remote area.

During that critical period, youth in South Vietnam faced hard choices: to stay in town and work for the French, perhaps to be killed by the indigenous Cambodians, or to join the communists to fight against the French. My two elder brothers chose the latter path.

For nearly three months, my family's boat wandered deserted waterways in the Dam-Doi and Nam-Can areas. Finally, we followed the Ong-Doc and Trem Rivers back to Thai-Binh, our natal village. Unfortunately, we could not resettle in our house because the communist guerrillas had occupied it as their head office. We had to live temporarily at the home of one of my father's relatives, located deep in the U-Minh forest. Only members of a few residential families could reach it so we were safe for a time.

Fortunately, my father and my eldest brother were able to follow and rejoin us at great peril from both the French and the communists before Tết (Lunar New Year) of 1946. Only my second brother was still allied with the communist "Committee for Resistance and Administration" of Bac-Lieu Province, where he remained for two more years.

Due to his detailed knowledge of the region, my father was able to evacuate our family safely to several areas in U-Minh forest where we avoided danger for one and a half years, before returning to Camau City in mid–August 1947. By that time, the French had changed their policy and called for the people to return to their cities and towns to reestablish their normal lives. Most families had no choice but to return to their hometowns; the nomadic jungle life, full of uncertainty, sudden evacuation, and little subsistence, was too much for anyone.

Most who resettled into their hometowns faced problems and could not easily recover their losses from the previous years of evacuation. Many had lost family members in addition to homes and property. In Camau City, three quarters of public buildings were destroyed, included the hospital and the beautiful primary school. Ninety percent of private homes had been burned down since the day the communists began their scorched earth policy. The northern bank of Canal 16, where our town house had been located, had become a wasteland covered with weeds and bushes. People begin their lives again, from scratch. Like our fellow citizens, my family suffered the loss of both our homes and all assets and properties, including a few hundred hectares of uncultivated land in my natal village which had become the communist guerrillas' lair.

Nevertheless, life continued for everyone despite the hindrances and the developing communist guerrilla warfare. My father rented a small house on the outskirts of town and created a forging furnace as a temporary means of subsistence for my family. Thus, a rich and happy farmer before the war became an empty-handed and humble forger in a devastated town. My eldest brother and I had to help him in his hard work. As a result, I could not return to primary school, which had temporarily been built on its former foundation with scrap wood, bamboo, and thatches.

However, we could no longer live in this new home because the communists began to increase their nightly executions of suspected "Việt-gian" by "Mò-Tôm." They threatened to kill all who had any contact whatsoever with the French. My father decided to move my family to Bac-Lieu provincial city in November 1947. There, he applied for a job at the provincial police station and became a police officer, second to the provincial chief of police. My eldest brother had a job at the provincial office of administration and I went back to primary school.

Many in our small town moved to larger cities in search of better livelihoods. But most residents continued to live in this small city and witnessed more changes to its face, while remembering its now-ruined images and its now-wounded soul. One of them was my second brother. Indeed, after he fled from the communist embrace in December of 1948, he returned to Camau City where he has lived to this day. Now, at age seventy-eight, he can tell us the most moving remembrances of the ups and downs of this small city.

In this sorrowful narrative I can tell only a fraction of what occurred in our city during the very first years of the Vietnam War. At that time, as a child, I did not understand that to gain independence we had to pay a price. But the price we paid in 1945 was too high, both physically and spiritually. We lost enormously: a city burned down, innocent lives sacrificed, and many properties destroyed for nothing. However, our biggest loss was the inspiration the word "independence" had given, because we were ashamed and frightened by the unimaginable cruelty of the communists, acting in the name of independence. We considered this "communist-claimed independence" a tragedy or a delusion. We lost confidence in those who pretended to be "saviors" of independence and liberty for our country. In reality, they were the planters of all seeds of misfortune, suffering, and disaster for the Vietnamese people day after day. We had seen enough shameless hypocrisy, and suspected anyone who claimed to fight for our independence.

THE YOUTH AND THE WAR

Prior to 1955, the French educational system was complicated and difficult for Vietnamese students. Also, there were many differences between students of French colleges and Vietnamese colleges, public institutions and private institutions, and a lot of other problems concerning the different programs of education. All of these issues would be summarized in one word: "restriction," which was associated with the French colonial policy of "restraining intellectual education" for the people of their colonies. This restriction was seen more clearly in higher education. In Vietnam, prior to 1945, there were only a few higher level institutions in Hanoi, Tonkin (or North Vietnam), such as "École de Droit and Administration," "École de Médecine Indochinoise" and "École Normale Supérieure," respectively training indigenous judges and administrators, local doctors, and teachers of high schools (in Vietnam these teachers were called "professors"). At the same time, none of these institutions existed in Saigon, Cochinchina (or South Vietnam). Thus, those who had the Baccalaureat Complet and wanted to attend higher education in science, engineering, advanced medicine, or other majors had to travel to France. However, the number of Vietnamese allowed to go was kept to a minimum and places were reserved only for those who had French citizenship or those who belonged to wealthy families. These problems led to several demonstrations by "collégiens" (high school students) in Saigon during the first months of 1950, the year after the first State of Vietnam was established.

In retrospect, I would say that these student demonstrations in Saigon were new events in Vietnam's political life. For the first time in history, student demonstrations erupted in the streets of the former capital of the French Federation of Indochina, the new capital of the State of Vietnam. Moreover, these heated demonstrations became the prototypes for many subsequent demonstrations by Vietnamese students in the 1960s.

At first, students of several public and private collèges (before 1954, high schools in Vietnam were called "collèges" for junior students, and "lycées" for senior students) in Saigon organized moderate demonstrations at public places demanding reform of the outmoded French system of education. Although Vietnam was then a newly independent state within the French Union, the French continued to handle all important matters, such as the education system, and economic, political, and military affairs. They also controlled the country's security forces, including the Army of Vietnam, the National Police, and the Federal Security Services. However, war with the Vietnamese communists came into a new phase in North and Central Vietnam with increased guerrilla activity in South Vietnam. Facing a new form of struggle from the masses, the French reacted firmly. Police, firefighters, and secret agents of their Federal Security Services were dispatched to crush these demonstrations. In one such action, those men shot down a student, beat or injured hundreds of others, including schoolgirls, and arrested several dozens more.

After the death of the student, a second phase of demonstrations involving thousands of students with more political demands occurred in front of the palace of the prime minister. These demonstrations were more intense and popular opinion said that many communist cadres had joined in. The repression by the French security and police forces was also more violent. Finally, the struggles of the Saigon students were shut down. Hundreds of students were arrested and tortured by the French Security Services, sending a great wave of other students in Saigon and in other cities fleeing to the communist-free zone (called the "movement of going to the maquis" or "phong trào thoát ly ra bủng biển"). This movement was emerging like a pest. Hundreds of secondary students, most of them belonging to middle-class families, fled their homes and took sides with the communists to fight against the French.

Like other students at collèges and lycées, I faced pressure from pro-communist students who engaged in a sort of "whispering propaganda," urging us to join one of the secret communist organizations in town in order to take action against the French and the Government of Vietnam, or to fly to the communist-free zone to fight for the "independence and liberty" of the country. At the same time, students faced scrutiny by Federal Security Services operatives who disguised themselves as students to monitor the activities and movements of other students in these collèges and lycées. As a result, the actions of these clandestine agendas led to hundreds of students leaving their families and joining the communists and hundreds of others being arrested.

In six years, from August 1945 to August 1951, thousands of students fled to the communist side. The first wave occurred in the two years of 1945 and 1946, when the French came back to Vietnam, and the second wave occurred in the two years of 1950 and 1951, after the students in Saigon failed in their struggles for the reformation of the national system of education. Thus, the French neglected the challenge of "winning the hearts and minds" of the Vietnamese people, particularly the youth — the hope of the country — when they came back to Vietnam after World War II. Indeed, the arrogant actions by the colonists pushed many of the city's elite students to the open arms of their foes while they also failed to control the youths in the countryside. (Later, those who had fled to the jungle with the communists became their active political and military cadres; however, after the war, most of them were excluded from important organizations in the communist regime, especially those who were from South Vietnam. Since these people had been originally belonged to the "little-capitalist" class, or middle-class families, they were denied acceptance in any proletariat institution but could be used by the communists in wartime).

A more damaging consequence of this French policy was that a majority of secondary students who remained in towns and continued the French system of education later became the strongest anti-colonist and anti-communist proponents in the national forces of South Vietnam. They had seen clearly the corrupt ambitions of both the French and the communists. In early 1950, only a few years after the harsh suppression of student demonstrations in Saigon, the French had to face both the Vietnamese communists in the battlefields and the Vietnamese nationalists on the political front, the latter were fighting for true independence for Vietnam.

LIFE IN UNIFORM

I was one of the secondary students who remained in Saigon during that critical period. In May of 1954, I received a draft order to be trained as a Reserve Officer Cadet (Élève Officier de Réserve, EOR) at Thu-Duc Reserve Officers' School (École des Officiers de Réserve de Thu Duc) located about 15 miles northeast of Saigon, South Vietnam.

At that time, those who graduated from collèges and lycées, or had a higher degree of education, were called into the army as "EORs" at Thu-Duc Reserve Officers' School in South Vietnam or at Nam-Dinh Reserve Officers' School in North Vietnam. In 1951, the latter was dissolved and all of its EORs were integrated with those in Thu-Duc. From First to Fifth Class, EORs who graduated became second lieutenants in the Army of Vietnam. Many famous generals of the later Republic of Vietnam Armed Forces had graduated from this military academy. Those who wanted to become regular officers from the beginning were required to have the same basic degree of education as EORs, and also had to pass an entrance examination to be admitted as cadets of the "École Militaire Inter-Armes de Dalat" (EMIAD) that formed career officers for the army of the new State of Vietnam. The educational and military abilities of the reserve and regular officers of Vietnam at that time were not much different, since all of them were educated through the same French system of education and the same French military training programs.

I provide these details about training to point out an important fact: most officers graduating from these military institutions belonged to the class of intellectual and elite students in Vietnam. Although all were educated in public and military schools by the French, officers of this generation were recognized as anti–French because, first and foremost, they knew the ambitions of the French after returning to Vietnam in 1945 had devastated their country. Consequently, while fighting against the communists, they were also trying to support the government of the State of Vietnam and, for the sake of the Vietnamese people, expel the French from the country instead of serving French interests. They might have liked French civilization, language, and literature or appreciated the spirit of liberty and equality of' the French people, but they rejected the colonialism of French political and military leaders of that time. This was the difference between these officers and the first generation officers created by the French in previous years, prior to the establishment of the State of Vietnam in July 1949.

After two months of training in Thu-Duc, we learned that the French and the Vietnamese communists had signed the Geneva Treaty on July 21, 1954. This treaty cut Vietnam into two parts, after the communists totally defeated the core of French Expeditionary Forces at Dien Bien Phu garrison. The Ben-Hai River became the demilitarized zone (DMZ) between the communist Democratic Republic of Vietnam (DRV) in the North and the nationalist State of Vietnam in the South. This was a very bad news for all of us.

I was one of 1,200 EORs in the Fifth Class. One-third of these EORs were North Vietnamese intellects or students. The Geneva Treaty proved disastrous for them as they were cut off from their families in the North and risked losing them forever. Blessedly, nearly a million people from the North migrated to the South. I did not know how many of my peers would be able to reunite with their families due to the migration. However, I was sure of one thing, that in the following years they might have to fight against those they had once loved, their brothers, sisters, relatives, and friends who had remained in the North and were later forced into the war in the South by the communist leaders.

In January 1955, about eighty-five percent of the EORs, including myself, graduated with the rank of second lieutenant. During ten days on leave I returned to Bac-Lieu City to visit my parents before being assigned to an infantry unit. I learned that Camau District, my hometown, had become a transit place for the communist cadres and guerrillas in the Mekong Delta to congregate before regrouping to the North with their "comrades" and "Uncle Ho" (Ho Chi Minh). All bodily organizations of the Government of Vietnam (GVN) at Camau City had been temporarily moved to Bac-Lieu City. My hometown again suffered from turmoil. Worse, it would have to witness deadly fights between its sons in a near future. Indeed, in this small town, where everybody knew everybody else, many residents were taking sides to fight with either the communists or with the nationalists. I had many friends from primary and secondary school who became communist and formed into several units and regrouped to the North. They became my foes. Thus, my lovely hometown became spiritually divided by the division of my country. However, just a few months after the regrouping of these communists to the North, Camau District was upgraded to a "province," called An-Xuyen Province.

After my short leave in Bac-Lieu, I returned to Saigon to receive orders for my first assignment of my long journey in the army. I began as a platoon commander at the 61st BVN ("Bataillon Vietnamien," or Vietnamese Battalion), located at Duc-Hoa District of Cholon Province, for one year. In January 1956, I was reassigned as a company commander to the 1st Battalion, 43rd Regiment of the 15th Light Infantry Division at Duc-My, Nha-Trang, in Central Vietnam. In January 1958, I attended an intelligence course at the Military Intelligence School at Fort Cay Mai in Cholon. After graduation, I was retained at this school as an instructor. From that time I began a humble and silent career backstage, as if I was walking under the shadow of the smoke of war but not within it, for more than ten years. As a result, I was promoted more slowly in the military compared with my classmates who were commanding combat units.

However, in this ten-year period in Saigon, I had the opportunity to attend four intelligence courses with the most advanced military intelligence agencies of that time. The first time, I took the "Territorial Intelligence Course" in Singapore offered to Vietnamese intelligence officers by the British Royal Forces in the Far East. The second and third times, I attended, respectively, the "Counter-Intelligence Course" and the "Field Operations Intelligence Course" in Okinawa with the U.S Forces in the Pacific at USARPACINTS (U.S. Army Pacific Intelligence School). The last time, I traveled to the United States to take the "Allied Senior Officers Intelligence Course" at the U.S. Army Intelligence School in Maryland, which trained senior intelligence officers to take leading roles in the field of operational intelligence for units the size of a division or larger. All of these intelligence courses enriched my knowledge of the conflicts between the communist world and the free world. I knew that the United States had no choice but to involve itself in the war in Vietnam to save Indochina and safeguard freedom for other nations in Southeast Asia.

During that period, I often suffered anguish as I witnessed many disastrous events that threatened our democracy. I saw unimaginable demonstrations in the streets of Saigon; the two coups d'état of the "generals" (in 1960 and 1963) to overthrow President Ngo Dinh Diem and a series of consecutive coups in the following years; and unrest around the country whenever communist saboteurs came too close to urban areas or inside the capital. In addition to these misfortunes, the arrival of tens of thousands of U.S. combat troops into the country brought a flow of dollars that changed the face of every city and town. Hundreds of snack bars sprang up like the mushrooms in fertile ground, which severely altered the economic life of the social classes and led to corruption. Our society faced new challenges involving the choice between good and evil, justice and crime, and conscience and malfeasance.

For two years, 1966 and 1967, as deputy commander of the Military Intelligence Center (MIC), which belonged to the J2 JGS RVNAF (Joint Staff Intelligence of the Joint General Staff of the Republic of Vietnam Armed Forces), I was commissioned by the Chief Staff J2, who was concurrently Commander of MIC, to organize a dozen Military Intelligence Detachments (MIDs) to work alongside each Staff S-2 (intelligence) of every allied grand unit fighting in Vietnam. Vietnamese officers and NCOs of these intelligence detachments were to help their allied partners with interrogation of prisoners and in understanding documents captured in the battlefields. I often visited them to encourage them in their duties around the four military regions of South Vietnam. On these tours, I always remembered my father's words about "heaven or hell" and the first history lessons on the "spirit of the land" that I had learned from my old teacher at my natal village. Yes, I did fly from one horizon to another, and I felt the presence of that spirit in every corner of the land, but everywhere I just saw flames, blood, tears, suffering and misery. Saigon was hell and everywhere in my country was hell. If there was a place called "heaven," it seemed to exist only in my dreams.

The misfortunes of Vietnam that I witnessed inspired me to compose poetry. I did not care if I was a good or a bad poet. What I wanted to do was to give voice to the hardship, agony, and misfortune of the Vietnamese people who were suffering during the war. In each word, I felt propelled by unremitting turbulence that led to calamity and suffering — the blaze of violence and war afflicting our motherland, changing the face of our society, and disrupting the lives of the people, even as I was evolving painfully in the midst of it all.

In such a troubled time, "war and peace," "love and hate" and "life and death" were the main themes of Vietnamese literature. Many writers and poets at the time wrote to appeal to the conscience of the Vietnamese leaders, both communists and nationalists. Their voices were unheard and sometimes their lives were in danger. In fact, under the communist regimes in North Vietnam, during the two decades of the 1950s and 1960s, many famous writers and poets were imprisoned under harsh conditions or simply disappeared. Meanwhile, in South Vietnam, men of letters were free to write, although their voices were deeply buried in the sounds of battles that raged around the country. Decades after the end of the war, the mainstream writings of Vietnamese in exile in any corner of the world involve memoirs or research and discussion on the Vietnam War. Yet the common purpose of these writings is to help the younger generations of Vietnamese understand why the war left such a bloody mark in their country's history. This too is my purpose: by tracing the war's events I hope to convey an understanding and clarity that will help younger generations of Vietnamese to be more reconciled with the past so they can make even better progress in the future.

2

Vietnam, the Arena of Confrontation Between the East and the West

American historians have written volumes of books, articles, and theses on the Vietnam War. Retired history teacher John Dellinger described pre-war Vietnam in "The War Makers," published in *Vietnam Magazine* in April 1996, depicting a country struggling to emerge from the framework of colonial rule to establish a new identity as a free nation. This transition became a primary reason for the war. The Americans argued that their involvement in Vietnam mobilized military forces and political will to safeguard freedom and promote democracy against the communist aggression. The war in Vietnam was due to different motives, according to each side's policy and strategy. My research reveals that any country's involvement in the First and Second Wars in Vietnam was due mainly to economic interests rather than political or military purposes. Otherwise, the Vietnamese communist party and nationalist parties fought each other for their separate aims and aspirations: the communists for the establishment of the communist regime in Vietnam and in the rest of Indochina, while the nationalists fought for the independence, freedom, and prosperity of the country. The different motives of these Vietnamese parties were the prime reasons that foreigners came to exploit them. In addition, since Vietnam occupied a strategic geographic position in the Asia-Pacific region and Southeast Asia, it could at any time be the arena of confrontation between the East and the West, especially during a time of war.

Regarding America's agenda, Dellinger asserts that five presidents of the United States "owned the war in Vietnam": Dwight D. Eisenhower, John F. Kennedy, Lyndon B. Johnson, Richard M. Nixon, and Gerald R. Ford, Jr. He writes: "None of them owned the war in the traditional way that American presidents had owned earlier wars. But each of them, to a greater or lesser extent, shared the responsibility for the Vietnam War."[1] However, my research suggests Presidents Roosevelt and Truman had been deeply involved in Vietnam & Indochina during World War II. Their involvement shaped the political status of Vietnam long before the Vietnam War began. The policies of these two presidents during World War II would also affect the future "First" and "Second" Vietnam Wars.

Most American historians define the Vietnam War (or the Second Indochina War) as extending from March 1965 to August 1972. American ground forces were committed to battle in March 1965, with the landing of two marine battalions of the III Marine Amphibious Force, at the important seaport of Danang — approximately 380 miles northeast of Saigon. The withdrawal of the last U.S. combat unit, the army's 3rd Battalion, 21st Infantry, occurred in August 1972.

Some historians expand this definition to include the prior United States military involvement in Vietnam, which had begun some 15 years earlier with the establishment of the U.S.

Military Assistance Advisory Group Indochina (MAAGI) in the capital city of Saigon in September 1950. They argue that when the Marines went ashore in 1965, there were already some 23,300 U.S. military advisers in the country. And, although U.S. ground combat forces began a scheduled withdrawal from Vietnam in 1969, all ground forces did not withdraw until August 1972, and the war continued for almost three more years, until the fall of Saigon on the last day of April 1975.

Many Vietnamese historians consider the war in their country as one war instead of two: the First Vietnam War and the Second Vietnam War. For them, the war began March 9, 1945, the day on which the Japanese suddenly attacked the French colonial garrisons in Indochina. The Japanese Ambassador to Saigon came to Hue, the former capital of the Nguyen dynasty, and announced to Emperor Bao Dai that Vietnam was now "independent." However, the Japanese "independence" and their weakening of the French in Vietnam aroused more secret movements among the Vietnamese people, including the nationalists and the communists in country, overseas, and especially in South China, who were struggling for their own true independence. The earliest recorded contacts between the United States and Vietnam occurred in the summer of 1941, under the Roosevelt administration. However, in the beginning, U.S. policy was one of "non-involvement." The following details will explain this U.S. policy.

VIETNAM UNDER THE UNITED STATES' VIEW

During World War II, the Germans overran France in the spring of 1940. The French colonials in Indochina could no longer count on any help from France. In addition, uncoordinated defense measures in the South Pacific between the British and the French decreased the real possibility of an effective defense of Southeast Asia and Indochina against Japanese aggression. Although French Indochina hoped for an alliance with the United States, President Roosevelt still clung to his non-involvement policy. The United States repeatedly refused to join Britain and France in an anti–Japanese alliance to protect the South Pacific and the Far East. This opened the door for disaster in Southeast Asia.[2]

The Roosevelt administration, more than twice, refused all demands to help French Indochina. Pleadings came from French Marshal Jean Pétain of the Vichy government, which had signed an armistice with Hitler in June 1940, and from French governors in Indochina General George Catroux and Admiral Jean Decoux. Several historical events surrounded French requests for help. First, on June 19, 1940, the Japanese addressed an ultimatum to the French governor-general in Indochina, General Catroux, demanding joint control up to the Tonkin borderline provinces of Cao-Bang and Lang-Son that had been under the French domination from 1886 to 1945. Tonkin, with its Yunnan railroad, was Nationalist China's artery on which flowed supplies from the Allied Forces. The Japanese used this strategic region as a primary base from which to launch attacks on Chiang Kai-shek's forces in the southwest provinces of China and to control French military activities in Indochina. Without orders from Paris and with the refusal of war equipment from Washington, Catroux acceded to the Japanese demands. He was replaced by Admiral Jean Decoux, who was faced with similar Japanese demands. Decoux, however, applied the tactic of "delaying and parleying," and told the Japanese to take up the problem with the French government in Vichy. Before they were forced to concede to the Japanese, the Vichy ambassador in Washington once more beseeched the United States to strengthen France's hand in Indochina. On August 22, 1940, U.S. Under-Secretary of State Summer Welles let Vichy know that the United States was unable to come to aid of Indochina. On August 30, Vichy signed an accord with Japan recognizing Japan's "pre-eminent position" in the Far East and granted the Japanese in principle certain transit facilities in Tonkin. In Saigon, Decoux ordered General Martin, the French commander in Tonkin, to negotiate with the Japanese delegate, General Nishihara. Franco-Japanese negotiations began on September 5, 1940, in Hanoi and dragged out for weeks. However, the conditions of the initial accord with Japan could not be re-negotiated.

With the Vichy government of Marshal Pétain under the control of Japan's ally, Germany, Indochina was totally isolated from outside help. The Japanese were growing impatient with the slow progress of the negotiations and decided to provide a demonstration of their power in Tonkin. On September 22, Japanese troops in neighboring Kwang-tung and Kwang-si suddenly attacked the French border forts along the borderline of Cao-Bang and Lang-Son Provinces. Japanese aircraft bombed Hai-Phong, the main military and commercial seaport of Tonkin, and began to land troops to occupy the port. Outnumbered and outgunned, the French border forts were overrun after two days of fighting and lost more than 800 men with thousands more wounded and arrested. This surprise attack was only the beginning of Japan's ambition in Indochina.

Japan sought to assimilate two main targets under the "Greater East-Asia Co-Prosperity Sphere": China and Southeast Asia. Indochina, especially Vietnam, was an important target due to its geopolitical position and its two favorable natural naval bays — Ha-Long in Tonkin (North Vietnam) and Cam-Ranh in Annam (Central Vietnam). Once the Japanese occupied Vietnam, they would use these bays as adjoining bases to advantageously launch their operations in any direction by heading north to China, south to Southeast Asia, east to the Philippines, Indonesia, Borneo, and farther to Australia and New Zealand. After the September attack on the frontier of Tonkin, when the Vichy government wired Admiral Decoux to accept the Japanese demands without delay, Japan quickly occupied three air fields in Tonkin and deployed its 6,000 man occupation force in Tonkin, Cochinchina (South Vietnam), and Cambodia. Moreover, 25,000 Japanese troops were authorized to move through Indochina at any time.

Subsequently, Japan brought pressure on the Vichy government to sign a cease-fire agreement in Tokyo on March 11, 1941. From the moment that agreement was signed, the Japanese "negotiated" over Decoux's head, directly with the Vichy regime. In a July 29, 1941, agreement signed with the Vichy, Japan acquired de facto "control and utilization" of all airports and port facilities in Indochina.

VIETNAM, THE ROOT CAUSE OF THE JAPANESE SUDDEN ATTACK ON PEARL HARBOR IN DECEMBER 1941

Japanese ambitions to occupy strategically located Indochina were very clear to the United States authorities. When it became certain that Vichy would no longer resist Japanese demands to control airports and port facilities in Indochina, President Roosevelt could no longer maintain an attitude of non-involvement. He laid down a series of decisions that would eventually lead to the surprise attack by the Japanese Air Force on Pearl Harbor on December 7, 1941, igniting the Second World War in the Asia-Pacific region between Japan and the United States (and its Allies). On July 26, 1941, three days before the Vichy government signed its agreement with Japan, President Roosevelt ordered the freezing of all Japanese assets in the United States and an embargo on petroleum exports to Japan. Two days before that, the Japanese ambassador to Washington, Admiral Kichisaburo Nomura, was summoned to a meeting with the president of the United States. The president proposed to Nomura a "Complete Neutralization of Indochina" in exchange for a guarantee of Japan's "right of acquisition of … supplies and raw materials therefrom on a basis of equality."[3]

The proposition of a complete neutralization of Indochina continued to be negotiated between the United States and Japan in November 1941. Not surprisingly the political solution was unacceptable to the Japanese government, which considered it merely as an extension to Indochina of the "open-door policy." In Paragraph 2, Section II, of the Proposition, the United States proposed negotiations between Britain, Japan, China, the Dutch government in exile, and Thailand in order to guarantee Indochina's neutrality. It demanded "for each of these signatories equality of treatment in trade and commerce with French-Indochina."[4] The proposal would totally ignore the role of France. In reality, had such a political solution be enrealized, it would have completely obstructed the Japanese plan to occupy Indochina. That was the primary cause of the conflict between Japan and the United States.

A secondary, but vital, cause was the issuance of the Executive Order on July 26 (mentioned above) by the president of the United States. While the proposition of neutralization of Indochina might politically harm the Japanese "Greater East-Asia Co-Prosperity Sphere" project, the embargo on petroleum exports to Japan was a death-blow to the Japanese Navy, which was the major expedition force of the Japanese at the Pacific. In other words, the embargo resulted in the Japanese Navy's insistence on achieving control of Southeast Asia before its petroleum supplies were entirely exhausted.

War between the two strongest powers in the Pacific was inevitable. The details of the causes for the attack on Pearl Harbor and the ensuing war in the Pacific were probably little known or unknown by the majority of the American people. Many did not know how crucial a role Indochina played in the collision between the superpowers in World War II.

The war exploded. On the morning of the Japanese strike on Pearl Harbor, the Japanese also surrounded all French garrisons in Indochina. Governor Decoux was faced with yet another ultimatum: to cooperate with the "Greater East-Asia Co-Prosperity Sphere" in order to keep France's role in the colony, or face the immediate destruction of his garrisons. Decoux yielded, thus saving 40,000 of his countrymen from the immediate ordeal of incarceration in Japanese concentration camps or death, and saving at least the appearance of French sovereignty over the local population.

As a result of these events, Roosevelt's political goal for a "complete neutralization" of Indochina failed and the war in the Pacific increased its intensity during the ensuing years from 1942 to 1945. A wave of new United States policies toward the French administration in Indochina surfaced and caused a surprised reaction by the Japanese.

Indochina became the focus of several high-level decisions of consequence to its postwar development. On the United States side, Roosevelt sought to substitute powers other than the colonial French. On January 3, 1943, the British ambassador to Washington, Lord Halifax, asked U.S. Secretary of State Cordell Hull for clarification on America's Indochina policy. President Roosevelt took up the matter personally with Halifax and later informed Hull that "he had confirmed to the British ambassador that Indochina should not go back to France but that it should be administered by an international trusteeship."[5] The idea of substitution was officially broached at the inter–Allied level during a conference in Washington on March 27, 1943. The U.S. president suggested to British foreign secretary Sir Anthony Eden that a "Trusteeship" be established for Indochina. The president also instructed Cordell Hull to present the trusteeship idea to the Russians at the Moscow Conference in October 1943. Later, General Joseph W. Stilwell, the U.S. commander in the China Theater, reported that President Roosevelt had in mind a trusteeship under three commissioners — an American, a Briton, and a Chinese.[6] British Prime Minister Winston Churchill objected that such a solution that would eliminate the French from Indochina. He stated simply that "he could not conceive of a civilized world without a flourishing and lively France...."[7]

In the following year, pushing his trusteeship approach, Roosevelt brought up his solution at the Yalta Conference in February of 1945. This time, he proposed an "Indochinese Trusteeship Council" of four international members: Chinese, Russian, French, and Philipino. Again, Churchill apparently vetoed the whole proposal. Roosevelt's new policy toward Indochina was finally discarded.[8] However, the Japanese considered Roosevelt's new solution as another obstruction to their plan for Indochina. They reacted by staging another sudden attack on all French garrisons in Vietnam, Cambodia, and Laos. On March 9, 1945, at 21:30 hours, the Japanese struck without warning. French garrisons in the colony were surrounded by Japanese troops and the French senior commanders were captured. In just one night, the Japanese overwhelmed and occupied French military camps, airports, and naval bases throughout the three countries of Indochina. All French colonial authorities, military governors, and civilian administrators at the provincial level were killed or arrested. Only in Tonkin were some French generals able to evade the coup with their small units, and escape through the Thai-Highlands area, which was close to Dien-Bien-Phu. The evading French generals established themselves around the airfield of Dien-Bien-Phu, and began calling for Allied supplies and air support. Among them were General Sabattier and his headquarters crew.

In the vital Tonkin area, Japanese action was particularly brutal. Lang-Son was the center of the tragedy. After the last message calling for help was sent to General Sabattier's headquarters, the Lang-Son garrison was completely massacred by the Japanese; only one man survived. The last message of the doomed Lang-Son was a request for a supply of water and air support. It was a hopeful call for an American intervention. But there was no response.

The nearest American field commanders to Lang-Son at that time were General Claire L. Chennault, the famous father of the "Flying Tigers" and commander of the 14th Air Force in Yunnan, and his direct superior, General Albert C. Wedemeyer. General Wedemeyer was commander-in-chief in the China Theater at Kunming; he also was the senior military adviser to Chiang Kai-shek and was nominally operating under Chiang's authority. After receiving the call for help from French General Sabattier, Chennault immediately sent liaison officers with light aircraft to make contact with Sabattier's headquarters at Dien Bien Phu. These U.S. officers had made a rapid survey of the most urgent needs of the French and arranged for air supply drops and coordination of air support. However, in the following days neither air supply nor air support were allowed, which left many French messages unanswered. Thus, the French troops were left unaided to face their tragic destiny in Indochina, especially in Lang-Son.

After the Japanese take-over on March 9, 1945, the total number of French troops massacred or captured in the country exceeded 35,000. More than 250 officers and 4,000 soldiers were killed or massacred while retreating to China. Only 320 officers, 2,150 Europeans, and 3,300 Vietnamese soldiers survived the 800-mile trek to Yunnan.[9] In the three countries of Indochina, the Japanese forced all Frenchmen into concentration camps and treated them severely.

The French, who were unaware of the United States' presidential policies, could not believe the unwillingness of the United States to assist and respond to their vital requests from Indochina in March 1945. After the war, General Chennault explained why he cut all contacts with French General Sabattier just after he had sent his liaison officers to Sabattier's headquarters: "Orders arrived from Theater headquarters [the China Theater of General Wedemeyer] stating that no arms and ammunition would be provided to French troops under any circumstances.... General Wedemeyer's orders not to aid the French came directly from the U.S. War Department. Apparently it was then American policy that French-Indochina not be returned to the French. The American government was interested in seeing the French forcibly ejected from Indochina so the problem of postwar separation from their colony would be easier."[10]

General Albert C. Wedemeyer also conveyed the reasons for his rigid refusal to aid the French. He had met President Roosevelt in March 1945. Roosevelt admonished him not to provide any supplies to the French forces operating in the area. This instruction to General Wedemeyer was only an extension of Roosevelt's previous order on that matter. Indeed, on October 13, 1944, Roosevelt had addressed a memorandum to secretary of state Cordell Hull that the United States should not do anything with regard to resistance groups or any other matter in Indochina. This instruction was transferred to the U.S. War Department and became a military order which restricted American military from ever authorizing support for any French military mission that could be accredited to the U.S. South-East Asia Command. This is why French requests for American assistance and military supplies to fight the Japanese in Indochina were unanswered. President Roosevelt's policy of eliminating the French from Indochina was clear.

As far as the Free French were concerned, General De Gaulle promised a bloody return to Indochina: "As painful as that development was locally, I must say that from the point of view of national interest, I willingly envisaged that hostilities would commence in Indochina ... in view of our position in the Far East, I thought it essential that the conflict should not end without us become, there also, involved as belligerents.... French blood shed on Indochinese soil would give us an important voice in later settlements."[11] Later, he would keep his promise.

After neutralizing the French forces in Indochina, the Japanese declared Vietnam, Laos, and Cambodia independent of colony rule. France lost control over these three countries after 60 years of rule. In Vietnam, on March 11, 1945, Emperor Bao Dai declared Vietnam "independent" and called in scholar Tran Trong Kim to form the first cabinet for the government of the State of Vietnam. However, the Japanese manipulated all military and economic activities of the country. They controlled the flow of rice and other food that led to the biggest mass starvation in Hanoi and several provinces in the North; through the end of March 1945, two million people died according to Vietnamese historian Cao The Dung.[12] These disastrous events were certainly observed by Washington.

Most American historians disregard the affects of policy decisions made by the Roosevelt administration regarding Indochina. However, President Roosevelt's preoccupation with eliminating the French from this colony certainly changed the course of history of the three countries of Indochina, especially Vietnam.

SECRET DEALS WITH THE COMMUNISTS OF VIETNAM

The death of President Franklin D. Roosevelt, on April 12, 1945, created a hiatus for months of American postwar planning for Indochina. During that period, a historic fatal meeting occurred between an American Office of Strategic Services (OSS) officer, Major Archimedes Patti, and the Indochinese Communist Party's leader, Ho Chi Minh. Their meeting evolved out of the disorder and confusion between the groups of the Chinese and the Vietnamese communists and nationalists who were struggling against the Japanese for their independence. With 8,500-man colonial garrisons under Japanese captivity after their coup in Indochina in March 1945, Major Patti was left without any potential ally until Ho Chi Minh approached him. They met in secret at the Vietnamese border.

This critical meeting affected for two decades the decisions and policies of the various presidents of the United States toward Indochina. It also affected the American media and American students in their anti-war campaigns and movements during the 1960s.

In spring 1945, Major General William J. Donovan, the head of the Office of Strategic Services, the forerunner of the Central Intelligence Agency (CIA), needed experienced men for Indochina. Major Patti was selected because of his previous successful missions in North Africa and Italy. Patti's specific instructions were to establish an intelligence network throughout the entire peninsula of Indochina. The assignment was a high priority since Indochina was strategically centered between the three vast political theaters: mainland China, the South Pacific, and Southeast Asia. Major Patti arrived at the OSS branch of Kunming in mid–April 1945, with his special team OSS-202, called the "Deer Team," to expand intelligence operations into Indochina. At that time, Kunming was the strong ally of the forces of Chiang Kai-shek and the focal point of the Allied Forces' activities to support Chang's resistance against the Japanese.

Before setting up the first secret rendezvous with Ho Chi Minh on April 30, 1945, Patti had several contacts with a French intelligence officer, Major Jean Sainteny. Sainteny was his counterpart and leader of a Free French intelligence team in Kunming. Sainteny's team was called M-5, or Mission 5, and had been establishing a sizable intelligence network along the border of Indochina. Sainteny appealed to Patti since the French had prepared clandestine units and needed weapons. At that point, Major Archimedes Patti would come to a historic decision not to rely on the French but on the Viet-Minh and their leader, Ho Chi Minh.

Later, Patti recalled his historic meeting with Ho Chi Minh: "From a practical viewpoint, Ho and the Viet-Minh appeared to be the answer to my immediate problem of establishing relations in Indochina. I started to work with them very, very closely."[13] Certainly, as a new American authority in Kunming, Major Patti did not know exactly who Ho Chi Minh was, but he had some of Ho's records in the OSS files. What he needed was a suitable way to establish an intelligence network behind the lines of Indochina. He was faintly aware that Ho was a communist and had been in Moscow for some training there. In addition, his Viet-Minh had a party front line. Patti saw that Ho's ultimate goal was to attain American support for the cause of a free Vietnam and felt that desire presented no conflict with American policy.

At that time, Dean Rusk, deputy chief of staff with the Allied Command in Asia at Kunming, sent a message to Washington to seek advice on American policy toward Indochina. For months, nothing happened. Finally, after Patti had been in Kunming for a few months, Rusk received from his Joint Chiefs of Staff an equivocal memorandum suggesting that "America's anti-colonial policy had been abandoned." This would mean that "the British went back to India and Burma, the Dutch back to Indonesia, the French back to Indochina, and the United States reverted to the pre-war situation," Rusk concludes.[14] There was no evidence that Major Patti had been aware of this policy change. In fact, he was left alone in charge of US affairs in Indochina with contrary instructions that he previously received from the White House through his superior, General Donovan. That was the first paradox.

Major Patti decided to work for the mutual interests of both the Deer Team and the Viet-Minh. He was mesmerized by Ho's oratory and hypnotic quality during their meeting. Ho let Patti know that the Viet-Minh would make available an equal force of 1,000 guerrillas to assist any American operation in Indochina. Ho also agreed to provide guides and give protection and shelter to Patti's Deer Team. In turn, Patti sent a fifty-man OSS group led by his deputy to parachute into a small village that was about 75 miles northeast of Hanoi, to establish a headquarters for the Viet-Minh. This mountainous village was called Tan-Trao and Ho's headquarters was placed at Pac-Po. The Deer Team then spread out with Vo Nguyen Giap's troops to secure and protect Pac-Po. Later, in 1946, Pac-Bo became Ho Chi Minh's main headquarters and base during the First Indochina War.

At Ho's headquarters, Patti felt that the Viet-Minh could do more for the Deer Team. He decided to train and arm them with modern weapons for joint combat operations. In just one month his OSS team trained about 200 handpicked future leaders of the Viet-Minh, who would lead the war against the Americans twenty years later.

However, the most catastrophic aspect of the Ho-Patti liaison that devastated the United States anti-communist efforts in Indochina in the 1960s and the early years of 1970s were the "credentials" Patti collected on Ho Chi Minh. During the period of joint operations at the border of Vietnam in June 1945, the OSS mission's collective final report advised Washington of extraordinary statements regarding Ho Chi Minh's qualifications. The report stated that Ho was the only legitimate national leader of Vietnam. Major Patti himself believed that Ho Chi Minh was not a hardened communist but was foremost a nationalist. His opinion was fully supported in field reports by other OSS operatives, which only became public at a Senate hearing in 1972. These OSS reports became the basis for anti-war marches and movements against the government by American students. These reports also crucially influenced the United States Legislature, which sought to decide the fate of South Vietnam.

Interviewed by the American media in 1972, Patti remembered that he met Ho Chi Minh for the first time on the last day of April 1945. Between April 30, 1945, and April 30, 1975, more than 2.8 million American troops followed Major Archimedes Patti to Vietnam. More than 58,000 of them and at least 2 million Vietnamese died in the controversial Vietnam War.

The OSS, especially Major Patti and his Deer Team and later the CIA, did not know the real Ho Chi Minh. They considered Ho first a nationalist and second a communist. In reality, Ho Chi Minh had always been a dedicated international communist behind his Vietnamese manners and patriotic zeal. Indeed, for all his life Ho had used the nationalist catchphrases in almost every one of his public utterances and meetings to attract and excite the Vietnamese populace. His speeches motivated the Vietnamese to sacrifice their lives for the nation's independence and he tried to convince international opinion to support his justification for the war, but all the while he never lost sight of his communist party's goals. The OSS failure to recognize Ho Chi Minh as a potential international communist leader would only be learned by U.S. politicians and intelligence officials some thirty years later.

In summary, the death of President Franklin D. Roosevelt in April of 1945 left the American policy toward Indochina in a prolonged hiatus and created uncertainty for six successive American presidents. Furthermore, the OSS's Major Archimedes Patti left Washington for an intelligence mission in Indochina that created a paradox regarding the U.S. stand against communism and led to the loss of tens of thousands of American lives in the Vietnam War.

3

Aggression and Deterrence

On August 10, 1945, Japan collapsed and declared their intention to surrender to Allied Forces after the United States dropped atomic bombs on Hiroshima and Nagasaki on 6 and 9 August 1945. The war in the Asia-Pacific region had ended.

THE VIETNAM WAR WAS BORN FROM WORLD WAR II

In Vietnam, on August 7, 1945, Prime Minister Tran Trong Kim of the Central Government resigned and his cabinet disbanded. Tran Trong Kim, a well-known scholar who had been appointed to the premiership by Emperor Bao-Dai on April 7, 1945, was an excellent architect of administrative regulations and educational formations. However, without a national army he could not accomplish his difficult job. After he resigned and after the Japanese forces in Vietnam surrendered on August 15, regional administrative authorities could not control their regions. At that critical juncture, the communists staged a brief uprising on August 17 and seized control of Hanoi on August 19, 1945. On August 26, Ho Chi Minh left Tan-Trao and came to Hanoi with Vo Nguyen Giap's troops and the OSS Deer Team of Major Archimedes Patti. Ho declared independence for the Democratic Republic of Vietnam (DRV) on September 2, 1945 in a festive ceremony held at Ba-Dinh Square. The Americans were the only foreign guests given places of honor at the ceremony; Major Patti stood next to General Vo Nguyen Giap.

News of Ho's declaration of independence spread to every corner of the country, even to remote places like Camau City that I described previously. People heard the news and tearfully celebrated this "fateful" independence. The enthusiasm and adulation of the crowd at Ba-Dinh Square in Hanoi that day may have surprised Major Patti. However, it did not last long, and the people of Vietnam began suffering the atrocity of the Vietnamese communists for decades to come. After the declaration of independence, Ho Chi Minh and the newly formed government would face the political chaos caused by the allied controlling forces in the country.

According to the terms of the Potsdam Agreements of July 1945, from August 18, 1945, the Chinese Nationalist forces of Chiang Kei-shek would occupy North Vietnam and a part of Central Vietnam north of the 16th parallel, while the British forces would control the southern half of the Indochinese peninsula below the 16th parallel. In Tonkin (North Vietnam), troops of Chiang Kai-shek, under the command of General Lu Han, came to Hanoi and became the burden of Ho Chi Minh. After a serious deal with Lu Han, Ho declared the dissolution of his Indochinese Communist Party and formed the new coalition government with the participation of leaders from other Vietnamese nationalist parties.[1] In Cochinchina

(South Vietnam) on September 12, the British Gurkha Division from Rangoon came to Saigon to disarm the Japanese. A French company of paratroopers accompanied it. The British forces' commander, Brigadier General Douglas Gracy, ordered the liberation of all French prisoners of war held by the Japanese and rearmed them for the protection of their civilian compatriots. This caused serious problems for Tran van Giau, the leader of the communist "Administrative Committee" in South Vietnam (Uỷ-ban Hành-chánh Nam-bộ; this committee soon changed its name to Uỷ-ban Hành-chánh Kháng-chiến, or Committee for Resistance and Administration). Skirmishes occurred at several places in Saigon. The French appeared to take control over the city by the end of the month.

During this chaotic period of September 1945, an important event happened that disrupted Ho Chi Minh's hope to lean on the support of the United States. On September 4, eight days prior to the arrival of the British forces, the American OSS Team 404 led by Major A. Peter Dewey was sent to the Saigon area to liberate more than two hundred American prisoners of war (POWs) held in Japanese camps. This intelligence team accomplished its mission. The POWs were flown out of Vietnam the next day.[2] Unfortunately, three weeks later Major Dewey was mistaken for a French officer and was killed in an ambush by the communist guerrillas of Tran van Giau. Ho Chi Minh faced a dilemma; he had to convey his excuse to the American Command in Southeast Asia. U.S. Navy Captain James Withrow replaced Dewey. Withrow was ordered not to interfere with the French re-occupation plans in Vietnam. Later, in mid–December, all OSS teams — the OSS 202, or Deer Team, in Hanoi and the OSS 404 Team in Saigon — were ordered to leave Vietnam.[3] This was the first sign of the American unwillingness to help Ho Chi Minh and his coalition government.

In reality, after the death of President Roosevelt in April 1945, the United States changed its policy toward the colonies of several Western powers in the Pacific and Asia, especially those of Great Britain and France. Roosevelt's successor, President Harry S. Truman, after a couple of months of indecision, began to listen to the advice of several important leaders in the Department of State and the Department of War and Navy, who considered the cooperation of Great Britain and France in Europe more vital for the United States "to meet the growing Soviet threat" than anti-colonialism in Asia.[4] However, the cooperation of these important allies should have materialized both on the Western front and on the Eastern front. On May 6, 1945, President Truman met with French foreign affairs minister Georges Bidault and let him know that the United States preferred the cooperation of French forces on the Oriental front. On June 2, U.S. secretary of state Edward Stettinius also informed French ambassador Henry Bonnet and Georges Bidault that the United States would not further touch French foreign policy toward their colonies.[5] The problem of the "independence" of colonies in Asia was then ignored by the United States.

In October 1945, a bilateral British-French agreement recognized French administration in South Vietnam, which included the old Cochinchina and a portion of territory of the old Annam, or Central Vietnam. In addition, British admiral Sir Louis Mountbatten, supreme allied commander in Southeast Asia, promised French general Jacques Phillipe Leclerc — who was assigned by De Gaulle as commander in chief of the French Expeditionary Forces in Indochina — to arm his troops and provide transportation for them to return to Indochina.[6] French forces returned to Saigon in mid–October 1945.

First, Leclerc's forces had to face the communist guerrillas of the Nam-bo Committee for Resistance and Administration led by Tran van Giau and his deputy Nguyen Binh (Le Duan was then under the command of these men). Giau declared a "scorched-earth policy" (sách-lược tiêu-thổ kháng-chiến) and withdrew his guerrilla forces to fight against the French. However, within a few months, from mid–October to December 1945, the French re-occupied the majority of provinces in South Vietnam. Their march toward the lowlands of the Mekong Delta continued. Other French units invaded Cambodia and Laos and quickly pacified these two countries.

Being on the verge of losing all territories in South and Central Vietnam and lacking foreign support, Ho Chi Minh had to turn to the French. On March 6, 1946, Ho Chi Minh signed, with Jean Sainteny, the French official delegate in Vietnam, a "temporary agreement" which recognized Vietnam as a free state that formed part of the Indochinese Federation and the French Union and allowed the French forces to relieve Chinese troops in North Vietnam. The agreement stated that it would "enter into effect immediately upon exchange of signatures."[7] The term "free state" would later lead to more talks between Ho's government and France, but French troops could move over the 16th parallel to North Vietnam immediately. However, to avoid confrontation with the Chinese Nationalist troops of Chiang Kai-shek in that part of Vietnam, a month before, in February 1946, France signed an agreement with China whereby all Chinese forces would withdrawal from North Vietnam and allow the French to return to Indochina in exchange for the restoration of various concessions, including the "renunciation of French extra-territorial claims in China."[8] Thus, with the temporary agreement signed, France immediately sent large elements to North Vietnam. In June, the French sent a Vietnamese-born officer in the French army, Brigadier General Nguyen van Xuan, to Saigon to form a government. They wanted to set a "self-governed state" in the South — the so-called "Nam-kỳ Quốc," or Nam-ky State. Later that year, in November, after French General Jean-Etienne Valluy had established a series of garrisons and outposts on the border of China and Vietnam and along the Route Coloniale #4 (RC #4), from Cao Bang to Lang Son and Lao Kay in Viet Bac (northernmost region of North Vietnam) and also after the sudden bombardment, attack, and seizure of the Seaport Hai Phong (November 26; 6,000 innocents killed), the French dropped their "scheme" of a Nam-ky State.

The relation between Ho Chi Minh and the French promptly deteriorated. Consecutive negotiations in Vietnam between Ho's delegations and French officials about the independent status of Vietnam (April–May 1946) as well as negations in France at Fontainebleau (June–August 1946) all failed. Ho Chi Minh himself was involved in the last phase of negotiations.

After the French raid in Hai Phong, the fighting spread to Hanoi by early December. Ho Chi Minh, after the failure of the political talks in France, returned to Hanoi and appealed to the United States to support his regime. He received no response. More excessive demands from the French made Ho Chi Minh and his lieutenants decide to go to war rather than satisfy them. On December 19, 1946, Vo Nguyen Giap ordered the Viet Minh to launch the first attack on the French in Hanoi that night. Ho Chi Minh returned to Pac Po, Tan Trao in Viet Bac to begin the "long resistance" against the French.

By late 1946, the world outside Vietnam had drastically changed. A new world order had been formed.

THE NEW WORLD ORDER AFTER WORLD WAR II

Soon after World War II, the political and military strategies of all nations were decisively influenced by the confrontation between the United States and the Soviet Union. The two super powers surpassed the other nations of the world, and the most strategic fact of life for each was the existence and power of the other. The covert conflict between these super powers became the Cold War.

The Cold War was not only caused by the race to develop nuclear power and by the race for outer space, but also by the large-scale conflict between "International Communist Aggression" conducted by the Kremlin leaders and the "Deterrence Strategy" originating from the White House and the Pentagon. In reality, this "containment" strategy in Washington was rooted in a report from a young and aspiring American diplomat in Moscow — George F. Kennan.

Starting in February 1946, Joseph Stalin announced a five-year plan to secure his Soviet regime in Russia, but his plan was analyzed as a scheme to conquer the world, beginning with Europe and make it communist. This communist supreme leader would use force to invade and occupy neighboring countries or ideological propaganda to mesmerize people in far away and underdeveloped countries — mostly the colonies — to "wake up" and fight for their independence and the social-class struggle. George F. Kennan, as assistant to Averell Harriman, then U.S. ambassador in Moscow, "had watched Stalin at close hand, and sent Washington an analysis of Russia that became the most famous telegram in U.S. diplomatic history."[9] Kennan's telegram, named the "Long Telegram" — of about 7,000 words — detailed Stalin's actions and visions to conquer the world. Kennan also proposed measures to "contain" Stalin's schemes. It became the "X" article in American Foreign Affairs — the anonymously written basis of the American policy of "containment" which was pursued by consecutive administrations for forty years with ultimate success around the world, except in South Vietnam.

Thus, the Cold War also saw former colonies call for independence and liberty. The rapid break-up of large colonial empires created many new countries that had to choose between the free-world democracy system and the communist socialist system. The geopolitical position of each new nation influenced its final fate. In some areas of the world, former colonies had to fight for their democratic independence or embrace the communist doctrine.

Starting in 1950, the Soviet Union and the People's Republic of China (PRC) took advantage of the unrest and disorder in key regions to set up a network of communist parties. They developed communist doctrine, concepts, and war strategies known as the "Revolutionary War." From this the communists launched their international aggression. In the primary phase, the master communists, either the Soviet Union or Communist China, selected and indoctrinated fellow leaders of underdeveloped countries with communist ideology and "Revolutionary War" concepts to become their international disciples. Any underdeveloped country that embraced the "Revolutionary War" fought not only for the "nation's liberation" but also for a "social class liberation," which the communists called the "people's liberation." The communists used this so-called "liberation" slogan to attract underdeveloped countries for the purpose of establishing a "Communist Empire" throughout the world. Examples of this can be seen in Eastern European countries after World War II. In the East, Mao Tse-tung used this concept of liberation and revolutionary war as a tool to dislodge the Nationalist forces of Chiang Kai-shek to Formosa and gain power in mainland China in December 1949.

During this period, the United States successfully restored and maintained peace in some troubled parts of the world. Applying the "Domino Theory" developed from the Truman-Doctrine & Marshall Plan and the concept of "containment" from Kennan, the United States created the strategy of "Regional Political and Military Organizations." In Europe, the North Atlantic Treaty Organization (NATO) emerged; in the Middle-East the Central Treaty Organization (CENTO) developed; and in the Asia-Pacific region the South-East Asia Treaty Organization (SEATO) also formed.

The new communist regime in China was a key issue for the United States in formulating its deterrence policy in the Asia-Pacific region. Although the Middle East was a very important zone because of its wealthy mineral oil resources, the enormous Chinese nation was crucial to the United States' foreign policy in the East. After completely taking control over mainland China, Mao Tse-tung, the chairman of the Central Committee of the Chinese Communist Party (CCP) and president of the People's Republic of China (PRC), decided to change old China. He described China as a "semi-colonial and feudal" country. Mao's social revolution was to deeply smash this four-thousand-year-old Confucian society.

In internal affairs, Mao Tse-tung acknowledged that the Chinese peasants would rebuild the country. Mao's approach emphasized the primary communist doctrine of Marx and Lenin but added key ideological derivations. Many historians named these derivations Maoism. According to Mao, the revolution of Chinese society was to be based upon the 450 million peasants in their immense agricultural country who needed liberation from the oppressive landowners.

In external affairs, Mao Tse-Tung's vision was not just limited to the border conflicts with India, but also targeted countries as far as the China Sea and Southeast Asia. The United States paid little attention to the first phase of the revolutionary wars, which started in the Philippines, Indonesia, and Malaysia, but could not ignore the direct involvement of Communist Chinese ground troops in the Korean War in 1950.

Mao Tse-tung's speech before the Politburo of the Central Committee of the Chinese Communist Party revealed China's true ambitions and the extent of its external policy: "We must by all means seize South-East Asia, including Vietnam, Thailand, Burma, Malaysia, and Singapore.... This region is rich in raw materials, it is worth the costs involved. After seizing South-East Asia, we can increase our strength in the region. And we shall be strong enough to confront the Soviet and East Europe bloc; the East wind will prevail over the West wind."[10] Mao's statement was very concise and his ambitions very clear. The United States, on the other hand, applied its containment policy to Southeast Asia by assisting allied "dominoes" to become strong enough to resist communist aggression, as it had done in Western Europe. Vietnam was one of these allies.

According to some American historians, this containment theory was applied in Southeast Asia during the height of the Cold War as the communist revolutionary war in China spread to Vietnam in the spring of 1947. The Truman Doctrine attempted to link the defense of Europe with collective security in Asia. In March 1947, President Truman explained his policy toward Indochina, saying: "It must be the policy of the United States to support the free people who are resisting attempted subjugation by armed minorities."[11] Although Truman's statement could be read both ways, the French interpreted it as meaning the U.S. supported them in Indochina. While Great Britain had peacefully withdrawn from its colonies in India, Burma and Pakistan, and the Netherlands had liberated the Dutch East Indies (now Indonesia), France still clung to its old colonies in Southeast Asia.

THE VIET-MINH AND THE FIRST VIETNAM WAR

Unaware of the principles of revolutionary war that the Viet-Minh such as Ho Chi Minh, Truong Chinh, and Vo Nguyen Giap were using in Indochina, the French still envisioned using the old tactics of conquering land through pacification operations, but not truly winning the hearts and minds of the Vietnamese people. This last vestige of colonialism was a major factor in the American reluctance to wholeheartedly help the French in their war against the communists of Vietnam despite the total "liberation" of mainland China by the communist forces of Mao Tse-tung in December 1949.

Meanwhile, Vo Nguyen Giap, the first Viet-Minh commander, combined the popular militia with the main force of the People's Army and by 1947 claimed that his forces totaled one million men. Nobody believed him because this million-man army was not to be found. The French could not "catch or crush" its large units by superior firepower and large-scale operations, except once in the first year of the war. On October 7, 1947, the commander of the French forces, General Jean-Etienne Valluy, mounted a coup de main, Operation Lea, in Viet Bac (the northernmost region of North Vietnam), with a force of 20 battalions. French paratroopers almost captured Ho Chi Minh and Vo Nguyen Giap in Bac Kan or Cho Moi. This French operation was successful: the Viet Minh suffered 9,500 casualties and many supply depots were destroyed. On October 22, Operation Lea ended and French operational units moved back to the lowlands, but a string of French garrisons, base camps and outposts along the Sino-Vietnamese border were reinforced. The Viet Minh regrouped and strengthened again in the following years, especially after Mao Tse-tung established the People's Republic of China (PRC) in mainland China, and offered the Viet Minh safe sanctuaries in several provinces bordering North Vietnam. There, Giap's large units could be trained, armed, and supplied by the Chinese Red Army, or the People's Liberation Army (PLA).

According to Qiang Zhai, a Chinese-born professor of history at Auburn University Montgomery in Alabama and author of the history book, *China and the Vietnam Wars, 1950–1975* (2000), after Ho Chi Minh paid a secret visit to Beijing and Moscow from mid–January to early March 1950 to meet Liu Shaoqi, Mao Tse-tung, and Stalin, most of his requests for political, diplomatic, economic, and military support were granted by these communist leaders. Particularly, the Chinese Communist Party (CCP) was in charge of these matters for Ho's government or the Democratic Republic of Vietnam (DRV), as well as the Communist Party or the Vietnam Workers' Party (VWP; Ho re-established it in November 1951), and the Viet Minh army or the People's Army of Vietnam (PAVN), which was commanded by General Vo Nguyen Giap.[12]

On January 18, 1950, the new PRC formally recognized the DRV with Ho Chi Minh as its leader. The USSR did the same on January 30, 1950. They were followed by communist countries in Eastern Europe and North Korea. Leaders of the CCP primarily organized two very important groups — the "Chinese Political Advisory Group" (CPAG) and the "Chinese Military Advisory Group" (CMAG) — that crucially helped the VWP and the PAVN to develop and be effective during their first phases of resistance against the French and to ultimately defeat them. Luo Guipo, the director of the General Office of the CCP Central Committee, came to Vietnam in mid–January as the CCP's representative, and became the head of the CPAG in the DRV. The famous General Chen Geng, commander of the PLA forces in Yunnan and head of the administration of Yunnan, was assigned as senior military advisor and representative to the PAVN, even though the senior leader of the CMAG was General Wei Guoqing. General Chen came to Viet Bac in July 1950, but he had previously prepared an operational plan for the PAVN's first and most important offensive phase against the French along the border and on Route Coloniale #4 (RC#4) in the northeastern region of North Vietnam.[13] General Chen's operational plan was based on the tactic of "encircling a small outpost and attacking the large rescue force," which was translated as "công đồn đả viện" and became the PAVN's main tactic during the two Vietnam Wars. In the first border offensive campaign along the RC#4, the outpost of Dong Khe was the target to be encircled and assaulted to lure large French units from their garrisons in Cao Bang and Lang Son to open fields whereby they would be attacked and destroyed. Chen's plan was appreciated by Ho Chi Minh and Vo Nguyen Giap. It was also approved by the CCP Central Military Committee that ordered the deputy commander of the Guangxi Military Region, General Li Tianyou, to form a "Logistics committee" for providing logistical support for the PAVN in the campaign.

On August 12, the CMAG led by General Wei Guoqing, arrived at General Giap's headquarters at Quang Nguyen on the border to meet General Chen Geng. Chinese advisors from this group were immediately dispatched to the PAVN's 304th, 308th, and 312th Divisions: another infantry division, the 316th, and the large Engineering and Artillery 351st Division also had their Chinese advisors by the end of the year. On September 16, 1950, General Giap launched the assault on Dong Khe, as planned by General Chen, with 10,000 troops. Two days later, Giap's troops captured this outpost of only 260 French defenders. The PAVN units suffered 500 casualties. The RC#4 was cut from the Cao Bang Garrison in the north and the Lang Son Garrison in the south. On their side, the French ordered Lieutenant Colonel Lepage of the Lang Son Garrison to lead his core units to recapture Dong Khe via outpost That Khe. On October 3, Lepage's column was ambushed by Giap's large force. In the north, French Lieutenant Colonel Charton left Cao Bang Garrison and moved his units southward on RC#4 to link up with those of Lepage. The rendezvous never happened. Both French columns moving on RC#4 to Dong Khe were encircled, assaulted, and cut to pieces; Lepage and Charton were captured. General Marcel Carpentier, Commander in Chief of French Expeditionary Forces in Indochina, ordered the abandonment of the string of French garrisons, base camps, and outposts along the Sino-Vietnamese border and along RC#4. Some 6,000 of 10,000 French troops were killed or captured on their retreat from the northeastern region to the Red River Delta, including those of Lepage and Charton's units. Meanwhile, 3,000 French troops from Lao Kay Garrison in the northwest border completed the retreat to the lowlands with few casualties. The French also lost a great quantity of war materials, artillery guns, light rifles, and ammunition. But the biggest loss would be their ability to win the war due to the growing size and strength of General Vo Nguyen Giap's PAVN that had the backing of the CCP leaders and the PLA generals. Otherwise, in reading the greater part of Chapter 1 of Qiang Zhai's book, one might think that the previously mentioned Chinese communist leaders and generals led the PAVN fight against the French but not Ho Chi Minh or his commanders, including General Vo Nguyen Giap.[14]

It is necessary to mention that the CCP leaders not only exercised a leading role in the Vietnam War but also in the Korean War. Since October 1950, the war in Korea seriously intensified after the PLA committed a force of 400,000 Chinese People's Volunteers for the "intervention" of the North Korean Army that invaded South Korea on January 25, 1950 and captured its capital and seized the peninsula in September. However, when this army was crushed by United Nations forces and pushed back to the 38th parallel, and then farther to the Yalu River in Manchuria, the Chinese Red armies led by Peng Dehuai met them on the northern bank of the Yalu River in October, 1950. Beijing threatened an "intervention" should the 38th parallel be crossed by General McArthur's forces. Starting in November, this war was "handled" by the CCP leaders. The "scholar general" Chen Geng was made second to Peng, serving as his deputy commander of the People's Volunteers forces. The Red Chinese threat appeared very real in East and Southeast Asia, both in Korea and in Vietnam.

In November 1950, as the Chinese People's Volunteers armies prepared to cross the Yalu River to attack United Nations forces, the PAVN leaders and their CMAG advisors in Vietnam prepared a "general offensive" to follow their victorious offensive campaign on the border in September–October, 1950.

In December 1950, France sent General De Lattre de Tassigny to Saigon as commander in chief of French Forces and high commissioner in Indochina. Independence was granted to Vietnam, Laos, and Cambodia six months before, but in "A Call to Vietnamese Youth," De Lattre declared: "Certainly people pretend that Vietnam cannot be independent because it is part of the French Union. Not true! In our universe, and especially in our world of today, there can be no nations absolutely independent. There are only fruitful interdependencies and harmful dependencies. Young men of Vietnam … the moment has come for you to defend your country."[15] This middle part of De Lattre's speech made sense; we later knew this when the Americans replaced the French in Vietnam.

At first, the United States was inclined to a "real independence" for Vietnam but was hesitant to endorse the "Bao Dai solution" until France granted autonomy and supported the creation of a genuinely independent and non-communist state for Vietnam. But after French President Vincent Auriol signed, with Vietnam's former Emperor Bao Dai on March 8, 1949, the "Elysee Agreement" in which "France yielded control of neither Vietnam's army nor its foreign relations," the United States began to view the Bao Dai solution "with greater sense of urgency."[16] Bao Dai returned to Vietnam as chief of state and formed the "Government of Vietnam" in June, 1949. The Elysee Agreement was ratified by the French National Assembly on January 29, 1950. On February 7, 1950, the United States formally recognized Vietnam, Laos, and Cambodia. On February 16, 1950, France requested United States military and economic assistance to fight the communists in Indochina. On May 1, 1950, President Truman approved $10 million for urgently needed war materials for Indochina with the hope that French forces in Vietnam would fight the communists and win the war with United States advice and guidance.

Britain and Australia also recognized Vietnam as an associate state within the French Union. The political lines had finally been drawn within Vietnam: Ho Chi Minh with the government recognized by the communist bloc, and Bao Dai with a government recognized by the free world. The first hint of the Vietnam War, from the beginning, lay on these political lines.

The French had confidence in being able to defeat the Viet Minh in Vietnam in fifteen months as De Lattre himself expected to "save it from Peking and Moscow."[17] Nevertheless, Mao Tse-tung and Stalin had divided their roles in the East and West, and the French could not win the war in Indochina. Specifically, after General Marcel Carpentier had abandoned Viet Bac or the upper half of North Vietnam, this area then became the Viet Minh's stronghold from which General Giap could launch other offensive campaigns to the west into Laos and to the south into the Red River Delta. Perhaps anticipating Giap's intention, General De Lattre ordered the reinforcement of French outposts in the Thai-Highlands and Lai Chau, and the construction of a line of fortified defensive positions to protect the rich and populated Red River Delta; it was the "De Lattre Line." (See Map 1.)

In early spring 1951, General Giap launched the so-called "general offensive" on French positions in the Red River Delta with three divisions. On January 13, the PAVN 308th, 312th, and 316th totaling 30,000 men attacked 8,000 French troops in Vinh Yen, 40 miles northwest of Hanoi. French air support played a major role in supporting ground troops. These communist divisions suffered heavy losses: 6,000 to 9,000 killed, a similar number wounded, and 600 captured. On March 23, Giap's force attacked Mao Khe in the northeast of the De Lattre Line and suffered losses not less than at the first defeat. However, the campaign continued through May and June with more than four divisions attacking French positions along the Day River on the left flank of the De Lattre Line in Phu Ly, Ninh Binh, Nam Dinh, and Phat Diem. Another 10,000 were killed and captured. General De Lattre's tactics were based on counter-attacks by his reserve paratroopers, who had been airlifted from Saigon, and the use of napalm bombs. Later, Viet Minh leaders blamed the disastrous failure of this premature "general offensive" on their Chinese advisor, Luo Guipo.[18] Nevertheless, Giap's force of several divisions could again stab into the vital area of the Red River Delta. Their attacks continued after the death of General De Lattre (from cancer) on November 20, 1951.

General Raoul Salan replaced De Lattre as commander in chief of the French Forces, and Jean Letourneau as high commissioner Indochina (he was also French cabinet minister for the Associated States). General Salan faced fierce attacks from General Giap's divisions in the lowlands of the Red River Delta. This most significant was the encounter of Salan's sixteen battalions composed of 15,000 troops and Giap's more than three divisions of 35,000 men at Hoa Binh Province, 45 miles southwest of Hanoi, from December 9, 1951, to February 26, 1952. Both sides suffered heavy losses. In the following months, a dozen or more French counter-attacks into the Viet Minh's controlled areas were in vain, including "Operation Lorraine" in the Phu Doan area and Thai Nguyen, respectively located 80 miles northwest and 40 miles northeast of Hanoi, from October 29 to November 14, 1952. The latter operation was a diversion to draw Giap's forces back to their bases in Viet Bac, from where Giap had sent three of his divisions westward to attack French outposts Nghia Lo and Lai Chau in paving the way for his entry into Laos during the next offensive campaign against the French.

Perhaps due to the pressure by the CCP leaders through their generals in Viet Bac, Ho and the VWP ordered General Vo Nguyen Giap to attack Nghia Lo and several nearby outposts. On October 24, Giap concentrated eight regiments and overwhelmed French units in the area. After losing Nghia Lo, the French abandoned Son La. By mid–December, Giap's divisions could move up to the Thai-Highlands, attack Lai Chau, or invade Laos.

In April 1953, in combination with several small units of the Pathet Lao, three PAVN infantry divisions — 308th, 312th, and 316th — waged war in Laos by attacking French positions south of Luang Prabang, in Samnuea, and in the Plain of Jars. By this campaign, Ho and Giap would regularly test French abilities, movements, and air support. Politically, Ho and other leaders of the VWP would join forces with the Pathet Lao to transform them into an armed force struggling for the liberation of Laos in the communist design. Laos then became an important strategic arena receiving attention from both Beijing and Washington. Mao of Red China and President Eisenhower of the United States paid most attention to Laos and envisioned Laos as crucial for their respective strategies of "aggression" and "containment." However, Vietnamese nationalist parties' leaders in Hanoi and Saigon regarded this PAVN invasion in Laos differently. In the beginning of the war, they considered Ho's communist party and his army as tools of the international communists to bring communism not only to Vietnam but also the rest of Indochina. This view resulted from cooperating for quite a while with Ho Chi Minh in the struggle to gain independence for Vietnam.

In retrospect, before the 1930s there were a dozen large anti-colonial movements in Vietnam against the French led by revolutionaries, both the communists and the nationalists. The most significant would be the armed revolution of the Việt Nam Quốc Dân Đảng, or the Nationalist Party of Vietnam (VNQDD, or NPVN). The VNQDD was organized by a group of intellects and writers, and led by Nguyen Thai Hoc. The organization was secret but developed largely in both urban areas and in the countryside, and as well as among the Vietnamese troops within French units in North Vietnam. For some reason, the "General Uprising" of the VNQDD prematurely started on February 12, 1930, in several cities in North Vietnam, but mainly in Yen Bai, 80 miles northwest of Hanoi. The attack failed. Hundreds of VNQDD members were arrested, including Nguyen Thai Hoc. Later, on June 16, he was executed with 12 other important VNQDD members. They became regarded as historical heroes. The French began to arrest and suppress Vietnamese revolutionaries, communists and nationalists. Thousands were arrested and sentenced. The majority went underground and most parties' leaders fled to China. In China they were allowed exile and these leaders were supported by Chiang Kai-shek in reorganizing their parties. Chinese soil was the first medium where these communists and nationalists could meet and cooperate. But later, Ho Chi Minh betrayed the nationalists.

Truong Boi Cong, Nguyen Hai Than, Ho Hoc Lam, and other nationalist parties' leaders, along with Ho Chi Minh, organized the key organization of this united front at Liwchow, in Kwang-si Province, in October 1943. It was the "Việt-Nam Cách-Mệnh Đồng-Minh Hội" (Vietnam Revolutionary United Association), which was composed of the "Việt-Nam Quốc Dân Đảng" (Nationalist Party of Vietnam) of Vu Hong Khanh, the "Việt-Nam Phục-Quốc Đồng-Minh Hội" (United Association for Reconquering of Vietnam) of Bo Xuan Luat, and the "Việt-Nam Độc-Lập Đồng-Minh Hội" (United Association for Independence of Việtnam), or "Việt-Minh," of Ho Chi Minh. After forming the newly united front and sending Ho Chi Minh back to the frontiers for a new phase of action, the Viet-Minh secret organization drew many nationalist revolutionaries and students, rather than communists.

In reality, Ho Chi Minh exploited the prestige and patriotic goals of these great nationalist revolutionaries to develop the Viet-Minh and strengthen his control over the organization. The Viet-Minh took over Hanoi and Ho Chi Minh declared "independence" in 1945. The presence of American senior officers at the ceremony and the flying of the American flag beside the "one-red-star flag" made it easy to convince the Vietnamese population that the United States had established "official relations" with the Viet-Minh regime. Emperor Bao Dai and his nationalist supporters believed that the United States had backed Ho. With this belief, Bao Dai gave up the reins of government to the Viet-Minh in August 1945, without a struggle.

By June 1946, when it became obvious that American support was not forthcoming, Ho Chi Minh became troubled and began to show the violent nature of a communist leader. Before leaving Hanoi for the "independence talks" in Paris, he ordered his loyal collaborators in Hanoi, Hue and Saigon, such as Vo Nguyen Giap, Pham Van Bach, Tran Van Giau and Nguyen Binh, to liquidate all nationalist elements who had cooperated with the communists in the Democratic Government. Along with leaders of religious sects, intellectuals, Trotskyites, and leaders of other nationalist parties, these elements were considered to be "internal enemies." The "purge" was extremely cruel and barbaric. In many areas, victims were tied together alive in bundles like logs and thrown into the river, to float to the sea while slowly drowning. This was called "Mò-Tôm" ("shrimp-catching," or "crab-fishing," as a French historian named it). Around the country nearly twenty thousand elite nationalists or unaffiliated innocents were killed. Among the deceased were well-known personalities such as Ngo-Dinh-Khoi, elder brother of the future first president of South Vietnam, Ngo-Dinh-Diem, scholar and politician Pham Quynh, and sect leader Huynh Phu So. The political and ideological purge by the communists continued for years even after Ho gained control of North Vietnam in 1955.

The communist path that Ho Chi Minh and his disciples followed was summarized in this slogan: "Chasing external enemies and crushing internal enemies for the liberation of the nation and the liberation of the working class" (the Viet-Minh's slogan in the war: "Đánh Thù Trong, Đuổi Giặc Ngoài Để Giành Độc-lập Quốc-gia và Giải-phóng Giai-cấp Công Nông"). War with the French greatly simplified Ho's political activities in Vietnam, uniting the Viet-Minh by their common hatred for the French (and later, the Americans), whom they called "white invaders," and the nationalists, for them the "internal enemies" or "Việt gian" (traitors to the country), and "puppets."

The more "white invaders" fighting in conjunction with the "puppets" that Vietnamese soil received, the more Ho Chi Minh united the Viet-Minh around him. As long as the Vietnamese believed that the source of "slavery and misery" was coming from abroad, Ho won

Vietnamese hearts and minds. They would sacrifice their lives to fulfill his demands for national unity and freedom. His Marxist slogans were of little importance in comparison to his overwhelming appeal to national pride and the traditional xenophobia of the Vietnamese. Ho's lifelong deceit was to conceal his true intentions and his real communist agenda, in order to control Vietnam and the masses.

This aspect of Ho's success was too abstruse and complicated for the American policymakers. They could not understand why the nationalist leaders of South Vietnam suggested that the United States not send combat troops to fight in Vietnam. Nationalist leaders sought only political, economic, and military support from the United States, just as the Vietnamese communists had been provided material support from the Soviet Union and Red China. The war then, according to this logic, would become a "Pure Vietnamese War of Ideologies." Unfortunately, during the length of the two Vietnam wars, the nationalists had their own problems, because the French and (later) the Americans did not trust them.

THE SHADOWY "STATE OF VIETNAM"

Those who escaped from the communist purge in 1946 had very few options. Some collaborated with the French, but the majority reunited into a political front called "National United Front" in Saigon in May 1947. The front included leaders and members of several nationalist parties such as the Vietnamese Democratic-Socialist Party with Đảng Dân-Chủ Xã-Hội Vietnam, the Nationalist Youth Association with Liên-Đoàn Thanh Niên Quốc-Gia, the Social Democratic Reconstruction Party with Đảng Dân-Chủ Xã-Hội Cấp-Tiến, and the Works' Personal Spirit Party with Đảng Cần-Lao Nhân-Vi. The two strong political religious organizations in South Vietnam, the Cao-Đai and the Hoa-Hao sects, plus the independent intellectual class of professors, doctors, lawyers, and engineers joined in. This front was more anti–French than Ho Chi Minh's forces. On May 17, 1947, the National Vietnamese Front issued a manifesto advocating the return of Bao Dai and the creation of a republican government for Vietnam. Bao Dai, the last emperor of the Nguyen Dynasty, had previously abdicated his throne in September 1945, and was honored by Ho Chi Minh as his "Supreme Advisor." However, 6 months later, on March 18, 1946, while leading a delegation to discuss with Chiang Kai-shek the Chinese troops in North Vietnam, Bao Dai decided to stay in exile in Hong Kong until 1948. Finally, Bao Dai returned to power in 1949. A non-communist State of Vietnam was born slowly and painfully.

Big problems faced the founders, leaders, protectors and supporters of this regime. Vietnamese nationalists were unable to deal with challenging problems such as:

1. The national economy, since the wealth of the country had been completely drained by an exhaustive war.
2. France's inconsistent policy toward Vietnam. The French argued they could not transfer all power to Bao Dai because of the perilous circumstances of war in the country. Those close to Bao Dai no longer felt that they could support him to repeatedly negotiate with the French for the full independence of Vietnam. Furthermore, the struggle at the conference table could not compete with the Viet-Minh in terms of patriotic appeal. Ho Chi Minh's creed was very simple; he wanted total independence for Vietnam even at the price of a long and bloody war.
3. The dilemma of a republican political power based on small numbers from the urban intellectual class, the middle class, and the civil-servant class situated in large cities and dis-

tricts. The masses of people in vast rural areas, especially peasants in small villages, were enticed or threatened by the Viet-Minh's two-edged approach: patriotic appeal and the threat of death. Rural and remote areas became sites of both physical and psychological battles between the Viet-Minh and the French.

4. Lack of a republican government army to protect the regime and its people. When the French agreed to allow the build up of a national army, they also permitted the Cao-Dai and the Hoa-Hao sects to organize their own armies, each reaching the strength of 40,000 men. The National Army still numbered about 80,000 men. In contrast, more than 200,000 Vietnamese, Cambodians, and Laotians served in the French Union Forces, by the end of 1950.

5. How to justify the struggle between these two Vietnamese forces, since both were fighting for the common cause of national independence. The presence of tens of thousands Vietnamese soldiers who fought besides the French Expeditionary Corps in the battlefield made it easy for the Viet-Minh to dub the nationalist government as "The Puppet" and the nationalists as "Việt-gian" for many years.

However, with the American recognition of the Republic State of Vietnam on February 7, 1950, Vietnam became a member of six United Nations specialized agencies and was recognized by 40 nations of the free world. These external gains granted and consolidated Bao Dai's regime as the first legal foundation of a free nation. In June 1950, the Korean War broke out, as the North Korean army crossed the partition line of the 38th parallel to invade South Korea. The United States became immediately involved in the war, providing armed support to the South Korean army. In the meantime, fearing wider communist expansion, the United States announced a program of military aid for Indochina. The starting amount was a modest $10 million worth of equipment given in 1950, but the American military involvement had begun.

Nevertheless, with the initiation of the American aid-program in mid–1950, both the Vietnamese nationalists and the French held great hopes for a rapid delivery of funds and military equipment. The United States' policy toward Indochina previously had been "tied to Europe." Now the United States had a true commitment to the "communist" situation in Indochina. American secretary of state John Foster Dulles believed it to be the only way to hold the line and to contain China and the Soviet Union. The commitment to Vietnam quickly became part of the overall American policy toward the Asia-Pacific region. The fighting in Vietnam was seen in a new light, transforming it from a colonial war into an anti-communist war for freedom. The United States hoped the Vietnamese nationalists would eventually dismiss the French from their country and fight the communists by themselves, fulfilling the words of President Truman that the U.S. intent was "to support the free people, who are resisting attempted subjugation by armed minorities."

A United States Military Assistance Advisory Group (MAAG) arrived in Saigon in July 1950, to coordinate aid to the French in Vietnam and to train the Vietnamese. Dulles himself called for the official formation of a Vietnamese National Army with the implication that the United States would then arm it. A Vietnamese Military Academy, which had opened in 1949, began to improve its training program and increase the graduation rate of new Vietnamese officers. Previously, all officers had been trained in French military schools. Many of them later played major political and military roles in South Vietnam, including generals Tran Van Don, Duong Van Minh, Nguyen Khanh, Tran Thien Khiem, and Nguyen Van Thieu. General Nguyen Cao Ky was among the first class of graduating officers to be trained by both the French and the Americans in their new combined training program.

In the meantime, the French hoped that with American military aid they would quickly win the war over the Viet-Minh. Notwithstanding this, in announcing military aid to the French, American secretary of state John F. Dulles conceived the fact that "Vietnamization" was a doorway to the region. At that time, the French did not know exactly what Dulles meant by using the term "Vietnamization." In 1961, Dulles' successor, Dean Rusk, tried to explain it: "On the one hand, we were giving France assistance for postwar reconstruction. On the other hand, we pressed them very hard to make a political settlement with Indochina to work out on the same basis on which the British were working out their relations with India and Burma. We did not press the French to the point where they would simply withdraw and say 'alright it is yours, you worry about it.' We didn't want them that far because we didn't want Indochina on our hands."[19]

In short, according to Rusk, Vietnamization in the 1950s meant the French would withdraw from Vietnam and the Vietnamese would fight the war for themselves with the indirect backing of the United States, since the United States did not want Indochina in its grip. However, the United States became deeply committed to the war in Vietnam. Just five months after the first American Advisory Group came to Vietnam, American military aid to the French in Vietnam rose one-hundred-fold. The initial $10 million increased annually by hundreds of millions, and cumulatively exceeded $1 billion by 1954. French expenditures in Indochina roughly equaled what the Americans had given them through the Marshall Plan for aid and reconstruction.

Despite American political concern and military aid, it became clear that the French could not win the war in Vietnam because of their outmoded colonial policy in Indochina and their limited strategy in North Vietnam. This became particularly evident at the battle of Dien-Bien-Phu. General Henry Navarre, commander in chief of the French Expeditionary Corps in Indochina and the architect of the set-piece outpost Dien-Bien-Phu, had previously stated that there was no possibility of winning the war in Indochina. He knew the Viet-Minh had gained a considerable advantage over the French in mobile forces, and he intended to find an honorable exit from the war, creating a military situation that would allow an honorable solution.

A French historian, Jean Lacouture, had the same view but for a different reason: "the war was nearly impossible to win because the Viet-Minh, with China behind them, had a great enormous sanctuary. So the war became more and more unpopular from 1950 and very expensive, though of course the United States paid."[20] In addition to financial aid, the Americans provided military equipment to the French in Indochina in the amount of 1,400 tanks, 340 aircraft, 240,000 small arms, and 150 million bullets. The American military aid to the French reveals how deeply the United States had committed in Vietnam. Obviously, by the late 1960s its decisions to directly engage in the war in this country had become inevitable.

American assistance to Indochina continued even after the French completely withdrew in May 1955, and the United States was dragged deeper into the war. At the time, Dean Rusk explained how the United States rationalized aiding the French in Indochina to avoid directly involving itself in the war. Many strategists suspected otherwise. They further argued that the basic commitment of the Truman administration to the French was not only based on material military assistance to the French in Indochina but also based on the political commitment with its allied European governments as a solution for the Far East after World War II. American involvement in Vietnam was so deep it could not be stopped without a strong collective will of the whole nation.

Indeed, twenty-five years later American General Bruce Palmer revealed in his book *The 25-Year War: America's Roles in Vietnam* that in October 1951, while a student at the Army

War College, he was part of a group assigned to study American policy in Southeast Asia. The group found that the United States had "probably made a serious mistake in agreeing with its allies to allow French power to be restored in Indochina" and that "Indochina was of only secondary strategic importance to the United States." The study concluded that the United States "should not become involved in the area beyond providing material aid."[21] The study was insightful. The war in Vietnam could not be won either by the French or Americans, because neither understood the nature of the war conducted by the communists and the endurance of the Vietnamese with their tradition of fighting against foreign invaders. Only American General Edward Lansdale, a foremost counter-insurgency expert, had very strong feelings that a colonial power — which the French were — couldn't win the people's war that was being waged. Only the Vietnamese themselves could win such a war.

The Vietnamese nationalists actually wished to fight the war for themselves. This did not please their rich and powerful fellow allies in Washington. Choosing their ways of fighting and trying to handle a war in which they knew their enemies better than anyone in the White House or the Pentagon would not be permitted. The men who ran that war were American politicians and bureaucrats, not even military professionals. American generals certainly knew how to fight to win a war, but the U.S. civilian leadership would not allow them to do that.

In summary, Truman's political philosophy of "Strategic Containment of Communist Aggression" was rigidly applied by his successors in order not to provoke a new, enormous war directly with China or the Soviet Union. Thus, American military strategy consecutively became a defensive one for almost twenty years, until the war became "unwinnable." The Truman policy of containment against communist expansion would remain the bedrock foundation of the United States' national policy toward Vietnam for the next 25 years.

4

The Two Vietnams

Indochina, located south of the vast mainland China, was an important geopolitical arena and a primary concern of the United States. Vietnam, which occupied the eastern Indochinese Peninsula along the South Sea, played an especially key role in the war of Indochina. When the outmoded colonial rule left the French unable to hold onto the region, the leading power in the free-world — the United States — stepped in. The U.S. would not allow Indochina to fall into the hands of the international communists — the Chinese or the Soviets. Previously, the U.S. had opposed the Japanese attempt to occupy the peninsula as an adjoining base to expand their control over the Far East and South Pacific. Many may pose the question why the United States had the primary concern for deterring any expansionist powers from occupying Indochina. The following was emphasized by U.S. leaders themselves prior to the meeting with the Japanese ambassador to Washington in 1941, prior to the sudden Japanese attack on Pearl Harbor on December 7: "the occupation of Indochina by Japan possibly means one further step to seizing control of the South Sea area, including trade routes of supreme importance to the United States for rubber, tin, and other commodities. This was of vital concern to the United States."[1] Clearly, the United States' involvement in the Indochina War (or Vietnam War) was mainly due to its economic interests rather than political or military interests. If a worldwide super-power takes some political, economic, diplomatic, or military strategy somewhere at sometime, it can only be to gain or to protect its own economic interests. This becomes a "rule" or "law" of its government. After World War II, in the 1940s, the Truman Doctrine practiced "economic means" to help other countries, including former enemies, recover their economies; this was not an exception. A primary example of this concept is the Marshall Plan, which helped Western European countries and included the restoration of West Germany's heavy industry and reorganization of their armed forces, while in Asia it helped Japan re-establish its economy. In alignment with American political, economic, and military plans in Europe, the United States also provided the French with military aid in Indochina. However, at the end of 1949, when the Chinese communists of Mao Tse-tung defeated the Nationalist forces of Chiang Kai-shek and occupied mainland China, the United States foreign policy toward Asia had to be revised, particularly its policy toward Southeast Asia and Indochina.

In general, American historians and strategists note that American foreign policy toward Southeast Asia at the time was one of containment toward Chinese expansion. Five consecutive U.S. presidents after Truman formulated and implemented this policy (see Chapter 3). However, each president had a distinct philosophy, style of leadership, and military strategy, and so owned the war in Indochina in a different manner. According to commentators, the "flawed strategies" of these presidents would lead to inconsistency in American policy toward this important region, resulting in the complete loss of South Vietnam, Laos and Cambodia.

Contrary to common opinion, I believe that the United States stuck to its primary policy from the beginning to the end. The U.S. succeeded in its goals of blocking the Chinese at their borders and saving peace and freedom for other countries in Southeast Asia.

THE UNITED STATES AND
THE BATTLE OF DIEN BIEN PHU

After the end of the Korean War in July 1953, President Dwight D. Eisenhower, who had taken office on 20 January 1953, adopted the lasting Truman Doctrine and the Marshall Plan for his foreign policy toward Europe and toward Asia and the Pacific. But Eisenhower followed his predecessor's policy with broader considerations for the dominant strategy of "containment" against the expansion of the communism both in Europe and Asia. The initial military aid for the French in Indochina to fight the Viet Minh in Vietnam under the Truman administration — in return for their reluctant participation in the North Atlantic Treaty Organization (NATO) and their agreement with the European Defense Community (EDC) — increased in the two years following the North Korean Army's invasion of South Korea (June 1950), and increased considerably due to the invasion by the Viet Minh into Laos in April 1953.

President Eisenhower and his most anti-communist aides, including vice president Richard M. Nixon and secretary of state John F. Dulles, were concerned about the situation in Laos and viewed the Viet Minh of Ho Chi Minh as the particularly active Southeast Asian component of the worldwide communist movement. In April 1953, Vice President Nixon visited Vietnam and encouraged the French to believe that they could win the war. John F. Dulles, who strongly supported a forthright anti-communist policy, made clear that he would not permit the loss of Indochina. French forces were then considered to be an anti-communist compulsion that would be able to deter the communist expansion in this doorway to Southeast Asia. The Eisenhower administration also suggested that the French develop the Associated States' armies, especially the Army of Vietnam. Moreover, there was increased focus to unite a number of free nations in the region and in the South Pacific into a collective defense organization using the "domino theory" as outlined by President Eisenhower: "You have a row of dominoes set up. You knock over the first one, and what will happen to the last one is the certainty that it will go over very quickly."[2] Thus, the loss of Indochina or a single nation in Southeast Asia to the international communists would eventually lead to the other nations of the area falling under communist control.

In March 1953, French prime minister René Mayer, minister of foreign affairs Georges Bidault, and minister for the Associated States in Indochina Jean Letourneau came to Washington to demand additional military aid for the French in Indochina. Their request was granted with $385 million. By the end of 1952, the United States had paid 40 percent of the French war cost in Vietnam of about $700 million.[3] Washington, in turn, recommended that France reinforce their strength in Indochina with two more infantry divisions, draw pacification plans to win the Viet Minh in two years, and develop the Army of Vietnam. All were agreed to and promised by the French delegation, but none materialized. Later, we learned that the "dictator in Indochina," Jean Letourneau, did nothing with his pacification plan, the so-called "Letourneau Plan," but exercised more control over the Associated States.

In May, French prime minister Mayer appointed General Henri Navarre to assume command of the French forces in Indochina. Navarre went to assess the situation in Vietnam a month before taking his command post and upon returning to France reported to his boss that "there was no possibility of winning the war in Indochina."[4] Nevertheless, Navarre came to Vietnam with a strategic plan. In North Vietnam, French forces and defensive measures would be strengthened to secure the lowlands of the Red River Delta, counterattack in Viet Bac, and control the northwest region to bar the access of General Giap's forces entering Laos. In Central Vietnam, pacification operations would be launched into areas controlled by the

Viet Minh. Within three months Navarre mounted several "search and destroy" operations with limited success. The French government authorized only ten battalions instead of two divisions as promised, while the Army of Vietnam slowly developed.

In the meantime, the PAVN of General Vo Nguyen Giap developed considerably and it could perform distantly combined operations — between infantry and artillery — in large-scale at the corps-sized level, or larger. They could quickly maneuver both in attack and in retreat. In the summer of 1953, the Central Military Committee of the VWP and General Giap planned to launch the winter-spring offensive campaign (1953–1954) on the French in the Red River Delta, but for some reason, three divisions of Giap's army moved westward to the north region. According to Professor Qiang Zhai, the CPAG senior advisor Luo Guipo, who facilitated the meeting of the VWP Politburo held on August 22, 1953, reported to Beijing that General Giap had proposed to launch this campaign in the lowlands of the Red River Delta, ignoring Lai Chau and downplaying the campaign in Laos. On August 27 and 29, Beijing leaders sent two messages to Luo that analyzed the situation of Vietnam after the arrival of French General Navarre and insisted that the PAVN stick to its initial campaign that focused on the northwest region and Laos. Qiang quotes a message (or part of it) that read, "By eliminating the enemy in the Lai Chau area, liberating the northern and central parts of Laos, and then expanding the battleground to the southern part of Laos and Cambodia to threaten Saigon."[5]

In mid–November 1953, the PAVN 304th and 316th Divisions and parts of the 325th Artillery Division moved to the northwest region and Lai Chau. This information was reported to General Navarre by his staff intelligence. The commander in chief of the French forces then decided to occupy Dien Bien Phu with his core units in North Vietnam to control the routes that lead to the northern part of Laos.

Dien-Bien-Phu was a small valley village in a remote area straddling the crossroads between the Vietnamese and Laotian borders, some 188 miles west of Hanoi. General Henri Navarre, French commander in chief in Indochina, chose it as bait to entice the Viet-Minh into the area in order to destroy them with crack French infantry and French superior air power. Navarre had gathered into this garrison a defensive force of 10,000 men, and when the Viet-Minh attack began, he strengthened it with his full reserve of 5,000 parachute troops. He expected to be confronted with two Viet-Minh divisions, but the garrison actually dealt with more than four divisions. Viet-Minh's General Vo Nguyen Giap had at least three-to-one superiority of both firepower and manpower in his offensive against Dien-Bien-Phu French forces.

The importance of the Dien-Bien-Phu battle was described by General Navarre himself: "The Viet-Minh understood that if the French command could be seriously defeated at Dien-Bien-Phu, that would allow them, politically, to win the war."[6] On the Vietnamese communist side, Ho Chi Minh, answering a British war reporter, simplified his thought: "Dien-Bien-Phu is a valley, and it's completely surrounded by mountains. The cream of the French Expeditionary Corps was down there, and we are around the mountains. And they'll never get out."[7]

At 1700 hours, on March 13, 1954, the Viet-Minh began their attack on Dien-Bien-Phu. Within two weeks the French garrison was cut off from the rest of the world, except for unreliable parachute supplies. After days and nights of fierce fighting and heavy casualties on both sides, by mid–March it became apparent that only American intervention could save the garrison from annihilation. The defeat and destruction of Dien-Bien-Phu would create dangerous political consequences for the whole Indochinese region and perhaps for all of Southeast Asia.

President Eisenhower was placed in a delicate situation. On April 7, 1954, in a speech to Congress, he declared that the loss of Indochina would cause the fall of Southeast Asia "like a set of dominoes." On April 11, he sent his secretary of state John F. Dulles to London to discuss with British foreign secretary Sir Anthony Eden the possibility of a "united action." Eden, however, argued that military intervention in Indochina might give China "every excuse" to invoke its alliance with the Soviet Union and possibly precipitate a world war. Moreover, the issue of intervention caused disagreement among top White House aides, congressional leaders, and top Pentagon commanders. Among these were Senator John F. Kennedy and House Speaker Lyndon B. Johnson, two future presidents of the United States, who opposed intervention.

In the meantime, the Pentagon formulated a massive bombing scenario, under the code name "Operation Guernica Vulture." The United States prepared to send 200 bombers from Manila to destroy General Giap's positions, troops, and artillery around Dien-Bien-Phu. Vice president Richard M. Nixon states in his memoirs, "In Washington the Joint Chiefs of Staff devised a plan, known as Operation Vulture, for using three small tactical atomic bombs to destroy Viet-Minh positions and relieve the French garrison." The "Pentagon Papers" uncovered no official record of the operation. However, French historian Bernard Fall asserts that Admiral Arthur B. Radford had prepared a secret plan of "large-scale" airstrikes, targeted around Dien-Bien-Phu, perhaps on a "one shot" basis, like "that first used by German and Italian aircraft to destroy the Spanish town of Guernica on April 26, 1937."[8] British prime minister Winston Churchill opposed such intervention as impossible and extremely dangerous. The British refusal gave Eisenhower a convenient reason to escape a dead end military intervention for the French in Dien Bien Phu.

According to many American historians, the most eloquent rhetoric that led Eisenhower to change from his initial intention to provide military intervention to the French was a report from General Mathew B. Ridway, the army chief of staff. Ridway estimated that the cost for such a military intervention would eventually exceed what the United States had paid in Korea. The implications of the report were clear to his commander in chief. Eisenhower wisely refused to consider a military commitment to Indochina without the participation of United States allies, especially Great Britain, and without the consensus of the United States Congress.

Once America abandoned the idea of intervention and rendered no aid, Dien-Bien-Phu fell. Indeed, the end came when the Viet-Minh violently attacked the central command of the garrison on May 7, 1954. General Navarre instructed General De Castries, commander of the garrison, to surrender to the Viet-Minh at 1700 hours the same day. In the fifty-five days of fighting the French lost 3,000 men and an equal number were permanently disabled; the 8,000 survivors had to march hundreds of miles to the Red River delta to be held as prisoners of war.

Qiang Zhai writes in his book that the Battle of Dien Bien Phu, from the beginning to the end, was overseen by General Wei Guoqing, head of the Chinese Military Advisory Group and General Giap's advisor. General Wei Guoqing's planning and execution was like the offensive campaign on the border and along Route Coloniale #4 in September 1950 that was led by General Chen Geng. All of these campaigns as well as other important strategic and tactical issues were directly decided on or approved by Beijing leaders. In reading the first two chapters of his book, one may think that Ho Chih Minh and his lieutenants, including General Vo Nguyen Giap, played secondary roles in the First Vietnam War while Mao Tse-tung and the CCP leaders and generals fought the war and defeated the French. Qiang clarifies the matter: "The Chinese military advisers actually planned and helped direct Viet

Minh operations, and there was direct transmission of strategy and tactics from China to Vietnam."[9]

At the Geneva Conference beginning May 8, 1954, a "final" political solution for Vietnam was negotiated. A "temporary partition of Vietnam" was to be created and on July 21, 1954, the French and the Viet Minh signed the Geneva Accords. The partition line was to be the 17th parallel, which became the border between the Communist North Vietnam and the Republic of Vietnam. The United States, however, refused to sign. On the whole, the United States reserved the right to take whatever action was necessary in the event that the accords were breached. Tran Van Do, foreign minister of the Republic State of Vietnam who attended the conference from the beginning, also refused to sign the Geneva Accords. Overall, the American and South Vietnamese refusal to sign at Geneva "was to have beneficial consequences for the new administration, a building south of the 17th parallel."[10]

In the end, the French were the biggest losers. After almost a decade of war in Vietnam they had 172,000 casualties. The monetary cost of the war doubled what the United States had pumped into the French economy during this period — some ten times the value of all French investments in Indochina. As the last French ship left Hai-Phong, on May 15, 1955, the last French colonial bastion in Southeast Asia disappeared. Over the past several months, North Vietnamese refugees numbering 860,000 poured into South Vietnam. More than 600,000 of these were Catholics who had long experienced persecution at the hands of Ho Chi Minh's Viet-Minh.

General Henri Navarre claimed that the United States should not have abandoned Dien-Bien-Phu. Had it intervened, it later would not have had to become involved in the war in Vietnam. Many French and Vietnamese historians also comment that it was at Dien-Bien-Phu that the political dilemma of Vietnam went unsolved in the next two decades for the United States.

Many American historians believe that in refusing to intervene in Indochina, President Dwight D. Eisenhower exercised a kind of negative ownership of the Vietnam War. French historians hold an opposite view, particularly Bernard B. Fall. In chapter 11 of his book, *The Two Vietnams*, he implies that the United States' refusal to save Dien-Bien-Phu and to sign the Geneva Accords directly reshaped the political atmosphere in Indochina. After the First Vietnam War, President Eisenhower was the first and foremost creator and director of the first act in the long tragedy of Vietnam.

By not committing large numbers of Americans in Vietnam for a military intervention, President Eisenhower combined both Roosevelt's and Truman's policies: the "termination of the French role in Indochina by whatever means" and the "containment of communist expansion" in Southeast Asia. Eisenhower crystallized the two policies into a new one — that of "replacing the French in Indochina and holding it." With this policy Eisenhower was hoping to transform the rest of Southeast Asia into democratic "dominoes" for the region, especially setting up an efficient South Vietnamese regime to face the communist North Vietnam. The Vietnamese nationalists learned to appreciate Eisenhower's policy in Indochina, because it was necessary and logical to save the rest of Indochina, especially after the signing of the Geneva Accords.

The Geneva Accords contained basic agreements for complete armistice in Indochina and a temporary partition of Vietnam. An additional "unsigned" article in the final "Declaration" read: "The military demarcation line is provisional and should not in any way be interpreted as consisting of a political or territorial boundary." There was also an article requiring that a national election be held in July 1956, to reunite Vietnam.[11]

According to American historian Lieutenant General Phillip B. Davidson, these articles might have been the benevolent intent of the conferees at Geneva. He writes: "The lax control and feeble enforcement measures prescribed by the Accords guaranteed two separate, competing states. The refusal of the United States and the government of South Vietnam to ratify the treaty only confirmed the inevitability of the permanent division."[12] By 1956, the existence of two separate Vietnamese states became apparent. Each had a constitution, elected assemblies, governmental regulations and laws, police forces and armed forces. Each state sent and received ambassadors to and from other nations. In 1957, the Soviet Union proposed the admission of both North and South Vietnam to the United Nations. Its proposal used these terms: "In Vietnam, two separate States existed, which differed from one another in political and economic structure."[13] By 1957, the 17th parallel became a "de facto" international boundary; and, if North Vietnam attacked South Vietnam, it would become an outright invasion of one country by another.

The United States and the Republic of Vietnam did not accept the 1956 elections. South Vietnam's foreign minister Tran Van Do stated to the Geneva Conference that the South Vietnamese opposed the arbitrary division of the country, as well as any fixed date for nationwide elections. Thus, from 1954 onward, the provisions of the accords and the position of South Vietnam were totally clear and known to the signatories at Geneva and other nations of the world.

Prince Norodom Sihanouk was the head of state in neighboring Cambodia. Sihanouk had accepted military aid from the communist bloc while placing restrictive conditions upon the reception of aid from the United States. This led to continual conflict between Cambodia and its neighbors, especially with South Vietnam.

From 1953 to 1954, Laos became the central ground upon which the communists of Vietnam could exploit a tactical advantage over the French. Laos continued to be a crucial strategic buffer zone for Ho Chi Minh's troops, who used it to as an arterial supply line and a way to infiltrate networks into South Vietnam. These Vietnamese communist units had the support of 4,000 Pathet-Lao troops. Prince Souphanouvong was the leader of the Pathet-Lao. Ho Chi Minh had trained him in Tuyen-Quang in March 1950, along with the Cambodian communist leader Sieu Heng. After the Geneva Accords, General Vo Nguyen Giap remained in Laos with four regiments in joint operations with the Pathet-Lao to begin to survey and plan construction of the Ho Chi Minh Trail. Souphanouvong organized the Pathet-Lao but Giap trained them, and they were now supported by China and the Soviet Union through the PAVN, or North Vietnamese Army (NVA). His half-brother, Prince Souvanna Phouma, became prime minister in 1956 and leader of the neutral force, and was also backed by Beijing.

As these events unfolded in Indochina after the collapse of French colonial rule, many feared communist insurgencies might break out in other countries in Southeast Asia. To prevent further communist gains in the area, the United States took the lead in sponsoring an anti communist regional organization. The Southeast Asia Treaty Organization (SEATO) was established on February 19, 1955. The eight members were Australia, New Zealand, Indonesia, Thailand, the Philippines, France, the United Kingdom, and the United States. The purpose of the organization was to provide collective defense and economic cooperation in South-East Asia, and to protect the weakest nations of the region against communist aggression. South Vietnam was placed under the umbrella of SEATO for military action against the Communist North Vietnam. SEATO was the first organized body implementing the policy of the United States in Southeast Asia. South Vietnam became the front line of deterrence against communist aggression in the region.

NGO DINH DIEM AND
THE REPUBLIC OF VIETNAM

After the Geneva Accords but before Ho Chi Minh's troops entered Hanoi, a new Saigon-Washington alliance began taking shape. On July 7, 1954, at the suggestion of President Eisenhower, Bao Dai, head of South Vietnam, replaced Prince Buu-Loc with Ngo Dinh Diem as his prime minister. Ngo Dinh Diem was born in Central Vietnam in January 1901, the third son of Ngo Dinh Kha, the grand chamberlain and minister of rites of the Nguyen Dynasty. Ngo Dinh Kha was a well-educated mandarin and an intense nationalist, who had developed a deep resentment of the French. Ngo Dinh Kha passed on to his sons, especially Ngo Dinh Khoi and Ngo Dinh Diem, his ardent nationalism, which was based on reforms through the Vietnamese elites. He resigned his government positions in 1907 and supported Phan Boi Chau, a celebrated nationalist, who became the founder of the first nationalist groups to be organized along modern Oriental lines (A meaning modernization of military concepts, training, and weaponry similar to that of Japan). Phan secretly selected and sent several dozens of elite students to study at the Japanese Military Academy, at Waseda University of Tokyo, and at Whampoa Political and Military Academy of China. Historians name Phan's movement "Đông Du," or movement for "Oriental Studies Abroad." Scholar Hoang van Chi terms it the "Pan-Asian Movement." According to him, Phan had close relations with Ho Chi Minh in Canton, China. However, in June 1925, Ho arranged to betray Phan to the French secret police in Shanghai for a petty sum of 100,000 Indochinese piasters, that would have been enough at the time to purchase 20,000 buffaloes. Phan was held and sent back to Vietnam to be sentenced to death, but the sentence was ultimately changed to lifetime house arrest in Hue. Phan died there in October 1940.[14]

Ngo Dinh Diem adopted his father's uncompromising stance against foreign occupation of his country. In 1929, Diem graduated from the School of Law and Administration and immediately entered the provincial administration as a district chief. In 1929, he was appointed governor of a province in Central Vietnam, and in May 1933, Emperor Bao Dai appointed him to the post of minister of the interior. But a month later, he disagreed with Bao Dai about the reforms of the country and resigned. In July 1949, on his return back to power, Bao Dai offered the premiership to Ngo Dinh Diem. Diem turned it down and refused to participate in shaping the new Vietnamese state on any terms. Thus, Diem once more withdrew his support from Bao Dai. In August 1950, Diem left Vietnam with his older brother, Monsignor Ngo Dinh Thuc, after his small political party, the Nationalist Extremist Movement (Phong-Trào Quốc-Gia Cực-Đoan) was disbanded by the French. Diem and Monsignor Thuc were in exile first in Japan, then later in the United States, France and Belgium. In 1951, with the increasing American involvement in the Vietnam War, Ngo Dinh Diem returned to the United States, where he embarked on an energetic speaking campaign at American universities and lobbied congressmen and government officials for the cause of Vietnamese independence.

In 1954, when Ngo Dinh Diem rose to power in South Vietnam, the political theme that he had spoken about at American universities became firm policy: expel the French and consolidate nationalist forces to struggle against the communists of Vietnam. Diem did not step into the fight unarmed. On June 16, 1954, when Bao Dai called upon Diem to form a new government, Diem demanded full and complete civilian and military powers. Bao Dai hesitated, but finally Diem received absolute powers on June 19, 1954. Ngo Dinh Diem arrived in Saigon on June 26, 1954, and on July 7, 1954, he completed the appointment of his first cabinet, just two weeks before the signing of the Geneva Accords. Colonel Edward Lansdale, from the United States Central Intelligence Agency (CIA), was immediately sent to South Vietnam by secretary of state John Foster Dulles, as senior military advisor to Diem and as CIA chief in Vietnam. Before being assigned to Vietnam, Lansdale had previously led the United States OSS counter-insurgency, which helped to achieve independence for the Philippines. Lansdale helped shape not only military affairs but also political, social and economic matters for the Philippines. A shrewd advisor like Lansdale was ideally suited for prime minister Ngo Dinh Diem.

The finest hours came to Diem and his American advisor in the fall of 1954 and the spring of 1955. At Geneva, France had agreed to withdraw all its troops within one year and the Viet-Minh had agreed to a three-month period of legal migration between North and South before the formal partitioning at the 17th parallel on October 11, 1954. Lansdale went to North Vietnam in August to stimulate a refugee exodus to the free land. French premier Mendes-France sent Major Jean Sainteny to Hanoi to establish new cultural and economic relations with Ho Chi Minh. On the other hand, Mendes-France assigned French chief of staff General Paul Ely to South Vietnam as high commissioner and commander in Chief of the French Expeditionary Corps.

In North Vietnam, the French and the Viet Minh signed the Cultural and Economic Agreements in November of 1954. After that, French troops began to withdraw as previously agreed. Ho still regarded French ties as his best guarantee to the Geneva terms. On their side, the French were still trying to persuade the United States that its involvement in Vietnam was "naive" and that Ngo Dinh Diem was an unrepresentative figure in the South. In addition, French authorities craftily argued that if Ho Chi Minh could not look to France and the West, he would be forced to build a stronger alliance with the communist bloc.

In South Vietnam, France had made French air force colonel Nguyen Van Hinh three-star general and chief of staff of the Vietnamese National Army only a few months before Diem took the premiership. General Hinh defied the prime minister. Hinh was forced to quit the post in December 1954, after the United States threatened to cut off all but humanitarian aid to Vietnam. Bao Dai personally intervened with a message from France in Diem's favor, which allowed Hinh to return to France.

While Ngo Dinh Diem was consolidating his hold on the Vietnamese National Army, the French tried supporting the two major armed sects in South Vietnam and an armed band in Saigon, all of which opposed Diem. The French were hoping that a "coup" would put an end to Diem and the American presence in the country. Their coup would not materialize.

After the Geneva Accords, the French policy in Vietnam was to reconcile with Ho Chi Minh and to hold South Vietnam. This unrealistic policy was based on the Geneva agreement to hold elections to reunite Vietnam in 1956, although the United States and South Vietnam were opposed to such a solution. The French thought that Ho could win the elections and they could remain in Vietnam along with their economic interests.

The result of this back-stabbing by the allies was mutual suspicion that would last for decades. The Eisenhower administration took crucial measures to bar the French conspiracy, mostly in South Vietnam. Secretary of state John F. Dulles informed the French, in Franco-American technical talks in Washington in late September of 1954, that henceforth American aid would be given not through the French but would go directly to Ngo Dinh Diem's government as of the following January 1955.

Prior to that date, in June of 1954, the United States had decided on measures to train and finance a 234,000-man Vietnamese National Army and to work through the French only if necessary. For a short while, the joint American-French training program for the Vietnamese Army (the Training Relation Instruction Mission, or TRIM) headed by Lt. General

John O'Daniel, was placed under the overall authority of General Paul Ely, the French commander in chief in Indochina. However, mutual antipathy quickly built up between French and American military personnel. Shortly after the Dulles' announcement, in January 1955, American officers replaced most of the French experts at the "Ecole Inter-Armes de Dalat" (which later became the National Military Academy) and Thu-Duc Reserve Officers' School. TRIM was dissolved, with all the ground force training changing into American hands. The MAAG, under the command of U.S. Lt. General O'Daniel, was placed in charge of training and building up the South Vietnamese National Army.[15]

Ironically, even as the United States announced its direct military aid for Ngo Dinh Diem, General Joseph Lawton Collins, the American ambassador in Saigon, was highly critical of Diem. The "Pentagon Papers" shows that by the late 1954, General Collins was advising Washington that an alternative to Diem's government "should be urgently considered," because of Diem's unwillingness to delegate authority, the influence of family, and the opposition of powerful sects. The American authority that saved Diem's government was the CIA chief in Vietnam, Colonel Lansdale. Lansdale was the right-hand man of secretary of state John F. Dulles in Vietnam. He opposed Collins' proposition. Dulles agreed with him and told Collins that the United States had no choice but to continue to support Diem because there was no other suitable leader known to Washington. He was probably right. No one in South Vietnam had such an admirable personality, a concrete policy, and a perfect ideology to face Ho Chi Minh and the communists as Ngo Dinh Diem. Ngo Dinh Diem, son of an intellectual like Ho Chi Minh, and likewise a bachelor, also spent years in exile in foreign countries to find a spiritual philosophy. It was a philosophy applicable to the construction of a better society for Vietnam, propagated as "Spiritual Personalism." It emphasized human spiritual dignity or the value of humanism in modern society, which is in direct contrast to communism, which heightens the proletariat but in reality, treats humans as tools of an absolute dictatorship.

Ten days before Ho Chi Minh's troops entered Hanoi for the transfer of power of North Vietnam from the French, President Eisenhower of the United States sent Ngo Dinh Diem a letter, dated October 1, 1954. In this letter, Eisenhower explained the rationale for his support of South Vietnam: "The purpose of this offer is to assist the Government of Vietnam in developing and maintaining a strong, viable state capable of resisting attempted subversion or aggression through military means.... Such a government would, I hope, be so responsible to the nationalist aspirations of its people, so enlightened in purpose and effective in performance, that it will be respected both at home and abroad and discourage any who might wish to impose a foreign ideology on your free people."[16] After this American presidential letter, the American foreign policy toward Vietnam was clearly determined. The problem of Vietnam became exclusively the responsibility and the burden of the Untied States.

France itself, with the new burden of Algeria also dependent on American aid, had agreed on January 1, 1955, to dissolve Indochina's status within the French Union, turning over sovereignty in South Vietnam to Ngo Dinh Diem. According to the Geneva Accords, the French would not be allowed to maintain any military base in Vietnam. The very presence of French troops in South Vietnam after the war hurt the national pride and the status of Diem as the new country's leader. In the ensuing negotiation, Diem remained adamant and agreed for the French troops to group at an aero-naval seaport for one year before withdrawing from South Vietnam.

After the French Expeditionary Force concentrated in Co May-Vung Tau, Ngo Dinh Diem began campaigns to deal with various pirate gangs and political religious armies, both in Saigon and the countryside. He did this with the backing of the Vietnamese National Army, and with the help of the CIA in Saigon and its chief, Colonel Lansdale.

The first objective was to tackle the Binh-Xuyen force in the heart of Saigon. Binh-Xuyen was a huge pirate force that was tolerated and armed by the French. With a large fleet of riverboats, this group controlled much of the commerce, opium dens, gambling and lavish brothels of the Cholon region of Saigon. Its leader, Le Van Vien, or Bay Vien, had been assimilated as a two-star general by the French. He later rose as a warlord, or as a mafia "godfather," who had 5,000 armed members and handled not only the whole business activities of the capital but also the national police force. Promptly after Prime Minister Ngo Dinh Diem promulgated a decree outlawing prostitution in March 1955, Bay Vien's armed forces were quickly swept out of Saigon and forced to surrender to the national force of four regiments that surrounded them at the Rung-Sat area. The commanders of these national units were Colonel Duong Van Minh and Lt. Colonel Nguyen Khanh. Both of them later became four-star generals and successively headed the military council that ran the country for months after a coup d'etat in November 1963.

Ngo Dinh Diem next targeted the armies of the two main political sects, each with at least 40,000 members. The Cao Dai was situated in the northeastern provinces of South Vietnam and the Hoa-Hao was in the southwestern provinces, mainly in the Mekong River Delta. The leaders of the sects were a coalition of militant religious leaders and vice-lords whom Bao Dai had always treated indulgently. They controlled these large regions with total authoritarian powers over the population's daily activities and beliefs.

Through a series of edicts, and by carefully placing capable civilian and military personnel in positions of power in the regions, Diem divided the sects and curtailed their activities. Finally, by military campaigns, also under the command of the newly promoted two-star General Duong Van Minh and Colonel Nguyen Khanh, pacification efforts were successfully underway during the three months from May to July of 1955. All the sect's armed forces were disbanded. Officers of these armies were reintegrated into the national army after undergoing retraining at the military centers. This benevolent and courteous behavior toward his nationalist opponents earned Ngo Dinh Diem the admiration and the support of the whole national army. Only one Hoa-Hao warlord was indicted and executed by court-martial on a charge of treason, based on his several deceitful surrenders to Duong Van Minh's operational forces. After the fact, Bao Dai cabled Ngo Dinh Diem from Paris, accused him of "selling the blood of the Vietnamese," and ordered his prime minister to resign.

Ngo Dinh Diem, who had received much popular support after cleaning up the political warlords, refused to comply with Bao Dai's order. On the contrary, at the advice of Colonel Lansdale, Diem conducted another step in an anti–Bao Dai movement by creating a Revolutionary Committee, composed of 200 delegates of 18 political parties and groups. The Committee convened as a "National Assembly." The assembly voted for a platform demanding the dismissal of Bao Dai, the formation of a new republican regime under Ngo Dinh Diem, and the total withdrawal of the French.

Following the proposition of the assembly, Ngo Dinh Diem proclaimed, on July 7, 1955, that a national referendum would be held on October 23, 1955, on the issue of a new republican nation and its leadership. The October 1955 plebiscite gave Ngo Dinh Diem more than 98 percent of the votes. It gave him the power to be the first president of the new "Republic of Vietnam." He informed Lansdale that he would hold parliamentary elections in the South instead of joint elections with the North in order to reunite Vietnam. Lansdale strongly urged Washington to support Diem. In March 1956, elections were held throughout South Vietnam to select 123 members of a "Constituent Assembly" that would formulate a republican constitution for the country, and then would transform itself into a regular legislature upon ratification of the constitution. On October 26, 1956, President Ngo Dinh Diem signed the text and it became operative. "Constitution Day" became an official national holiday of South Vietnam. In Hanoi, communist prime minister Pham Van Dong viewed the South Constituent Assembly's elections in March 1956 as a United States conspiracy, calling it "a blatant violation of the Geneva Accords."[17]

In Paris, on April 3, 1956, France informed Britain and the Soviet Union, co-chairs of the Geneva Conference, of its intent to dissolve the French High Command in Indochina. On April 26, 1956, all French forces completed their last withdrawal from South Vietnam. With the departure of the French forces, all remaining French influence was rapidly dissipated.

Through the effective help of Colonel Lansdale, Ngo Dinh Diem gradually and successfully gained complete power in South Vietnam, now established as a free republican regime. By 1956, he brought order out of the chaos in the country he took over in 1954. President Diem consolidated his regime while providing safe haven for almost one million refugees from North Vietnam. He installed a strong republican government, drafted a new constitution, and pledged to initiate extensive social reforms.

In the ensuing years, from 1957 to 1961, with the support of President Eisenhower, Ngo Dinh Diem continued to do very well in South Vietnam; he gained immense help from his younger brother, Ngo Dinh Nhu, an erudite strategist. The most important additional success in South Vietnam by the Ngo Dinh Diem administration was the clearing out of the communist insurgency. According to a communist document captured in 1960, more than 16,000 communist cadres were in South Vietnam as early as in 1955 to wage a new revolutionary war.

Indeed, immediately after the Communist Party seized power in North Vietnam, Ho Chi Minh initiated a new war in the South, sending to South Vietnam his elite collaborators such as Le Duan, Pham Hung, and Van Tien Dung. Ho ordered them to enlist a considerable number of southern-born cadres in order to reopen a new insurgency phase. In addition, Ho ordered Vo Nguyen Giap to keep more than one division in Laos in order to support the Pathet Lao in a liberation war against the Laotian Royal Army. According to this captured document, by the end of 1958 almost all of the 16,000 communist cadres left in South Vietnam were eliminated by Ngo Dinh Diem's armed forces, extirpating the communists' first phase of insurgency. Evidently, on April 7, 1959, Major General Samuel L. Mayer, MAAG–Vietnam Deputy Commander, testified before the American Senate Foreign Relations Committee that the guerrilla problems in South Vietnam had almost completely disappeared.[18]

In reality, the communist insurgency in South Vietnam had changed little after William Colby replaced Colonel Lansdale as chief of CIA–Saigon at the end of 1958. Colby realized that to replace the communist cadres eliminated by South Vietnamese force, Ho Chi Minh would have to send back many of the same cadres who had gone North in 1954. The CIA estimated that about 5,000 southern-born cadres infiltrated back in 1959. They first began the process of political organization at the basic level by going through the villages. New tactical measures were taken such as propaganda against Americans and Diem, death threats, and murdering village chiefs, officials and antipathetic villagers.

Colby coordinated with President Diem's political adviser, Ngo Dinh Nhu, to set up a strategic program in a new anti-insurgency phase called "the Strategic Hamlets." In remote and insurgency-active areas, peasants in small villages were relocated into larger "agrovilles" or fortified villages, enclosed with ditches, barbed wire fences or spiked bamboo hedges. Each hamlet had its militia guards to protect the villagers and help them to go out to cultivate their piece of land during daytime. This strategic measure was targeted to separate the communist cadres from the peasants. The program was successful, with remarkable results.

Beside efforts to clear the communist cadres from the countryside, President Diem built up his army with units made up by a new generation of young officers. Over 80 percent of those officers were trained by American officers of the MAAG-Vietnam. Instruction teams doubled in size to 685 officers and non-commissioned officers (NCOs) in 1959. MAAG's commander, Lt. General Samuel Williams, focused on making the South Vietnamese Army, which was composed of eight well-organized divisions, capable of withstanding a North Vietnamese invasion long enough to permit the intervention of the United States within the framework of SEATO.

According to Colby and President Diem, in order to face the communist "liberation war" (or revolutionary war), these two important strategic measures had to be taken. The Strategic Hamlets were essential to separate the "fish from the water," and a strong regular army, well trained in both jungle-war and conventional war, was necessary to crush the communists. The final phase of any war with the communists would be a conventional form of war such as the communists had conducted in China and in Korea.

However, the primary aim of President Ngo Dinh Diem was to fight such a war himself with his own South Vietnamese troops. He and his brother, Ngo Dinh Nhu, had a deep understanding of the Vietnamese mentality. They hated to see foreign troops in their country. Diem and Nhu's view was that "as the presence of foreign troops, no matter how friendly they may be, was the target of the communist propaganda, [it was] therefore incompatible with Vietnam's concept of full independence." What Diem and Nhu needed from the United States was political, economic, and military aid. Indeed, Diem's press secretary Ton That Thien, a prestigious Vietnamese journalist, later stated that from 1960 on, the Americans started more intense consultation, proving they were thinking of moving into Vietnam at the time. President Diem and especially his brother Nhu were dead set against the Americans moving in and taking over.

In only five years, from 1955 to 1960, President Ngo Dinh Diem had miraculously re-established order in a fractional and chaotic South Vietnam, and consolidated it into a constitutional nation. Diem believed South Vietnam had the ability to thwart Ho Chi Minh's attempt to make the country communist. Unfortunately, the situation dramatically changed after the United States foreign policy toward Vietnam changed under the Kennedy and Johnson administrations. Kennedy's policy of "escalation of military commitment in Vietnam" developed into Johnson's so-called policy of the "limited war," and the "defensive war." The situation worsened under the Nixon and Ford administrations with their policies of "honorable withdrawal" (Nixon) and "forget about Vietnam" (Ford).

The intervention by the United States in Vietnam had two basic objectives: to prevent North Vietnam from overthrowing by invasion the anti-communist Saigon regime and to permit the South Vietnamese people to live in freedom under a government of their own choice. The success of South Vietnam during President Eisenhower's time in office demonstrated that his foreign policy to "Advise and Support" a free-world nation in Southeast Asia had definitely succeeded. "Support" to an allied free nation like South Vietnam in building up its military forces, in advising its leaders to formulate their own military strategy, and letting them fight their own war against the communist aggression — these were the best ways for the United States to advance its interests in worldwide containment.

President Truman's doctrine was needed, but President Eisenhower's vision and policy in allowing Diem to reorganize South Vietnam was superb. Although Truman and Eisenhower did involve U.S. troops in Vietnam and created a "precedent" for their presidential successors to commit military forces, they did not, however, engage American troops on the battlefield. The United States' involvement in South Vietnam was an ambitious undertaking. However, the misdirected policies and the flawed military strategies of the four presidential successors of President Eisenhower would exact a heavy price: loss of South Vietnam to the Communist North. "Perhaps the worst failure in foreign policy in the history of our nation was our well-intentioned involvement in Vietnam," says Colonel Harry G. Summers, Jr., in his *On Strategy: A Critical Analysis of the Vietnam War.*"[19]

COMMUNIST NORTH VIETNAM'S AMBITIONS: "TO CONSOLIDATE THE NORTH, TO AIM FOR THE SOUTH"

Although the Indochinese Communist Party (ICP) was organized as far back as February 3, 1930, by Ho Chi Minh in Hong Kong, then dissolved in 1945 and reestablished with the new name of "Vietnamese Workers' party" (VWP or Đảng Lao-Động Vietnam), the long-term objectives of the Party did not change. "The basis of the VWP and its guiding line in all fields of its activities is the doctrine of Marx, Engels, Lenin, and Mao Tse-tung, adapted to the realities of the Vietnamese revolution," says Nguyen Kien Giang, a North Vietnamese historian.[20]

The regional objectives of the VWP in Southeast Asia were defined during the early 1950s. In the spring of 1952, the French Deuxième Bureau captured a secret VWP document that stated: "The ultimate aim of the Vietnamese communist leadership is to install communist regimes in the whole of Vietnam, in Laos, and in Cambodia."[21] To accomplish this ambitious aim, as the VWP gained control of North Vietnam in November 1954, its Politburo immediately formulated a new strategy, "to consolidate the North, to aim for the South" (Củng cố miền Bắc, chiếu cố miền Nam).

To consolidate the North, Ho Chi Minh had to strengthen the internal organization of the party and the government before he carried on with the reforms of the land, agriculture, the art, and the education. Ho kept the 1945 government status quo as the Democratic Republic of Vietnam. Almost all leading members of the government were also members of the VWP Central Committee. Ho relinquished the premiership to his faithful companion Pham Van Dong, but he retained full powers. The People's Army had remained in the hands of Vo Nguyen Giap. The presidency of the National Assembly went to Truong Chinh, who had been removed from the secretary-generalship of the VWP after the land reform errors in 1956. Ho also divested himself of the party's secretary-generalship, which he had held since 1956, and handed this key post to Le Duan in 1961, after Duan returned from his leading mission in South Vietnam.

This restructuring system evolved down the line to all executive and administrative levels, from central to provinces, to districts, and to villages. The system was called "parallel hierarchy." It permitted the VWP to control all activities, to handle security for all organizations, and to keep discipline under control of its personnel. The dogmatic "parallel hierarchy" was also strictly applied in the army with an authoritarian political cadre over the head of each unit commander. In addition to this controlling political system, new organizations were created to assume control over various layers of the population, from schools to urban streets, from cities to villages, from children to old women, to workers and peasants, who were not readily integrated into the VWP. A Soviet Union–like society from the 1930s was integrated into North Vietnam shortly after the Geneva Accords, by 1955. Moreover, a new control apparatus named the "People's Control Organs" was set up as the Civil Division and the Military Division. The twofold mission of these divisions was to "watch the execution of the law" by the whole executive branch, "as well as by the citizens," and to "watch the execution of the party's military orders" by all military units and personnel. They had the power to "bring to justice all cases to inquiry, may suspend prosecution and may participate in judicial operations, and may appeal judgments of lower courts to higher tribunals."[22]

Ho Chi Minh's second step in consolidating the North was the crucial re-application of the "Land Reform" that he adopted from Mao Tse-tung and applied firmly in communist controlled areas of Viet Bac (Northernmost Region of North Vietnam) in the first campaign in 1953–1954. That campaign was premature. This time, the VWP had in its control the northern half of Vietnam's territory and population. Ho and his disciples in the VWP's Politburo decided to steadily transform this "semi-colonial and feudal society" into a "socialist society" with a strong "proletarian dictatorship" in the countryside and to destroy all "internal enemies," whom they named "reactionaries" of the regime.

The second "Land Reform" Campaign started with ferocity and bitterness ten days after the Democratic Republic of Vietnam (DRVN) issued the new "Population Classification" Decree No. 422-TTG on March 1, 1955, that replaced the provisional Decree No. 239-TTG issued on March 1, 1953. This decree reclassified all of North Vietnam's rural population into five classes: landlords, rich farmers, medium farmers, poor peasants, and laborers. Landlords were classified further into three categories: (1) traitorous, reactionary, and cruel landlords; (2) ordinary landlords; and (3) resistance landlords, or those who participated in the Resistance (against the French, 1946–1954). The decree reclassified people in urban areas into three classes: intellectuals, professionals, and artisans. The "Land Reform Law"—Decree No. 197-SL issued on December 19, 1953—was again applied in this second "Land Reform" Campaign.

Ho Chi Minh and members of the VWP's Politburo entrusted Truong Chinh, secretary-general of the party, to direct this "Land Reform" Campaign. He had under his mandate a large number of expert cadres who had been sent months before to mainland China to learn "Chinese Land Reform." In theory, the Land Reform Campaign would be realized in two stages: (1) The "Land Rent Reduction" stage, and (2) the "Land Reform" proper stage. The first stage aimed to destroy the most dangerous "reactionaries," or landlords whom the VWP named "Enemy Number One" of the regime ("Enemy Number Two" being the urban bourgeois, or those who were rich and practiced foreign trade in cities and towns; later, by the end of 1975, they were known as "Capitalists and Sellers," or Tư-sản và Mại-bản). Resistance landlords might think they would have some privilege, but when the land reform came forth they were all condemned as first category landlords who were living in former French occupied areas. It was clear that the VWP attempted to purge landowners both in newly liberated areas and in already liberated areas in the countryside. Therefore, cadres who were rich or medium-size farmers might avoid sentences in the first stage "Land Rent Reduction" but could not escape annihilation from the second "Land Reform" proper stage. The VWP threw a stone to kill two birds at once — the landowners of the old "Feudal society" and the "possible" enemies in its ranks — to pave the way for further development of "socialism" in the countryside. Apparently, from 1955 on this "Land Reform" Campaign forced people in ten thousand villages of the North to experience fear and bereavement for years.

Truong Chinh and his land reform experts knew how to do their jobs. Chinh presided over the "Land Reform Central Committee" at Hanoi and sent his expert cadres down to chosen provinces and villages — or experimental sites — to lead poor peasants and landless peasants (bần cố nông) in enacting the reform. Leaders in neighboring provinces were ordered to learn land reform practices from these experimental sites and to enact the land reform in their provinces with the help of experts from the "Central Committee" and Chinese advisors. With this "oil-stain" process, land reform progressively spread over North Vietnam.

Usually, a landlord was arrested, treated like a mad dog, and badly tortured to extract confessions on his hidden wealth before being dragged to an open area — usually a soccer field — to be denounced for all kinds of crimes by the masses. A denouncer could be a landlord's tenant, a debtor, an opponent, a friend, a relative, or anyone else who was poor or landless and had been selected in advance by the land reform cadres. After that, the landlord was sentenced to be executed or jailed. If he was sentenced to death then he was shot immediately after the trial. All of his lands, rice fields, orchards, houses and gardens, furniture, rice and other agricultural produce, animals, agricultural tools, money and jewelry — apparent or hidden — were completely confiscated.

The land reform procedures in both stages were the same; but, in the second stage the "Central Committee" ordered an increase in the minimum number of landlords to be sentenced to death from one to five at each village. Thus, rich and medium-size farmers were reclassified as landlords and suffered the same fatalities. There were no official records of the number of victims in these two stages of the land reform. It was estimated that there were 20,000 victims in the first stage and fivefold that number in the second stage. However, the number of family members and connected individuals who died in this Land Reform Campaign was innumerable due to the Land Reform Central Committee's policies of "Isolation" and "Connection," which was enforceable in both stages. These policies posed even more terror in the countryside. "Isolation" meant that all family members of a "criminal landlord" must be severely isolated in his house during his arrest. His parents, siblings, wife, children, and other relatives were forbidden to go out of the house for any reason, even to work or to purchase food. Isolation of the landlord's family might last three or four months. As a result, most of these victims died by starvation; elderly people and children died first, and then the others. "Connection" meant that those who had previous relations with any "criminal landlords" must be punished. They were condemned as landlords or subject to isolation if they had very close relations to the landlord; those who had lesser relations would be sent together with their families to remote farms for hard labor, or were simply chased out of the "Peasants' Association" — a new infrastructure organization. That also meant they were economically isolated and usually died from starvation. A large number of victims committed suicide because of the Isolation and Connection policies.

The death of landlords and their family members increased drastically from the fall of 1955 to the spring of 1956, to the point where Ho Chi Minh had to order the postponement of the Land Reform Campaign in March 1956 and the release from prison of twelve thousand former cadres who were condemned as landowners. The VWP entrusted confided General Vo Nguyen Giap to rectify the reform with the so-called "Rectification of Errors" Campaign. Truong Chinh resigned from his secretary-generalship and was assigned to hold the presidency of the National Assembly. Though the remedy was taken, bloodshed continued for a year more at each village in the countryside between former cadres who just returned home and new cadres who had denounced and condemned them before.

Many historians saw Ho Chi Minh's land reform as a major failure for the VWP, but some suspected and stated that Ho launched the land reform to eliminate those who were considered dangerous "enemies" of the communist regime. It was a way for Ho to consolidate his powers, much as Stalin and Mao Tse-tung had done in the Soviet Union and China.

Scholar Hoang van Chi, in his book provides a reasonable number of victims in this 1955–1956 Land Reform Campaign: "half a million Vietnamese (4% of the population of North Vietnam) were sacrificed."[23] However, nobody knew even roughly the number of "reactionaries" in urban areas who were purged by the VWP in those years. The majority of them were intellectuals, influential people (Buddhist monks and Catholic bishops and priests), rich people, urban bourgeois, and merchants and traders living in Hanoi and other cities and towns before and during the Resistance (1946–1954) who, for whatever reason, could not migrate to South Vietnam during the 300-day "official evaluation" from August 1954 to May 1955. Of course, the VWP prepared policies for them. The less cruel policy was the nation-wide "brainwashing campaign." The most dangerous "reactionaries" were sent to isolated re-education camps in forested areas in Tây Bắc and Việt Bắc (the northwest and northern-most regions of North Vietnam) to be brainwashed; in reality, they were forced to perform hard labor in penal servitude without terms. Their family members were also relocated to remote economic sites to labor for their livelihood. Least dangerous reactionaries had to receive brainwashing before being ordered to leave the capital, cities, and towns with their families and go to their natal villages or to new economic sites. All of these measures were quietly enforced at night so that the normal life in urban areas was not agitated. It was estimated that about 300,000 people in North Vietnam were forced to leave Hanoi and other cities and towns for their ordered sites to endure harsh and miserable lives. Still, the most effective policy that overcame the city bourgeois and all classes urban traders, sellers, and private enterprise owners was a series of financial and industrial measures such as the restriction of small amounts of new bank notes to each citizen, the imposition of an exceeding tax on "remaining goods" in each store, and the creation of the so-called state and private enterprise system in industry (there were small craft and art factories in North Vietnam at that time with few employees in each factory). These measures transformed every rich bourgeois into an empty-handed man, every small store owner into a tax debtor, and every enterprise owner into state servitude with minimum payment. Finally, the DRVN banned all private commercial activities and organized a "state trade office" in each North Vietnamese city and town to manage all kinds of purchasing and selling of goods, including food and other necessities. Thus, with the formation of "collective farms" and "peasant associations" in the countryside and the creation of a system of "state trade offices," "trade shops," and "trade restaurants" in cities and towns, the VWP completely controlled the stomach of the North Vietnamese population and consolidated the bases of a "socialist society" in North Vietnam.

However, the land reform campaign in the countryside and the purging of reactionaries in cities and towns ignited peasant revolts in several provinces such as Nam Dinh, Ninh Binh, and Nghe An, and a serous reaction by intellectuals and men of letters in Hanoi that historians named "The Nhân văn and Giai phẩm Movement"—or the anti-regime movement of the "Humanity Paper and the Literacy Pieces Selection."

While the revolts by peasants in Nam Dinh and Ninh Binh during the "Rectification of Errors" period (after March 1956) were not big enough and were promptly repressed by communist provincial militia units, the revolt by peasants in Nam Dan District, Nghe An Province, a few miles from Ho Chi Minh's birthplace, was the largest ever seen in North Vietnam. Like some other international communist leaders, Ho Chi Minh exercised manslaughter when he ordered his forces to ruthlessly crush such revolts. On November 2, 1956, a number of peasants fearing land reform surrounded the jeep of an International Control Commission (ICC) and asked that they be allowed to go to South Vietnam. Shots were fired when a small communist militia unit tried to disperse them. By nightfall, the protest movement composed of more than 20,000 peasants armed with bamboo sticks had swept over the whole district.

The communists feared that the rebelling peasants would march on to the provincial capital of Vinh. Ho Chi Minh surpassed Stalin's approach in Budapest, Hungary, by sending the whole 325th Division to Nam Dan to crush the "rebels." More than 6,000 peasants were killed and executed, and a large number of them were deported and imprisoned. This communist massacre was unknown to the rest of the world.

While the revolt by peasants at Nam Dan District of Nghe An Province was brutally suppressed by the People's Army with little sound echoing, the literary revolt by intellectuals and men of letters in Hanoi was largely known in several countries in Asia and in Europe. According to common opinion, the objective causes of the literary revolt by intellectuals in North Vietnam were the "De-Stalinization" campaign (February 14–25, 1956) of the new leader Nikita Khrushchev in the Union of Soviet Socialist Republics (USSR), the "Hundred Flowers" campaign (since May 25, 1956) of Mao Tse-tung in China, and the "Liberation Revolts" in several Eastern European countries (Poland, June 1956, and Hungary, November 1956). In reality, the self-ignited literary movement against the North Vietnamese regime started in early spring of 1956, prior to any of the previously mentioned events. Thus, the real cause of this literary revolt was the VWP's humiliation, disgrace, and oppression of intellectuals in addition to the atrocious policies of purging nationalists and "reactionaries" and terrorizing of the people of North Vietnam.

Even though the majority of intellectuals who joined the communists in their nine-year resistance had played an active part in the development of the VWP and the People's Army, they were always suspected by them of being "internal enemies." The sole reason was that most of them were of landowner, bourgeois, or some capitalist background; they were subjects to be eliminated from the ranks. Those who survived the VWP's purging campaigns in the communist controlled areas of Vietnam — the "Political Struggle," the "Thought Reform" in 1953, and the "Land Reform" in 1953–1954 — came to live in Hanoi from October 1954. However, after the division of Vietnam these people continued to be treated badly — morally and materially — by the party. Men of letters were especially denied adequate living standards and sought jobs for months, except those who tiptoed around Ho Chi Minh and other party leaders. Among these flatterers was To Huu — the most brazen master of the "Personality Cult" (tệ Sùng bái Cá nhân) — who appeared like a brilliant star and gathered around him other well-known and submissive poets, writers such as Huy Can, Huy Thong, Xuan Dieu, Che Lan Vien, Hoai Thanh, Nguyen Huy Tuong, Nguyen Dinh Thi, Nguyen Cong Hoan, Nguyen Tuan, Hong Cuong, and several dozen others. The party offered them good living conditions and high positions in North Vietnamese literary circles. The great disparities between these two groups of men in arts and letters, both in political stature and material conditions, would become another important cause of the literary revolt, which was known as the "Nhân văn and Giai phẩm" Movement.

This literary movement started in Hanoi in February, 1956 with the appearance of "Giai Phẩm Mùa Xuân," or the "Spring Selection of Literacy Pieces," from a group of talented composers, artists, writers, and poets. Organizers and editors were Le Dat, a cadre of the Central Propaganda and Training Directorate (Cục Tuyên Huấn Trung ương), and Hoang Cam, a well-known poet and playwright of poetry-dramas; contributors were Van Cao, Tran Dan, Tu Phac, Si Ngoc, Nguyen Sang, Tran Le Van, To Van, Quang Dung, Huu Loan, and Phung Hoan. The most impressive pieces that To Huu, who was then a member of the VWP Central Committee and director of the Central Propaganda and Training Directorate (Uỷ viên Trung ương Đảng, Chủ Nhiệm Cục Tuyên Huấn Trung ương), accused of rebellious "plots" against the party and its top leader, Ho Chi Minh, were the two poems "Nhất Định Thắng" ("To Win Decidedly") by Tran Dan and "Ông Bình Vôi" ("Mr. Lime-Pot") by Le Dat. The long poem (500 verses) by Tran Dan hinted that Ho Chi Minh, who was always lacking self-confidence and patience, had stabbed people in the back during his commitment to cut Vietnam into two parts. This led to the migration of a large number of North Vietnamese to South Vietnam, and transformed Hanoi into a sullen place that blurred with incessant rain falling on the dreary immensity of the red national flags while shadows of communist cadres bore down on the fate of every one of its residents. Just days later, many students and learned men in Hanoi and other cities could fluently recite the refrain that repeated many times in the poem:

> "Tôi bước đi
>   không thấy phố
>   không thấy nhà
>   Chỉ thấy mưa sa
>   Trên màu cờ đỏ"

The English translation might read:

> "I was getting out
>   seeing neither streets
>   nor houses
> But blurred rains
>   Pouring on the immense red of national colors."

The short poem of Le Dat was more accurate in comparing the aging Ho Chi Minh, who became more cruel and less discerning year after year, to a lime-pot that narrowed day by day from the dehydration of the lime used by betel-chewers in many Vietnamese families. Scholar Hoang Van Chi translated the last four verses of "Mr. Lime-Pot" into English, as follows:

> "People who live too long
> Are like lime-pots
> The longer they live
>   the worse they grow
> And the narrow they become."[24]

The Vietnamese original version is:

> "Những người sống lâu trăm tuổi
> Y như một cái bình vôi
> Càng sống càng tồi
> Càng sống càng bé lại."

Consequently, all issues of the *Spring Selection of Literacy Pieces* were seized. Le Dat was held at his office fifteen days to write the "self-criticized confessions" (viết "kiểm thảo") but Tran Dan and Tu Phac, a composer, were arrested and jailed. Tran Dan cut his throat to commit suicide, but survived. Other contributors were disregarded for a while. Perhaps, after Ho Chi Minh canceled the land reform, the VWP was concentrating more on solving the perilous unrest in the countryside during the "Rectification of Errors" campaign rather than focusing on a handful of young writers and poets of a new magazine who used literature to vaguely criticize the Party and its leadership. Otherwise, one might imagine that Ho Chi Minh would cast a large net to catch "bigger fishes" — or more important figures of the anti-regime intelligentsia in North Vietnam — just as Mao Tse-tung set the trap in the "Hundred Flowers" Campaign in May 1956 to purge the "Right Wing" in Red China. The VWP subsequently organized an eighteen-day conference in August 1956 for men of letters in Hanoi to study the "democratic freedom" in writing and the "elimination of the personality cult" in literature. The biggest "fish" was then emerging: Nguyen Huu Dang, a long-standing communist and former minister of propaganda of the DRVN first cabinet. He gave an explosive speech attacking the VWP's policies of oppressing intellectuals and handling the "arts and letters" activities to consolidate and develop their totalitarian powers. His speech was a real wake-up call for the North Vietnamese intellectuals to fight the party, which was seriously influenced by Maoism.

On August 29, 1956, the *Giai Phẩm Mùa Thu* Số 1, or the "Fall Selection of Literacy Pieces" No. 1, appeared in Hanoi with excellent articles by two heavyweights of the literary circle Phan Khoi and Truong Tuu, that forcefully attacked the VWP and its leaders. Phan Khoi — a veteran journalist, writer, poet, and advanced Confucian scholar who had deep knowledge of both Eastern and Western cultures — criticized the party and its leaders with the editorial "Comments on the Party Leaders in Arts and Letters," while Truong Tuu or Nguyen Bach Khoa — a well-known theoretician, Marxist critic, writer, and university professor — wisely attacked the party with the critique "The Personality Cult Disease." Prime editors of this "Fall Selection" were the same poets, Le Dat and Hoang Cam. Nguyen Huu Dang then suggested these two young poets establish another magazine to reinforce their voice. The three of them organized the *Bán Nguyệt San "Nhân văn,"* or the Biweekly "Humanities," and invited the notable and experienced Phan Khoi to preside on the editorial board and the young and dynamic writer Tran Duy to take part as editorial secretary. The *Humanities* No. 1 premiered on September 15, 1956, carrying several articles supporting Tran Dan, who then became famous. Tran Dan's release on November 2, 1956, was unexpected; also, the VWP promulgated the "Hundred Flowers Blossom" all over North Vietnam. Nobody would have suspected that the "net" of Ho Chi Minh had opened wider.

From September to December 1956, more editions of *Nhân văn* and *Giai Phẩm* were published by the private publishing house Hong Duc of the generous activist Tran Thieu Bao with contributions by publishers in other papers and donations of ink and printing materials. Two more notable intellectuals engaged in the fight: Dao Duy Anh, a scholar, lexicographer and professor of several universities in Hanoi, and Tran Duc Thao, a philosopher and professor who taught for a time at the distinguished Sorbonne in Paris; both were widely known in Vietnam and overseas. Then *Nhân văn* and *Giai Phẩm* also gathered more contributors who were talented artists, composers, writers, and poets such as Hoang Tich Linh, Dang Dinh Hung, Chu Ngoc, Phung Cung, Nhu Mai, Nguyen van Ty, Ta Huu Thien, and Bui Quang Doai.

The *Nhân văn* contained more political articles than the *Giai Phẩm*, but both papers revealed the real aspects of a fearful and unjust society under the communist regime and carried rich information on the malign VWP and its vicious leaders. These two papers formed a potential literary and political movement attacking the VWP leaders for corruption and nepotism, their policies of oppression and despotism, and the whole communist regime for their atrocities and totalitarianism. The movement fought for the liberation of "arts and letters" and other specialized issues in medicine, science, and law from the autocracy of the "political cadres"; demanded personal liberties for the people; criticized the murdering of innocents from the "Land Reform"; attacked the "State Trade Office" system (Hệ thống Mậu dịch Quốc doanh) of being speculative and corruptible; and finally, rejected the very dogma of Marxism and implicated a political alternative — democracy.

All issues of *Nhân văn* and *Giai Phẩm* were warmly received by the public who had hungered for years for picturesque literature and illustrative politics. The majority of the readers were urban, learned people and university and high school students who loved the beautifully written political articles and literary pieces. Specifically, these papers contributed to national literature the eminent and impressive poems, short stories, and fictions that were composed around rhetorical figures or metaphors never seen before. In addition to the poem of Le Dat that compared Ho Chi Minh to a lime-pot, the fiction of Tran Duy described other VWP leaders as the "giants without a heart"; the short fiction of Nhu Mai insinuated that the VWP literary cadres who became trite with monotonous and formulated terms in the writing style of To Huu were "robot poets"; and the short story of Phung Cung alluded that every faded-talent poet or writer who served the VWP — such as Huy Can, Huy Thong, Xuan Dieu, and Hoai Thanh — was like the "Old Horse of Lord Trinh," a former, unmatched race horse that was over-fed as the cart horse of a viceroy and finally could not race, but hit the gloomy ground due to corpulence, exhaustion, and senility.

However, when Hanoi students became involved with the first edition of Đất Mới, or the *New Land Magazine* No. 1— which was organized by university students Phung Hoan and Bui Quang Doai, and supported by Professors Tran Duc Thao and Truong Tuu Nguyen Bach Khoa — the VWP took immediate action by seizing all issues of the magazine. A month later, after the literary movement clearly became a political movement that strongly attacked the communist regime with a series of new analyses, comments, and editorials by the previously mentioned university figures and by Nguyen Huu Dang and Tran Duy in *Giai Phẩm Mũa Đông*—(*Winter Selection of Literacy Pieces*) and *Nhân văn Số* 5 —(*Humanities* No. 5), Ho Chi Minh signed a decree on December 9, 1956, to ban the liberty of the press. On December 15, the VWP ordered the closing of the *Giai Phẩm* and *Nhân văn*.[25]

From February 20 to 28, 1957, the VWP organized the second "Conference" for men of arts and letters. Truong Chinh then called for the destruction of the *Nhân văn* and *Giai Phẩm* movement. However, the true retribution against the organizers and contributors of the *Nhân văn* and *Giai Phẩm* were applied only after the trap "Hundred Flowers" Campaign of Mao Tse-tung in China and concluded with Mao's orders to annihilate the Right Wings in December 1957. Just days later, the party conclusively resolved the literary "revolt" with its usual heavy-handed measures. All founders, contributors, supporters, and anyone else who had any connections with the *Nhân văn* and *Giai Phẩm* movement were expelled from their associations, sent to remote labor camps, or arrested and taken into custody. Nguyen Huu Dang, Tran Duy, and Phung Cung were each sentenced with jail terms for twelve to fifteen years; Tran Duc Thao, Dao Duy Anh, and Truong Tuu Nguyen Bach Khoa were dismissed from Hanoi universities and sent to remote labor camps for unknown terms; Le Dat, Hoang Cam, Tran Dan, Van Cao, Nhu Mai, Phung Hoan, and several dozen other composers, artists, writers, and poets were expelled from their arts and letters associations and sent to remote labor camps with terms; Phan Khoi died three days before he was to go on trial and his son, Phan Thao, editor of another newspaper, died in prison seven months later under unexplained circumstances. An uncountable number of supporters and readers of *Nhân văn*, *Giai Phẩm*, and *Đất Mới* were also arrested and ill-treated in remote labor camps. The majority of these unfortunate people were students; many of them never returned home and were never heard from again, and many committed suicide.

Thereafter, the VWP regained control of all "Arts and Letters" associations and activities. The purging of anti-regime intellectuals continued for many years. Though the "spirit" of *Nhân văn* and *Giai Phẩm* subsequently lasted for decades, its slogan "arts for arts sake" disappeared after that time. The VWP determined that arts and education must serve only the regime's political aims. The words education, culture, and teaching only meant "indoctrination." North Vietnamese youth were indoctrinated with Marxist-Leninist views, and extreme hatred against Americans and the South Vietnamese regime was nurtured.

All in all, over the five years from 1955 to 1960, Ho Chi Minh consolidated North Vietnam by means of "iron and blood," transforming it into a solid communist bastion in Southeast Asia, which threatened its neighbors and the whole region, especially South Vietnam, its real and immediate target. The most important objective of Ho Chi Minh and his Vietnamese Communist Party was to "liberate" South Vietnam. However, they would not conduct an "invasion war" through the 17th parallel at this time as had been done in the Korean War. Instead they would engage in a revolutionary war to acquire South Vietnam. This meant applying military, political, diplomatic, and psychological strategies, using various kinds of warfare, and exhausting the enemy through a long and comprehensive struggle. The most vital means was to "maneuver the mass of population" both in the North and in the South to endure a long-standing war (chiến tranh trường kỳ). It was the primordial factor to assure the final victor by a link of the "General Offensive" (Tổng Công Kích, or TCK) of the revolutionary armed forces with the "General Uprising" (Tổng Nổi-Dậy, or TND) of the population. Another important means was the North Vietnamese communists' dialectic and scientific methodology. Together, the exhaustion of a long-standing war with the exploitation of Indochina's political and geographic conditions, with the support of the communist bloc, and the help of the inconsistent policy of the United States in Vietnam would all prove to be the downfall of free South Vietnam.

The VWP utilized special tactics in the preparatory phase. Ho Chi Minh and his Communist Party prepared to engage in strategic psychological warfare to reinforce their point of view to liberate South Vietnam. To win favorable international opinion and to stimulate a mob psychology within Vietnam, the VWP and the DRVN government drafted and promulgated a new constitution in 1960. Their main emphasis was on the independence and reunification of Vietnam, as clearly described in the constitution's Preamble: "Vietnam is a single entity from Lang-son to Camau. The Vietnamese people consistently united and struggled against domination by foreign aggressors in order to liberate their country. In the last few years, our people in the North have achieved many big successes in economic rehabilitation and cultural development. At present, socialist transformation and construction are being successfully carried out."[26] "Meanwhile, in the South, the U.S. imperialists and their henchmen have been savagely repressing the patriotic movement of our people. They have been strengthened military forces and carrying out their scheme of turning the southern part of our country into a colony and military base for their war preparation. They have resorted to all possible means to sabotage the Geneva Agreements and undermine the cause of Vietnam's reunification. But our southern compatriots have constantly struggled heroically and refused to submit to them. The people throughout the country, united as one, are holding aloft the banner of peace, national unity, independence, and democracy, resolved to march forward and win final victory. The cause of the peaceful reunification and the Fatherland will certainly be victorious."[27]

"Under the clear-sighted leadership of the Vietnam Lao-Dong Party, the government of the Democratic Republic of Vietnam, and President Ho Chi Minh, our entire people, broadly united within the National United Front, will surely win glorious success in the building of socialism and the struggle for national reunification."[28]

Thus, the Vietnamese Communist Party's resolution, "To aim for the South," was exposed very clearly, through its official viewpoint.

Second, as a master of schemes and plots, Ho Chi Minh set up several veiled political organizations to mask the true activities of the Vietnamese Communist Party leaders and their cadres. Under the cloak of these organizations, they mobilized all the North's natural and human resources for the war effort in order to "liberate" of South Vietnam. The first such organization was the Mặt-trận Liên-Việt, the National United Front. The Liên-Việt, organized in 1951, was refurbished in 1955 to facilitate the changes of the VWP in its liberation goals. The newly reformed organization was composed of youth groups, groups of mothers, farmers, workers, resistant Catholics, war veterans, and other associations. It was placed under the complete control of the party's leaders and cadres at all levels in order to control and manage the whole population of North Vietnam, and to channel them directly into the war. No one could escape this regimentation or resist the party's decisions. Caught in the fine mesh of that party structure, everyone was obliged to execute docilely their "civil rights and duties" to consolidate the North and to go to the South to liberate their "southern fellow countrymen who are living in slavery."

The second organization, more important than the first, was the Mặt-trận Giải-phóng Miền Nam, namely the Southern National Liberation Front. The front was organized in December 19, 1960, in order to conceal the new VWP policy of military-political subversion of South Vietnam. Ho Chi Minh and his fellow communists used it to mastermind the war in South Vietnam. They claimed that South Vietnamese revolutionaries were responsible for the "revolution" in the South, rather than the communist units of North Vietnam. In reality, all of the communist war activities, psychologically, politically, and militarily carried out in the South were directed and controlled by another organization, the Central Office of South Vietnam (COSVN). The COSVN was the most important organism of the VWP's Political Committee in South Vietnam. It was the political and military "high command" and the headquarters for all the communist forces fighting in South Vietnam. The communist forces were composed of infiltration regular units of the North Vietnamese People's Army combined with regional and local communist guerrilla and militia units, the so-called Liberation Front Army units. All the leaders of the COSVN were members of the VWP's Political Committee, such as Le Duan its founder and first leader, General Nguyen Chi Thanh, Pham Hung, and Nguyen van Linh. In short, all aspects of the "liberation war" staged on South Vietnam's territory were under the overall responsibility of the COSVN, which meant under the clear direction of the Vietnamese Communist Party, or Đảng Lao-Động Vietnam.

The formative "founders" of the previously mentioned Southern Liberation Front were Attorney Nguyen Huu Tho, Engineer Huynh Tan Phat, Attorney Truong nhu Tang, Doctor Phung van Cung, and Professor Nguyen van Hieu. All were dissidents of Diem's regime, arrested by Diem, and later sent to North Vietnam through the DMZ. These "saloon politicians," or opportunist politicians, were introduced to Ho Chi Minh and sent back to South Vietnam to organize the Liberation Front. Despite this, at COSVN's meetings, they were regarded as third-class cadres of the North regime.

Ho Chi Minh's fabricated "Southern Liberation Front" (which later changed into the "Southern Provisional Revolutionary Government") succeeded in convincing international opinion about the war in Vietnam, not only among American congressmen, politicians, media reporters, and the population, but also among American generals and officers who were fighting in Vietnam. However, many American lower-ranking officers had a clear vision of the front's real purpose. As Chief Warrant Officer Sedgwick Tourison, Jr., relates it in his book *Talking with Victor Charlie*: "The National (Southern) Liberation Front was a smoke screen that served the Democratic Republic of Vietnam well in the international arena because many in the West found it a convenient justification for their own support of the North over the South.... The Front was not a large group of citizens organized to oppose Diem government. It was formed, directed, and managed by the Lao-Dong Party. It never was a force independent of the Party's control and direction."[29]

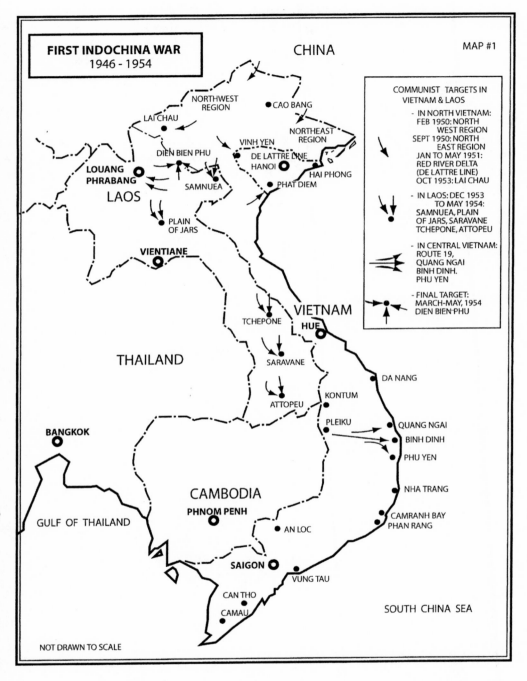

Discussing these "revolutionary forces," Sedgwick writes: "The armed forces of the communist movement in the South, the VC or 'Liberation Army' were the creation of the Democratic Republic of Vietnam, the North."[30] The knowledge of Sedgwick Tourison, Jr., was accurate. Unfortunately, it did not clear the dark cloud of confusion in Washington. Compounding this confusion, the South Vietnamese Army simply considered the "Viêt-cộng" or VC, as the Vietnamese Communists, without distinction between northern and southern communists, while MACV authorities distinguished the "VC" as those of the Liberation Army and the "NVA" as those of the North Vietnamese Army. Sedgwick also points out: "The emergence of the terms 'VC' and 'NVA' is a reflection of flaw in our [U.S.] policy. We sought to emphasize the legitimacy of the Republic of Vietnam and illegitimacy of the North. It didn't work. The terms, rather than helping Americans understand the single-mindedness of the North's activities, supported the North's claim that there was a viable and significant group against President Ngo Dinh Diem within the South who was independent of control by the North Vietnam. Nothing was further from the truth."[31]

Sedgwick emphasized: "The ability of the National [Southern] Liberation Front to pass itself off as an offspring of popular discontent to President Ngo Dinh Diem and devoid of Party [the VWP] direction is a reflection of the political ignorance of those who accepted such statements as face value. It is history, not this writer, who had made such a judgment."[32]

Unfortunately, many American civilian and military authorities ignored this little nuance of history. They either did not know, or chose to ignore their true opponents in a true war. Throughout the Second Indochina War, U.S. leaders blindly led the American and South Vietnamese troops to fight the "shadow" of the their enemy, as a Vietnamese proverb says: "bỏ mồi bắt bóng" (to drop the substance for the shadow).

In North Vietnam, Ho Chi Minh and his communist fellows seriously prepared a total war to "liberate the South" that would engrave in the minds of their younger generations these iron fated words, "born in the North to die in the South." Meanwhile, American leaders such as Kennedy and Johnson, who had inherited Truman's and Eisenhower's policies, led the youth of America into an extraordinary war fought with flawed strategies and without the will to win, but only to fight and sacrifice.

5

Counter-Insurgency Strategy

American foreign policy toward Vietnam under the four presidents after Eisenhower consisted of a patchwork of indecisive strategies. Inconsistent military strategies prevented US forces from winning the war in the field. "The different personalities and politics of different presidents, along with their varying military strategies, led to an inconsistency in presidential philosophy and leadership that the U.S. military could not overcome," said American historian John Dellinger.[1]

Their communist opponents, on the contrary, maintained a consistent policy with the firm objectives of liberating South Vietnam and building a socialist and communist society. Ho Chi Minh wrote in 1960:

> In the beginning it was patriotism and not Communism which induced me to believe Lenin and the Third International. But little by little, developing step by step in the course of struggle, and combining theoretical studies of Marxism-Leninism with practical activities, I came to realize that Socialism and Communism alone are capable of emancipating the workers and downtrodden people all over the world. There was in Vietnam — as well as in China — the legend of the magic bag; anyone faced with a great problem would simply open the bag to find a ready solution. For the Vietnamese revolution and Vietnamese people, Marxism-Leninism is not merely a magic bag, or a compass, but a real sun which lights the road to final victory, to Socialism and Communism.[2]

From the beginning, the Indochinese Communist Party (ICP) was created to fulfill these objectives (later, in 1951, it changed its name to the Vietnamese Workers' Party, VWP). Its Central Committee's members knew the war was a political war fought for ideological objectives. Therefore, the practical means to gear the war via the armed forces would be to develop a political army with extreme discipline hardened through indoctrination. Soldiers of the VWP's People's Army became ready to fight with fanaticism, to the point of sacrificing their lives for the sake of the party. Vo Nguyen Giap, the commander in chief of the People's Army, wrote in his book, *People's War, People's Army*: "The People's Army is the instrument of the Party and the revolutionary State for accomplishment, in armed form, of the tasks of the revolution. Profound awareness of the aims of the Party, boundless loyalty to the cause of the nation and the working class, and a spirit of unreserved sacrifice are fundamental questions for the army, and questions of principle. Therefore, the political work in its ranks is the first importance. It is the soul of the army."[3]

In 1947, Truong Chinh formulated a doctrine called "The Resistance Will Win" which was adapted from Mao Tse-tung's "On Protracted War," also termed the "People's War" or the "Revolutionary War." The ICP applied this "Resistance" (Trường-kỳ Kháng-chiến) as its "doctrine of war" in its struggle in Vietnam like the Chinese Communist Party did in China. This kind of war laid out 3 phases of transformation: (1) a strategic defensive phase of prolonged attrition from insurgency and guerrilla warfare; (2) the "war of movement," to gain equilibrium of force, and (3) a "general offensive" and "general uprising" phase (Tổng Công-Kích vā Tổng Nổi-Dậy).[4]

The most important stage of this doctrine was the first phase of strategic defense or insurgency and guerrilla warfare, which had a twofold purpose. First, the party sent out politico-military cadres to carry on the so-called armed propaganda approach (Võ-trang Tuyên-truyền). These communist cadres went among the mass in order to recruit, organize, and develop armed forces from village militia to become area guerrilla units (du-kích quân); then, from district (huyện-đội) to provincial (tỉnh-đội) and regional units (bộ-đội Miền). Vo Nguyen Giap stressed that "the development of this organized system of political militia and guerrilla units would largely precede the building of a regular army."[5]

Second, as the propaganda spread, the party — which then became the VWP — continued to terrorize the South Vietnamese people, mostly in the countryside. The party's terrorist policy had two important goals: intimidation of the populace and elimination of enemies throughout the village and district infrastructure. This policy of terrorism was officially outlined in one of the COSVN's resolutions and practiced by both the People's Army and VC regular units. The most skillful were the secret assassination squads (tiểu-tổ ám-sát) found at most communist local units including the Du-kích xã (village guerrillas), the Huyện-đội (district units), and the Tỉnh-đội (provincial units). The resolution's strategy stated that "integral to political struggle would be the liberal use of terrorism to weaken and destroy local government, strengthen the party apparatus, proselyte among the populace, erode control and influence of the South Vietnam Government and its armed forces."[6] These communist units carried out barbarous acts of terrorism, such as killing and cutting the victim's body to ribbons or leaving his head dangling from a bamboo pole in the middle of the village. Others simply gunned down the victim after reading his "death sentence." These violent acts of terrorism were more effective for their political and psychological effects among the masses than for their military effects.

Communist insurgency in South Vietnam increased considerably from 1960, after the creation of both the Southern Liberation Front and the Liberation Army, the latter formed by hard-core officers such as General Tran van Tra, Le Trong Tan, and Tran Do. These officers infiltrated into the South, with more than 10,000 southern-born cadres, passing through the DMZ by crossing the Ben-Hai River in Quang-Tri Province and then using the Ho Chi Minh Trail. Infiltrations by the front's cadres and North Vietnamese Army (NVA) troops went undetected until mid–1960.

Until that time, the communist insurgency had not directly defeated any South Vietnamese battalions or regiments but simply aimed to eliminate the government rural officials such as hamlet and village chiefs, district policemen, schoolteachers, recalcitrant villagers, and those who sympathized with the South Vietnam regime. In the Central Highlands and remote areas of the Mekong Delta, they intimidated villagers by assassination, abduction, kidnapping, or harassment in order to force their cooperation, to collect taxes, food, and other supplies; and to discourage them from giving intelligence to the government officials. This first phase of the insurgency, which had been the Viet-Minh's source of success against the French in the 1940s and 1950s, now became a real threat for Ngo Dinh Diem's administration and the American authorities in South Vietnam. This was especially true after the "arc of insurgency" was established around Saigon that killed, maimed, or kidnapped several American officers and officials in November and December 1960. The newly appointed American ambassador to Saigon, Frederic E. Nolting, narrowly escaped a hand grenade thrown at his car in early 1961.

Official estimates of the number of South Vietnamese village officials killed by communist insurgents, from May 1957 to April 1961, exceeded 8,000. Countless innocent villagers and farmers were also killed or kidnapped.

At this point, the war was one of insurgency, staged by the North Vietnamese Communists disguised as the Liberation Front. Faced with this situation, John F. Kennedy, the new president of the United States, had trouble formulating a suitable military strategy. The war conducted by the communists in North Vietnam was clear but the subversion of the people "inside" South Vietnam was not. Common opinion held that the VC (Việt-Cộng) in South Vietnam fought the war for independence with the "help" of the NVA (North Vietnamese Army). Accordingly, the true nature of the "liberation war," or "revolutionary war," was not grasped by the United States. In fact, the war in South Vietnam was a unique war conducted by Ho Chi Minh and the VWP, or really the Vietnamese Communist Party. This was the true nature of the Second Vietnam War.

Although the true opponents were misidentified and the nature of the war misunderstood, the Kennedy administration was credited by some historians for its prompt action in South Vietnam and in Indochina, especially in Laos, which was then in a state of war, involving the Royal Laotian Army and the Pathet-Lao.

COUNTER-INSURGENCY: CONCEPTS AND MEASURES

On May 11, 1961, a United States presidential memorandum set forth the Kennedy administration's policy for South Vietnam, essentially affirming the previous Eisenhower policy. It stated: "The U.S. objective and concept of operations stated in the report are approved: to prevent communist domination of South Vietnam, to create in that country a viable and increasingly democratic society, and to initiate, on an accelerated basis, a series of mutually supporting actions of a military, political, economic, psychological and covert character designed to achieve this objective."[7]

All supporting activities by the U.S. were accelerated. An inter-agency "Vietnam Task Force" was set up, military aid was accelerated, and an endless stream of inspection missions of all kinds began to invade Saigon. In addition to these activities, one week before issuing the memorandum, President Kennedy declared in a press conference on May 5, 1961, that he would consider the use of U.S. forces if necessary "to help South Vietnam resist communist pressure." But after an overwhelming majority had re-elected Ngo Dinh Diem (on April 9), Diem let Ambassador Nolting know that the people of South Vietnam did not want combat troops from the United States. This was the first direct conflict between these two presidents. Their disagreement would later deeply affect the "termination" of Diem and his brother Nhu. At the time, vice-president Lyndon Johnson left Washington immediately for talks with Diem on the subject.

Back in Washington on May 20, 1961, Johnson proposed to increase the ARVN (Army of the Republic of Vietnam) to 170,000 men, double the provincial Civil Guards (Bảo-an Đoàn) around the country, from 60,000 to 120,000 men, and equip the village Militia (Dân-vệ) with modern small weapons. His most interesting proposition to President Kennedy was that he construct more strategic hamlets and "increase ... the agrovilles from 22 to 100 in one year."[8] The problem of "American combat troops" was not discussed at that time. However, President Diem was told to accept the "pacification plan" involving the ten Mekong Delta provinces known as the "Delta Plan" and the Central Highlands project, called the "Boun Enao Project" and involving the participation of U.S. "Special Advisory Teams."

On December 15, 1961, in officially exchanged letters, President Diem stressed that South Vietnam faced the "most serious crisis in its entire history," while President Kennedy promised that "the United States would promptly increase its aid" and expressed his "full confidence in the determination of the people of South Vietnam."[9]

French historian Bernard B. Fall emphasizes the United States' expansion of military involvement in Vietnam after the exchange of these presidential letters. President Kennedy informed Saigon of plans to increase the number of American advisers from 900 to 16,000 over a two-year period. Within weeks, Kennedy dispatched the first helicopter units, called "Eagle-Flights," to Vietnam. More than 300 American pilots were ordered to lead Vietnamese troops into battle but not engage in combat — unless in "self-defense." By early 1962, the number of American advisers increased to 4,000, including Green Berets units, or Special Forces, especially trained to deal with guerrilla warfare. They belonged to the new Counter-Insurgency Council chaired by General Maxwell D. Taylor. On February 8, 1961, MAAG-Vietnam became the Military Assistance Command, Vietnam (MACV), bringing the American role from a few hundred advisers, as started by President Truman, to thousands of Americans committed to the field.

Professor Arthur Schlesinger Jr., who was then Kennedy's political adviser, used a metaphor to compare Kennedy's "gradual escalation" policy in Vietnam to a drink; he wrote: "It's like a drink. The effect wears off, and you have to take another. Yet, he felt obligated to offer a small drink himself and he increased the number of military advisers."[10] Bernard Fall further developed Schlesinger's idea, "it could well be argued that it was the Kennedy administration that brought the bottle to the party."[11] Fall also stated in *The Two Vietnams* (1964) that: "And thus, degree by degree, the United States slid into the Second Vietnam War."[12] Later, in a retrospective article in 1967 on President Kennedy's military commitment to Vietnam, he commented: "It was he (or men under him) who made all the decisive mistakes in the Vietnam situation. Probably no chief executive in recent memory was so badly informed about an increasingly serious situation as JFK was about Vietnam. It was during his administration that the politics of inadvertence blossomed into full-gear commitment."[13]

After the war, many American scholars and politicians agreed with Fall's comment, but polls from the early 1960s showed that a large majority of Americans favored going to war, if necessary, to prevent a communist takeover of any friendly nation. Ostensibly, the United States' reason for military involvement in Vietnam was based on the general philosophy of strategic containment of communism. However, the lure of building a personal "theory of war" suitable to a new arena, in which the so-called wars of liberation largely developed, also influenced President Kennedy. His aim was to be the father of a new worldwide theory of "Counter-Insurgency," which he realized by "giving birth" to the Green Berets Corps of the U.S. Armed Forces. South Vietnam became an appropriate and timely turf upon which he could test his "theory" and his "tool." Indeed, his secretary of defense, McNamara, had confirmed in mid–1962: "We still win even on present ground rules.... South Vietnam is a test of U.S. firmness and of U.S. capacity to deal with wars of liberation."[14]

Thus, South Vietnam became the "testing-ground" of a new concept of war for the United States under the Kennedy presidency. This was one of the root motivations of his policy of military escalation in South Vietnam. Degree by degree he slid into the Second Vietnam War. Not with the out-of-control manner, as stated by Schlesinger in his metaphor of "a drink after a drink," but with a well-planned intention, as secretary of state Dean Rusk said: "Vietnam posed for us a serious question about where we're going in respect of collective security. If the US had done nothing about Vietnam then its allies would have been the first to say 'You see, you cannot trust the Americans.'"[15] And, Rusk's deputy, Roger Hilsman, a close Kennedy aide, stated that the president was extremely sensitive over Vietnam and saw it in a global context, with the thinking that "the world [was] deemed to be exploding into wars of national liberation and communist-led insurgency."[16]

A new concept of war in South Vietnam and in other Indochinese countries was sorely needed, with effective countermeasures against communist "revolutions." This was especially true after Soviet Premier Khrushchev made a pointed speech in support of world revolution just days before Kennedy's presidential inauguration on January 20, 1961. However, Kennedy's new initiatives turned out to have serious psychological and political ramifications for the outcome in South Vietnam and in Laos.

First, in South Vietnam, President Kennedy decided to firmly handle the war despite the opposition of South Vietnamese president Ngo Dinh Diem and his brother Ngo Dinh Nhu. Peter Brush, a U.S. Marine Corps veteran, wrote a remarkable observation in *Vietnam Magazine*: "The more the US took control of the war to avoid the defeat of the GVN [Government of Vietnam] by the communists, the easier it was for Hanoi to portray the United States as a neocolonialist power and the GVN as merely as puppet regime."[17] It was ironic but it was, in fact, true. President Kennedy's second big mistake was his initiative to neutralize Laos.

THE NEUTRALIZATION OF LAOS IN 1962

In Laos, the pro–Chinese regime of Prince Souvanna Phouma was replaced, in July 1958, by the right-wing reform regime of Prince Boum Oum and General Phoumi Nosavan. From May 1959, Laos was in the midst of a bizarre war between three different forces. The United States backed the rightist forces of General Phoumi Nosavan. Nosavan fought both the neutralist forces of rebel Captain Kong Le (later major general), who was backing Prince Souvanna Phouma, and the Communist Pathet-Lao under Prince Souphanouvong, who were backed by both the Soviet Union and Red China. The Pathet-Lao was greatly influenced by the North Vietnamese Army. There were at least 4,000 NVA officers and soldiers serving in Pathet-Lao units.

Most of the fighting and an endless series of inconclusive clashes occurred in the Plain of Jars area in north central Laos. Meanwhile, in the southeastern panhandle and Laotian border, the 559th Special Groups of the North Vietnamese Army, with a total of 35,000 men, continued to expand and improve the existing trails along the Truong-Son Chain (Day Truong-Son) into a major road network known as the Ho Chi Minh Trail. During that period (1959–1961) this invasion and exploitation of Laotian territory by the communists of North Vietnam for their purposes in South Vietnam was of critical importance.

According to Roger Hilsman, assistant secretary of state for Far-East Affairs, ex–President Eisenhower had given incoming President Kennedy urgent advice about Laos. Eisenhower warned that Laos was important and would be a big problem for the Kennedy administration. If Laos fell to communism, he feared that other Asian nations would follow, toppling like a row of dominoes. He also suggested to Kennedy that the United States might have to send troops to Laos.

In the eyes of master strategist Eisenhower, Laos occupied an area in Indochina that was very important militarily and geographically. Were the United States to fight a ground war, the best place for it would likely be in Laos instead of South Vietnam. Had President Kennedy advanced and directed an open war in Laotian territory at that time, he would have won the war. First, North Vietnam's invasion of Laos meant the United States would be engaged in the cause of helping a free nation against communist invaders. Such an undertaking would gain global support and the cooperation of the Western allies. Second, the 40,000 North Vietnamese communist troops in Laotian territory would be considered conquerors of Laos. Accordingly, they could not retain their purported nationalistic "reason" of a "liberation war." Third, by fighting in Laos, the Kennedy administration could gain more easily the support of the U.S. populace, the media, and the Congress.

While there may have been other reasons such a course would have been a winning solution, the Kennedy administration unfortunately chose a narrow path in Indochina: neutralizing Laos and fighting a "limited war" in South Vietnam. Kennedy wished to avoid a "second" Korean War by drawing Red China into an intervention in Indochina. Also, Kennedy had been elected president by a very small margin and "realized that in his first term he needed to make sure he would become a popular president so that he could address more difficult issues in his second term," wrote Dr. Jane Hamilton Merritt, a Pulitzer Prize winner.[18]

Under the Kennedy presidency, the U.S. followed two contrasting strategies in Indochina, a formal official one and a tacit one, especially in Laos. In fact, one of Kennedy's advisers, under-secretary of state Averell Harriman, proposed that Laos be "neutralized." He assured Kennedy that the neutralization of Laos would "block the use of Laos' territory against South Vietnam," making it possible to "solve the South Vietnam problem in South Vietnam, rather than by military action in Laos."[19]

On May 16, 1961, a fourteen-nation conference on Laos convened in Geneva. American delegates were two men who had damaged American policy toward Indochina from the beginning: Averell Harriman and his assistant William Sullivan, who later became American ambassador to Vientiane. These aides to Kennedy designed and controlled the application of Laos' neutral treaty, which ensured Hanoi's success in waging its long-term conquest of South Vietnam.

The Geneva Accords, signed on July 23, 1962, supposedly neutralized Laos by stipulating that no foreign troops were to be on Laos' soil and by setting up a neutral government in Laos with the purpose of ending its civil war. Accordingly, on October 5, 1962, all 800 American advisers to the Royal Laotian Army withdrew from the country. However, it quickly became clear the North Vietnam would not follow suit, but would insist on keeping large forces in Laos. Although the coalition government was officially neutral — under the premiership of Prince Souvanna Phouma and two vice prime ministers, the rightist General Phoumi Nosavan and the Pathet-Lao leader, Prince Souphanouvong — Laos remained divided. The Royal Laotian Army held the few cities and provinces in the western part of the country and the Pathet-Lao controlled the countryside and the mountainous regions in the eastern part. The nexus between these two opposite sectors was that North Vietnamese troops already held southeastern Laos. They had the capacity to intensely resist any forces, including those from the United States.

In order to deal with this troubling dilemma; the United States decided not to stick with its initial and official solution of "neutralization." A second solution, one of a tacit strategy, was then adopted by President Kennedy based on Harriman's recommendation. Harriman persuaded the president to carry out, on the surface, United States obligations under the Geneva Treaty terms, but covertly to engage in a secret war with the NVA in Laos. This would defend the status quo of the neutral government in Laos until the war in South Vietnam was resolved. Hanoi continued to send troops and supplies through Laos to South Vietnam. Norman B. Hannah, a retired State Department foreign affairs officer, related Harriman's argument: "[Only i]f the Communists [North Vietnam] using the Laos routes should lose in South Vietnam could Laos ever become neutral."[20] To realize this tacit strategy, a north-south line was drawn through Laos, based on the de-facto holding line between the Royal Laos forces and the Pathet-Lao. This became known as the "Harriman Line" and was supposed to protect

Vientiane and Luang-Prabang, the two capitals of Laos, although it admittedly conceded half of the country to Hanoi's use. This was, as Hannah pointed out, "Ironic, but inevitable as the Harriman Line paralleled and protected the Ho Chi Minh Trail."[21]

Later, in March 1964, Robert McNamara, secretary of defense, confirmed this Harriman strategy: "As a consequence of these policies [on Laos] we and the Government of South Vietnam have had to 'condone' the extensive use of the Cambodia and Laotian territory by the Viet-cong both as a sanctuary and as infiltration routes."[22] The Harriman Line and the concept of "condoning" the communists' extensive use of Laotian territory were a reality that allowed the North Vietnamese to officially deny their presence and involvement in Laos. They continued to construct and develop the Ho Chi Minh Trail with extensive networks of roads, trails, and support stations for movement of tens of thousands of troops and materiel to battlefields in South Vietnam.

The damage from this strategy was made clear when William Sullivan was assigned to Laos as ambassador. According to Michael Maclear, author of *The Ten Thousand Day War* (1981), Sullivan, as ambassador in Laos, exercised total control over all American political and military activities in the large but unacknowledged war in Laos. Sullivan had no coordination of actions with any American military or diplomatic authorities in South Vietnam, but only within his embassy in Vientiane. Since the Geneva Accords would only superficially be carried out and the war against North Vietnamese in Laos was kept secret, Ambassador Sullivan determined that Laos was his own field of responsibility and jurisdiction. In fact, he opposed Pentagon plans to use ground forces against the Ho Chi Minh Trail. Sullivan placed restrictions on U.S. ground activities and air strikes in Laotian territory, particularly in the east sector of the Harriman Line and the panhandle along the border of Laos and Vietnam, which was occupied by communist North Vietnam. His restrictions worked to the distinct advantage of the NVA's logistics operations and troop infiltrations along the Ho Chi Minh Trail — to the point that American troops dubbed the trail "Sullivan Speedway." This strategic network of trails and roads fed the communist revolutionary war in South Vietnam.

All American and South Vietnamese authorities in Washington and in Saigon agreed that the infiltration of North Vietnamese Army supplies and troops through Laos had to be barred and the Ho Chi Minh Trail demolished. However, the awkwardly inconsistent policies and the incredibly self-imposed restrictions on U.S. ground combat forces in Laos (and Cambodia) by American politicians prevented a fully effective strategy to eliminate this serious external threat to South Vietnam.

The 1962 Geneva Accords did not aid the United States' cause in Laos. Instead, they betrayed that cause by giving communist North Vietnam virtual immunity against ground attack on their main supply line, the Ho Chi Minh Trail, through the Laotian panhandle. Many scholars contended that the Geneva Accords marked the beginning of the downfall of Laos and resulted in North Vietnam's ability to develop and use the Ho Chi Minh Trail to sustain the war in South Vietnam. Some stressed that the accord was one of the most self-defeating aspects of the entire Second Indochina War. Indeed, the Ho Chi Minh Trail was more important than the communist revolutionary ideology. Scholars point out that the communists of Vietnam could not win the "hearts and minds" of the South Vietnamese people, but they won the war by sending hundreds of thousands of soldiers down the Ho Chi Minh Trail to sustain and prolong the war. Thus, the United States failed in Vietnam because the American people were just not prepared to support a prolonged war of attrition.

THE HO CHI MINH TRAIL

Military experts from the U.S. Defense Intelligence Agency (DIA) described the Ho Chi Minh Trail as a network of forested and mountainous trails, crude paths, gravel roads and sophisticated highways some 3,500 miles (5,645 kilometers) in length. However, Hanoi's first ambassador to the United Nations, Ha van Lau, asserted that the network of roads making up the trail extended to more than 13,000 kilometers. The trail paralleled the thousand kilometers of Laos' border with South Vietnam and spread along the Trường-Sơn Chain (or the Long-Mountains range), that forms Indochina's bony spine and dominates the whole southern part of Laos, Central Vietnam, and the northern part of Cambodia.

The trail originally began with crude trails used by tribal hunters and smugglers moving contraband from China to the port cities of Southeast Asia. During the First Indochina War, these trails were expanded to serve as a primitive communication path for the Viet-Minh in their "To the South Movement" (Phong-trào Nam-tiến). They used local tribesmen as guides to evade French outposts along the border and the French Deuxième Bureau's intelligence networks. During the initial stages of "insurgency" in South Vietnam that followed the 1954 Geneva Accords, North Vietnamese General Vo Nguyen Giap kept some of his valuable regiments in Laos. In addition to training the Pathet-Lao, he made plans to construct a strategic network of supply routes to South Vietnam in order to carry out the Vietnamese Workers Party's goal "To Aim for the South." The Ho Chi Minh Trail became a complex web of narrow jungle paths throughout Laos, on which the VWP, at first, sent back southern-born cadres, who had migrated North in 1955, and brought modest shipments of small arms to organize guerrilla resistance in the South.

The real construction and development of the modern Ho Chi Minh Trail and military relay stations, or Binh-trạm, began in the spring of 1959. This work was done under the protection of the NVA 301st Division and a specially combined group known as Group 559, 35,000 men strong, commanded by Colonel Vo Bam. All of these NVA units were placed under the direction of Colonel Dong Si Nguyen, the architect and commander of this extensive construction project. Group 559 expanded and improved existing trails into a major road network with spurs leading into base areas in the Ashau in South Vietnam's I Corps & Region, the Duc-co Pleime in II Corps & Region, and war-zones D and C in III Corps & Region (see Map #2).

Colonel Dong Si Nguyen, who later became a member of the VWP Political Committee and minister of construction in Hanoi after the war, brought in engineer battalions equipped with up-to-date Soviet and Chinese machinery to build roads and bridges. Anticipating powerful American bombing of this supply route, Colonel Nguyen placed sophisticated anti-aircraft defenses, underground tunnels and barracks, hospitals and bunkers, garages, and storage facilities all along the trail.

Military relay stations (Binh-trạm) manned by engineers, transportation staff, and anti-aircraft crews were located at intervals of approximately one-day's march, or about 15 or 20 kilometers, depending on the terrain along the trail. Each Binh-tram was mainly protected by two anti-aircraft battalions armed with 12.7mm, 23mm, and 37mm guns and a SA-2 missile battalion, but also typically had two engineer battalions, two truck transportation battalions, a signal battalion, a communication liaison battalion, a security battalion, and a food-production unit.[23] Group 559, which was also in charge of all infiltration groups all along the Ho Chi Minh Trail, operated these military relay stations.

Group 559 provided complete management of the Ho Chi Minh Trail. Responsibilities included construction and repair of roads and bridges; air defense and security of the Binh-tram; transportation of all supplies and war materials and equipment to South Vietnam; communication and liaison among Hanoi, the COSVN headquarters, and other communist regional headquarters; and complete support and guides for any infiltration groups at any site throughout their journey on the trail. At its maximum strength, the Group had an estimated 50,000 troops assigned to 20 Binh-tram and an addition of supportive forces of 100,000 civilian workers.[24] The continual functioning of the trail depended on the regular management of each Binh-tram.

In the early 1960s, transportation of supplies to the South along the trail depended upon thousands of human porters with ponies, and occasionally, bicycles. The first groups used elephants to help carry supplies over the first barrier, the crossing of the 1,300-foot Mu-gia Pass on international Road 15, into Laos. The elephant-led groups entered the Laotian town of Tchépone (or Sépone), which is located near the border of South Vietnam, a few miles south of the DMZ. This became the northern terminus of the Ho Chi Minh Trail.

Protected by the Harriman Line, the Communist North Vietnamese greatly exploited the trail. The transportation network developed elaborate footpaths, river-ways and even two-lane highways that wound along the 7,000-foot heights from above the 17th parallel to the 11th parallel. These roads were capable of supporting the heaviest of tracked military vehicles that poured interminable supplies and troops to the battlefields in South Vietnam.

The growing number of North Vietnamese Army soldiers fighting in South Vietnam reflected the subsequent high rate of traffic on the Ho Chi Minh Trail. In 1959, an estimated 5,000 political cadres born in the South infiltrated back from the North. From 1962, the cycle of escalation greatly increased in response to the American military escalation in South Vietnam. Considering replacements for casualties as well as new units committed to the battlefields, at the heights of the war from 1964, the trail became the principal entrance for as many as 60,000 to 90,000 infiltrators a year.

In the meantime, most American foreign policy advisers knew that the Ho Chi Minh Trail carried into South Vietnam all kinds of weaponry, equipment, and materiel manufactured in the Soviet Union and in China and used by North Vietnamese soldiers. But no one "accepted" the direct solution to cut off the trail by ground forces. The Ho Chi Minh Trail became legendary as a myth with two particular characteristics. First, the trail was invisible but progressively developed; second, it was indestructible and ever-lasting.

American pilots who executed flying missions on the trail related the first characteristic. Sol Sanders, a former pilot of an American T-28 had been flying regularly over the trail. He wrote for *U.S. News & World Report* that he had been astonished by what he did not see. U.S. military intelligence reported that tens of thousands of North Vietnamese troops and massive supply trucks were known to be using this jungle web of man-made roads. But Sanders could not see any men or trucks moving on the trail. "The whole flight had an eerie quality. Although there was no doubt that we were flying over a heavily traveled road, I saw no sign of life during the entire time," Sanders wrote.[25]

The rate of infiltration by the North Vietnamese Army along the Ho Chi Minh Trail was estimated to have tripled since 1962, so in early 1964 the U.S. began a secret air campaign of strafing missions. Flights of American T-28 propeller aircraft, which were funded by the CIA to support the Royal Lao Air Force, surveyed the Ho Chi Minh Trail within Laotian territory. The code-name for this operation was Steel Tiger and, like other conflicts between the United States and North Vietnam in Laos after the neutralization, was kept secret. The complete silence on the Ho Chi Minh Trail at daytime could be explained by the 559 Group's well-organized and disciplined movement along the trail. Infiltration efforts began at nightfall. Daily, hundreds of loaded trucks with war goods waited to make the nightly run into

South Vietnam from their staging points at each Binh-tram in the Laotian panhandle. The truck drivers were expected to know every turn and obstacle along the route, covering only about a 20-mile stretch of the trail during each nightly run. At dawn, the whole movement stopped. All trucks pulled off the roads and were hidden in camouflage truck parks, or in any of the thousands of caves carved into the hillsides along the trail. The mysterious and secret movement along the Trường-Sơn Range created the "eerie silent quality" all along the Ho Chi Minh Trail.

The second characteristic of the Ho Chi Minh Trail, "immortality," was inexplicable to the Americans. No one could understand how the trail could survive the heavy and regular bombings of the American B-52s. After the war, Ha van Lau, Hanoi ambassador to the United Nations, explained: "The routes were permanently maintained by groups of young pioneers, men and women, who were ready every moment to repair the roads immediately after every bombing in such a way that despite the very strict surveillance by American planes, this roads network was never cut. Every night the roads were immediately repaired."[26] The Ho Chi Minh Trail, constructed by turning ancient paths into a sophisticated logistic network, was continuously repaired for years with no expense but the sweat, tears, blood and bones of generations of North Vietnamese youth who maintained the trail's "immortality." According to the communist press, the road repair gangs, or the so-called Youth Shock Union (Đoàn Thanh-Niên Xung-phong), permanently numbered more than 50,000. They were teenaged men and young women who volunteered to work along the trail for three years' service. With males drafted into the army at eighteen, the majority of the Youth Shock groups were young women. The casualties from American bombing and sickness among these civilian workers on the trail must have been enormous. American firepower deployed to cut the trail was unprecedented in history. The bomb ordinance expended along this single network exceeded what had been used in all theaters of war during all the years of World War II. From 1965 to 1972, under the Johnson and Nixon administrations, 2,235,918 tons of ordinance was dropped in vain over the trail, including 171,000 tons of B-52 bombs (in World War II, two million tons of air ordinance were dropped). The Ho Chi Minh Trail was unshakable and ever-lasting as the communist North Vietnam's glorious way to their final victory.[27]

Later, after the Paris Accords came into effect by January 1973, the NVA began a massive build up of roads and highways in order to reinforce their units in South Viet Nam. What they established was called "Trường Sơn Đông" (the Long Mountain Eastern Route, or Corridor 613). The Corridor 613 ran along the eastern side of the Trường-Sơn Range in parallel with the old Ho Chi Minh Trail on the western side. The two were connected by a network of crossroads. This new corridor, which started from Dong Hoi and ran all the way south to Loc Ninh, was completed by early 1975.

After the war, General Van Tien Dung, NVA General chief of staff who commanded the communist final offensive in South Vietnam in 1975, described the trail in his account of that campaign: "The strategic route east of Trường Sơn Range [i.e., the Long Mountains or the Annam Cordilla] was the result of labor of more than 30,000 troops and shock youths. The length of this route, added to that of the other old and new strategic routes and routes used during various campaigns built during the last war, is more than 20,000 kilometers [12,500 miles]. The eight-meter [24.4 feet] wide route of more than 1,000km [625 miles], which we now see, is our pride. With 5,000 km [3,125 miles] of pipeline laid through the deep rivers and streams and on the mountains more than 1,000 meters [3,300 feet] high, we were capable of providing enough fuel for various battle fronts. More than 10,000 transportation vehicles were put on the road."[28]

Without the neutrality of Laos, the Harriman Line, or the self-restricted deployment of ground forces in Laos, communist North Vietnam would not have been able to construct the Ho Chi Minh Trail. If this were the case, communist guerrilla warfare in South Vietnam would have followed a course similar to that in Malaysia: it would have been crushed in a few years and history would have changed for the three countries of Indochina.

Thus, the biggest mistake of the United States in the whole Second Indochina War, that led to military failure in this far land, especially in South Vietnam, was the Kennedy administration's foreign policy toward Laos. President Kennedy overemphasized the "counter-insurgency" process in South Vietnam and ignored the important position of Laos that allowed North Vietnam to build up the strategically vital Ho Chi Minh Trail. Thus, the Johnson administration had to take the onerous task of cutting the trail. Since 1964, the United States foreign policy toward Indochina turned on the absurd "existence of a Laos neutrality" and all military strategic measures taken by President Johnson were based upon the menacing existence of the Ho Chi Minh Trail.

The second important mistake of the Kennedy administration was its arbitrary and brutal handling of South Vietnamese leadership. The United States' previous judicious policies under the Truman and Eisenhower administrations were turned into a policy of oppression and rude interference in an allied country. This deep interference was the primary cause of the dangerous situation in South Vietnam during the critical period of 1963–1965, and it created the precedence of military escalation for the following administrations of the United States.

In the eyes of South Vietnamese intellectuals, the American oppression and interference in their country were considered a new form of foreign autocracy that concentrated all political, military, economic, and diplomatic powers of the country within the American embassy in Saigon. The American ambassador became a new colonial governor. As a result, South Vietnamese officials were reticent to cooperate with the American authorities in South Vietnam and the efficacy of the combined anti-communist measures was diminished.

THE "ELEVEN POINT PROGRAM"

The creation of a "full-fledged" American Military Assistance Command, Vietnam (US-MACV), to take control of the rapidly rising American military build-up, showed that the Kennedy administration intended to stay in the struggle for South Vietnam and win it. "We are going to win in Vietnam, we will remain there until we do win," said Robert F. Kennedy, U.S. senator and President Kennedy's younger brother, on February 15, 1962.[29] But this point of view was based upon President Kennedy's thinking about the war as one of "counter-insurgency." According to an American historian, the president himself viewed Vietnam as an almost perfect place to use counter-insurgency warfare: "There he could show his interest in the Third World, demonstrate conclusively that America lived up to her commitments, and play the exciting new game of counter-insurgency."[30]

Counter-insurgency warfare was overestimated in the early 1960s as the U.S. Army's doctrine or dogma. It received enormous attention in the military schools and training centers, and was envisioned as the United States' primary response to internal wars promoted by the communists in underdeveloped countries. Noted historian Harry G. Summers, Jr., a retired U.S. Army colonel, remarked: "It stultified military thinking for the next decades."[31]

This counter-insurgency was not readily accepted by South Vietnamese leaders, particularly Ngo Dinh Nhu, President Diem's brother and political adviser. President Diem and his brother Nhu actively resisted this counter-insurgency program and instead implemented the "Strategic Hamlets" project, which concentrated peasants into newly built hamlets in the countryside to protect and isolate them from communist guerrillas. Assistant United States secretary of state Roger Hilsman described those hamlets as "concentration camps," as did North Vietnamese prime minister Pham van Dong.

The Kennedy administration appeared to underestimate the efforts of Ngo Dinh Diem and his brother Ngo Dinh Nhu in their strategy. Ngo Dinh Diem's regime was accused of arrogant autocracy by Kennedy's important aides and many reporters in the American press. Those who opposed Diem's regime wished to see in South Vietnam the liberal democracy of the United States. Many had extensive knowledge, wide learning, or were clever upper-class intellectuals. But they lacked knowledge and understanding of Asian culture, and did not see that Western-style democracy could not be applied to any Asian country during a time of war, such as Vietnam in the early 1960s, where people lived in an anarchic, disoriented and chaotic society. In such times, any liberal freedoms offered to them would be a double-bladed knife that would be dangerous for them. In the first steps of democracy, a moderate freedom with the respect of the ancient traditions, habits and customs in addition to some fundamental conditions such as a true independence, a Vietnamese leadership, and socio-economic development, would satisfy them and encourage them to work for their future.

The first period of democracy under Ngo Dinh Diem sought to satisfy these fundamental aspirations of the South Vietnamese people. The ideological "personalism" then must be considered as a viable political doctrine that would face communism in Vietnam. President Diem stated in his message to the Constitutional Assembly of April 17, 1956: "Democracy is essentially a permanent effort to find the right political means of assuring to all citizens the right of free development."[32] He meant that socio-economic development must precede political freedom. Mrs. Ngo Dinh Nhu, President's Diem's sister-in-law, likewise said: "Political democracy must be entirely reorganized on the basis of an effective economic democracy to modern[ize the] structure of production."[33]

However, the application of the personalism in Diem's regime gave rise to much confusion, particularly in the intellectual circles of Washington and in the White House. The personalism concentrated national power in the hands of the Ngo family's members. Monsignor Ngo Dinh Thuc, President Diem's older brother, preached in the Mekong Delta. Another brother, Ngo Dinh Can, unofficially ruled Central Vietnam. His most confident brother and political adviser, Ngo Dinh Nhu, the real theoretician of the regime, actively opposed the presence of American ground combat forces in South Vietnam and Kennedy's military strategy. Diem and his regime faced a dilemma.

The regime was accused of autocracy, nepotism, and corruption. The deep sense of pride the Ngo's family had earned recently was replaced by a deep sense of shame, the result of these allegations by the American press and American officials. It provoked a fierce response from the Ngo family, especially Mrs. Ngo Dinh Nhu, and from supporters, such as some Saigon's newspapers and the Vietnamese Democratic Party, a reputable political party in South Vietnam in the 1960s. Mrs. Nhu answered those who constantly criticized South Vietnamese leaders in an editorial in the *Times of Vietnam* of March 1962:

> For years, I, like others in this country, simply clenched my teeth and shut up when I had to listen to all accusations of communist propaganda against the regime and the ideal of the Personalist Republic, all reported with glee by the U.S. press. And I should continue to do this if the strange and wild behavior of the U.S. press had calmed down. But, on the contrary, it has increased to a point where it risks harming the fighting spirit of our people. The Vietnamese people do not have to be taught solidarity toward their allies ... but they cannot allow the prestige of their leaders and their ideals to be unjustly and foolishly besmirched by irresponsible elements.[34]

Before that, during the third week of November 1961, the South Vietnamese press had erupted in a wave of anti–American articles, especially after a U.S. military mission led by General Maxwell D. Taylor, military adviser to President Kennedy, returned from Saigon with a critical report that was extremely hard-hitting toward the Diem regime. The report criticized severely the absence of long-overdue political reforms in South Vietnam, including the reform of freedom of speech and a more effective decentralization. The Taylor mission's report shocked not only Ngo Dinh Diem's cabinet but also the whole of South Vietnam's middle and upper classes. *Tự-Do* (*Liberty*) and *Thời-Báo* (*Times*) newspapers in Saigon and others, in a series of late November and December articles, accused Americans of "interference with the internal affairs in Vietnam" and also labeled American officials in South Vietnam (and in Washington) as capitalist-imperialists.

Washington attributed the viciousness of these attacks to political adviser Ngo Dinh Nhu. By December 6, 1961, there were hints that under the pressure of U.S. Department of State, U.S. ambassador to Saigon Frederic E. Nolting had personally asked President Diem to fire some of his relatives, particularly Ngo Dinh Nhu and his wife, from any official or unofficial positions in the regime. On December 12, Diem called in Nolting and told him that all further reforms suggested by Washington would temporarily have to be reexamined and that Ngo Dinh Nhu's powers would remain unchanged. As a result, the honeymoon between the United States and Ngo Dinh Diem's regime during the previous eight years lasted only until the end of 1962, despite an immense public relations effort on both sides.

In essence, the fierce opposition by Ngo Dinh Diem and his brother Ngo Dinh Nhu to the Kennedy administration's political and military positions in South Vietnam was a real obstacle to United States efforts to apply its new anti-communist theory in this testing ground. Only one alternative solution remained: an American-induced changeover toward a more "docile" and "responsive" government, even at the price of seeking out replacement leaders. Everyone knew that the United States would directly control South Vietnam because President Kennedy wanted it to become the testing ground for his new concept of war. In mid–May 1961, France's president Charles De Gaulle warned Kennedy: "The ideology that you invoke will not change anything.... You Americans wanted, yesterday, to take our place in Indochina, you want to assure a succession to rekindle a war that we ended. I predict to you that you will, step by step, be sucked into a bottomless military and political quagmire."[35] Later, the United States' commitment in Vietnam became even more disastrous than predicted by De Gaulle.

All the while, the problem "leadership" in South Vietnam divided Kennedy's advisors into two distinct camps. One strong group argued that: "You can't win with Diem," and suggested Diem and Nhu be immediately replaced. The other group acknowledged that the United States perhaps could not win with Diem, but in the words of General Taylor, "if not Diem — who?" The question had no answer, but President Kennedy became sympathetic to the idea of a coup, provided that the Americans were not responsible and were not involved in it. A quarter of a century later, history proved it to be the other way around.

During those days, a temporary reconciliation between the Kennedy administration and Ngo Dinh Diem's regime was achieved and lasted for nearly twenty more months. In early 1962, General Taylor declared that he and Diem had agreed that Washington and Saigon would make "a new start," which meant political reforms in South Vietnam in return for new forms of American military aid. In Saigon, Ambassador Nolting, speaking at the Saigon Rotary Club on February 15, 1962, assured the local upper-class audience and international media's reporters that "the Vietnamese Government, under the devoted and courageous leadership of President Ngo Dinh Diem, attempts to realize, under difficult conditions, political, social, and economic progress for the people, with the help of the United States." He emphasized that the United States was giving its fullest support to the "elected and constitutional regime of Vietnam."[36] Overall, the speech was well received in South Vietnam. By the end of February, official American opinion made a 180-degree about-face and the American press changed their unfavorable comments about Ngo Dinh Diem's regime.

On the South Vietnamese side, President Ngo Dinh Diem signed the Accords of "Eleven Point Program" with the United States on January 2, 1962, and published it on January 4. In implementing the terms of the Accords, the United States offered to South Vietnam routine basic economic assistance. Two of the eleven points concerned the training of village officials and the formation of the mountaineers (Montagnards) in the Central Highlands. This contributed the most to the "elevation" of American advisers in South Vietnams. The January Accords therefore gave Washington some grounds for hope. (See the Appendix, "Summary of the Eleven-Point Program Accords, January 1962.")

In the next six months the United States saw the activation of counter-insurgency activities, starting from the Highlands in Central Vietnam. Moreover, the United States hoped that the Diem administration would implement the desired reforms. It was obvious that neither of these two points satisfied President Diem and his political adviser, Nhu. They had to accept the presence of American advisers who were detached to each of the forty-four province chiefs of South Vietnam. Beginning with the First Republic (the Diem administration) a middle-ranking ARVN officer, from major to lieutenant colonel, was assigned to the post of province chief. The province chief position served both functions as provincial administrator and territorial military commander under direct supervision of the Military Tactical Zone, or Military Region commander. In March of 1962, each province was "reinforced" by an American group called the "Military Advisory Training Assistance" (MATA) group, whose major duty was emphasizing "civic action" in rural areas and training the provincial civil guard (Bảo-an Đoàn) and village militia (Dân-vệ) to become more effective in counter-guerrilla operations.

Each provincial MATA group needed several more American officers and non-commissioned officers (NCOs) to perform these civic and training duties. However, the American provincial advisory team chief's activities were not limited to training and civic actions but also worked in coordination with the Vietnamese province chief in any domain of the province's activities: military organization, supply, planning and operations, administrative and economic complicated and difficult problems. He collaborated closely to help the province-chief accomplish his responsibilities and to improve the province's counter-insurgency conditions. "Any activity must be known to be helped" was the unspoken message between the lines. Vietnamese authorities and American advisers worked in an atmosphere of harmony or reluctance, depending upon the personal relations between them. Normally, in most instances, the relationship was fair. This aspect did not satisfy Ngo Dinh Nhu. He knew that this system of cooperation between American advisers and Vietnamese officials at the provincial level would permit the United States to "penetrate" deeply in South Vietnam and interfere into Vietnamese governmental affairs, politically, economically and militarily. All initiatives in these domains, from the basic infrastructure, would be "known" and "re-examined" by American authorities in the country. South Vietnam, therefore, would gradually lose its command, national pride and sovereignty.

THE "BOUN ENAO PROJECT" AND THE CIDG CONCEPT

The other point of the Accords, Article #8, addressed the mountaineer minorities in Vietnam's Central Highlands, the important area adjoining the Ho Chi Minh Trail. The Montagnard tribes in this region were composed of five main groups of 50,000 to 70,000 each — containing some twenty distinct ethno-linguistic elements. They were the Rhade, Jharai, Bahnar, Sedang, and Bru. At that time, Montagnard tribesmen were trapped between the communists and the government of South Vietnam (GVN). They feared the NVA and VC more than they supported them.

During the summer of 1961, the American ambassador in Vietnam and advisers from various American agencies in Saigon held different solutions for securing the Central Highlands, but the best was a project proposed by a young American agricultural specialist, David A. Norwood, who was familiar with the region. His proposed project would simply give the Montagnards the opportunity to defend themselves by forming them into self-defense forces. By order of the ambassador, the CIA station's chief in Saigon chose Norwood to lead a special combined group of U.S. Army Special Forces officers and NCOs, CIA specialists, and U.S. Army Medical Group specialists, in cooperation with a Vietnamese Survey Office (the GVN's Central Intelligence Services) team, to realize the project.[37]

The project was started in a Rhade tribe called "Boun Enao," in Darlac Province, in October 1961. The tribe's chief and elders requested that the ARVN and Vietnamese Air Force (VNAF) stop attacking Rhade tribes and that medical, educational, and agricultural assistance programs be provided to the tribesmen. These actions were taken in conjunction with the construction of a fence around the village and the military training of a 30-man village-defense force and four medics. The project proceeded at Boun Enao essentially as planned. The villagers constructed fences, shelters, and a dispensary. Most of the needed materials came from the jungle but the Americans were requested to provide any developmental aid during the experiment. The first village-defense group was formed, equipped with rifles and shotguns, and led by US Special Forces NCOs, to protect the village.

Norwood's project was officially dubbed the Boun Enao Project. The Boun Enao complex was the beginning of what proved to be an effective counter-insurgency network in the Central Highlands. In three months, forty other Rhade tribes within a 15-kilometer radius of Boun Enao entered the program on a voluntary basis under essentially the same terms used for Boun Enao and became new village complexes. Any village's volunteer unit, called a strike-force, was used as a reserve force to assist villages under attack. The CIA paid the majority of these strike units monthly. By April 1962, the 40-village complex had been completed. William Coleman, the chief of the Saigon CIA station, officially labeled these village defense forces the Civilian Irregular Defense Group (CIDG) program. Later, the Boun Enao Project was transferred to the U.S. Military Assistance Command, Vietnam (MACV) to handle, after which the project would largely expand.

A few weeks prior to President Ngo Dinh Diem's signing of the January 1961 "Eleven-Point" Accords, Adviser Ngo Dinh Nhu visited the Boun Enao complex. Impressed by the progress of the new village complex, especially by the formation of the village defense force, he authorized an expansion of the Boun Enao's concept to the entire Vietnam Central Highlands, in the Mekong Delta, and in some special coastal areas.

On the American side, in the summer of 1962, an official delegation from the Department of Defense–Defense Intelligence Agency (DOD–DIA) visited the Boun Enao complex to assess the progress and to help the project develop. Close air support was requested for the project. Immediately, a U.S. Air Force Air Commando unit was assigned to the "Boun Enao Project" headquarters. Air support was also ready: an L-19 observer to spot enemy concentration, a C-47 flare gun ship to assist villages attacked at night, and two helicopters to facilitate strike-force mobility. The project was then expanded to 200 villages with a total population of 60,000, village defenders of 10,600, and strike-force of 1,500. Each village participating in the programs was given a two-way voice attack alert radio by the U.S. Overseas Mission (USOM); the village radio operators were trained by U.S. Special Forces. The expansion was completed by October 1962.[38]

The project appeared to be a success. However, only 150,000 out of the 700,000 in the Central Highlands sought refuge in government-controlled areas. During 1962, the communists maintained strong positions in the mountainous border areas between Central Vietnam and Laos, and between Central Vietnam and Cambodia, to protect and develop their sanctuaries along the Ho Chi Minh Trail. They had close support from the mountaineer tribes still outside of government control. In addition to this suspect situation, from May 1961 to June 1962, at least three NVA regiments were identified infiltrating the Highlands and the mountainous region between Quang-Ngai and Binh-Dinh. These regiments were named Mountain Regiments and were made up of Jarai, Rhade, and Hre mountaineers who had gone north in 1954. One of these was the 120th Regiment commanded by Colonel Y-Bloc, a Hre mountaineer. This regiment was operating in conjunction with the 126th Mountain Regiment in An-Lao Mountains, west of Quang-Ngai Province, while the famous 803rd Mountain Regiment was in Southern Mountain Plateau of the Central Highlands. This regiment's activities gravely affected the development of the Boun Enao Project by conducting company-size attacks on new projected villages, platoon-size ambushes on villages' strike-force units, and propaganda activities among the mountaineers. A significant number of village defenders deserted to this Mountain Regiment.

For these reasons, by August 1962, Adviser Ngo Dinh Nhu ordered a 30-day halt to the arming of Montagnards. He felt that the Montagnards were not to be trusted and suggested the U.S. MACV to abandon the Boun Enao Project in the Central Highlands. The defenders of the projected-villages were required to return their weapons to the government and strike-force personnel would be drafted in the ARVN. The disagreement between American authorities in Saigon and Ngo Dinh Nhu intensified. The Boun Enao Project failed and died two months later. After one year in operation, the Boun Enao Project had absorbed a great number of American military and civilian personnel into South Vietnam: Special Forces, Air force, CIA, USOM, and other agencies. The project failed, but its spirit — the CIDG program's concept — became the American ideal counter-insurgency practice in South Vietnam for a decade later in parallel with other tactics.

U.S. military authorities in Saigon admitted that the CIDG programs were efficacious to protect and control the population in remote areas in different parts of South Vietnam. They encouraged the ARVN to absorb the CIDG program.

The concept of CIDG (Civilian Irregular Defense Group), also called the Mike Forces program, was the standard formation of a unit of natives, initiated by the U.S. Army 1st Special Forces Group — the famed Green Berets. This supposed local irregular unit was called an "A-Detachment" and commanded by an American leadership group of 12 Special Forces troops, or an A-Team. This system of formation was similar to the formation of a company of indigenous commandos of the French Army's "Groupement de Commandos Mixtes Aeroportes" (GCMA), or Composite Airborne Commandos Group in the First Vietnam War. American authorities imagined that men of Mike Forces units could win the "minds and hearts" of the Vietnamese in the countryside. By such an imagination, many A-Detachments would be formed and stationed wherever around the country and working out of their own fixed bases. An A-Detachment (company-sized unit) comprised a number of local people that varied from 60 men to 230 men. Several A-Detachments formed a B-Detachment (battalion-sized unit) and several B-Detachments formed a C-Detachment (regiment-sized unit).

Before August 1962, in performing the counter-insurgency missions given by presidential directive in 1961, the U.S. 1st Special Forces Group formed, in each Military Region of South Vietnam, a number of A-Detachments, B-Detachments, and C-Detachments. All of these Mike Forces units were funded and supervised by the U.S.–CIA in Saigon. After the U.S. Military Assistance Command, Vietnam (MACV) was created, the new commander, General Paul Harkins, and the new chief of the U.S. CIA in Saigon, John Russell, realized that CIDG programs were too complicated for civilian control. They agreed to transfer the command and support of these Mike Forces units to the U.S. MACV. By November 1962, one C-Detachment, three B-Detachments, and 26 A-Detachments in various parts of South Vietnam completed the takeover of the chain of command determined. All others were to be completed by July 1, 1963.

General Paul Harkins suggested the ARVN create its own Special Forces and organize its own mountainous, coastal, and rural CIDG units. U.S. MACV would support their training, equipping and funding. A plan was devised and approved by the Vietnamese government. The U.S. 1st Special Forces would add one more mission: training first Vietnamese Special Force soldiers at the Commando Training Center at Nha-Trang. Those trainees would form the core of the ARVN Special Forces units. The CIDG program with the A-Team formation concept subsequently became the counter-insurgency practice throughout South Vietnam.

With the same notion of an unconventional warfare, American authorities in Saigon suggested President Diem organize Ranger units for the ARVN. The 77th Mobile Training Team of the U.S. 7th Special Forces Group was sent to Nha-trang to train the first Vietnamese Ranger groups. The U.S. 1st Special Forces Group organized them into companies for counter-insurgency and counter-guerrilla warfare, and later took over the complete training of all Vietnamese Ranger units in Duc My, Nha-Trang. Nha-Trang, in the early 1960s, became the base for both American and Vietnamese Special Forces training centers. It was also the base for U.S. Air Force and U.S. Navy detachments to train Vietnamese Air Force (VNAF) and Vietnamese Navy (VNN) officers, NCOs, and specialists to develop the Republic of Vietnam Armed Forces (RVNAF).

In addition to these training efforts, a system of American Advisory Teams was developed to attach to RVNAF units. The system really needed a great number of American military and civilian personnel for South Vietnam. They were committed piecemeal along with any old and new military, administrative and economic units or organizations of the Republic of Vietnam (RVN) as advisers or counterparts to their chieftains, if not officially considered as "supervisors" of almost all activities of these units or organizations. By late 1962, President Kennedy had 15,000 military "advisers" in South Vietnam and an estimated 3,000 civilian personnel, in all agencies in Saigon and around the country, with official and unofficial missions. The free "comings and goings" to and from various Vietnamese airports and seaports were unlimited for the Americans after that.

The RVNAF was strengthened considerably by the presence of American advisers and Green Beret forces in the country. But, it was generating increasing difficulties for their war against the communists. Also, this created tremendous unrest in the society. For example, Professor Vu Quoc Thuc, Dean of Saigon Law School pointed out how this would affect the economy: "The American-Vietnamese eleven-point program of January 4, 1962, will absorb some unemployed labor, and so will the newly planned industrial projects. The presence also, of close to 15,000 American troops and of additional thousands of American civilian person-nel, with their extensive requirements for house servants and clerical labor, is likely to have cushioning effect on inflationary pressures as long as the United States continues to funnel sufficient amounts of consumer goods into the economy. In other words, South Vietnam is rapidly returning to an artificial war economy."[39] Many Vietnamese in the capital and cities were very quickly aware of the value of the "U.S. green dollars." The RVN had to accept de facto devaluation of the Vietnamese piaster (national currency) from the 35-to-1 official exchange rates to about 65-to-1, and the population accepted the exchange rate of 100-to-1 on the black market. In any city where American troops were present, people began to deal for U.S. "green dollars" while in the countryside peasants were caught between the RVN forces and the communists.

Under the new living conditions, the society's traditions began to fall. New social classes surfaced, ranking in order from the highest: the prostitutes, the bonzes — or Buddhist priests, the fathers or Catholic priests, and the generals. In Vietnamese original terms, which were known everywhere in the country, these "new social orders" were "Nhất Đỉ, Nhì Sư, Tam Cha, Tứ Tướng." The number of prostitutes increased considerably with the increased num-ber of GIs in South Vietnam. This was ironic, bizarre, and nauseous, but it was also true. This social phenomenon of South Vietnam might go unmentioned in Western historical books or newspaper articles. However, it was one of the main causes leading to the political deteri-oration of the South from the spring of 1963, the Buddhist evolutional crisis in summer, and the Americans' abolition of the First Republic of Vietnam in the fall of the same year. After all, the Eleven-Point Program had latent effects.

Some historians commented that until the spring of 1963, the United States did not have a grand design in South Vietnam beyond the mechanics of developing the counter-insurgency theory: the use of U.S. Special Forces to establish a series of CIDG units in remote areas, the deployment of the "Eagle Fighter" helicopter units to reinforce the mobility of the ARVN, or the introduction of a hierarchical "Advisory Teams" system into then RVNAF. Other com-mentators viewed the Eleven-Point Program as the greatest design of the Kennedy adminis-tration in South Vietnam. Indeed, it was a totally progressive plan concerning several important standpoints that concentrated into a single purpose — to fight an unconventional war, or a counter-insurgency war. In other words, the program encompassed all of President Kennedy's planned counter-insurgency measures, from military tactics to separate the VC from the peas-ants and eliminate them, to the reconstruction of the economic, industrial, and agricultural structure for South Vietnam. Further, the program would improve the living conditions of the people, especially in the countryside, with the hope of realizing total social reformation in South Vietnam. It was a perfect program with the essential strategy "to win the hearts and minds" of the Vietnamese. Roger Hilsman, U.S. assistant secretary of state for Southeast Asia, once blamed General Paul Harkins and the West-Pointers, who fought in South Vietnam but disregarded this strategy. They considered there could only be a military solution and that "winning hearts and minds" was not their job. He said: "I think the strategy is greater than that. President Kennedy sent me out specifically to try to explain the theory behind this pol-icy to [commander in chief] Paul Harkins. I don't think he misunderstood the policy. I came to the conclusion years later that he and people under him thought that it was somebody else's business."[40]

Theoretically, this strategy was excellent. However, Hilsman did not know that the Viet-namese, for the thousand years of their history, would not permit any armed strangers who came to their country to win their hearts and minds, except their own leaders. This explains why the distinct strategy of the Kennedy Administration could not easily be applied in South Vietnam to win the war. Instead of carrying weapons to perform civic action missions to win the hearts and minds of the Vietnamese, the Americans needed to give their weapons to the Vietnamese leaders and let them do their job with their compatriots so that the war might be won. Moreover, Kennedy's entourage was supposed not to consider too much the problem "win with Diem, swim with Diem, or sink with Diem." They should have considered, however, that even if only 10 percent of the South Vietnamese supported Diem's regime, 20 percent hated him and his family, 20 percent liked the communists, and 50 percent feared them, the war could also be won with Diem without the direct U.S. military personnel involvement in the country.

In addition to the Geneva Accords of neutralization in Laos, the presence of American armed servicemen in South Vietnam destabilized the situation in Saigon. The war increased its intensity in the countryside as an uncontrolled number of NVA troops infiltrated through the Ho Chi Minh Trail from the beginning of 1963.

Another type of unconventional warfare was also waged in Vietnam by the Kennedy administration planners. They expanded Special Forces secret missions to North Vietnam and to Laos with small action groups of eight to fifteen men each. Members of each group were South Vietnamese Special Forces Airborne Commandos who were all northern-born and immigrated to South Vietnam after the Geneva Accords, in 1954–1955. They belonged to the 1st Observation Group-Special Forces (Liên-đoàn Quan-sát, lực-lượng Đặc-biệt) of the ARVN but were handled and trained by the CIA sponsored American Saigon Military Mission (SMM), which was formed in the mid–1950s by Colonel Edward Lansdale, the first American military adviser to President Ngo Dinh Diem. These small observation groups parachuted into areas near the Laotian and North Vietnamese border to survey the Ho Chi Minh Trail, or into North Vietnam's soil to take the first step toward psychological warfare operations and sabotages against NVA supply systems such as railroads, bridges, and harbors.

This type of unconventional secret mission was the "deformation" of Kennedy's counter-insurgency theory. The CIA–controlled 1st Observation Group of the ARVN of the early 1960's fielded more than 19,000 personnel, included CIA agents, U.S. Green Berets and South Vietnamese Special Forces Airborne Commandos (Biệt-kích Dù). It specifically targeted North Vietnam, as well as border control over the Vietnamese, Laotian and Cambodian borders.[41]

From 1962, this type of unconventional warfare, mastered by Washington's planners such as Defense Secretary McNamara and the chairman of the Joint Chiefs of Staff, General Maxwell Taylor, led to the execution of secret missions inside enemy territory by the U.S. Green Berets and the South Vietnamese Special Forces. Combined projects between U.S. Green Berets and the ARVN Special Forces included Project Delta, Project Omega, Project Sigma, and Project Gamma. Each had its special structure, purpose, and modus operandi for conducting clandestine operations behind enemy lines. The most important and top secret organization was the Military Assistance Command Vietnam's Studies and Observations Group (MACV-SOG). MACV-SOG incorporated U.S. Army Special Forces, U.S. Marine Corps Force Recon Marines, U.S. Navy Sea-Air-Land commandoes (SEALs), and U.S. Air Force Special Operations. This secret organization, an organ of MACV, was directed by the U.S. secretary of defense and the chairman of the Joint Chiefs of Staff through an organization called the Office of the Special Assistant for Counter-insurgency and Special Activities. The Pentagon delegated day-to-day direction to the MACV-SOG commander who commanded and controlled all American and Vietnamese special missions deep into North Vietnam, Laos and Cambodia. All action groups or teams' members were normally U.S. volunteer Green Berets, Marines, and South Vietnamese Special Forces Airborne Commandos. In its early missions, MACV-

SOG planned operations in a large measure based on the performance of the two previous organizations, the CIA–controlled First Observation Group and the Saigon Military Mission, characterized by airborne operations: dropping small commando teams into Laos for intelligence collection along the Ho Chi Minh Trail or into North Vietnam for propaganda and modest physical destruction of specific targets.[42]

Later, at McNamara's recommendation, the United States president ordered the MACV-SOG to carry out Operations Plan 34A (OPLAN-34A), which the Pentagon called "an elaborate program of covert military operations against the state of North Vietnam." It was hoped that progressively escalating pressure from clandestine attacks "might eventually force Hanoi to order the Viet-cong guerrillas in South Vietnam and the Pathet-Lao in Laos to halt their insurrections," related U.S. Army Colonel William Wilson.[43] The secret operations ranged from flights over North Vietnam by U-2 spy planes, to airborne operations code-named Midriff, and maritime operations code-named Plowman. These operations were given the innocuous name "Operation Footboy." Footboy air operations consisted of: dropping commando teams to recover downed American pilots in Laos; commando raids to rescue American POWs in North Vietnam or to kidnap North Vietnamese citizens for intelligence purposes; dropping supplies to in-place teams; and parachuting in special teams for short term reconnaissance and for psychological warfare, to create the illusion that numerous teams of agents were operating freely throughout North Vietnam. Footboy maritime operations consisted of commando raids from the sea to blow up rail and highway bridges and to bombard North Vietnamese installations, naval assets, coastal air defense and radar, beached civilian and military vessels, and the like by patrol torpedo fast boats (PTFs). Meanwhile, the more unusual long-term Footboy operations that required the combined assets of Midriff and Plowman was the "Sacred Sword Patriot's League" (SSPL; in Vietnamese terms it was "Đoàn Gươm Thiêng Ái-Quốc"). SSPL operations were covertly carried out by SOG-PTF boats manned by South Vietnamese maritime commandoes of the Vietnamese Coastal Security Service, which was a division of the RVNAF's Strategic Technical Directorate (Nha Kỹ-Thuật Quân-lực Việt-nam Cộng-hoà), flying the flag "Gươm Thiêng Ái-Quốc," enthusiastically plied the northern waters of the DMZ from the 17th parallel to the 20th parallel as an anti-communist internal movement within North Vietnam with activities of sabotage and terror warfare against the communists. On the other hand, SSPL also conducted psychological warfare and operated daily both "black" and "white" radio broadcastings over North Vietnam. "Thirty-minute 'black' radio programs purported to voice the views of dissident elements in North Vietnam, while 'white' radio broadcast the 'Voice of Freedom' daily."[44] The SSPL radio broadcasting program (Chương-trình Phát-thanh Gươm Thiêng Ái-Quốc) was the most efficacious of all MACV-SOG secret operations in Vietnam. The program lasted until the last day of the Republic of Vietnam, on April 30, 1975.

Operation-Footboy of MACV-SOG, from its inception in the early 1960s, was under the jurisdiction of the Strategic Technical Directorate (Nha Kỹ-Thuật), the Psychological Warfare Division (Cục Chiến-tranh Tâm-lý), the General Political Warfare Department (Tổng-cuc Chiến-tranh Chính-trị) of the RVNAF, and other secret organizations of the government of South Vietnam. "Footboy, like so many other so-called South Vietnamese programs, was [in fact] run by the United States," says Charles F. Reske, a former officer of the top secret U.S. Navy Security Group.[45]

Politico-military commentator A.K. Dawson, in his magazine article, "The Fatally Flawed OPLAN-34A Commando Raids on North Vietnam Were a Disaster with Lasting Consequences" (which reviewed the book *Secret Army, Secret War* by former DIA officer Sedgwick Tourison, Jr.) remarked: "OPLAN-34A, the flawed and failed operation designed to 'send a message to Hanoi,' in the words of former Secretary of Defense Robert McNamara, left a disastrous swath of human destruction and suffering in its wake."[46] In fact, most of the U.S. Green Berets and ARVN's Special Forces Airborne Commandos were captured or killed during their secret missions in Laos, frequently in North Vietnam. They are all heroes, although the U.S. government for decades refused to recognize their bravery and their heroic sacrifice or disappearance in this bizarre "secret war" in Indochina. The Pentagon established an official "Theater Service Calendar" following the Gulf of Tonkin Resolution of August 7, 1964. Many U.S. Green Berets who served in clandestine operations in Indochina and survived before this, that is, during the Kennedy presidential term, were denied all medals, honors, recognition, and benefits accorded to Vietnam War veterans. In a pragmatic sense, they are the United States' forgotten soldiers of the Vietnam campaign. This is also the case of thousands more U.S. military personnel of different secret services in Vietnam. A former agent of the Army Security Agency, who had served in Vietnam from December 1961 to December 1962, states: "If you served in Vietnam before August of '64, you're not considered to be a real Vietnam vet. That is, unless you [got] killed."[47] It is ironic, but it is also the fatality of the war. United States Green Berets are believed to have the most American KIA/MIAs in Indochina during the Second Vietnam War. "No MACV-SOG POWs were released. MACV-SOG also suffered casualties that exceeded 100 percent, every MACV-SOG recon-man was wounded at least once, and about half were killed," relates Rob Krott, another politico-military commentator, in his magazine article, "MACV-SOG Was Once So Secret That the U.S. Government Denied Its Existence."[48]

Besides, the recruitment of South Vietnamese Special Forces Airborne Commandos by the U.S. CIA in Saigon, or by MACV-SOG, to carry out secret missions behind enemy lines during the Vietnam War, also created problems. As volunteer commandoes who performed secret operations planned by these two U.S. organizations, they parachuted deep into North Vietnam. They were captured or killed, more because of their American planners' ignorance of village defense systems of North Vietnam under the communist regime and by inadequate planning than by the leaks that were usually blamed on South Vietnam's government. Although hundreds of Vietnamese airborne commandoes were known to be held as POWs, they were declared dead. After more than 20 years in communist prisons, all of them were released and most of them made their way to the United States.[49]

When the United States was using this tactic of war in Indochina, the mistaken notion of using U.S. Green Berets was revealed by Graham Martin, a confidant of President Kennedy. Graham Martin, who was then State Department liaison official with the Pentagon on updating military strategy, recalled later advising President Kennedy that the Green Berets were a mistake, because they had been used as guerrillas but not anti-guerrillas. The Americans really were not capable of understanding and coping with that kind of war.

Still, Graham Martin was not the only confidant of President Kennedy. Other Kennedy advisers convinced the president that the U.S. military strategy in Indochina was right but that Ngo Dinh Diem was ill-suited for South Vietnam. They argued that Diem and his younger brother, Nhu, could not fight the communists with their own strategic hamlets because the South Vietnamese people did not support them. Two of those advisers were General Maxwell Taylor and assistant secretary of state Roger Hilsman. However, some supported Diem and his anti-communist strategy. One of these voices belonged to General Paul Harkins, the first Commander of U.S. MACV (COMUSMACV). He recognized that Diem's strategic hamlets constituted proof that his administration had grass roots support and that the war in Vietnam could be won within one year after the (Vietnamese) army attained a fully offensive footing. In addition, U.S. ambassador to Saigon, Frederick E. Nolting, after visiting three-

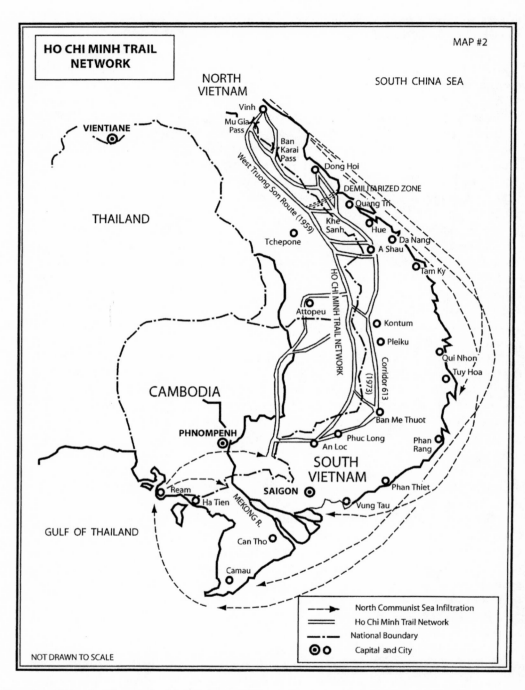

fourths of South Vietnam's 44 provinces, became convinced that President Diem was most respected as a leader.

Wavering between the two contrary opinions, in early 1963 President Kennedy sent a two-man mission to South Vietnam consisting of General Victor Krulak of the Marine Corps and State Department official Joseph A. Mendenhall. After returning from that mission, these two who held opposite opinions briefed the president and the U.S. National Security Council. General Krulak said that everything in Vietnam was going fine, Diem's morale was high; the United States needed to support him to the end and he would win the war. Meanwhile, Mendenhall reported that Diem was extremely unpopular, his regime was very precarious; the Buddhists disliked him; and the liberal democrats disliked him. The most important "observation" was that "Diem does not provide any kind of possible basis for a successful American policy."[50] This statement would mean that "Vietnam is property of the United States but the local guardian could not perform his ordained job, we might kick him out or eliminate him."

The reports of this two-man mission came out just days after an important military event happened in South Vietnam. On January 2, 1963, at Ap-Bac, a small village of My-Tho Province in the Mekong Delta, the biggest battle since the Geneva Accords in 1954 was fought between an ARVN combined element of an infantry battalion plus an armored company and a communist battalion. The fight was fierce. The losses by both sides were high. A paratroop (airborne) battalion and other infantry units reinforced these two Vietnamese units on the battlefield. American advisers, amphibious carriers, and helicopters supported all. The remainder of the communist unit, composed of about 200 men, shot down five American helicopters, killed three Americans, and broke through the ARVN units' encirclement. The problem became serious. American authorities in Saigon were quick to blame the setback of the ARVN units. The U.S. embassy in Saigon and MACV recommended the US military exercise control over Vietnamese forces in any future joint-operations. President Diem promised, "henceforth the Vietnamese commanders would heed the counsels of their American advisers."[51] In reality, Vietnamese commanders of all levels received orders not to inform their American advisers before conducting future operations in any terrain. Some operations failed because of the lack of helicopter support. American advisers, who handled tactical control over the use of U.S. helicopter units, decided whether American craft were "available" or "unavailable" to support any ARVN unit's operations. Orders went out to the Americans in the field to apply local pressure in order to implement the assigned programs, without engaging in debates about the fundamentals. Within the American Advisory Corps in Vietnam, this resistance became known as "helicopter diplomacy."

In the administrative field, in May 1963, American authorities suggested President Diem allow the rural population to elect its own representative to the "Communal Council" and the "Village Administrative Council" in each village. This new administrative reform, according to U.S. civilian authorities, was the only way to gain democracy for the people in the countryside and to give them the opportunity to share the responsibility with the government. The Saigon regime was obliged to yield to the American suggestion but find its own way to keep tight control over all village elected councils and provincial elected councils around the country. The last but important disagreement was American insistence that the Diem administration accept modest free speech in South Vietnam. An immediate furor broke forth in the Vietnamese press with unpredictable violence. The English-language newspaper, *Time of Vietnam,* accused U.S. secretary of state Dean Rusk of "indirectly aiding the Viet-Cong Communist guerrillas." The issue was quietly laid unresponsive again. Nevertheless, the fate of president Ngo Dinh Diem and his regime was sealed.

6

The Death of a President and a Democracy

In the morning hours of November 2, 1963, South Vietnamese President Ngo Dinh Diem and his brother Ngo Dinh Nhu were assassinated as part of a coup d'état orchestrated the previous day by a number of ARVN generals. Three weeks later, on November 23, U.S. United States president John F. Kennedy was assassinated in Dallas. Returning home from the funeral of President Kennedy, his successor, President Lyndon B. Johnson, arrived at the White House with vice-president Hubert Humphrey. He pointed at the picture of ex-president Ngo Dinh Diem, which was hanging on the wall of the house, and remarked to Humphrey: "We have had a hand that killed Diem. And now 'this hand' is showing up here."[1] President Johnson's statement is considered to be a confirmation of U.S. involvement in the November coup and assassination of President Diem and his brother, but the question remains as to who was responsible for the unjust deaths of the Ngo brothers. Which American hands, among Kennedy's aides, assistants, and advisers, were involved?

In January of 1969, upon taking up residence in the Oval Office, President Richard Nixon immediately ordered the director of the Federal Bureau of Investigation (FBI), Howard Hunt, to carry on an investigation of the death of President Diem in order to find out who in the Kennedy administration was involved. Nixon sought the orders from Washington that authorized the coup's joint-conspirators in Saigon to kill Ngo Dinh Diem. No trace of such orders were ever found.[2]

THE BUDDHIST CRISIS

Relations between the Kennedy administration and Diem's regime deteriorated after the Saigon press attacked U.S. secretary of state Dean Rusk and criticized U.S. policy in Vietnam. The Buddhist riots over alleged religious persecution and the events that followed during the summer of 1963 gave the United States the "necessary and sufficient" motives to eliminate Diem and Nhu. Nhu, especially, was accused of running the secret police force and directing the ARVN to kill Buddhist demonstrators and arrest Buddhist monks, nuns, and students, after the first spark of Buddhist opposition set up in Hue, the old capital of Vietnam.

In early May of 1963, government officials in Hue reportedly allowed Catholic churches to fly religious flags in celebration of the birthday of Archbishop Ngo Dinh Thuc, older brother of President Ngo Dinh Diem. However, on May 8, the government banned the traditional Buddhist flags at Tu-Dam pagoda marking the birth of the Buddha. The local Buddhist leaders complained the act was discriminatory. When city officials refused to remove the ban, thousands of Buddhists took to the streets in protest. Military units were used to disperse the demonstration and nine persons were killed. Riots then spread from Hue to Saigon. The crisis worsened after a 66-year-old Buddhist monk, Thich Quang Duc, set himself on fire in a busy Saigon street. Buddhist revolts were more intense in Saigon and Hue. On August 21, the government ordered a Special Force to stage raids against a number of Buddhist temples. Several hundred Buddhists, monks, nuns, and students were arrested. Meanwhile, Buddhist leaders took refuge in the U.S. embassy in Saigon and the U.S. consulate in Hue. Six more monks would sacrifice themselves before November.[3] These events were summarized in the words of assistant secretary of state Roger Hilsman: "Here you had a country's ninety-five percent Buddhist, led by French-speaking Vietnamese who were beating up pagodas, killing nuns, and killing priests. I would say certainly by the beginning of the Buddhist crisis he [Kennedy] was already discouraged; by the middle of it, I think he was totally discouraged."[4]

Through Hilsman's statement everyone knew that Diem's regime would not last long. The primary reason was that President Kennedy finally inclined toward the camp that continuously opposed Diem and Nhu. This camp was composed of politicians who had a biased knowledge of the Vietnamese society, culture, and history. Thus, their advice to the president was superficial and incorrect. For two millennia, Confucianism, Taoism, and Buddhism were the three great philosophical systems underpinning Vietnamese culture and social life. In practicing these philosophies, the Vietnamese commonly used such material objects as altars, likenesses, figures, lamps and incense in their ceremonies. Most would pray while holding burning incense and kneeling down before the altar adorned of figures or statuettes, in the same way a Buddhist did before an alter in a pagoda. Therefore, looking from the outside, a foreign observer might mistakenly assume that ninety-five percent of Vietnamese are Buddhists. A truly conscientious intellectual would perceive more clearly, especially when deciding the fate of a people.

A careful observation of Vietnamese society would reveal that on the altars of the majority of Vietnamese families were pictures, figures or nominated tablets of their ancestors and parents, figures of upright and loyal generals — Chinese or Vietnamese — and great sages from ancient times. This type of ordained altar proved that the Vietnamese had adapted the "cult of ancestors" and the cult of "heroes and sages," a social and ethical tradition rooted in Confucianism rather than Buddhism. A minority of Vietnamese families displayed Buddhas statuettes and other likenesses, or even figures of various fairies — symbols of the Taoist cult — on their altars, which were separated from their ancestors' altars.

Other studies also demonstrated that the majority of the Vietnamese were not Buddhists, but adopters of Confucianism. An observation of Vietnamese daily social life revealed that almost all Vietnamese practiced Confucian teachings, including the "three relations," or "Tam cương" in Vietnamese (relation between king and subject, father and son, and husband and wife); the "five virtues," or "Ngũ thường" (benevolence, righteousness, civility, knowledge, and loyalty) applicable for men; the "three followings," or "Tam tùng" (follow father, husband, and son's advice) and the "four virtues," or "Tứ đức" (proper employment, proper demeanor, proper speech, and proper behavior) applicable for women. Only a minority of Vietnamese practiced the Buddha's teachings such as Buddhist prayers, or "Kinh Phật" and Buddhist laws, or "Phật-pháp," which were high, deep, and transcendent, but were too difficult for the masses. Confucian teachings were taught in every national and private school for thousands of years under every regime including the Chinese domination, the Vietnamese consecutive monarchies, the French colonial rule, and the democracy of South Vietnam (except the communist regime of North Vietnam). Buddhist teachings, on the other hand were taught only in Buddhist pagodas or in few Buddhist institutes. Taoist teachings also played an important role in Vietnamese culture, helping the masses harmonize humans and nature, reveries and realities, metaphysics and Buddhism. Overall, in North Vietnam before 1955, and in South Vietnam before 1963, an estimated 95 percent of the Vietnamese population followed Confucianism. This percentage included about 25 percent of Buddhists who were also Confucian pragmatists, and five to six percent of Catholics and Protestants. The percentage of Taoists was difficult to estimate because the Taoists mingled within Confucians and Buddhists. The rest of the population, about four to five percent, was either atheist or communist.

In Vietnamese history during the Ly dynasty, there was a period during which Buddhism seemed to be the national religion. The first emperor of the Ly, Ly Cong Uan, had been the student of a Buddhist monk, before dethroning the last king of the Le (the First Le, or Tien-Le). He had intended to establish Buddhism as the primary faith for his subjects by building up many Buddhist temples and pagodas around the country and creating several institutes to teach Buddhist laws and prayers. But after a short period of time, Buddhism was overcome again by Confucianism for almost the next nine hundred years. The conclusion could be drawn that Vietnam was different from Tibet: 95 percent of Vietnam's population adopted Confucianism but not Buddhism. The "coming" of the American troops to South Vietnam in 1962–1963 profoundly changed the social life and social orders of South Vietnam. For hundreds of years the Vietnamese social order consisted of, from upper to lower class, scholars, farmers, craftsmen, merchants, and soldiers. Vietnamese scholars, despite their French education under French colonial rule, mostly kept the performance of Confucian traditions in their familial and social relations. From the beginning of the 1960s, when the United States started pouring "green dollars" into South Vietnam, Vietnamese intellectuals witnessed the decadent changes in their society. To maintain their composure and dignity, and to evade political and economical pressures, some withdrew into "ivory shells." Others transposed their social position to the new classes.

Some Vietnamese historians recognized that the Kennedy administration had the perfect vision regarding the leadership of the Vietnamese Buddhist monks of the time. They were seen as capable of leading the people in a political struggle against Diêm and his brothers. The populace, especially the Buddhists, believed that Diem's regime was anti–Buddhism. A scrutiny of the religious and spiritual practices of Vietnamese society demonstrates that those Kennedy advisers that belonged to the anti–Diem camp were badly mistaken in suggesting their young and brilliant president allow the 1963 coup against South Vietnam President Ngo Dinh Diem. Worse yet was allowing their local henchmen to assassinate Diem and his brother Nhu, and later execute his youngest brother, Ngo Dinh Can.

The three days in Hue on the Birthday of the Buddha (May 8–10, 1963) represented the bloodstained start of the 1963 Buddhist crisis. The self-sacrifice of Reverend Thich Quang Duc on June 11, 1963, in the heart of Saigon was the apex of the Buddhist "suicide policy" designed by the exalted Vietnamese Buddhist leadership. Ngo Dinh Diem and his brothers were caught in the Buddhist trap. Madame Ngo Dinh Nhu, President Diem's sister-in-law, publicly accused American authorities of manipulating the Buddhists into this scheme. U.S. ambassador to Saigon Frederic E. Nolting supported President Dien's opinion that the "Buddhist crisis" was a political rather than religious outbreak. The ambassador was abruptly relieved from his post by President Kennedy. Powerful people in the U.S. State Department, like Averell Harriman and Roger Hilsman, and others in the White House, wanted Nolting out of Vietnam for an easier handling of their plot against President Ngo Dinh Diem and his brother Ngo Dinh Nhu.

With the departure of Frederic E. Nolting, South Vietnam's president Ngo Dinh Diem lost his last lifeboat to save his regime and himself when he was in the middle of the politically dangerous waves that would engulf him. Indeed, Henry Cabot Lodge, the new U.S. ambassador to Saigon, just two days coming to his post — on August 24, 1963 — sent an urgent cable to his established chain of command in U.S. State Department, Roger Hilsman, reporting that the U.S. embassy in Saigon had been approached by several of RVNAF generals and that Lodge believed that the generals might take matters into "their own hands" and pull a coup against President Diem.

PLOTTING WITH THE GENERALS

Many sources recently have revisited the 1963 coup d'état in South Vietnam. Retired U.S. Army colonel William Wilson wrote in *Vietnam Magazine* of April 1997 that: "The United States gave its support to a cabal of army generals bent on removing the controversial Diem, whose rise to power Kennedy had backed and who had been the anchor of American policy in Vietnam for nine years. For weeks, with the president informed every step of the way, the American mission in Saigon maintained secret contacts with the plotting generals through one of the Central Intelligence Agency's most experienced and versatile operatives, Lt. Col. Lucien "Lulu" Conein."[5]

Lieutenant Colonel Lucien Conein was born in Paris, enlisted in the French Army, and deserted when France surrendered to Germany in 1940. The United States' OSS recruited him for its secret operations in France during World War II. In 1945, Conein was one of the OSS Deer Team officers under the command of Major Archimedes Patti, who had worked with Ho Chi Minh. Conein himself entered Hanoi in 1945 with the OSS team, and returned in 1954 on a mission to sabotage the communist transportation system. Reassigned to Vietnam in 1962, Conein played a shadowy role as adviser to the Saigon Ministry of the Interior, which commanded all South Vietnamese police and secret police forces. When Cabot Lodge came to Saigon, Conein was immediately chosen for the "American mission" to set up contacts with South Vietnamese generals for the coming coup d'état. Through Lucien Conein, Lodge's American mission maintained secret and close contacts with General Duong van Minh and General Tran van Don for almost three months before the coup. General Duong van Minh, alias "Big Minh," was the commanding general of the ARVN's Operations Command Headquarters, and General Tran van Don was the ARVN's chief of staff. Lodge stressed that Conein had been a friend of General Don, whom Conein held in high esteem, but General "Big Minh" was chosen to be the leader of the plot.

Although details of these contacts were not released, there was enough proof to substantiate that Lodge mastered-minded the coup against President Diem. A sensitive cablegram dated October 5, 1963, from Lodge to the State Department described a meeting with Lt. Colonel Conein and General Big Minh, in which Minh expressed that "he did not expect any American support, but he needed assurances that the United States would not attempt to thwart the plan, and that it would continue to provide military and economic aid."[6] At first, the American National Security Council was reluctant to lend their support, fearing the coup was unlikely to succeed. Indeed, in 1960, a coup d'état against Diem was conducted by the ARVN's Airborne Brigade, but it lasted only two days. Diem's regime was saved by some generals such as Nguyen Khanh, Tran Thien Khiem, Ton That Dinh, and Colonel Lam Quang Tho. On August 26, while in Saigon, Ambassador Lodge presented his credentials to President Diem and demanded Nhu's removal as senior political adviser. In Washington, the National Security Council convened at the White House and President Kennedy expressed his second thoughts after the green-light cable of October 24 had been sent to Lodge. There was a consensus between the president and members of the National Security Council that the situation in Saigon was changing too fast; Washington needed more accurate information about which generals were involved, precisely what they planned, and the possibilities of President Diem conforming. Ambassador Lodge was to be asked for more details on these problems.

On August 29, 1963, Henry Cabot Lodge advanced another step by sending a cable to Washington demanding decisive measures: "We are launched on a course from which there is no respectable turning back: the overthrow of the Diem government. There is no turning back because U.S. prestige is already publicly committed to this end in large measure, and will become more so as the facts leak out. In a more fundamental sense, there is no turning back because there is no possibility, in my view, that the war can be won under the Diem administration."[7]

In Washington the National Security Council immediately convened, and after a long day of debate, in the end decided to give Ambassador Lodge complete discretion to suspend U.S. aid to Diem. This gave him a mandate to determine American policy in South Vietnam. The same day, President Kennedy cabled Lodge as follows:

> I have approved all the messages you are receiving from others today, and I emphasize that everything in these messages has my full support. We will do all we can do to help you conclude this operation successfully. Until the very moment of the go signal for the operation by the generals, I must reserve a contingent to change course and reverse previous instructions. While fully aware of your assessment of the consequences of such a reversal, I know from experience that failure was more destructive than an appearance of indecision. I would, of course accept full responsibility for any such change as I must bear the full responsibility for this operation and its consequences.[8]

With the administration endorsing the coup and the president himself accepting any consequences, Lodge had absolute confidence to proceed with the American mission, involving Conein and the Vietnamese generals in the coup against Diem. But in the course of the proceedings, Lodge played games with the generals, with Diem, and even with the commander of U.S. MACV, General Paul Harkins, like an artful magician who was "throwing stones to someone's head, but hiding his hands." In particular, he had Lieutenant Colonel Conein secretly discuss the coup with General Big Minh.

On their side, the Vietnamese generals, without the credible endorsement of the U.S. embassy in Saigon, hesitated to go through with the plot. This lasted more than a month until the first "signal" appeared on October 3, 1963, when Washington removed Saigon CIA Station Chief Richardson, who was very close to President Diem and Adviser Nhu. On the same day, General Duong van Minh summoned Conein and informed him that a coup was being planned. It was the first time in which Big Minh outlined various possible courses of action, including plans to assassinate Diem's brothers Ngo Dinh Nhu and Ngo Dinh Can. Lodge reported the content of this meeting to Washington in a cablegram dated the same day. In Washington, CIA Director McCone came to meet President Kennedy and argued that Diem's removal would merely lead to a succession of coups. He argued to the president that the hint of "assassination" proposed by Big Minh in the coming coup would create serious consequences for Washington. Certainly, Ambassador Lodge knew all of this. He knew that Big Minh would kill Diem and his brothers Nhu and Can in the coming coup. On November 2, 1963, the second day of the coup, he delayed offering a plane to Diem and Nhu in order to leave the country, suggesting that he had the same intention as Minh: Kill Diem and Nhu, not out of hatred, but because politically they were afraid of them or, more specifically, they were afraid of their reputation that would motivate other Vietnamese commanders to wreck the coup. Lodge demonstrated more cunning than Minh by letting Minh do it himself, and purposely ignoring McCone's admonition. This was the trickery of a crafty political gambler.

Another important "signal" for the conspiratorial generals occurred on October 17 when the United States informed Saigon that military aid for Ngo Dinh Nhu's Special Forces, which was commanded by a confidant of Nhu, Colonel Le Quang Tung, would only continue if channeled through the ARVN Command. On October 25, General Tran van Don had the confirmation of Lieutenant Colonel Lucien Conein that he had been authorized by Ambassador Lodge to discuss the coup with him. On the next day, October 26, Don met Lodge at the airport; Lodge confirmed that Conein was his representative. Thus, confident that he had direct access to U.S. Ambassador Lodge, General Don planned the plot in details with General Minh and others. On October 28, Don informed Conein that the exact time of the coup would be made known to the U.S. embassy only hours before it happened. All in all, the meeting of October 26, 1963, between General Tran van Don and Ambassador Henry Cabot Lodge was the main catalyst of the November coup d'état in South Vietnam, even if the details of their discussion are not known. Neither of them ever disclosed their secret talks, but rather either conveyed the "truth" in paradoxical terms or lied. Without that meeting, the coup might may not have occurred.

As the countdown to the coup proceeded, these tacit arrangements infuriated General Paul Harkins. He sent an angry cable to the Defense Department suggesting that he trusted neither General Don nor Ambassador Lodge. Indeed, General Don and Lodge both lied, even to General Harkins, because they considered Harkins to be the last American in Saigon who opposed the coup against Diem. The White House was concerned over the rift between these highest American civilian and military authorities in Saigon. But it was too late, and Lodge prevailed over Harkins, despite the suspicions Harkins expressed in his cable about the leadership of the Vietnamese plotting generals, which had made the National Security Council, once again, think over the coup against Diem: "in my contacts here I have seen no one with the strength of character of Diem, at least in fighting communists. After all, rightly or wrongly, we have backed Diem for eight long years. To me it seems incongruous now to get him down, kick him around, and get rid of him.... Leaders of other underdeveloped countries will take dim view of our assistance if they too were led to believe the same fate lies in store for them."[9]

Similarly, in a meeting with the president and members of the National Security Council on the afternoon of October 29, Robert Kennedy had the same reservations. American biographer Richard Reeves, in his book *President Kennedy*, relates: "He stated that he could not see any difference between the situation now and back in July and August, when these same generals had proved incapable of organizing a coup. 'Supporting the coup,' he said, 'meant putting Vietnam, or even all of South-East Asia, in the hands of one man unknown to all of them. This risks so much,' he said. 'If it falls, Diem throws us out.'"[10] In another meeting on the same day, the president himself said, "If we miscalculate, we could lose our entire position in South-East Asia."[11]

In the end, President Kennedy was persuaded to let the coup happen. He was persuaded not only by his anti–Diems' advisers but also by his own pretensions of maintaining the U.S. position in Southeast Asia and especially in South Vietnam, when he knew that Diem was essentially in a struggle with him over which one would run South Vietnam. In addition, by early summer, the CIA had reported unconfirmed information that Diem and Nhu were trying to open secret negotiations with Hanoi about the possibility of a united Vietnam without any foreign advisers. He said in April 1963, "We don't have a prayer of staying in Vietnam. Those people hate us. They are going to throw our ass out of there at almost any point. But I can't give up a piece of territory like that to the communists and then get the American people to reelect me."[12] President Kennedy would also never forget words of Mike Mansfield, the Senate majority leader: "if these remedies do not work, it is difficult to conceive of alternatives, with the possible exception of a truly massive commitment of American military personnel and other resources — in short, going to war fully ourselves against the guerrillas — and the establishment of some form of neocolonial rule in South Vietnam."[13] The United States had troops in South Vietnam and a new type of neocolonial governor in the land — Henry Cabot Lodge — but the situation had not been remediable because the "barriers of U.S. policy in Vietnam, Diem and Nhu," existed. The coup to eliminate these political barriers was inevitable.

THE COUP D'ÉTAT KILLING PRESIDENT NGO DINH DIEM AND THE FIRST REPUBLIC OF VIETNAM

In November of 1963, the coup proceeded as scheduled. Ambassador Lodge himself played a role in the coup. He delayed his departure to Washington scheduled for 31 October. At 10:00 A.M. on November 1, Lodge called on President Diem with General Paul Harkins and U.S. Pacific commander Admiral Harry D. Felt. Later, President Diem's press secretary, Ton That Thien, recalled:

> Lodge kept President Diem busy until past twelve. Each time Admiral Felt goes to leave, Lodge asks another question and we know now from the 'Pentagon Papers' that Lodge knew all along that the coup would be staged and he was simply pinning down President Diem to deny him access to his staff. Downstairs, Mr. Nhu — this was a coincidence, a strange coincidence — was being asked all sorts of questions by [Colonel] Thieu. Afterwards I talked to people who wanted to get in touch with either Nhu or the President to tell him that there was something going on. And they couldn't get to him or any orders from the palace at all until the rebellious troops were on the outskirts of Saigon. You cannot say that this is sheer coincidence."[14]

It was very clear:

> the first stage of the coup — to pin down President Diem and his brother Nhu in order to deploy the coup plotting forces — was well played by the two most important players, ambassador Henry Cabot Lodge and Colonel Nguyen van Thieu. After the coup Colonel Nguyen was promoted to general, and in 1967, became the second president of South Vietnam. But their roles in this stage were dim in comparison with the following coup events which were timely recorded by most historians:

At 1:30 P.M., on Friday, November 1, in Saigon, coup forces surrounded key installations in the capital, such as the Defense Ministry, the headquarters of the Vietnamese Navy (VNN), the headquarters of the National Police, Tan Son Nhut Airport, and the Central Post Office; first, they seized the Central Radio Broadcasting Station and broadcast announcements about the "Revolution of the Armed Forces of Vietnam against the nepotistical regime of Ngo dinh Diem," while an infantry division, under the command of Colonel Thieu, surrounded the Presidential Palace.

An hour before, at 12:30 P.M., key generals of the ARVN such as Duong van Minh, Tran van Don, Tran Thien Khiem, and Le van Kim had summoned all other generals and senior officers to Tran Hung Dao Camp, the headquarters of the Joint General Staff of the Republic of Vietnam Armed Forces (JGS-RVNAF), to ask them or force them into pledging and supporting the coup d'etat. With the guns of a group of Minh's military policemen aiming at them, both the plotters and the few commanders still loyal to Diem let their voices be recorded declaring their support of the coup.

Important commanders loyal to Diem and Nhu were assassinated or detained. Navy Captain Ho Tan Quyen, commander of the Vietnamese Navy (VNN), was murdered just an hour before the coup started; Colonel Le Quang Tung, commander of ARVN's Special Forces, and his brother, Major Le Quang Trieu, were arrested by Big Minh's special group; the commanders of the Vietnamese Air Force (VNAF), the Airborne Brigade, and the Marine Forces were detained at Tran Hung Dao Camp, after pledging to transfer their units to General Minh's new assigned commanders. There were several key positions generals that could not be present at the camp, such as the III Corps commander, General Ton That Dinh, who was at Bien Hoa commanding all coup units around Saigon; the I Corps commander, General Do Cao Tri, who was at Danang; the II Corps commander, General Nguyen Khanh, who was at Pleiku; and the IV Corps commander, General Huynh van Cao, who was at Can-Tho. General Khanh and General Cao were considered the large unit commanders most loyal to President Diem. Until then, they kept their total silence toward the coup.

Colonel Lucien Conein, wearing his U.S. Army uniform and a revolver, was the only American officer who participated in the coup from its beginning at the headquarters of the Vietnamese generals. Conein used a special radio and a telephone line to maintain permanent liaison with the Vietnamese generals and U.S. embassy. Thus, Lodge was well aware of all details of the coup and he assuredly reported important coup events to Washington.

Important events unfolded in top-secret cables between the U.S. embassy in Saigon and the White House. The first cable concerning the coup in Saigon was received in the White House Situation Room at 2:34 A.M., on October 31 (or 3:34 P.M., November 1, in Saigon, which is thirteen hours ahead of Washington). It was the report from Colonel Conein to the U.S. embassy in Saigon, then conveyed to Washington: "Generals attempting contact Palace by telephone but unable to do so. Their position as follows: If the President will resign immediately, they will guarantee his safety and the safe departure of the President and Ngo Dinh Nhu. If the President refuses these terms, the Palace will be attacked within the hour by Air Force and Armor."[15] The concordance was that at 3:00 P.M. in Saigon, General Don had called the president, suggested he resign and surrender, and assured him that a plane was ready for him and his family to exit the country. Diem, however, refused to resign or surrender.

A second cable was received at 3:40, from Lodge: "Conein reports from JGS. Generals firmly decided there to be no discussion with the President. He will either say yes or no. Observed four AD-6 fighter bombers with munitions aboard at approx 10,000 feet over Saigon.... JGS Gens have monitored radio broadcast from Palace to First and Second Corps and 21st Division. Can hear fighting from Embassy. Can confirm insurgents not arrested. As of 15:35, fire reported Palace vicinity."[16] This cable was followed by another, received at 4:11 A.M., also from the U.S. embassy in Saigon: "Conein at JGS reports Big Minh called President on telephone but President allegedly not present and Big Minh spoke to Nhu. Col Tung was forced at gunpoint to announce he's a prisoner. Air Force Commander did not speak. Conein believes he has been eliminated.... Big Minh stated to Nhu if the President and Nhu did not resign, turn themselves over the coup forces within five minutes, the Palace would sustain a massive airborne bombardment. At this, Gen Minh hung up ... at 17:15 Gen Minh once more called Diem and Diem hung up."[17]

The last cable that McGeorge Bundy of the National Security Council brought to Kennedy's bedroom on the morning of November 1, 1963, came at 6:00 A.M. Washington, was the content of the final telephone conversation between Diem and Lodge at 4:30 P.M., November 1, in Saigon. It read:

DIEM: Some units have made a rebellion and I want to know: What is the attitude of the U.S.?

LODGE: I do not feel enough informed to be able to tell you. I have heard shooting, but am not acquainted with all the facts. Also it is 4:30 A.M. in Washington and the US Government cannot possibly have a view.

DIEM: But you must have some general ideas. After all, I am a Chief of State. I have tried to do my duty. I want to do now what duty and good sense require. I believe in duty above all.

LODGE: You have certainly done your duty. As I told you only this morning, I admire your courage and your great contributions to your country. No one can take away from you the credit for all you have done. Now I am worried about your personal safety. I have a report that those in charge of the current activity offer you and your brother safe conduct out of the country if you resign. Had you heard that?

DIEM: No. (and then after a pause) You have my telephone number?

LODGE: Yes. If I can do anything for your physical safety, please call me.

DIEM: I am trying to reestablish order.[18]

Ambassador Lodge lied to Diem in saying: "it is 4:30 A.M. in Washington and US Government cannot possibly have a view." In reality, when the first cable from Saigon came to the White House, McGeorge Bundy and his assistant, Michael Forrestal of the National Security Council, were immediately informed by the Situation Room's duty officer. They came to the White House before 2:00 A.M. that night with other cables from CIA Saigon Station and MACV. They waited until past three to awaken the president.[19] If the United States had "a view" regarding President Diem's situation and the "physical safety" of him and his brother Nhu, it had already been formed. In contrast, Lodge surely did not want to create more problems when everything, until then, was going so well for the supported plotters and for the United States' interests. Thus, the last act of the first scene of the coup d'état in Saigon fell in the darkness of night that Friday, November 1, 1963, with the empty promises of the generals and of Lodge to guarantee the physical safety and safe exit of Diem and Nhu if they surrendered. On the other side, Diem and Nhu believed that they could reestablish order.

The first act of the second scene continued in the darkness when Diem, Nhu, and some aides escaped from the Presidential Palace by a secret exit and fled to the house of their Chinese confidant, Ma Tuyen, in Cholon. From there, President Diem remained in touch with the Generals and called on them to surrender. Diem's last hope lay with the forces of the Central Highlands and the Mekong Delta. But General Khanh of the II Corps and General Cao of the IV Corps could not come to save him and his regime. The final scene would be as follows: At 5:30 A.M., Saturday, November 2, in Saigon, President Diem and Adviser Nhu moved to hide in a Catholic church, the Saint Francis Xavier Church in Cholon, located in the 6th Administrative District and the 7th Military Sub-Sector of the Capital Military Special Zone.

By the evening of November 2, everybody knew that President Diem and Adviser Nhu had been killed by one of Big Minh's aides inside a U.S. M-113 armored personnel carrier sent to escort them from Saint Francis Church to the JGS.

After the sad dawn of November 2, 1963, the coup's secrecies, particularly the assassination of Diem and Nhu, were discovered both in Saigon and in Washington. In Washington, at 6:05 P.M., Friday evening, November 1 (7:05 A.M., Saturday, November 2, Saigon time), the White House received a cable from Ambassador Lodge emphasizing that Diem had telephoned the generals at 5:30 A.M. (Saigon time) to offer his surrender, asking only safe passage out of Vietnam for himself and his brother Nhu. Lodge said that he did not know where the Diem call had come from, because the brothers had escaped the palace during the night and disappeared into the city. "General Minh had accepted this," Lodge reported.[20]

However, at midnight, November 1, the White House received a cable from CIA Saigon that read: "Best estimate this time is that Diem and Nhu dead. Radio announcement reports they committed suicide by poison. Bodies reported to be in JGS in armored personnel carrier or inside building. Feel with reasonable certain that they are dead and continuing to check by what means and where now located."[21]

At 9:00 A.M., Saturday, November 2, when President Kennedy came to the Cabinet Room, where the National Security Council members were waiting for him, he nodded to them and sat down. Michael Forrestal presented to him a cable from Lodge reporting the death of Diem and Nhu. "He handed it to the President, who look at it, stood up, and rushed from the room without a word, looking pale and shaken."[22] When he re-entered the room, Kennedy told his aides, who were in total silence, that Diem had fought the communists for nine years and he deserved a better end than assassination. William Colby, who was in the room, observed: "President Kennedy was obviously upset, distraught. I think that he felt a sense of personal responsibility for it. Certainly he hadn't anticipated it — whether he should have or not is another question."[23]

That evening, the White House received a more detailed and precise cablegram from CIA Saigon; it read: "Young Vietnamese Saigon businessman ... casual source exhibited set of snapshots morning 3 November which showed Ngo Dinh Diem and Ngo Dinh Nhu covered with blood, apparently bullet-riddled, lying dead on floor of armored vehicle with hands tied behind them. Photos appear authentic. Source states pictures taken approximately 10:00 o'clock on November 2. Pictures now being offered for sale to international press in Saigon."[24] That night, November 2, Roger Hilsman, then assistant secretary of State for the Far East, was asked by journalist Marguerite Higgins, who was present at the White House: "Which American hand was blood-stained?"[25] There was no answer for this question.

Naturally, the Kennedy administration had no choice but to recognize the new authorities in Saigon: a military junta headed by Generals Big Minh, Don, Kim, Khiem, and Dinh. President Kennedy learned that at six or seven o'clock on the morning of November 2, General Don had asked the American embassy in Saigon to provide Diem and Nhu safe passage out the country and into exile. The Americans could have saved Diem and Nhu. Notwithstanding, one half-hour later, David Smith, the acting chief of the CIA Saigon Station, told Conein to tell Big Minh that it would take twenty-four hours to get a suitable plane from Guam to Tan Son Nhat Airport. Big Minh told Conein: "We can't hold them that long," as Richard Reeves retells it, and he comments, "it sounded like a death sentence."[26]

After the assassination of the South Vietnamese leaders, Ambassador Henry Cabot Lodge sent a cable to President Kennedy congratulating all Americans that had helped the coup succeed, saying: "*All this may be useful lesson in the use of US power for those who have similar situation in other places in the future.* The President, the State Department, the military, the AID, the USIS, and the CIA deserve credit for this result. Without united action of the U.S. Government, it would not have been possible. My thanks to you and all those associated with you for comprehending and imaginative guidance and support."[27] This message of Lodge would confirm that the United States had used its power to transform South Vietnam from an efficacious anti-communist government into an ineffective coalition that could not help the United States win the war; a docile junta ready to work for the U.S. government. The tacit methods of the United States to eliminate the self-willed leaders of its supported nations were also revealed. Because of these dangerous measures, on November 20, Prince Sihanouk of Cambodia announced that he was rejecting all U.S. aid, and the military junta in Saigon led by General Duong van Minh lasted only three months.

Perhaps President Kennedy was unaware of the tacit methods and measures plotted by his confident aides. Nevertheless, there were solid works on which historians could base their deliberations and viewpoints that these measures were used as efficacious tools to eliminate opponents, at least in the case of President Diem and his brother Nhu. Of course, the coup against Diem was thoroughly staged by Ambassador Lodge, who was backed by Averell Harriman, under-secretary of state; Roger Hilsman, assistant secretary of state for the Far East; and Michael Forrestal of the National Security Council. The November 1963 coup ended with the death of President Diem and his brother Nhu, and the death of the First Republic of Vietnam.

President Ngo Dinh Diem would be the last strong leader of South Vietnam. The November coup d'état in 1963 to eliminate him and his brother Nhu was a tragedy not only for South Vietnam but also for the United States. William Colby, then the CIA's Far East director, hastened to Saigon after the coup and reported to Washington that the war would soon be over and lost. Looking back at the November-coup d'état sometime later, he said:

> It really sounds incredible today that we made those decisions about getting rid of Diem without really careful consideration about what kind of government would replace him.... The chaos and anarchy, which infected the Vietnamese government at that time, caused everything to fall apart. The assessments were very clear that the situation was going downhill very fast during 1964, and our assessment was that the communists would probably win the war by about the end of 1965. They began to send their military units — not just infiltrators but military units — down the Ho Chi Minh Trail in the fall of 1964 to begin to build up the military force to administer the 'coup de grace.' Now President Johnson who was in charge of it at that time was of course a very tenacious Texan, a very tough fellow, and he wasn't about to have that happen.[28]

The United States would not let South Vietnam fall easily. However, its thirty-sixth president, Lyndon Baines Johnson, had inherited the painful results of the Kennedy administration's foreign policy in Indochina and Vietnam in several domains: (1) the tacit war in Laos which resulted from the 1962 neutralization of the Geneva Accords; (2) the Harriman Line in Laos that allowed North Vietnam to exploit and develop the Ho Chi Minh Trail; (3) the chaotic political, economical, and social situations and the anarchy in South Vietnam that weakened the United States' efforts to fight the communists in the country; (4) the concept of "escalation of U.S. engagement" in South Vietnam, which was proposed by the National Security Council in Action Memo 249 of June 19, 1963, and approved by President Kennedy; and (5) Kennedy's circle of aides, who were generally talented policy-makers and military strategists, but were not suitable for directing the war in Indochina, and with their concept of "escalation" would push the Johnson administration to commit more combat troops in Vietnam. The war became more intense and irresolvable.

Ultimately, the coup d'état in South Vietnam in November 1963 that eliminated President Ngo Dinh Diem and established a militarist regime in Saigon was the third paradox for the United States that caused the first serious failure of its foreign policy in Indochina.

7

The Escalation of the War

On the afternoon of November 22, 1963, President John F. Kennedy was tragically assassinated in Dallas, Texas. Aboard *Airforce One* from Dallas to Washington, vice-president Lyndon B. Johnson was hurriedly sworn in as the thirty-sixth president of the United States. This abrupt transition made Johnson the most powerful leader of the free world. But it plunged him into the prolonged struggle in Vietnam that would ultimately crush his political life. The Vietnam War, in which Johnson played a crucial role, was the primary cause of the destruction of his presidency. The war itself was the most disputed conflict of arms in American history.

President Johnson's general policy on Indochina and Vietnam was to continue Kennedy's policy of deterring international communist aggression, preventing communist domination of South Vietnam, and promoting the creation of a viable and increasingly democratic society in South Vietnam by supporting its government with political, psychological, economic and military aid. Some Kennedy aides had argued that the elimination of Ngo Dinh Diem would produce a leadership in South Vietnam better at fighting the communists in order to achieve these common objectives, both serving the interests of the U.S. and promoting freedom in Vietnam. After the death of President Diem and his brother, the United States learned the coup did neither. On the contrary, the political instability of the unconstitutional government in Saigon coupled with the acceleration of NVA infiltration from Laos to South Vietnam, aggravated the situation and dogged the United States for the next several years.

A "LIMITED WAR" OR A "DEFENSIVE WAR"?

In his first address to the nation, President Johnson pledged to heal the wounds of the assassination of President Kennedy and to build a "Great Society" for the American people. He proposed to concentrate his efforts to solve racial issues, poverty, malnutrition and education. Vietnam was still abstract to the president. However, within twenty-four hours, the abstraction of Vietnam gave way to the painful reality as the president considered how to reconcile the nightmare of Vietnam with his dream of a Great Society. He seemed determined to handle both issues: resolve the chaos in Vietnam while realizing the American dream of a better society. This would consolidate his position in America's history. He could not let Vietnam be lost and to become the target of blame previously assigned to one of his predecessors, a Democrat who had lost China to the communists in 1949. On the second day of his presidency, Johnson announced that the United States' military support for the Saigon military junta would continue.

The concept of a "limited war" was said to be a philosophical legacy of the Kennedy administration that was left to the Johnson administration. Military historian Colonel Harry G. Summers, Jr., as related by Robert L. Hewitt in the June 1993 issue of *Vietnam Magazine*, suggested that the theories and policies of Kennedy administration's policy-makers who committed U.S. combat troops to Vietnam initially were irrevocably linked to a "defensive strategy." Summers quoted the words of McNamara: "The greatest contribution Vietnam is making — right or wrong is beside the point — is that it is developing the ability in the United States to fight a limited war, to go to war without the necessity of arousing the public ire." Hewitt's own view was: "When President Johnson escalated the war to the intensity he did, it precipitated a crisis for those theorists. A strategy for a prolonged, 'low-profile' defensive war was replaced by a strategy for a prolonged, 'high-profile' defensive war."[1] Hewitt also quoted Bernard B. Fall, that: "As soon as American advisers were engaged in combat operations, the fact that there were 20,000 under Kennedy and 400,000 under Johnson becomes of a little importance."[2]

Johnson's concept of "escalation" of a "high-profile defensive war"—to the point that historians name it the "Americanization" of the war — was just an imitation of the Kennedy administration's concept of a "low-profile defensive war." "Escalation" thus would be defined as a "development" of the current strategy, which was being applied in Vietnam by the Kennedy administration. Johnson's continuation of Kennedy's policies and theories would be explained by the fact that President Johnson had maintained almost all of Kennedy's team of advisers who had formulated war strategies for Vietnam.

Many American historians have observed that the result of these experts' advice to consecutive presidents of the United States from Kennedy on, was to demolish American foreign policy and hope in Indochina and Vietnam, and led to the defeat of the US Armed Forces in an illogical and negative war of defense and attrition. Indeed, John Dellinger has remarked: "Such was certainly the case in the Vietnam War, a hotbed of political intrigue. Civilians directly influenced presidential decisions or made decisions that had enormous consequences on the battlefield. Those decisions most often came from the ambassador to South Vietnam, the secretary of defense and the national security adviser."[3] According to Dellinger, these key "experts" were Henry Cabot Lodge, Maxwell Taylor, Robert McNamara, Clark Clifford, and Henry Kissinger. Four of them, except Kissinger, were Kennedy-Johnson aides. Historian Norman B. Hannah adds to that list Averell Harriman and William Sullivan. Hannah proved that their policy of "neutralization of Laos" and their concept to "condone the extensive use of the Laotian border" for the NVA to exploit the Ho Chi Minh Trail led to the "so-called McNamara Line."[4] The concept of a "defensive war" also grew out of Harriman and Sullivan's theories and applications in Laos, which helped lose the war.

Another American historian, H.R. McMaster, explained how these "civilian experts" so trusted by United States presidents, especially Kennedy and Johnson, led to defeat. In a *Vietnam Magazine* article of August 1997, he wrote: "Dismissed JSC [Joint Chiefs of Staff] access to the president reflected Kennedy's opinion of his senior military advisers.... The Old Guards in the Pentagon were relegated to a little influence."[5] After the Cuban missile crisis, President Kennedy told his brother Robert Kennedy, "If we listen to them, and do what they want us to do, none of us will be alive to tell them that they were wrong."[6] President Kennedy also warned Johnson: "To watch the generals and to avoid feeling that just because they were military men their opinion[s] on military matters were worth a damn."[7] Like his predecessor, President Johnson also relegated his Joint Chiefs of Staff to the background. Both Kennedy and Johnson appreciated civilian advisers such as McNamara, Harriman, and the Bundy brothers. Particularly, under Johnson administration, the Oval Office "Lunch Bunch" decided every important political and military decision in Indochina and Vietnam. Every Tuesday the president held a luncheon at the White House with a group of aides included the secretaries of state and defense, some national security advisers, his press secretary, and some more congressional figures or Washington's bureaucrats. They discussed and decided strategies, and even tactics that would be applied in Laos, Cambodia, North Vietnam, and South Vietnam battlefields. No military commanders, not even the Joint Chiefs nor the JCS's chairman, were present at any of these luncheons. Thus, the "civilian experts," or bureaucrats, and not the generals, decided how to wage the war. American media and historians name them the "Lunch Powers." McMaster concluded: "The war was lost in Washington, D.C., even before Americans assumed sole responsibility for the fighting in 1965 and before they realized the country was at war: indeed, even before the first American units were deployed."[8]

Among Kennedy and Johnson's top aides was a unique military expert, General Maxwell Taylor. According to McMaster and Dellinger, Taylor was author of the "limited war" strategy. Dellinger named Taylor "the foot-dragging" general, remarking: "Taylor was willing to up the ante, but he was never willing to win the pot."[9] General Taylor was brought back from retirement, first to serve as Kennedy's military adviser and then as chairman of the Joint Chiefs of Staff in October 1962. He played an essential role in U.S. political and military decisions in Indochina and South Vietnam. Other historians have identified Robert McNamara as the most important aide of presidents Kennedy and Johnson. McMaster writes, "Defense Secretary McNamara would dominate the [Vietnam] policy-making process because of three mutually reinforcing factors: the Chiefs' ineffectiveness as an advisory group, Johnson's profound insecurity, and the president's related unwillingness to entertain divergent views on the subject of Vietnam.... He would become Lyndon Johnson's 'oracle' in Vietnam."[10] A careful study proved that McNamara was neither the "brain" nor the "wisdom" of White House policy on Vietnam, but a masterfully political swindler who lied to the American people and the U.S. Congress by his deceptive notion of trying "to fight a war, to go to war without the necessity of arousing the public ire." McNamara's deceptive notion, however, pleased President Johnson, who was seeking such a solution to deceive the American people and the Congress.

Perhaps the most devastating aspect of Johnson's policy in Vietnam was the public revelation that America was suddenly plunged into a serious war in Vietnam. In the beginning, the president was influenced by the advice of Kennedy aides. He listened to their arguments and theories carefully before he decided to hold South Vietnam and escalate the war. Historian Norman B. Hannah described President Johnson: "The image of L.B.J. is not one of a man spoiling for a fight but of a man in agony over the necessity of pouring billions into a strange kind of bloody fighting he does not like or understand."[11] Just a few weeks into his presidency, the president found himself dealing with the political degeneration of the new military junta in Saigon and the serious increase of communist activities in Laos, along the Ho Chi Minh Trail, and throughout South Vietnam. The war would be lost, as Colby had estimated. Johnson had to choose either to renege on Kennedy's commitment in Vietnam and withdraw, or to increase the intensity of commitment to respond to the gloomy situation, and possibly dump South Vietnam in the very near future. Finally, he chose the latter.

In the meantime, Senator Mike Mansfield and American columnist Walter Lippmann proposed neutralization of South Vietnam. Lippmann's theory of neutralization particularly made the President worry. It was: "a) SEA [Southeast Asia] is destined to become a zone of Chinese control; b) we could not halt Chinese communist expansion; and c) that our best hope was to slow that expansionism down and make it less brutal."[12] The Johnson administration rejected Mansfield and Lippmann's proposals of neutralization of South Vietnam. However, Lippmann's theory became a very important "account" that would affect Johnson's aptitude and application in formulating political and military strategy for Indochina. Johnson's concept of war envisioned "an intensively defensive war" to stop Communist North Vietnam's expansion into the South but with "limits" so as not to provoke Red China to intervene in Indochina and transform it into a total war in Southeast Asia. Johnson's conduct of the war would later prove this remark. Johnson's concept therefore became his "own theory" rather than the one of the foot-dragging general, Taylor, or the bureaucrat McNamara. These experts were Johnson's "hands" but not Johnson's "brain." Thus — in my opinion — President Johnson owned the Second Indochina War with his own strategic and tactical modus operandi.

Using this approach, Johnson led his team into the war in Indochina having an apparent political goal of continuing Kennedy's policy and the enforcement of American will in Vietnam. His military strategy would be seen as a perilous adventure. Dellinger names Johnson's concept of war as some kind of war of attrition: "Escalating the number of American troops to more than a half-million while fighting a restricted war until the enemy could be defeated by attrition."[13] The United States had never experienced a protracted war. On the contrary, such a war was one designed by the communists of North Vietnam to fight their stronger enemy.

At the beginning of 1964, Johnson faced two difficult fronts in Indochina: (1) The tacit war in Laos, and (2) the second offensive phase of the communist revolutionary war in South Vietnam. *The connection between these two fronts was the Ho Chi Minh Trail. Consequently, the trail was really a critical problem for Johnson's war team. It became the main cause of the American "escalation" in Vietnam.* To face these threats, the Johnson administration developed a strategy of concentration of air-power efforts and MACV-SOG's secret operations to cut off North Vietnamese troop and supply movement to the South along the Ho Chi Minh Trail. American combat troops were sent to South Vietnam in order to protect the long border between South Vietnam and Laos. On the other hand, MACV held command over all "pacification" ground operations to search and destroy the VC National Liberation Front's army and guerrilla units while they improved the ARVN to secure the countryside.

In order to carry out these main military goals in Indochina, Johnson appointed his best men to the region. In Laos, at Harriman's urging, William Sullivan was assigned as ambassador to Vientiane to conduct the tacit war against the NVA and the Pathet-Lao and to support the Laotian Royal Army of General Nosavan. In South Vietnam, the chairman of the Joint Chiefs of Staff, General Maxwell Taylor, was assigned as ambassador to Saigon, and General William Westmoreland was made post commander of U.S. Military Assistance Command, Vietnam (COMUSMACV). Although the problems in the U.S. Command in Indochina were presumed resolved this was not the case. Sullivan did not get along with Taylor and Westmoreland. The "Harriman Line" and the "Sullivan Speedway" still existed, frustrating U.S. strategy in South Vietnam. Meanwhile, in Washington, the Johnson administration prepared military support for the war. However, escalation of the "defensive" war was the United States' fourth paradox.

THE UNITED STATES'
"STICK AND CARROT" POLICY

In South Vietnam, on January 6, 1964, the military junta commissioned the national power to the troika comprised of Big Minh, Tran van Don, and Tran Thien Khiem. Big Minh was on top but he was a suspected neutralist. On January 30, 1964, General Nguyen Khanh, II Corps Commander, with the help of Lt. General Tran Thien Khiem, Major General Nguyen Van Thieu and the Dai Viet Party, overthrew General Big Minh, dissolved the old troika and replaced it with a new one composed of himself, General Big Minh, and Lt. General Tran Thien Khiem. Khanh proclaimed himself chief of state and secured American support. In the meantime, General Khanh arrested five generals of the junta; Don, Kim, Xuan, Dinh, and Vy, whom he suspected of being inclined toward a neutralist solution for South Vietnam. These generals were confined at Dalat City for months. General Big Minh was kept as titular chief of state, but in the following months Minh continued to struggle to gain control of national power with General Khanh; he failed twice. On May 4, 1964, in a meeting with the U.S. ambassador to Saigon, Khanh suggested the latter to convey to Washington his opinion that the war could not be won in South Vietnam except by an invasion of North Vietnam. He also demanded an immediate bombing of Hanoi and a reinforcement of 10,000 American Special Forces to seal the border.

General Nguyen Khanh was probably unaware that Washington had already prepared a bombing plan against North Vietnam. In the first two months of 1964, when French president Charles de Gaulle, who may have had special contacts with both Duong van Minh and Ho Chi Minh, strongly appealed for a neutralist solution for Vietnam, and Prince Sihanouk announced that he would continue to accept U.S. military and economic aid providing Cambodia's neutrality could be respected. At the same time, William Bundy, assistant secretary of state for Far East Asia (replacing Roger Hilsman), reported to Johnson that since early 1964 North Vietnam had been continuously sending large number of arms and troops to South Vietnam and it appeared that it had already won the war. In March, President Johnson sent McNamara to South Vietnam when communist guerrillas moved their attacks closer to Saigon. In Saigon, McNamara cabled the president that the dangerous neutralist sentiments persisted. Johnson cabled back, ordering U.S. authorities to stop "neutralist talk" wherever possible by whatever means. After returning to Washington, McNamara proposed that South Vietnam begin general mobilization, that the ARVN receive the most modern of U.S. equipment, and finally, that an exact plan to take the war to North Vietnam be prepared. On March 17, 1964, President Johnson convened an extraordinary session of the National Security Council (NSC) and McNamara informed the NSC that South Vietnam was on the verge of a total collapse. The president immediately authorized war preparations and planning of the strategy for the bombing of North Vietnam. While the bombing Operation Plan 37-64 was being prepared, Johnson made his first direct and instantaneous combat moves, ordering the U.S. Navy and Air Force jets to fly reconnaissance support missions for the T-28 air operations that had been used years ago in Laos, along the Ho Chi Minh Trail. He also ordered the intensification of covert secret missions on land, sea, and air against North Vietnam by MACV-SOG, and signed the OPLAN-34A.

A week after President Johnson's orders, the Operation Plan 37-64 bombing scenario to North Vietnam was completed with a large target list. However, before the United States began its real war in Indochina, the president sent his senior aide, secretary of state Dean Rusk, to South Vietnam for a final assessment of the political and military situation in the region. On May 17, 1964, when Rusk flied to Saigon, in Laos the Pathet-Lao launched a new phase of attack against the Laotian Royal Army. The three-year-old neutralist government of Laos would be disregarded at any time.

The outgoing ambassador in Saigon, Henry Cabot Lodge, who was speculated to be a possible Republican candidate for the presidency, was briefed by Dean Rusk on the OPLAN 37-64 bombing of North Vietnam. Lodge advised Rusk that the United States could use the "solution" as a "stick and carrot" policy toward Hanoi. Rusk shared Lodge's idea. After his return to Washington, Rusk reported Lodge's advice to Johnson. The president and Dean Rusk agreed that the "bombing" should go along with the "dialogue" with Hanoi. Rusk called that a "psychological struggle" and he believed that the threat or initial use of the bombing would bring Hanoi to the conference table.

Actually, the "stick and carrot" approach would appear as follows: The United States declared it would initiate action by air and naval means against North Vietnam until Hanoi agreed to stop the war. If hostilities ceased, the U.S. would then undertake: (1) to obtain the agreement of Saigon to a resumption of trade between North and South, (2) to initiate a program of food assistance to North Vietnam, (3) to reduce control on U.S. trade with North Vietnam, (4) to recognize North Vietnam diplomatically and, if Hanoi were interested, undertake an exchange of diplomatic representatives, and (5) to remove U.S. forces from South Vietnam, on a phased basis, reducing the number of military advisors or trainers to the level of 350, as permitted under the Geneva Accords. In addition, the peace package required a guarantee of full amnesty for all Southern guerrillas, then estimated to number 103,000, and it proposed, that the DRV (Democratic Republic of Vietnam) could repatriate Viet Cong from South Vietnam over whatever period the DRV desired.

This peace package "message" versus the threat of a wider war was to be carried to Hanoi by a Canadian diplomat arranged by President Johnson and Canadian prime minister Lester Pearson on May 28, 1964 in New York. The "messenger" was the chief of the Canadian International Control Commission (ICC) delegation in Vietnam, James Blair Seaborn, who had the right to rotate between Saigon and Hanoi according to the Geneva Accords. Seaborn went to Hanoi twice. The first trip, on June 16, 1964, he met North Vietnam's prime minister Pham van Dong. After two hours of conversation, Dong suggested Seaborn convey to Washington the resolute determination of North Vietnam to pursue the war even if the United States increased aid to South Vietnam to wage war against the North. With his answer went a counter-proposal composed of three pre-requisites: (1) American withdrawal from South Vietnam, (2) peace and neutrality for South Vietnam — in the Cambodian manner — with the participation of the Liberation Front, such that the people of the South could arrange the affairs of South Vietnam without third-party involvement, and (3) a "just solution," meaning re-unification of the country, which was seen as fundamental. Pham van Dong's reply meant that communist North Vietnam would accept the "stick" but not the "carrot."

Seaborn's second trip occurred on August 18, 1964. Again he met Pham van Dong. The meeting occurred 16 days after the "Maddox Crisis" and 2 weeks after the Operation Plan 37-64 bombing against Hanoi had been performed by the U.S. 7th Fleet. Dong was furious and did not forget to deliver to Washington his Communist Party's warning that if the war came to North Vietnam, it would come to the whole of Southeast Asia. Returning to Washington, Seaborn reported that Hanoi had noticeably changed. People were ordered to conduct air-raid drills, dig street trenches, and constructing brick bunkers all around the city. All of these meant that North Vietnam had decided to continue the war at any price, both in the North and in the South of Vietnam. The United States' "stick and carrot" policy clearly affected the North Vietnamese communists psychologically. They accepted "the ante in order to win the pot" as it was demonstrated later. Reliably, the leaders in Hanoi had speculated the risks they might have faced while confronting an enormous adversary like the United States. However, they, and especially General Vo Nguyen Giap, had learned from the North Korean Army how a weak nation can vanquish modern American troops when a long war occurred through, as Giap named it, the "political psychological shortcoming" of the democratic system. The crucial weaknesses of the United States in a prolonged war, as Giap estimated, were: "Public opinion in the democracy will demand an end of the 'useless bloodshed,' or its legislature will insist on knowing for how long it will have to vote astronomical credits without a clear-cut victory in sight. This is what eternally compels the military leaders of democratic armies to promise a quick end — to bring the boys home by Christmas — or force the democratic politicians to agree to almost any kind of humiliating compromise."[14] Under the clear-sighted leadership of Hanoi the war would continue, at any price, until Vietnam could be reunified and a socialist regime could be established, not only in Vietnam, but in the whole of Indochina.

THE "MADDOX CRISIS" AND THE GULF OF TONKIN RESOLUTION

James Blair Seaborn's historic mission was never disclosed to the American public. All details of the "stick and carrot" policy were engulfed by the mysterious circumstances in the Gulf of Tonkin. On August 2, 1964, the U.S. Honolulu Pacific Command reported to Washington that the U.S.S. destroyer *Maddox* was attacked by three North Vietnamese PT-boats at thirty miles offshore North Vietnam in "international" waters in the Gulf of Tonkin. The U.S.S. *Maddox* was described as having been on a routine mission in international waters offshore Vietnam since July 31, 1964. It was midnight of August 2 in Washington; the joint chiefs aroused President Johnson. Immediately the president ordered another destroyer, the U.S.S. *C. Turner Joy*, to join *Maddox* in the region. Two days later, on August 4, also in the dark of midnight, Washington received the alert of a second North Vietnamese PT boats' attack against U.S.S. *Maddox* and U.S.S. *C. Turner Joy* when these two American destroyers linked up. This time the attack occurred at fifty to fifty-five miles off the coast of North Vietnam. Within minutes later, the National Security Council convened and President Johnson decided immediately to start phase one of the Operation Plan 37-64 bombing scenario against North Vietnam.

At 10:30 August 5, 1964, while American bombers from the 7th Fleet were in the air, President Johnson told the nation: "Renewed hostile actions against United States ships on the high seas in the Gulf of Tonkin have required me to order the military forces of the United States to take action in reply."[15] Thus, the United States directly entered the war in Vietnam without declaration at 11 A.M., August 5, 1964. The first American air strike on North Vietnam, by sixty-four U.S. naval aircraft, targeted Vinh, a northern province of the DMZ. Three days later, on August 7, 1964, the Gulf of Tonkin Resolution was passed first by the House by 416–0, then the Senate by 88–2. The resolution authorized the president of the United States to take all necessary measures to repel any armed attack against U.S. forces in Southeast Asia and approved in advance all necessary steps, including armed forces in meeting any requests by the SEATO nations for assistance.

The claim that the Johnson administration intentionally triggered the Vietnam War by orchestrating the *Maddox* incident and deluding the Congress has remained a topic of discussion. At least two books and more than one hundred newspaper and magazine articles have been written about this unimportant matter. The important point was that the United States had entered into a non-essential war in Vietnam that was supposed to be fought by the South Vietnamese themselves. President Johnson himself knew that he should not commit ground forces to Vietnam. At his birthday party on August 27, 1964, he said: "I've had advice to load our planes and bomb certain areas that I think would enlarge and escalate the war and result in our committing a good many American boys to fight a war I think ought to be fought by the boys of Asia."[16]

Serious political and military problems in Indochina were thought to have changed Johnson's initial intentions. Washington policy-makers had their own reasons for taking new measures to hold onto United States goals in Southeast Asia. First, the political situation in South Vietnam was a burden for the United States. There were consecutive coups d'état and the national power consecutively changed hands after the death of President Ngo Dinh Diem. This situation eroded the vital force of the ARVN to fight a war and created irremediable problems. The clashes between Buddhists and Catholics in the last week of August 1964 killed almost a hundred people. The Buddhists initiated anti-government riots in Saigon and Hue. In Saigon, students of the Buddhist university and elsewhere organized several riots against the military junta, demanding "peace for Vietnam" and "GIs go home." On August 27, 1964, thousands of student demonstrators tried to attack the ARVN headquarters near Tan-Son-Nhut airport for the same reasons. In addition, during the last two weeks of November 1964, tens of thousands of people of divergent nationalist clans rioted in Saigon to demand "reforms" and "elections." In this chaos, only the ARVN's junior officers held their units in safe order. As the generals tried to purge each other for power, the fighting against the communists at that time was dubbed "La Guerre des Capitaines" by the French press.

Second, the NVA activities along the Ho Chi Minh Trail markedly increased. During the last six months of 1964, the number of infiltrators increased to 34,000 and the trail itself developed. Communists attacked the CIDG and ARVN outposts along the border of the Central Highlands and in the Mekong Delta. The VC guerrilla circle approached the Capital Special Zone (Biệt-Khu Thủ-đô, composed of Saigon, Cholon and Gia-Dinh Province) and VC sabotage was targeted at American installations in Saigon and at U.S. air bases around the country.

Third, North Vietnam had advanced in conducting retaliation in South Vietnam, after the first phase of U.S. bombardment at Vinh. The Joint Chiefs of Staff alerted President Johnson that Hanoi leaders had changed the ground rules in South Vietnam and MACV commander General Westmoreland reported that North Vietnamese troops had engaged into the war directly. Four NVA divisions had been sighted in South Vietnam.

General Maxwell Taylor, as ambassador in South Vietnam, advised Washington of a "gradual" bombing of North Vietnam. He convinced President Johnson that a bombing strategy would raise the morale of Saigon leaders and give South Vietnamese people the feeling of trust toward the United States' strong support; second, it would, if not totally cut off the manpower and equipment activities of North Vietnam to South Vietnam, at least slow down these infiltrations; and, finally it would convince Hanoi leaders that the cost of the war could be too great to pay, including the obliteration of their capital, that could force them to come to the negotiating table for peace talks. MACV commander General William Westmoreland, on the contrary, argued that the bombing of North Vietnam would not be enough, but it would logically bring communist retaliation in South Vietnam. He requested U.S. Marines for South Vietnam. In supporting Westmoreland, the Joint Chiefs of Staff stressed that combat troops were needed to deter communist retaliation to the U.S. air strikes. Defense Secretary McNamara, who had promoted the bombing strategy, now supported General Westmoreland. Assistant secretary of state for the Far East William Bundy excited both strategies. President Johnson had to choose the "air war," or the "land war," or both.

A MILITARY REGIME IN CHAOS

While the Johnson administration in Washington considered strategy options for the war in Vietnam, in Saigon the political turmoil worsened by the day. The new leader of the "Armed Forces Council," General Nguyen Khanh, having neutralized Big Minh's power, went further by replacing Minh's choice for prime minister, Nguyen Ngoc Tho, with his own choice. To consolidate power he appointed more of his men to key posts in the armed forces and the government. Lt. General Tran Thien Khiem was promoted to the rank of general and Major General Nguyen Van Thieu became lt. general. These two generals were respectively assigned commander in chief of the ARVN and chief of staff of the Joint General Staff. Khanh also rewarded a number of young colonels who had supported him for power with the rank of one-or two-star general. Colonel Cao Van Vien, commander of the Airborne Brigade, was promoted to major general after the brigade victoriously returned from the battle of Hong Ngu in the Mekong Delta in February of 1964. Navy Captain Chung Tan Cang, CNO of the VNN, was promoted to commodore and Colonel Nguyen Cao Ky, commander of the VNAF, to brigadier general. Ky was the most famous among the young, newly promoted one-star generals; others were Nguyen Chanh Thi, Le Nguyen Khang, Vinh Loc, Ngo Du, Nguyen Duc Thang and Nguyen Bao Tri. The American press referred to this group of young generals as the "Young Turks." In the meantime, Khanh fired from his cabinet Dr. Nguyen Ton Hoan, the leader of the Đại Việt Party and his deputy prime minister in charge of pacification, and did not reward several of this party's members who served in the army. The main reason was that the two political parties, Đại Việt and Cấp Tiến, had not supported Khanh in his desire to be "chief-of-state for life" after he proclaimed the "Vung Tau Constitution" (Hiến Chương Vũng Tàu) that granted him this lifetime power. As a result, his constitution was dumped.

These political bounties and penalties, in addition to Khanh's ineffectiveness in politics, generated discontent, displeasure, and indignation among party leaders, generals and colonels of long standing, who subsequently plotted military coups against Khanh. The first military conspiracy exploded on September 13, 1964. Lt. General Duong Van Duc, IV Corps commander; Major General Lam van Phat, former minister of the interior, Colonel Huynh Van Ton, 7th Infantry Division commander, and his chief of staff Lt. Colonel Pham Van Lieu; and Lt. Colonels Ly Tong Ba and Duong Hieu Nghia — both men armored unit commanders — had their infantry and armored regiments moved from the Mekong Delta to Saigon in the early morning, blocking several access routes to the city, occupying some unimportant places and encircling the Joint General Staff Headquarters at Tân Sơn Nhứt, in which was located the residence of General Khanh. The conspirators sought to capture him but fortunately, just minutes before the siege began, Khanh escaped and rushed to General Ky's home in Tân Sơn Nhứt Air Base. Ky saved Khanh by flying him on a VNAF C-47 to Vung Tau. From there Khanh took another flight to Da Lat. General Ky flew back to Bien Hoa Air Base and called Lt. General Duc and Colonel Ton threatening to bomb and destroy their units if they did not withdraw back to the delta. By night, Colonel Ton took his troops back to My Tho. He was followed by General Duc and General Phat and the armored units of Ba and Nghia. The coup failed. Leaders of the coup and most unit commanders of the "revolutionary forces" were subjected to different levels of punishment.

Although the coup on September 13, 1964 had failed, it significantly impacted the political situation. General Khanh began to suspect even those who had supported him before. He dispatched General Tran Thien Khiem to the United States to serve as ambassador which led to the breaking up of the troika. After that, General Khanh forced a number of generals, who had pro–French backgrounds and just had been released from the house arrest in Da Lat, to retire. The most important point was that Khanh still continued to hold national power by keeping the position of president of the Armed Forces Council and the leader of Council of Generals. However, he delegated the role of administration of the country to a civilian government in October 1964.

In complying with the U.S. requests, General Khanh and the Council of Generals agreed to form a "National High Council" to oversee the activities of the civilian government. This council was composed of nine members who were well known politicians and was believed to have broad popular support in South Viet Nam. Phan Khac Suu was invited to become the president of the new council and also to assume the role of chief of state. Professor Tran Van Huong was also invited to be a member of this council, and at the same time, to serve as the new prime minister. In the meantime, General Khanh stepped back to the post of commander in chief of the armed forces. Only a short time later, on December 23, 1964, General Khanh called a number of the Young Turks into his office at the JGS headquarters and let them know there were four members of the National High Council who supported General Big Minh and were plotting to depose chief of state Phan Khac Suu and prime minister Tran Van Huong to take over the government. After a heated discussion, the young generals agreed to arrest these politicians and place them on detention in Pleiku. Also, they put prime minister Tran Van Huong under house arrest in Vung Tau for unknown reasons.

These events led to two important developments. First, the level of trust between the military leaders of Saigon and the United States suffered, affecting the relationship with Ambassador Maxwell Taylor and the U.S. State Department. This type of crisis had happened under President Diem's administration, which led to the U.S.–sanctioned coup of November 1963. General Khanh's fate seemed to be little different. Only a few days after the arrest of the four politicians and Prime Minister Huong, Ambassador Taylor invited General Khanh to the U.S. embassy. General Khanh declined and instead sent four generals, Thieu, Ky, Thi, and Cang, to see the ambassador. When the four generals arrived at the U.S. embassy, Ambassador Taylor addressed them using a superior tone of voice and condemned them for creating a "real mess" in the Saigon political arena. General Ky's recollection of this evening as described in his memoir, *Buddha's Child: My Struggle to Save Viet Nam*, was that he did not raise his voice but explained simply, "What is done is done. We can not return to the past." This embarrassing occurrence was reported to General Khanh. An angry General Khanh immediately called a press conference the following day intending to declare Ambassador Taylor persona non grata. Instead of using these terms, General Khanh only said that Ambassador Taylor possessed a "colonist's attitude." Perhaps because of this event, Ambassador Taylor was called back to Washington and replaced by ambassador Henry Cabot Lodge. Before he left Saigon, Ambassador Taylor followed the orders of the U.S. State Department requesting a civilian government in Saigon, despite the belief held by the Vietnamese generals that a civilian government was ineffective in directing the country's effort in the war against the communists. The generals conceded and on January 27, 1965, invited Dr. Phan Huy Quat, another well-known political figure in Saigon, to become the new prime minister and to form a new cabinet. Phan Khac Suu remained as chief of state. Although still in power, Khanh lost the unconditional support of the United States.

A second coup to overthrow General Khanh took place on February 19, 1965. This time, it was led by Major General Lam Van Phat, Colonel Pham Ngoc Thao and Colonel Bui Dinh. The "revolutionaries" included an infantry regiment with some armored units under the command of Colonel Bui Dinh, a battalion of intelligence students of the An Nhon Center (a branch of the Military Intelligence School Cay Mai), and an Airborne Recon company under the command of Major Ho Van Kiet, commander of Intelligence Special Unit 924 of J2/JGS RVNAF. They occupied a number of places in Saigon and surrounded the JGS Headquarters and Tan Son Nhut Airbase with the intention of capturing General Khanh and General Ky. Although the latter two units belonged to the JGS/J2 under the command of Brigadier General Nguyen Cao, he was not aware of their plot. Later, it was revealed that the coup was planned by Colonel Pham Ngoc Thao and Professor Nguyen Bao Kiem. Colonel Pham Ngoc Thao, before 1954, was a communist battalion commander. After 1954 he returned to town and was trusted by Bishop Ngo Dinh Thuc. Under the Ngo Dinh Diem administration, Thao was made provincial chief of Ben Tre and promoted to the rank of lieutenant colonel. During the coup of November 1, 1963, Lt. Colonel Pham Ngoc Thao turned against President Ngo Dinh Diem and became one of the most devoted members of the coup. After that, Pham Ngoc Thao was promoted to full colonel and assigned to the Vietnam embassy in Washington, DC, as military attaché. After Khanh came to power, Colonel Pham Ngoc Thao was recalled to Saigon and was not entrusted with any position of power. His resentment led to his planning of the coup against Khanh. But who was the mastermind behind this coup, Hanoi or the United States? No one had the answer. According to General Ky, only a few hours after the armor units of General Phat were put on the move, Major General Robert Rowland, American advisor to the VNAF Headquarters, called General Ky at Bien Hoa and on behalf of the U.S. government asked whether General Ky would support General Phat. General Ky refused and let Rowland know he had sent a message to General Phat that if the latter had not withdrawn from Tan Son Nhut Air Base by 7 A.M. the next morning, he would have the place bombed. General Ky also requested General Rowland leave the place by then. By 6 P.M. General Rowland called General Ky again and told him that Colonel Pham Ngoc Thao would like to meet Ky. After dark, Thao and Colonel Samuel V. Wilson, a famous CIA spy, arrived at the Bien Hoa Airbase. Colonel Thao tried desperately to persuade General Ky to support the coup by saying that it was necessary for the country because the current government was incompetent. Ky refused and declared that Thao and General Phat must withdraw their troops or he would take action. After that, Ky let Thao and Wilson leave.

The next morning, February 20, at about 8 A.M. all units of General Phat and Colonel Thao withdrew. Both leaders escaped into hiding. Most of the unit commanders and officers who participated in the coup were punished. Later, Colonel Thao was captured after being wounded. He died in his cell at the ARVN Security Directorate. After April of 1975, the communists confirmed that Pham Ngoc Thao was one of their spies in the South and granted him the posthumous rank of army colonel.

Many people thought that even though General Khanh had escaped the coup safely, he would be unable to run the country. This came true sooner than expected. Immediately afterward, another coup deposed General Khanh and forced him to leave Viet Nam. In his memoir, General Ky did not mention this coup of the Young Turks. However, in a memoir by General Lam Quang Thi, *The Twenty-Five Year Century*, published in February 2002, General Thi briefly recollected the event. On February 21, 1965, Brigadier General Nguyen Bao Tri, commander of the 7th Division Infantry, told Thi that he was about to take an infantry regiment and one armored squadron to support General Ky in the coup to depose General Khanh. General Tri left with the troops to Saigon and Thi, then a full colonel and deputy commander of the 7th Division Infantry, stayed in My Tho to command the remaining troops of the 7th Division Infantry. General Thi wrote: "This time the coup was a success. On February 25, General Khanh left the country as ambassador-at-large after having been elevated to the rank of four stars general. Ultimately, Khanh ended up as a restaurateur in Paris."[17]

History had turned to a new chapter. The national power was in the hands of the generals who were members of the Armed Forces Council. Chief of State Phan Khac Suu and Prime Minister Phan Huy Quat remained in their positions. The new leaders of the Armed Forces Council were Lt. General Nguyen Van Thieu and other senior generals. The Young Turks did not yet appear on the national political ground until the sudden break-up of the civilian government on June 19, 1965. Therefore, in the first three months of 1965, the political situation was temporarily settled while the military situation remained critical. Dean Rusk, American secretary of state, thought the South might be cut in two after the general elections in the United States. General Nguyen van Thieu, the new military and political "power" in Saigon said the communists had controlled seventy-five percent of the country-side and the Vietnamese government controlled only the chief towns, which meant the urban areas of provinces and districts.

8

The "Lunch Bunch War"

Military events occurring during this period of political chaos in South Vietnam incited the Johnson administration to make several fateful decisions. On November 1, 1964, at Bien-Hoa Airbase, close to Saigon, a series of guerrilla mortars killed four Americans and destroyed five U.S. B-57 bombers. This was the first strike by the communists against U.S. military personnel and materiel. Although the Pentagon urged President Johnson to order an immediate air strike against air bases near Hanoi, Johnson only ordered an updated bombing scenario against North Vietnam. However, when a communist guerrilla blitz on the U.S. compound at Pleiku on February 7, 1965, killed nine Americans and wounded seventy-six others, President Johnson authorized a new phase of bombing above the 17th parallel that swept out the Dong-Hoi barracks, North Vietnam's major troop dispersal base. On the same day, the president ordered the countdown to "Rolling Thunder," the phase two sustained bombing of North Vietnam. At dawn on March 2, 1965, a hundred American fighter-bombers crossed the DMZ and within minutes bridges, rail-lines, port and supply facilities at Vinh were flattened down. Rolling Thunder had begun its first stage.

Many in the U.S. Defense and State Departments, including the Joint Chiefs of Staff and MACV commander General Westmoreland in particular, argued the need for combat troops for South Vietnam. Ambassador Taylor, who opposed a ground war, finally agreed to the first landing of two U.S. Marine battalions in Danang on March 8, 1965. Thus, within the space of a week, President Johnson had decided to wage both an "air war" and a "ground war" in Vietnam. Weeks later, the Pentagon asked the president for forty-four additional Marine battalions. According to Bui Diem, then chief of staff of Premier Phan Huy Quat, U.S. combat troops grew to 82,000 in the first six weeks, 120,000 within four months, 184,000 within that first year (1965), 300,000 by mid–1966 and more than 500,000 by 1967, when he became ambassador to Washington. From the beginning of 1965, General Westmoreland, COMUSMACV, had taken primary steps for a ground war. In addition to the U.S. combat troops in Vietnam, the United States' allies in the Asia-Pacific region and the SEATO nations, sharing a secret commitment with the United States, sent combat troops or Peace Corps staff units to South Vietnam. Nearly 60,000 allied combat troops from Australia, New-Zealand, and South Korea, and Peace Corps from the Philippines and Thailand were placed under the command of General Westmoreland, plus 500,000 of the ARVN in joint operations with the U.S. combat forces since January 1966.

Westmoreland's plan consisted of three stages: (1) securing base areas; (2) deep patrolling and an offensive phase; and (3) search and destroy operations. Although this way of conducting the war has been called "Westmoreland War" by many American historians, the label is inappropriate. As field commander, General Westmoreland had to perform his duty in accordance with the real military situations in South Vietnam. His search and destroy strategy was needed for South Vietnam to stand three years after the death of Ngo Dinh Diem and the abandonment of the Strategic Hamlets strategy in the countryside. When more than four NVA regular divisions infiltrated South Vietnam from 1964 to 1965, the number of communist forces, including the Liberation Army, rose to more than 120,000 men who were armed with modern weapons from the communist bloc. They began their second phase, the "war of movement," in the South and controlled the Central Highlands and the Mekong Delta, except for the province and district urban areas. They created several secret zones (mật-khu) or war zones around Saigon. These included War-Zone D and War-Zone Duong Minh Chau in Bien-Hoa, Binh-Duong and Tay-Ninh Provinces, secret zones Tam-giac-sat and Long-nguyen in Binh-Duong and Binh-Long Provinces, and the Rung-Sat secret zone right at the door of Saigon Naval Port.

General Westmoreland's first search and destroy operation swept War-Zone D on June 27, 1965. By continuing these operations, in just over one year he pushed all communist regular units to their sanctuaries in Cambodia and Laos. In the meantime, he reorganized the ARVN into the RVNAF (Republic of Vietnam Armed Forces) and doubled its strength to more than 500,000 men in 1965, and to almost one million by the end of 1967. However, the war that Westmoreland really wanted was not in South Vietnam but was in the southern part of Laos and North Vietnam. General Westmoreland's most significant vision was to urge President Johnson to rally the U.S. public behind the U.S. war in Vietnam. Unfortunately, while he commanded U.S. troops in South Vietnam, the bureaucrats in Washington fought the war in Vietnam. Thus, it became the "Lunch Bunch War" instead of the "Westmoreland War."

General Maxwell D. Taylor left Vietnam in July 1965, after reluctantly receiving the 101st Airborne Division's landing at Cam-Ranh Bay. General William C. Westmoreland, as MACV commander, had to greet Henry Cabot Lodge, who returned to Saigon as ambassador. The general had to endure the effects of the "Rolling Thunder" air campaign that pushed Hanoi not to retreat from the war but to advance into the South by developing the Ho Chi Minh Trail and deploying more NVA divisions to South Vietnam. In 1966 this escalation of North Vietnam's strength in the South through the trail forced the United States to establish the "McNamara Line." Thus, Westmoreland had to accept a complicated defensive war in South Vietnam while his initiatives to cut the trail were rejected by the "Lunch Powers" in Washington. This resulted in the communist Tet Offensive that completely extinguished President Johnson's morale.

THE ROLLING THUNDER AIR CAMPAIGN

The Rolling Thunder air campaign widened the war to North Vietnam while maintaining Johnson's "limitation" notion. Retired U.S. Army lt. general Philip B. Davidson, former chief of staff of J2-MACV, and retired U.S. Air Force colonel Jacksel Broughton (author of *Going Downtown: The War Against Hanoi and Washington*) named this Johnson notion "gradualism." General Davidson writes: "This strategy was one of 'gradualism' ... [intended] not to apply maximum force toward the military to defeat the adversary; rather it must be to employ force skillfully along a continuous spectrum ... in order to exert the desired effect on the adversary's will. In plain English, it meant that you start operations against an enemy by a limited attack, gradually increasing the pressure until the adversary does what you want him to do. It is, in essence, the use of limited means to attain a limited end."[1] In the August 1994 issue of *Vietnam Magazine* Colonel Broughton elaborated on the reasons for the failure of the Rolling Thunder air campaign against North Vietnam in an article entitled "Wasted Air Power." According to Broughton, Rolling Thunder's first phase, which lasted from March of

1965 through March of 1968, was theoretically launched to interdict North Vietnam's capability to wage war in South Vietnam. Its efforts would concentrate on North Vietnam's potential means of waging war without restriction of targets. But the bureaucrats in Washington neglected this important issue. The recommendations of military commanders were ignored. Admiral Grant Sharp, commander in chief of the U.S. Pacific Fleet, who was in charge of the Rolling Thunder air campaign, proposed a list of 94 targets related to the "six primary systems" in North Vietnam that should be promptly and decisively destroyed to prevent the North Vietnamese from supporting their forces and continuing the war in South Vietnam. These systems included the electrical networks, the limited industries with warmaking capabilities, the transportation network, the air bases and training centers, the petroleum, oil and lubricant facilities, and the constantly improving Soviet- and China-sponsored air defense network. After his proposal list was processed through the Joint Chiefs of Staff (JCS) it was rejected by the "Lunch Bunch," or delayed until the end of 1968. The Lunch Powers themselves chose the targets to be struck by air. Colonel Broughton estimated that if in the early stages of the Rolling Thunder air campaign, the United States had concentrated its effort to eliminate these systems, when the North air defense network was weak or nonexistent, the course of the war would have drastically changed.

In addition to these "six primary systems," two more arterial strategic networks in North Vietnam should have been considered: the railroad network from China to Hanoi and the sea transport that conveyed war goods from the Soviet Union to Hai-Phong Harbor in North Vietnam. Hanoi was almost totally dependent on these communist nations for economic and military aid to sustain the war, so these supply routes were crucial for a prolonged war.

In the beginning of the 1960s, the Sino-Soviet rift threatened problems for Hanoi's receipt of economic and military aid from China and the Soviet Union. Ho Chi Minh formulated a strategy to ensure the continual support from both Beijing and Moscow. War goods from China went to Vietnam via the Nanning-Hanoi and Kunming-Hanoi railway lines and by eight major roads to North Vietnam, with 80 percent of goods coming through railways and 20 percent by truck or bicycle. Roughly 80 percent of war goods from the Soviet Union in 1965 went by sea transport to Hai-Phong Harbor.

In 1963, Admiral Thomas Moorer, commander in chief of the U.S. Pacific Command, proposed mining Hai-Phong Harbor. But his proposal was passed over in favor of the air campaign to interdict the supply railways from China only. The Rolling Thunder campaign was later taken in this sense, and Hai-Phong Harbor remained intact until May of 1972. Allan B. Calhamer, a military historian, remarked in an April 1998 magazine article that "the United States feared that if, in response to closing of Hai-Phong Harbor, China permitted the Soviet Union to ship to North Vietnam by rail, China and the Soviet Union might simply draw closer together diplomatically."[2] A more accurate explanation was that the Lunch Bunch feared that a U.S. blockade of Hai-Phong Harbor would provoke a U.S.–U.S.S.R. confrontation. Thus, the two railroad lines from China to Hanoi became the main targets of the Rolling Thunder air campaign while the main purpose was more to scare North Vietnam into submission than to destroy targets. Colonel Broughton summed up the strategy of the Lunch Bunch: "They stuck with the 'gradualism,' which simply means don't hurt the enemy too much, then back off and see if they're ready to quit."[3]

To pursue their initial goals, Washington bureaucrats placed a number of restrictions on all air force and navy bomber and fighter pilots who participated the air campaign. First, they were forbidden to enter the restricted zones composed of a ten-mile circle around Hanoi and five-mile circle around Hai-Phong. Second, all American pilots were not allowed to strike MIG fighter facilities or to shoot MIGs on the ground if these Soviet-built fighter aircraft were not in action. Third, the American pilots were not permitted to attack a Surface to Air Missile (SAM) site in North Vietnam unless it was operational, which meant that it was firing missiles at U.S. fighters and bomber aircraft. During the first days of the Rolling Thunder bombings some wrong hits on friendly foreign embassies and hospitals in Hanoi resulted in civilian casualties. Hanoi immediately launched a diplomatic propaganda campaign against the United States. Secretary of Defense McNamara responded by increasing the restricted zone around Hanoi to a 30-mile circle. In addition, to prevent U.S. pilots from offending the Chinese population to the north of the China-Vietnam border, McNamara created a 30-mile-deep restricted buffer zone across the Vietnam-China border. These increasingly queer restrictions gave advantage to Hanoi in its anti-air actions and induced more casualties and losses for U.S. pilots and aircraft. American strategic bombers and tactical fighters had then only a ten-mile active portion in the middle of the 70-mile railroad from the Chinese border to Hanoi. On this ten-mile stretch between the northern restricted buffer zone and the southern restricted circle around Hanoi, there was an average of one anti-aircraft gun every 48 feet.

To organize the air-defense network against the Rolling Thunder campaign, the leaders in Hanoi ordered their armed forces to move military equipment and supplies into populated areas and set up anti-aircraft guns in the center of villages and on the roofs of hospitals. Relying on aid from China and the Soviet Union, they increased their air-defense web with an enormous number of SAMs, anti-aircraft artillery such as 37mm and 57mm guns, 80mm to 100-plus-mm radar-controlled guns, and a number of MIGs. Broughton remarked that after 1966 North Vietnam had the most formidable anti-air defense in the history of aerial warfare.[4] The dispersion of war equipment, materiel, and supplies permitted Hanoi to conserve enough potential to support its forces in South Vietnam for a prolonged war.

To sum up, the first phase of the Rolling Thunder campaign failed after 72 pauses and 17 cease-fires. North Vietnam was not forced to the negotiating table. On the contrary, the bombing strengthened popular support for the VWP leaders by rousing nationalist and patriotic enthusiasm to resist the American air attack on their motherland. The CIA reported on March 16, 1966, that "although the movement and supplies has been hampered and made somewhat more difficult [by our bombing], the communists have been able to increase the flow of supplies and manpower to South Vietnam. Air attacks almost certainly cannot bring about a meaningful reduction in the current level at which essential supplies and men flow into South Vietnam."[5] The Rolling Thunder air campaign ended on November 1, 1968. A special report from the DIA revealed that from 1965 to 1968 about 643,000 tons of bombs were dropped on North Vietnam targets, caused nearly 80,000 North Vietnamese casualties, including 80 percent civilians, but the United States lost 922 aircraft. The number of pilots dead and arrested was undisclosed. The Johnson Administration never achieved its intended objective with the Rolling Thunder air campaign due to a lack of focus on the politically accurate purposes and strategically crucial targets.

Another air campaign, code-named Igloo-White began at the same time as the Rolling Thunder air campaign. Targeting Laos, the operation was designed to cut the NVA supply line to South Vietnam. By early 1966, however, the CIA and DIA concluded that these air campaigns could not deter the flow of manpower and supplies along the Ho Chi Minh Trail.

In South Vietnam, General Westmoreland argued with Washington that a ground blockade of the Ho Chi Minh Trail would produce better results than bombing either North Vietnam or the trail. He proposed that American ground troops would enter Laotian territory deep enough to cut this NVA arterial route to South Vietnam and, in early 1966, prepared plans to make this happen. His master plan was to repair and develop the international Highway 9 from Quang-Tri in Central Vietnam through the central part of the Laotian panhandle to Savannakhet, on the east bank of the Mekong River. Westmoreland estimated he needed at least a corps-size force of three divisions to maintain the trail block. His proposed east-west line ran perpendicular to the projection of the Harriman Line (see Map #3) to cut the Ho Chi Minh Trail in the southern part of Laos. The war then would be a front-line battle along route number 9 and the Communists of North Vietnam could not deny their "invasion of Laos." Also, the war would not be prolonged in South Vietnam. Westmoreland's plan was supported by ambassador Ellsworth Bunker, who had recently replaced Henry Cabot Lodge in Saigon. Later, Bunker disclosed: "Shortly after I arrived, I sent a message to the President urging that we go into Laos. If we cut the Ho Chi Minh Trail, the Viet-cong — I thought — would wither on the vine. What kept them going were supplies, weapons, and ammunition from Hanoi."[6]

Another American general who had a strategically analogous vision was General Lewis W. Walt, commander of the 73,000 U.S. Marines in the critical I Corps & Region comprising the five northernmost provinces of South Vietnam. Indeed, from mid–1965 to mid–1967 General Walt had proposed the Pentagon permit the Marines enter Laos and cross the DMZ. This proposition reinforced Westmoreland's view on the battlegrounds of the Indochina-theater. These two generals were the right men on the battlefield but were apparently not the right men to decide how to wage the war. Other military leaders in the Pentagon and in the U.S. Pacific Command also urged President Johnson to consider invading Laos, Cambodia, or even North Vietnam, but Johnson and McNamara felt that such a widening war would intensify the situation in Southeast Asia and worsen the present stalemate in Indochina. Washington, hamstrung by Harriman's false neutrality ploy and Ambassador Sullivan's opposition, that invading Laos would violate its supposed neutrality, and fearing an escalation leading to Chinese intervention, rejected these proposals. Thus, while the United States tried to limit the ground war to the boundaries of South Vietnam, the North Vietnamese strategy encompassed all of Indochina as their battleground. And since Westmoreland's plan to invade Laos was rejected by Washington, the commander of the MACV had to fight a defensive war in South Vietnam.

Responding to the U.S. airstrikes on North Vietnam, in the first half of 1966, Hanoi increased its infiltration of supplies, equipment, and troops to South Vietnam by 120 to 150 percent compared to the previous year. To divert official U.S. attention away from the NVA flow of infiltration along the Ho Chi Minh Trail to the South's Corps & Regions II, III, and IV, Vo Nguyen Giap sent the 324B NVA Division to the DMZ and began massing forces in the northern provinces of the South Vietnam's I Corps & Region. The 324B Division infiltrated deeply into the area southeast of the DMZ while other NVA heavy artillery units deployed at least 130 pieces of Soviet 152mm and 130mm guns along the northern bank of the Ben-Hai River. The NVA artillery had played a major role in Giap's strategic and tactic operations at Dien-Bien-Phu, and that battle had given the VWP one half of Vietnam in 1954. Now, the fact that Giap put his best artillery units at the DMZ made the American leaders to think that Giap might do something new, or the war would change into a new phase. But sticking to the defensive concept, the Johnson administration had few options to choose to deal with the new military situation in South Vietnam. From July of 1966, General Westmoreland was ordered to send the U.S. 3rd Marine Division to the DMZ to open search and destroy operations and establish a series of base-camps and fire-bases along Highway 9, stretching from the coastal lowlands to the west highlands around Khe-Sanh, on the Vietnamese and Laotian frontiers. McNamara thought that the most important measure to prevent NVA infiltration into Quang-Tri, the northernmost province of the I Region, was to clear out NVA base camps along the DMZ by deploying the Marines to the region.

The myopic vision of the civilian leaders positioned the best Marine infantry "maneuver" battalions in base-camps from Dong-Ha, located about 12 miles from the coast, to Khe-Sanh in the west highlands, tying them down rather than harnessing their ability in the battlefield. The main mission of these implant battalions was to defend their base-camps and patrol their respective portions of Highway 9 to secure the supply from the forward headquarters of the 3rd Marine Division at Dong-Ha to their bases. In the meantime, General Giap was maintaining intensive artillery fire on Marine fixed positions and infantry ambushes against the Marine supply-convoys along Highway 9. From mid–1966 through the summer of 1967, Giap never launched a direct assault on the Marine bases. Some military writers implied that the Marines were posted in Con-Thien or Khe-Sanh conforming to the "set-piece strategy" of General Westmoreland. From the summer of 1967, the Marine force increased to 21 infantry battalions and nine artillery battalions and was coupled with two Vietnamese Marine battle groups at Gio-Linh, on the front-line DMZ.

THE "MCNAMARA LINE"

At a meeting of the U.S. Joint Chiefs of Staff in early March of 1966, McNamara divulged his plan to construct a high-tech barrier across the DMZ to stop the flow of NVA infiltrations of troops and war equipment into I Corps & Region of South Vietnam and to reinforce the Marine defensive system at the DMZ front-line. The "barrier" had initially been proposed by Roger Fisher, a Harvard Law School professor, submitted to the U.S. Department of Defense, as a measure to deal with the NVA infiltration down to the Ho Chi Minh Trail and across the DMZ. But with the appearance of the 324B NVA Division in the southern part of the DMZ, and Giap's artillery units on the northern bank of the Ben-Hai River in April 1966, McNamara turned the proposal over to the Jason Group, composed of more than forty academic scientists, with his view concentrated on the construction of a barrier only at the DMZ. Thus, General Giap's diversion was effective in drawing the attention of American civilian leaders' to the DMZ instead of the Ho Chi Minh Trail; North Vietnam would send more troops, war equipment, and supplies to other South Vietnamese military regions for a new offensive phase. The future McNamara Line was theoretically ineffective before construct even began.

After a short period of study, the Jason Group proposed an infiltration barrier consisting of two components: (1) an anti-personnel barrier manned by troops across the southern side of the DMZ from the South China Sea to Laos; and (2) an anti-vehicular barrier, primarily an aerial operation, imposed in and over the Laotian panhandle to interdict traffic on the Ho Chi Minh Trail.[7] The features common to both barriers were remote acoustic and chemical sensors, button bomblets, and gravel mines. These new technologic sensors were to help identify NVA personnel and truck movements for U.S. airstrikes or for artillery fires. However, the final plan of the barrier approved by McNamara in the end of 1966, the III MAF Operation Plan 11-67, which was known as "Dye Maker" or the "McNamara Line," consisted of only an anti-infiltration barrier below the DMZ.

General Westmoreland ordered the Marines to implement the construction of the supposed linear barrier, which "consisted of a 600–1,000-meter-wide stretch of clear ground [or "trace"] containing barbed wire, minefields, sensors and watchtowers backed by a series of manned strong points. Behind the points would be a series of fire support bases to provide an interlocking pattern of artillery fire. This part of the system would begin at the coast of South Vietnam below the DMZ and continue westward across the coastal plain for about 30-

kilometers to the beginning of a more mountainous area. From that point to the Laotian border, the barrier would be less comprehensive," reported military writer Peter W. Brush in describing the McNamara Line.[8] The McNamara Line was anchored in the east of Gio-Linh, manned by ARVN units supported by U.S. Marine artillery, and in the west by the U.S. Marine base-camp Con-Thien.

The construction of the McNamara Line was divided into two phases. The first phase was to extend from April to November of 1967. The second phase would begin after the monsoon season of 1967 to be completed in July of 1968. However, monsoon rains and General Giap's large unit attacks on Marine base-camps along the DMZ during the summer of 1967 hampered construction efforts by the Marines.

Senior Marine commanders opposed the concept of a linear barrier and a system of marine strong points to block the NVA, believing these defensive systems would waste resources, tie down the Marines in the line of their vulnerable base-camps along the DMZ, and result in unnecessary U.S. casualties. However, facing serious difficulties, the Marines implemented their orders, continuing the construction of the McNamara Line and fighting to defend their base camps under the fierce attacks of the NVA.

Immediately after the Marine 11th Engineer Battalion and the Navy Seabees (engineers) began to construct the McNamara Line, General Giap launched a series of attacks on important U.S. Marine base camps and fired on prominent fire support bases along Highway 9, such as base-camp Con-Thien, outpost Khe-Sanh, fire-bases Calu, Rockpile and Carroll. These three firebases positioned a number of artillery 175mm self-propelled guns that would effectively support the farthest Marine base camp, Khe-Sanh on the west highlands. To prepare a careful diversion, Giap ordered his large units to attack Khe-Sanh in April and Con-Thien in May. Con-Thien was saved by a joint operation between the U.S. Marines and ARVN units, called "Operation Hickory," from May 18 to 25. In early August, Giap's infantry units ambushed a large U.S. Marine supply convoy of 85 trucks on Highway 9, west of fire base Calu, placing U.S. Marine base camps at Khe-Sanh under siege. Marine supply convoys to Khe-Sanh ended for some nine months. The Marines at the Khe-Sanh "set-piece" garrison were isolated, except for air support and supply. However, Con-Thien and Khe-Sanh were not the crucial targets of General Giap in this phase of attack.

According to several American historians, the massing of large NVA units and their attacks on Khe-Sanh and Con-Thien in I Region, on Dak-To in II Region, or on Loc-Ninh in III Region of South Vietnam, were only measures designed to test the ability of American large units and the response of the United States toward North Vietnam before the VWP would prepare a decisive strategy in South Vietnam and launch its winter-spring offensive campaign of 1967-1968. When the first phase of this winter-spring campaign began with the fierce attack again on Khe-Sanh, General Westmoreland put the construction of the McNamara Line on hold. He ordered all the sensors and related equipment that was supposed to be installed along the DMZ transferred to the Marines at Khe-Sanh to use in the defense systems around the base-camps. As a result, the construction of the McNamara Line at the DMZ lagged far behind schedule. But even had this linear barrier been constructed on time, it would have been misplaced.

In early 1966, the U.S. Joint Chiefs of Staff estimated that more American combat troops would be needed for the planned construction of the McNamara Line, to block the DMZ and the Vietnam-Laos border, and for Westmoreland's search and destroy operations. Westmoreland himself requested more than 420,000 American troops by the end of 1966. Westmoreland was determined not to turn over the tactical initiative to the enemy by digging in the U.S. troops on the defense. That was seen as a measure that would result in defeat. Instead, he turned the mission of safeguarding the military bases, cities, towns, provinces and districts over to the ARVN and put his combat units into hitting the enemy in tactical offensive operations. By the end of 1966, Westmoreland had completed about 300 sweep operations throughout the four military regions of South Vietnam, which drove back the NVA and the Liberation Front Army, or Viet-Cong units, to their secret sanctuaries along the borders of Vietnam and Cambodia, and Vietnam and Laos.

THE ESTABLISHMENT OF THE
SECOND REPUBLIC OF VIETNAM

The ARVN became the Republic of Vietnam Armed Forces (RVNAF). On June 19, 1965, the Armed Forces Council, led by General Nguyen van Thieu, assigned Thieu as president of the National Leadership Committee (Chủ-tịch Uỷ-ban Lãnh-đạo Quốc-gia) acting as chief of state; Air Force commander Major General Nguyen Cao Ky, was made president of the Central Executive Committee (Chủ-tịch Uỷ-ban Hành-pháp Trung-ương) acting as prime minister of the War Cabinet. Chief of state Phan Khac Suu and prime minister Phan Huy Quat had resigned after having political disagreements between them lasting many months. Many members, or ministers, of the War Cabinet were RVNAF generals. General Ky had a shrewd view of the United States "escalation" of combat troops in South Vietnam. He said: "When South Vietnam, as part of the free-world, was attacked by the communists with China and the Soviet Union behind them, I think it was the duty of America to come to the rescue."[9] In reality, it is unlikely that the United States involved prime minister Nguyen Cao Ky in the decision to escalate combat troops in South Vietnam. He was really just trying to cope with the United States' strategy and cooperating with American ambassador Lodge or General Westmoreland in the role of "leading the war" against the communists. He did not decide the strategy but he could facilitate logistical problems. General Westmoreland regarded Prime Minister Ky as highly intelligent, aggressive, and willing to fight the war against the communists, even in North Vietnam. He failed to understand Ky's arrogance.

On the Republic of Vietnam side at that time, many Ky supporters in the RVNAF regarded Ky as a dynamic, clever, and exquisite, but unpredictable, leader. They believed Ky had made timely decisions that would resolve the political and economical difficulties facing the South Vietnamese government during the two years of turmoil following the collapse of the First Republic.

The event that clearly proved Ky's ability was his hazardous handling of the "Buddhist Struggle Movement" in Central Vietnam in the summer of 1965. That summer, during Ky's inspection tour in Danang and Hue, he noticed that Lt. General Nguyen Chanh Thi, commander of I Corps & Region, intended to split from the coalition of generals in Saigon. He gave orders relieving Lt. General Thi from command on March 10 and appointing Brigadier General Nguyen Van Chuan in Thi's place. Immediately, Venerable Thich Tri Quang and other Buddhist leaders in Central Vietnam organized a fierce and coordinated reaction in Hue and Danang. They assembled a series of demonstrations and demanded General Ky resign and General Thi be reinstated. Thich Tri Quang also influenced Brigadier General Phan Xuan Nhuan, the 1st Infantry Division commander in Hue and Quang Tri, a number of other unit commanders in Danang, and its Mayor, Dr. Nguyen Van Mau. The protesters occupied many parts of the city and took over the city's broadcasting station, using it to deliver anti-government propaganda. Many were armed with military weapons and were prepared to resist the pacifying force of the government.

The uprising began to spread to Qui Nhon, Nha Trang, Da Lat, and even to Saigon. If this movement spread, it might lead to the total collapse of the government. Some speculated that this uprising was the result of the General Ky's decision to relieve General Thi; actually, it was rooted in another cause. A few Buddhist leaders wanted important decisions made by the government to be overseen by the United Buddhist Church. Previously, this issue had been posed to General Khanh by Thich Tri Quang and Thich Tam Chau in exchange for their support. Thus, Khanh's departure might have been also a reason for this Buddhist uprising.

On April 5, two Marine battalions were sent to Danang, but General Chuan could not control the violence. Saigon then successively sent General Huynh Van Cao and General Ton That Dinh to I Corps. Like Chuan, they both were born in Hue, but both of them were ineffective in improving the situation. In the meantime, from early April to mid–May, General Ky had many meetings with Thich Thien Minh and Thich Tam Chau, leaders of the United Buddhist Church, that did not lead to any satisfactory solution. Each time they arrived at a compromise, the United Buddhist Church's leaders added new demands, asking for several unfeasible social and political reforms. Finally, General Ky decided to take a hard course of action. On the night of May 14, General Ky called in General Cao Van Vien, chairman of the Joint General Staff, and Colonel Nguyen Ngoc Loan, chief of the Security Directorate and commander of the National Police. General Ky gave them orders to subdue the uprising. In the early morning of the following day, General Vien and Colonel Loan arrived at Danang with two other Marine battalions and some armored units dispatched from Saigon. Within three days, they had successfully put down the uprising. A number of Buddhist leaders, together with most of the unit commanders of the ARVN who took part in the uprising, were arrested. General Vien then went on to Hue and was reinforced with two additional Airborne battalions. He ordered day and night curfew and isolated Hue by cutting all supply and transportation routes to the city. Three days later, on May 22, Thich Tri Quang and Brigadier General Phan Xuan Nhuan surrendered. Venerable Thich Tri Quang was taken to Saigon and put under the care of Dr. Nguyen Duy Tai, head of the Duy Tan Hospital. The generals were put under Military Disciplinary Council and were retired. They included Generals Thi, Chuan, Cao, Dinh, and Nhuan. General Nguyen Chanh Thi left the country and went into exile in Washington, DC, under the sponsorship of the U.S. government. The other unit commanders and officers were disciplined but not many were discharged from military duties. By then, Brigadier General Hoang Xuan Lam, commander of the 2nd Infantry Division was promoted commander of the I Corps. From then until April 30, 1975, the United Buddhist Church leaders were more conciliatory toward the government of RVN and did not stage any more uprisings. As the result, the political situation was stable for several following years.

Although from the middle of 1965, before the election, General Thieu and General Ky were both considered to be the leaders of South Vietnam, in reality national power was in the hands of General Ky. Not long after the Council of Generals delegated national power to General Ky, as prime minister, he persuaded other generals to establish a supreme power organization. Called the "Directorate," this organization was composed of ten senior generals who shared power equally. These were the chief of the National Leadership Committee, chief of the National Executive Central Committee, minister of defense, chairman of the Joint General Staff, four corps commanders, and two other generals. The "Directorate" replaced the "Council of Generals" and was the new name of the National Leadership Committee. The majority of Directorate members consisted of the "Young Turks," who solidly supported General Ky. Consequently, General Ky held more power than General Thieu by influencing the Directorate, and by holding the War Cabinet. In the meantime, the Armed Forces Council was growing with 1600 generals, colonels, and lieutenant colonels of all branches of the armed forces who were commanding units from regiment — or equivalents and above. These three national organizations, the Directorate, the Armed Forces Council, and the War Cabinet, worked together under the leadership of the Directorate from 1965 until the formation of the Second Republic.

Neither General Ky nor General Thieu were involved in the strategic level of decision making about the war. The United States supported them with only limited military and economic aid. They were expected only to stabilize the political situation in South Viet Nam while the U.S. escalated its involvement in the war by sending more U.S. and Allied troops into Vietnamese battlefields. By then, the Johnson administration began to realize that a civilian government could not stabilize the volatile political situation in South Vietnam; however, keeping the War Cabinet would show contempt for democratic principles. It was a major obstacle to the Johnson administration's efforts to win popular support in both the U.S. and South Vietnam and to convince allied nations to take part in the war.

For these reasons, President Johnson's invitation to Generals Thieu and Ky to meet him and his aides in Honolulu on March 7, 1966, was not so surprising. Many issues were put on the table during the summit to define the nature of U.S. help and support for South Vietnam. Plans of rural construction, economic stabilization, and medical and educational development were drawn. However, the prime issue of this highest summit, though unknown to public, may have been the problem of establishing a lawful regime in South Vietnam.

Indeed, right after resolving the Buddhist Crisis, General Ky began laying the groundwork for the election of the National Constitutional Assembly. On September 1966, 85 percent of voters went to the ballot boxes and voted to elect 118 representatives for the new Assembly. By the end of 1966, the Assembly began to draft a new constitution. In order to improve the Directorate's effectiveness in coordinating with the Assembly, General Ky suggested the generals add to the Directorate several civilian experts and politicians. By March 15, 1967, the new constitution was approved by the Directorate. The new constitution prescribed a democratic government consisted of the Executive Branch, the Legislative Branch, and the Judicial Branch. The Executive Branch was to be led by the elected president and vice president, who would direct the government activities of the prime minister and the Cabinet, composed of many ministers. The Legislative Branch was composed of the Senate and the House of Representatives and held the ultimate national power. The Judicial Branch was led by a Supreme Court composed of nine judges. In theory, the Directorate and the Constitutional Assembly would be dissolved after the September 1967 national election when the new government became active.

Only a few days after the proclamation of the constitution for South Viet Nam, another summit took place between President Johnson and Generals Thieu and Ky in Guam. President Johnson complimented the generals for passing the new constitution for South Viet Nam. However, when asked about the conduct of the war, including General Ky's proposal to attack communist North Vietnam, President Johnson either avoided giving a direct answer or changed the subject. The Johnson administration only wanted the military leaders of South Vietnam to establish a constitutional government to stabilize the political situation and had no intention of letting them take charge of the fight against the communist North Vietnam. This policy of the President Johnson would lead to the loss of the war. If U.S. leaders had understood the importance of involving South Vietnam's leaders in the conduct of the war efforts, the outcome would have been different. And if the U.S. had let the leaders of South Vietnam develop their own strategy and only had provided them with support in modernizing their armed forces, providing abundant supplies and adequate air power, they would prob-

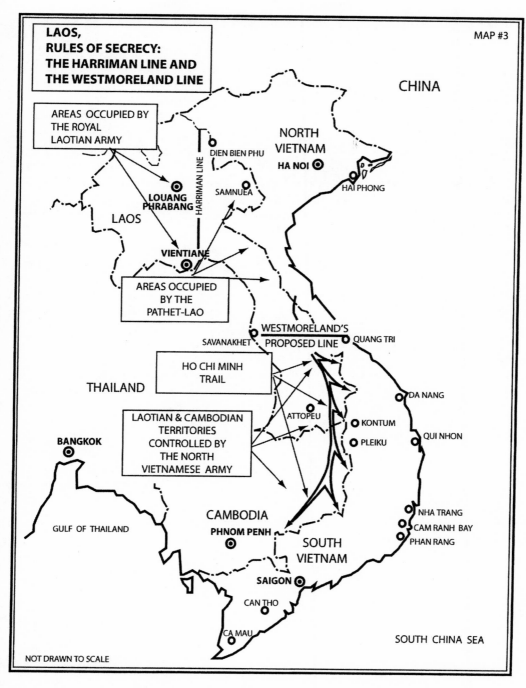

LAOS,
RULES OF SECRECY:
THE HARRIMAN LINE AND
THE WESTMORELAND LINE

MAP #3

AREAS OCCUPIED BY
THE ROYAL
LAOTIAN ARMY

CHINA

NORTH
VIETNAM

DIEN BIEN PHU

HA NOI

HARRIMAN LINE

SAMNUEA

HAI PHONG

LOUANG
PHRABANG

LAOS

VIENTIANE

AREAS OCCUPIED
BY THE
PATHET-LAO

WESTMORELAND'S
PROPOSED LINE

SAVANAKHET

QUANG TRI

HO CHI MINH
TRAIL

THAILAND

DA NANG

ATTOPEU

KONTUM

QUI NHON

LAOTIAN & CAMBODIAN
TERRITORIES
CONTROLLED BY
THE NORTH
VIETNAMESE ARMY

PLEIKU

BANGKOK

NHA TRANG

CAM RANH BAY

PHAN RANG

CAMBODIA

GULF OF THAILAND

PHNOM PENH

SOUTH
VIETNAM

SAIGON

CAN THO

CA MAU

SOUTH CHINA SEA

NOT DRAWN TO SCALE

ably have been able to fight the communists in any front; because no one knew how to win over the North Vietnam communists better than the South Vietnam leaders at the time.

After returning from the summit in Guam, both General Thieu and General Ky were busy in the campaign for the presidency. A schism began to develop in the relationship between Thieu and Ky. General Thieu knew that if he let the Armed Forces Council or the Directorate decide, General Ky would certainly be nominated for the top spot on the ticket. General Thieu then decided to campaign as an independent candidate with Trinh Khanh Vang as vice president. General Ky reacted by forming his own ticket with Nguyen Van Loc. Both Vang and Loc were politicians. The generals then tried to bridge the difference by convening a meeting for the Armed Forces Council and the Directorate. The reasonable result of the meeting was a single military ticket with General Ky as the presidential nominee and General Thieu as vice presidential nominee. But before the generals could declare the results of the meeting, General Ky, moved by General Thieu's speech and tears, declared he would give the presidential nomination to General Thieu. This may have been Ky's greatest mistake, and it was one of the moments that significantly contributed to his political downfall.

The election was held on September 3, 1967, and the result was as expected. The military ticket of General Thieu and General Ky won the election among the ten different tickets. In the Senate race, there were six tickets with 60 senators declared winners among 62 tickets that had been listed in the ballot. After the certification of the results, the Constitutional Assembly dissolved and was replaced by the newly elected Congress. Nguyen Van Loc was appointed prime minister and was to form a new cabinet. Thus, the Second Republic of South Vietnam was born with General Thieu as the president, General Ky as vice president, a civilian cabinet, a Congress, and an armed forces of 650,000 strong. The political situation gradually improved, but the social problems started mounting as the U.S. government started pouring in "green dollars" and American GIs. The rising star of the South Vietnam political stage, General Nguyen Cao Ky, began to fade. President Thieu slowly built up a network of support for himself. A number of generals such as General Tran Thien Khiem, General Do Cao Tri, and General Nguyen Huu Co were recalled to Saigon to hold important positions. A number of generals became politicians and became senators like General Tran Van Don, General Ton That Dinh, and General Huynh Van Cao. By then the struggle for power in South Vietnam became more subtle and conciliatory. Later, General Duong Van Minh also returned and decided the fate of South Vietnam.

9

The 1968 Tet Offensive: The Turning Point

Traditionally, the Vietnamese, like the Chinese, celebrate the first week of each new lunar year with a festival, or "Tet." New Year's Day, or Nguyen-Dan, is the most important day of the year. Nguyen-Dan varies every year and falls between the last week of January to the last week of February on the Western calendar. In 1968, the Nguyen-Dan came on January 31. There was a cease-fire of 36 hours during the Tet of 1968. Despite the cease-fire, the communists launched brutal attacks on 33 provinces, 64 districts, and 29 important military installations over four military regions in South Vietnam. Saigon, including the American Embassy, was hit during the pre-dawn hours of January 31. This communist campaign, the so-called General Offensive and General Uprising (Tổng Công-Kích & Tổng Nổi-Dậy, or TCK & TND), or 1968 Tet Offensive, according to American historians, was the turning point of the Second Vietnam War.

The Communist Party, or the Vietnamese Workers' Party (VWP), launched the TCK & TND campaign after a long discussion among its Politburo members and after a long military process that had begun in the beginning of 1966. This campaign was Ho Chi Minh's last before his death in 1969. Ho alluded to this secret war policy in his speech to the nation on Nguyen-Dan 1967. Ho called the people of North and South Vietnam to make a united effort for a new phase of war, which was assumed to be an initiation of "fighting and negotiating," to acquire the final goals of a "victorious liberation" of South Vietnam, a complete reunification of the country, and a total realization of a beautiful Vietnamese socialist society. The VWP implemented Ho's policy with Party Resolution 13 in July and Resolution 14 in October 1967. These two resolutions adopted the strategy of using the TCK & TND to "liberate" South Vietnam.

PLANNING

NVA General Nguyen van Vinh, commander of the VWP Central Office in South Vietnam (COSVN), came closest to discerning Ho's war policy. In a meeting with staff members in April 1966, General Vinh predicted that since the United States widened the air war to the North and escalated sending combat troops to the South, the VWP and the COSVN would study American policy and strategy. In the first phase, the flexible response phase, the United States would enjoy the upper hand. In the second phase, "fighting while negotiating" would be Hanoi's war strategy. Based on Ho's initiative, the VWP formulated a joint military-political-diplomatic strategy to face the U.S. escalation of the war. General Vinh concluded that at diplomatic and political warfare, the Americans were unsuitable. He said: "In a war of position, they can defeat us. But with our present tactics, we will win and they will be defeated.

It is the same as if we force them to eat with chopsticks. If we eat with spoons and forks like them, we will be defeated, if chopsticks are used ... they are no match for us," Vinh then explained "to defeat the enemy in the South is to basically ... smash the Americans' aggressive will ... we can push the Americans out of Vietnam by coordinating the political struggle with diplomacy [make them eat with chopsticks]."[1] Pushing the Americans out of Vietnam was the VWP's primary effort, but the reunification of Vietnam was its crucial purpose. Military measures were the primary means to satisfy their political and diplomatic goals. Therefore, the communists would not stop at this phase without military victory. North Vietnam had to concentrate their efforts on offensive campaigns, among which the Tet Offensive was very important. Vinh disclosed this campaign to his COSVN staff members: "With regard to the General Offensive [TCK] and General Uprising [TND], it was requested that a concrete plan, including the quantity of weapons needed, the number of armed forces needed, etc..., be made known in order to carry out the undertaking confidently. For secrecy's sake, it is not yet necessary to reveal information on these matters."[2]

In short, NVA General Nguyen van Vinh, COSVN commander — the highest VWP politico-military authority in South Vietnam in 1966–1967 — saw two ways for the communists to wage war in the South: (1) fighting and (2) negotiating. If fighting would allow them to win the final military victory, they would fight with maximum strength. If fighting would give them a moderate military victory, they might negotiate for a withdrawal of U.S. forces from South Vietnam. Indeed, throughout the summer of 1967, the VWP and COSVN prepared the National Liberation Front's leaders and cadres for a "coalition government" in case "negotiations would be made and treaties would be signed" alongside preparations to undertake weighty offensive operations, before starting the decisive TCK & TND campaign of 1968.

However, according to recently disclosed documents from Hanoi, after officially adopting the TCK & TND offensive strategy in the South by issuing Resolution 13 in July of 1967, General Vo Nguyen Giap, with his natural prudence, was hesitant to conduct a premature offensive without the possibility of winning. Giap believed that an American ground attack northward through the DMZ would be the logical next step for General Westmoreland after the Marine base camp Con-Thien was attacked by NVA large units in May 1967. He insisted that the defense of North Vietnam come first. But as commander in chief of the People's Army, Giap was obligated to implement VWP decisions. Giap had dispersed his artillery and infantry large units along the northern bank of the Ben-Hai River to prevent such an attack and to make a diversion in order to reinforce troops and equipment to the COSVN through the Ho Chi Minh Trail in preparation for the TCK & TND. But he had to again test the reaction of the United States, before the VWP Politburo would make their final decisions.

TESTING CAMPAIGNS

Giap's testing campaign was drawn up. Some American historians call it the First phase of the communist winter-spring campaign of 1967-1968. This testing campaign would therefore resolve two imperative demands: (1) to know exactly the Johnson administration's will for the war in Vietnam, and (2) to know Westmoreland's tactics and ability to deploy American troops over four military regions of South Vietnam. In September 1967, Giap launched forceful attacks on U.S. Marine positions along the DMZ with NVA large units, which were supported by artillery long range 130mm guns on the other side of the Ben-Hai River. Con-Thien base-camp was under fierce enemy assaults continuously from September 27. Attacks and counter-attacks were furious and both sides sustained enormous casualties. General Westmoreland declared that B-52 strikes on the NVA units at Con-Thien were devastating for the enemy and Con-Thien a "Dien-Bien-Phu in reverse"; which meant the General considered Con-Thien (and later Khe-Sanh) a second Dien-Bien-Phu, a "set-piece-outpost" staging "to wait for the enemy" to come, surround, and attack as he wanted. General Giap then would reason he could expect Westmoreland to continue operating in a defensive and reactive persistence instead of sending U.S. troops on the offensive across the DMZ or conducting a full scale invasion of North Vietnam. Westmoreland's reaction at Con-Thien proved that the United States did not have the will to attack North Vietnam by ground forces. Hanoi leaders concluded that the Johnson administration responded as they had hoped. The first demand was solved.

The VWP Politburo grew confident in the TCK & TND campaign, issuing Party Resolution 14 in October 1967, while Giap's testing campaign continued in South Vietnam. Giap opened three new fronts in three South Vietnamese military regions. Common opinion suggested this was done to test Westmoreland's defense systems and to draw American large units from urban areas in order to prepare concrete plans for the future TCK & TND.

In South Vietnamese III Corps & Region, in the late September 1967, COSVN was ordered to send its 9th Division and a regiment of the 5th Division into Binh-Long, Phuoc-Long and Binh-Duong Provinces harassing the U.S. Army 1st Infantry Division, or the Big Red One, and trying to overrun the advanced headquarters of the ARVN 5th Division at Song Be. In late October, these VC units tried to swamp U.S. Green Beret camp at Loc-Tan on international Route 7, 15 miles north of Loc-Ninh. At the same time, Loc-Ninh district headquarters, 75 miles northwest of Saigon, was attacked and overrun by other VC large forces. General Westmoreland immediately sent ten U.S. battalions into the region for several screening operations. A body count of nearly nine hundred VC was reported at the end of these operations and the 9th VC Division was pushed back to the Cambodian borderline. In II Corps & Region, in the first week of November 1967, four NVA infantry regiments plus a rocket artillery regiment approached Dak-To on National Road 14, 35 miles northwest of Kontum Province, and attempted to attack Dak-To and the U.S. Green Berets CIDG camps within the area. General Westmoreland moved the U.S. Army 4th Infantry Division to Dak-To, the 173rd Airborne Brigade, a brigade of the 1st Cavalry Division, and six ARVN battalions to the vicinity. In mid–November, NVA artillery rockets hit the 4th Division's base camp and the crowded airfield, destroying two C-130 and triggering a 1,000-ton explosion in the ammunition dump. At the same time, another NVA large force ambushed the reinforcements for two battalions of the 173rd Airborne Brigade. After 50 hours of impetuous fighting, the U.S. Airborne Brigade lost 124 killed and 347 wounded, the largest number of casualties since U.S. combat troops entered the battlefields in South Vietnam. The enemy casualties numbered 1,400 killed. These communist attacks in II and III Corps & Regions from September to November, were later explained by General Giap: "At the battles of Loc-Ninh and Dak-To in the Central Highlands in 1967, we were able to test our forces against defended positions. The next step was to move a larger force toward Khe-Sanh. Again the U.S. imperialists responded."[3]

In I Corps & Region, in December 1967, more than three NVA divisions began to mass around U.S. Marine outpost at Khe-Sanh: the 304th Division, which had fought at Dien-Bien-Phu, commanded by General Hoang-Dan; the 320th "Delta" Division commanded by General Sung-Lam; the 325th "Gold Star" commanded by General Nguyen Huu An; and a regiment of the 324th Division plus several artillery battalions. These large units were under the command of General Tran Qui Hai, Assistant Chief of Staff of the North Vietnamese

People's Army, who was newly assigned as commander of the "Route 9 Front." Thus, except for the 304th NVA Division, which had been at Khe-Sanh since the beginning of 1967, Giap moved to the region three more regular divisions. Later Giap disclosed his intentions: "Our main emphasis was to draw the American units away from the populated areas in the lowlands and, by doing so, make it easier for the Liberation Front to control the people. We deployed two divisions into the northern provinces of Quang-Tri and Thua-Thien, which drew in American troops from other areas."[4]

KHE SANH OR SAIGON, WHERE WAS THE COMMUNIST MAIN TARGET?

A careful study of Giap's deployment of NVA regular units around Khe-Sanh and the two northernmost provinces of the I Corps & Region, while leaving the lowlands for the Liberation Front units, made clear how the VWP would conduct the war in their offensive campaign TCK & TND. The VWP would give the Liberation Front Army, or VC units, then built up to regimental size and divisional size, the job of attacking South Vietnamese cities, towns, and military installations. The NVA regular large units would confront the U.S. forces at the border, on the DMZ, or within Quang-Tri and Thua-Thien Provinces. Later, U.S. military intelligence discovered that Giap had kept more than a corps-sized unit on the other side of the DMZ to prevent an American invasion of the North and as a counter-attack force. In the end of December, Giap completed his dispersal of NVA regular divisions along the DMZ and around Khe-Sanh and attempted to send other divisions to infiltrate deeply into Quang-Tri and Thua-Thien.

As the enemy built up at Khe-Sanh, General Westmoreland, believing that the climactic showdown of the war would take place mainly in the northernmost provinces of South Vietnam, planned for a massive and complicated concentration of American troops in I Corps & Region. In late November 1967, Westmoreland began to pull the best American units from II and III Corps & Regions and move them to the I Corps & Region, especially in Quang-Tri and the DMZ. By mid–December, Westmoreland had 50 U.S. battalions in place in the I Corps Region. He tripled the Marine defensive forces at Khe-Sanh Garrison by sending in five more Marine battalions and a Vietnamese Ranger battalion, and placed them under the command of an expert Marine officer, Colonel David Lownds. The general also reinforced a great number of U.S. Army artillery 175mm field guns to fire-bases Calu, Rockpile, and Carroll while preparing a careful aerial firepower plan, code-named Niagara, to support Khe-Sanh in case of an enemy attack like Dien-Bien-Phu. In mid–December, Westmoreland canceled projected operations in the II Corps & Region's Central Highlands and ordered the 1st Cavalry Division to move into Thua-Thien Province with a brigade of the 101st Airborne Division. Before that, a brigade of the South Korean Blue Dragon Division and two best ARVN large units, the Airborne Division and the Marine Division had been sent to Quang-Tri Province. Robert Pisor, a war correspondent in Vietnam, commented critically that in the last week of January 1968, General Westmoreland had in these northernmost provinces of South Vietnam a "half of all the American combat troops of South Vietnam. But while Westmoreland was moving tens of thousands of combat troops to the north, Vo Nguyen Giap was moving tens of thousands of combat troops to the south for the boldest stroke of the war: the Tet Offensive. Khe-Sanh was a feint, a magician's snap of the fingers to freeze the audience's eyes."[5] Many military writers did not think Khe-Sanh was a second "Dien-Bien-Phu," but at that time all Washington authorities' eyes were on Khe-Sanh.

Later, General Westmoreland explained his decision of to move American combat troops to I Corps & Region: "Some have claimed that the enemy instigated a series of border fights, Khe-Sanh in particular, to draw my forces away from the cities. I believe the opposite was true. The attack on the cities, and the earlier attacks at Loc-Ninh at III Corps in October 1967 and Dak-To in II Corps in November 1967 were designed strategically to divert our attention away from the vulnerable northern provinces of I Corps."[6]

In reality, in conducting the TCK & TND campaign in South Vietnam in January 1968, North Vietnamese communists hoped not only to gain a tactical military victory over the U.S. forces at Khe-Sanh or on the DMZ, but also to gain a strategic political victory over South Vietnam. This would assist them in future peace-talks as envisioned by Ho Chi Minh's "fighting while negotiating" with the purpose to "push the Americans out of Vietnam." If they could overrun the U.S. Marines at Khe-Sanh, it would be a second "Dien-Bien-Phu." Even if they could not defeat U.S. Marines at Khe-Sanh, with their attacks on Saigon and all over South Vietnamese provinces and cities, they would show their ability to wage a protracted war. They would win a political and psychological victory coming to the negotiating table for a "neutral government" solution in South Vietnam with the sharing of power between the current South Vietnamese government and the National Liberation Front. Capturing the two northernmost provinces of South Vietnam was another possibility of their offensive campaign. Accordingly, the VWP ordered Tran Bach Dang, a high-ranking political operator of the COSVN to make secret contacts with the U.S. embassy in Saigon for a "political solution." The VWP Resolution 14 stated: "The upcoming General Offensive & General Uprising will be a period, a process, of intensive and complicated strategic offensives by the military, political and diplomatic means ... a process in which we will attack and advance on the enemy continuously both militarily and politically as well as a process in which the enemy will ferociously counter-attack in order to wrest back and reoccupy positions that would have been lost."[7]

General Vo Nguyen Giap said: "Waging war is not easy, you know.... We chose Tet because, in war, you must seize the propitious moment, when time and space are propitious."[8] Tet 1968 was a propitious moment for the communists to open fire; 1968 was also a general election year in the United States. The Communist Offensive Campaign, or TCK & TND, was then realized under two planning phases:

- Phase I: From January to March 1968. Targets of the NVA regular units: U.S. Marine garrison Khe-Sanh on the western highlands of the DMZ, U.S. Marine base camp at Con-Thien in the center, ARVN Marine base camp at Gio-Linh in the lowlands east coast, and Quang-Tri and Thua-Thien capital cities. Targets of the Liberation Front Army, or VC units: Saigon and several provincial cities, districts and ARVN installations, including the U.S. embassy in Saigon.
- Phase II: NVA regular large sized units would cross the DMZ and assault the U.S. and ARVN forces after the General Uprising of the South Vietnamese people had begun. This plan could not be realized because there was not a general uprising of the people in the South and after the defeat of both the NVA in I Corps & Region and the VC in Saigon and other military regions. There were only several inconsistent attacks on Saigon and some provinces in May 1968.

The Communist Phase I Offensive had two stages. First, at dawn on January 21, 1968, two NVA divisions ferociously attacked Khe-Sanh Garrison. Con-Thien and Gio-Linh were also hit. Particularly, at Khe-Sanh, the NVA long-range artillery shelled the defensive forces with devastating accuracy. As Khe-Sanh was besieged, the U.S. media poured into the garrison. Their news, photos, and televised images of the battle began to psychologically attack the American populace day after day. The communists attacked Khe-Sanh but every American family was hurt. In Washington, President Johnson was deeply worried, not only by the prospect of losing Khe-Sanh but also by polls of the American public showing support for the war declining and the anti-war movement gaining momentum. As the 5,500 U.S. Marines and 1,100 ARVN rangers were pinned down inside the bunkers and barbed wire at Khe-Sanh, in Washington, a Gallup poll showed that fifty percent of these polled disapproved of the president's war conduct and only thirty-five percent approved. The president said: "This is the decisive time in Vietnam."[9]

Part of the significance of the Khe-Sanh battle to the whole Second Vietnam war lay with its impact on the general public in America. Before the communists attacked Khe-Sanh, a majority of Americans knew little about the war in South Vietnam and some did not even know where Vietnam was. After Ambassador Bunker arrived in South Vietnam to carry out Johnson's plan of de-escalating American involvement, the public believed that their fathers, husbands, sons, brothers and other relatives would come home before Christmas 1967. General Westmoreland convinced them, when he returned to the United States in late November and told the National Press Club, that the war in Vietnam would come to the end with a visible American victory, declaring: "We have reached an important point when the end begins to come into view. The enemy's hopes are bankrupt."[10] Vietnam-Khe-Sanh had come to the American minds first, before Vietnam-Saigon. Then, Khe-Sanh was the disastrous first shock to them and the first catastrophe that morally defeated President Johnson, his aides and his supporters.

Hanoi leaders certainly perceived this demoralization of the American people and its impact upon the Johnson administration. Under these circumstances, they knew Washington could not think of invading North Vietnam, except to increase aerial bombardment in the North. They were confident enough to launch the Tet-Offensive, the second stage of their Phase I Offensive.

If Khe-Sanh was not a surprise, the Tet Offensive, according to public opinion, was a real surprise for all. It came during the time when all attention was focused on Khe-Sanh. The Tet Offensive erupted throughout South Vietnam with more than 100,000 NVA and Liberation Army troops, or Viet-Cong units, of which 80 percent were new NVA infiltration troops. They began their first attacks by targeting Kontum, Pleiku, Qui-Nhon. Ban-Me-Thuot and Nha-Trang, in II Corps & Region on January 30, 1968. The next day, January 31, New Year's Day, every major South Vietnamese town, city, and U.S. and RVNAF installation came under attack. Among the hundred of targets, Saigon, Long Binh, Bien-Hoa, and Hue were the main objectives. If Saigon was the center of political, diplomatic, and administrative activities, Long-Binh was the heart of U.S. armed forces in South Vietnam with its materiel and supply depots and ammunition dumps. Bien-Hoa concentrated the majority of U.S. air-powers with its strategic airbase and the ARVN III Corps. Hue was the symbolic cultural, religious, and spiritual center of ancient Vietnam.

Saigon was hit by the 7th NVA Division, the 9th VC Division, 5 separate regiments, 12 regional battalions, and 11 special sabotage groups. The latter special units would be the main force to attack important installations in Saigon. At the same time, the U.S. II Field Forces headquarters and the 3rd Ordnance at Long Binh, Bien-Hoa, were attacked by the VC 5th Division. On the same day, Hue was overwhelmed by 5,000 NVA troops of the NVA 5th and 6th Regiments and two sapper battalions, which were reinforced the next day by a regiment of the NVA 325C Division and a regiment of the NVA 324B Division: sixteen battalions in sum. The only installations the communists failed to capture were the headquarters of the ARVN 1st Division and the U.S. MACV compound.

Hanoi and COSVN used only three divisions and a number of local battalions to attack Saigon-Long-Binh and Bien-Hoa, a combined target that was tenfold larger than Hue, on which they used two well-trained NVA divisions for the attack. By General Westmoreland's estimation, the logical explanation was that the offense in the new capital (Saigon) and its vicinity was a political demonstration of their military capability while the offense on Hue was a prime attack to seize the old capital to form a "revolutionary government" of the Liberation Front to further their political aims. Hanoi put hundreds of other provincial and district cities and towns in South Vietnam under attack, perhaps to incite a general uprising of the people.

In Saigon, many important installations were attacked, such as Tan Son Nhut Air Base, MACV compound headquarters, the RVNAF headquarters, the Presidential Palace, the National Police headquarters, the Vietnamese Navy headquarters, and Saigon broadcasting station. But the most important target of the communists was the U.S. Embassy in the heart of Saigon. Everywhere, in the first minutes of the communist Tet Offensive the gloom was made complete. MACV and RVNAF intelligence did not estimate that the communists could coordinate a total attack on the first day of the lunar New Year and get onto the U.S. embassy grounds or South Vietnam's National Palace. When the attack came President Thieu was not in the palace. At the U.S. Embassy, Ambassador Bunker was suddenly awakened at 2:30 A.M. and taken to a safe place while the fighting clashed at the main gate. Meanwhile, communist sappers blew a hole in a side wall and penetrated into the compound. Gunfights broke out within the embassy grounds and U.S. Marines had to reinforce the Embassy. For hours, the press, particularly the American reporters, observed the fighting. That day, the headlines of every major newspaper across America reported that the U.S. Embassy in Saigon was under communist siege. It was a huge shock for Washington and American public. But the American press was hugely mistaken. As General Westmoreland observed: "The enemy had attacked in force and he was going to be defeated. But the press was unbelieving. The character of the press reports was doom and gloom."[11]

From the DMZ to the Mekong Delta, the U.S. and RVNAF forces met with every NVA and VC major unit and everywhere the fighting was fierce. Everywhere, these communist units were held in place, crushed to pieces, or pushed back with in total defeat and with enormous losses of manpower, guns and materiel. An American general later summarized:

Main Force NVA and indigenous VC units had attacked our forces. The strikes were often suicidal, and the enemy suffered terrible carnage in the face of our superior firepower and air supremacy. Near Pleiku, the bodies of virtually an entire NVA infantry battalion lay on the battlefield when the conflict was over. There was one major exception to this. Hue, the old fortified city on the Perfume River in the extreme north of South Vietnam, had been taken and was still in the hands of the North Vietnamese forces.[12]

On February 11, 1968, the Communist Phase I General Offensive and General Uprising, or the Tet Offensive, was almost over, except at Hue and Khe-Sanh. Hanoi leaders expected that a general attack on all over south Vietnam would lead to a "general uprising" of the population; the bulk of South Vietnamese people would join communist units and dissolve the Republic of Vietnam, the ARVN would disintegrate and it troops would defect to their side. This course did not happen. On the contrary, when the fights occurred, everywhere people supported the ARVN troops and ARVN units at every level fought with great courage and distinction. Later, General Westmoreland gave credit: "Contrary to popular opinion, the Tet Offensive was the main Vietnamese fight. The South Vietnamese Army, other members of the South Vietnamese armed forces, Regional Force [RF] and popular Force [PF] militias, and the national police deserve the major share of credit for turning back the offensive, for they and the South Vietnamese people took the brunt of the attack."[13] The Liberation Front Army, or VC units, suffered the biggest of the casualties with more than 32,000 killed and 5,000 captured.

In the meantime, the battles at Hue and Khe-Sanh continued and seemed to be at a stalemate for President Johnson, particularly after the CBS News anchorman, Walter Cronkite, the most trusted figure in the American media and a significant shaper of public opinion, came to Hue in February, observed the battle and turned against the war.

In mid–February, after a meeting with President Thieu, General Westmoreland established a combined field army operational headquarters comprising of the U.S. Third Marine Amphibious Force (III MAF) and the Vietnamese I Corps & Region to retake the old capital. The combined headquarters was placed under the command of General Creighton Abrams, deputy Commander of MACV. On February 25, 1968, the battle at Hue came to an end when units of the 1st ARVN Infantry Division placed the Vietnamese national flag at the top of the Citadel. The communist Tet Offensive was completely over. But during the roughly three weeks they occupied Hue, the communists executed and buried alive more than 3,800 people, including government officials, ARVN officers, NCOs, soldiers, policemen, civil servants, priests, and young men of military age. They killed everyone they suspected of working for the South Vietnamese government. The barbarity of these atrocious and inhumane killings revealed the true face of Ho Chi Minh and the Vietnamese Communist Party's leaders.

Ironically, many serious observers thought that Khe-Sanh "was but a brief diversionary feint for the surprise Tet-Offensive." When the Tet Offensive faded in after a short time, the battle at Khe-Sanh continued to the end of March. The most decisive weapons General Westmoreland used to defeat Giap's forces were sensors, jet fighter strikes and B-52 bombardments. New wave sensors precisely registered every large NVA movement of men and vehicles approaching or massing around U.S. Marine positions. Jet fighters and B-52 were called to intercept immediately with precise destruction of requested targets. Colonel Lownds, commander of the defensive forces at Khe-Sanh, summarized: "Sensors had come into being and when they went to wild where I figured the enemy would come from. We took out our maps and figured out where the enemy would assemble. We'd wait until he had closed the assembly area because we wanted to get them all. The B-52 strikes would be a 'godsend,' miraculous thing. It's almost scary when you think of it. You don't even see them but, boy, the bombs sure come down right on target."[14] Some said that Giap was not stupid to hit Khe-Sanh. General Giap wanted to hit it and overrun it. Khe-Sanh was only saved by its architect and creator, General Westmoreland, and by its heroes, the U.S. Marines and ARVN Rangers, plus the power of American advanced high-tech detectors and air supremacy. On March 25, 1968, General Westmoreland decided to relieve Combat Base Khe Sanh and open Route 9 by the operation code-named "Pegasus." The operation started on April 1st, 1968, with a force composed of the U.S. 1st Calvary Division and two Marine regiments (the 1st and 26th) in combination with the ARVN 3rd Airborne Brigade. After several encounters with the NVA 9-Front's units along Route 9, U.S. and ARVN units under the command of Brigadier General J.J. Tolson completely cleared up this route from Calu to Khe Sanh and Lang Vei. NVA units around Khe Sanh were eliminated or pushed back to Laotian territory with huge casualties estimated to be from 12,000 to 15,000. However, while their casualties were certainly enormous, they were quietly buried under the dense forest of the borderline highlands and in the memories of their commanders.

THE TURNING POINT OF THE WAR

To sum up, the Communist General Offensive and General Uprising both in the cities and at the frontiers, Khe-Sanh and the DMZ, was militarily a total defeat for the North Vietnamese Communist Party and General Vo Nguyen Giap himself. However, this offensive campaign psychologically and politically defeated President Johnson. General Westmoreland also committed a severe mistake by requesting an additional 206,000 combat troops for Vietnam although victory was apparently in his hands. Had he not been defeated by the American media he would have been a great hero of the United States. But President Johnson was defeated by a public opinion that was shaped by the fourth power of the American democracy. On February 27, 1968, at the White House, President Johnson followed attentively the CBS News broadcasting the comment of Walter Cronkite on the war in South Vietnam. Cronkite said: "It is simply clear to this reporter that the only rational way out ... will be to negotiate, not as victors but as an honorable people who lived up to their pledge to defend democracy, and did the best they could."[15] Cronkite had passed one night at the field headquarters of General Abrams and said that the battle at Hue was "a World War II battlefield."

The day after hearing from Cronkite, President Johnson ordered his newly assigned secretary of defense, Clark Clifford, to form immediately a Tet-inquiry "Task Force" to be operative on March 1 when Clifford took office in the Pentagon. Clifford made clear that the Tet inquiry resulted from General Westmoreland's request for a huge number of additional troops for Vietnam. On March 10, the *New York Times* disclosed Westmoreland's request. This news shocked the nation. On March 19, the House of Representatives passed a resolution calling for an immediate review by Congress of U.S. war policy in Vietnam. That same day Senator Robert Kennedy declared his presidential candidacy. The Defense Department Task Force had finished the Tet inquiry and Clifford claimed that the Pentagon had no plan to win the war; that the Vietnamese communists could withstand a war of attrition and if the United States sent an additional 200,000 troops to Vietnam it might send more; nobody knew how long the war would last. He decided to convince the president to change U.S. policy in Vietnam. Clifford had supported Johnson's war policy, now turned against it. The hawk became a dove.

On March 22, President Johnson formally announced that General William C. Westmoreland was promoted to army chief of staff and was to leave Vietnam by June. General Creighton William Abrams was going to replace Westmoreland as commander of U.S. MACV (COMUSMACV). After a couple of weeks working with Clifford, on March 31, 1968, President Johnson addressed the nation that he had decided to freeze troop levels, limit the air war against North Vietnam, and seek a negotiated peace. Finally, the President announced that he would not run again for the presidency. He told the people:

> With America's sons in the fields far away and with America's future under challenge here at home; with our hopes and the world's hopes for peace in the balance every day, I do not believe that I should devote an hour or a day of my time to any personal partisan causes, or to any duties other than the awesome duties of this office — the presidency of your country. Accordingly, I shall not seek, and I will not accept, the nomination of my party for another term as your president.[16]

The Communist Tet Offensive was the turning point of the war and President Johnson did "the best he could" to defend democracy. But in the end he did as Walter Cronkite and Clark Clifford wanted, pursuing peace talks with North Vietnam. This was the fifth paradox of the United States.

United Nations secretary-general U Thant and the French government arranged peace talks that began in Paris on May 12, 1968, mainly between the United States and North Vietnam, with the presence of South Vietnam and the National Liberation Front. In the same

ARVN 81st Special Airborne troops counter-attack in Gia-Dinh, Saigon Special Military Zone, during the Communist 1968 Tet Offensive. Courtesy Nguyen Cau and Sao Bien.

month, the communists launched the Phase II Offensive against Saigon and several South Vietnamese provinces in order to demonstrate their power and so to gain an advantage at the negotiating table. This time, the NVA regular units played a key role since tens of thousands of VC deserters came over to the South Vietnamese side after the Tet Offensive. This communist offensive was quickly crushed by U.S. and ARVN forces.

Later, General Frederic C. Weyand, the last MACV Commander and the U.S. general most trusted and admired in South Vietnamese intellectual and military circles, described the communist Tet 1968 Offensive campaign:

First, by attacking everywhere at once, they [the communists] fragmented their forces and laid themselves open to defeat in detail. Second, and most important, they believed their own propaganda and thought there would be a "great general uprising" wherein the South Vietnamese people would flock to their banner. There was a great general uprising all right, but it was against them rather than for them. The vast majority of South Vietnamese people wanted nothing to do with VC. During the entire course of the war there were never any mass defections by the South Vietnamese. But it is interesting to note that in the aftermath of the Tet-Offensive more than 150,000 VC deserters came over to our side."[17]

After President Johnson gave up on the war, some said that the United States had been stabbed in the back from within, possibly by the media and the anti-war movement. Some historians asserted that the lack of American will and a politically defective policy finally turned the American people against the war. The real battle Johnson had fought and lost was not the communist Tet Offensive in South Vietnam, it was the conquest of the hearts and minds of his own people.

10

"Honorable Withdrawal"?

In the United States, Democratic presidential candidate senator Robert F. Kennedy was shot down in the Ambassador Hotel in Los Angeles on June 6. Many felt that had Kennedy not been assassinated, he would have been elected president and he would have ended the war in Vietnam in 1969. This supposition would be probable only if Kennedy planned to abandon South Vietnam. A few weeks later vice-president Hubert Humphrey beat senator Eugene McCarthy, one of three leaders of the anti-war movement, for the Democratic Party presidential nomination. But in the general election, Republican candidate Richard M. Nixon won the presidency by a narrow margin over Humphrey, on the platform of "progressive de–Americanization" of the war in Vietnam and "peace with honor."

President Nixon inherited from the Johnson administration domestic discontent with the war. In foreign policy matters, the Nixon administration continued the previous administration's concept of containment against international communist aggression. A flexible "détente" was pursued with the largest communist nations, especially with the Soviet Union through the Strategic Arms Limitation Talks, or SALT, and with the People's Republic of China for re-establishment of diplomatic relations. Nixon's political approach exploited the rivalry between the Soviet Union and China. The hope was to decrease international tensions between communist and non-communist nations and weaken the potential support to North Vietnam of the communist bloc in order to solve the war in Vietnam that so entangled every corner of American society. Nixon's policy in Vietnam was to turn the war back to the South Vietnamese people gradually through "Vietnamization" and through the threat of massive military measures against North Vietnam so that a political solution could culminate in the "honorable withdrawal of American military force from South Vietnam."

In his inaugural speech on January 20, 1969, President Nixon stated: "The greatest honor history can bestow is the title of peacemaker. This honor now beckons America — the chance to help lead the world at last out of the valley of turmoil and on to that high ground of peace that man had dreamed of since the dawn of civilization."[1]

However, history proves that the peace in Vietnam cost more than 58,000 American sons, hundreds of billions of American taxpayer dollars, several million Vietnamese lives, and the flight of more than 2,000,000 South Vietnamese to every corner of the world. During the last seven years of the Vietnam War, one U.S. presidential adviser, German-Jewish immigrant Henry Kissinger, actively contributed to the disaster. Some have argued that the policies of Nixon and Kissinger might eventually compel a different conclusion.

In the mainstream of international conflicts at the time, President Nixon and Henry Kissinger considered Vietnam to be a "sideshow." However, it would be a cruel sideshow to be solved with extreme priority in order to calm the rage of the Americans who demanded "peace" and peace immediately. The anti-war movement reached its highest level.

THE ANTI-WAR MOVEMENT
IN THE UNITED STATES

On the first day Nixon arrived in the White House he heard the echoes of anti-war demonstrators from the Lincoln Memorial demanding peace. The president recognized the continued decline of American public support for the war in Vietnam rooted in the Johnson administration's deceitful war strategy for the intervention in South Vietnam by ground combat forces in the previous years.

The anti-war movement was launched on college campuses by separate protest groups. At first it only expressed strong sentiment against the war and there was no structure or coordination among these groups. However, in March 1965, when President Johnson sent the first combat unit to Danang, some 25,000 people immediately demonstrated in Washington; the majority were students. Thereafter, anti-war sentiment congealed into a "movement" with the emergence of several anti-war organized groups on several campuses around the country. These groups were led by intellectuals, social and political activists, including several congressmen. Some of them were: David Dellinger, a journalist and founder of a pacifist newspaper, who first came to Hanoi and met Ho Chi Minh in 1966; senator Eugene McCarthy, a Democratic Party liberal and presidential candidate, who had given the mass of young Americans the faith of "New Politics"; and Jerry Rubin, a newspaper reporter and socialist activist who led the "teach-in" speeches at Berkeley University and founded the Yippies, or Youth International Party.

The anti-war movement largely opposed U.S. government on several crucial issues:

- The war policy in Vietnam, attrition strategy, random air strikes and civilian massacre, U.S. troop casualties.
- The draft of mostly poor black and white students for military services in Vietnam while favoring the sons of the rich and upper class by the so-called "deferment" system which allowed them to continue their studies in college.
- Defense spending had cut into the domestic budget that pushed Congress to refuse to pass some civil right measures. The cuts gravely affected the "Great Society."
- The claim that Ho Chi Minh was a nationalist rather than a communist and the United States involvement in the war in Vietnam was illegitimate.

Several Democratic congressmen joined the anti-war cause, such as Senators William Fulbright, Robert Kennedy, Mike Mansfield, Morse Wayne, and George McGovern. They were few in number but strong in power, bringing the anti-war movement from the streets to Congress. Also, through 1966–1967, opinion polls revealed that Americans still supported Nixon's policy in Vietnam. Across the country, there were hundreds of small demonstrations in support of or against the war by different groups. After the communists of Vietnam launched the Summer-campaign of 1967 attacking U.S. forces at Loc-Ninh, Dak-To, and along the DMZ, which resulted in huge casualties on both sides, a great number of U.S. soldiers came home in "canvas bags." Anti-war leaders David Dellinger and Jerry Rubin sensed that the time had come to let Americans know the truth about the war in Vietnam and to push them to react against it. The anti-war movement grew dramatically with the formation of a leading committee. Committee members represented several anti-war groups: student and teacher associations, women's groups, war veterans, movie stars, notable authors and intellectuals, doctors and psychologists, radicals and anarchists, civil rights pacifists, and black militants. The leftist activist, Jerry Rubin, in particular thought that the anti-war movement should become bolder and more confrontational in an effort to close down the Pentagon.

On October 21, 1967, more than 50,000 people from different groups rallied at the Lincoln Memorial. After hearing speeches given by anti-war speakers, a diverse crowd marched toward the Pentagon, with white professors alongside black students. Ten thousand U.S. army troops and state marshals were deployed to safeguard the Pentagon with unloaded rifles, tear-gas and truncheons. Young girls from the crowd placed flowers in the rifle barrels of thousands of soldiers. The voice of one of the anti-war movement leaders, David Dellinger, was heard demanding peace, with a chorus from the crowd, "Peace Now, Peace Now." However, the peace demonstration turned into a running battle that lasted for many hours with more than 1,000 demonstrators arrested. This demonstration was the most violent dissent in the United States since the beginning of the Vietnam War. Rubin saw it as the turning point of an anti-war effort that would capture the imagination of the young.

Ten months later, the anti-war movement Leadership Committee set up another huge demonstration in Chicago. The communist 1968 Tet Offensive and the siege of Khe-Sanh shocked the nation. General Westmoreland's request for massively more troops, disclosed in March by the *New York Times*, also shocked the nation, particularly young people. They, poor black and white students, were mostly against the draft. The anti-war movement now entered a new phase. Counseling centers were created to advise students on how to avoid the draft. Draft cards were sent back to the Department of Defense or burned. As many as 250,000 students avoided draft registration while 1,000,000 openly resisted the draft. Twenty-five thousand of them were indicted and more than three thousand went to prison. Almost one hundred thousand others chose exile in Mexico, Canada and Sweden. All of these events led to the demonstration at Chicago's Grant Park on August 29, 1968.

Anti-war movement activist and leader Jerry Rubin thought that the demonstration held in Chicago would end the war by serving as a trumpet-call for young people to rise up. Although he called for 500,000 people to show up, the actual number of demonstrators was fewer than 10,000. Chicago Mayor Richard Daley anticipated 100,000 protestors would show up and called out 26,000 police and state National Guard troops to face them. The early rally by the demonstrators at Grant Park was bloodied. Senator McCarthy, the Democratic presidential candidate, turned his convention office at the Hilton Hotel into a kind of "field hospital" for his sympathetic voters. The next night, the protestors reassembled and marched toward the Democratic Party's convention hotel, where Vice-President Humphrey, another candidate for the presidency, was giving his acceptance speech. They were halted. The march turned violent when the police suddenly appeared and charged the crowd, clubbing and beating up protestors without restraint. Senator McCarthy ascertained that in a few minutes more than 800 of the anti-war protestors had been injured. He finally decided to join them and became one of the anti-war movement leaders; his phone was wiretapped after that.

The scenes of this demonstration and terror were televised and widely shown. This worked unconsciously for the interest of the communists of Vietnam and encouraged them to prolong the war and stiffen their voice at the Paris peace talks. Upon taking the Oval Office in January 1969, President Nixon inherited this legacy from the Johnson administration. The American people had turned against the war.

THE "VIETNAMIZATION"

General Frederic C. Weyand, former U.S. Army chief of staff, once remarked: "Vietnam was a reaffirmation of the peculiar relationship between the American Army and the American people. The American Army really is a people's army in the sense that it belongs to the

American people, who take a jealous and proprietary interest in its involvement. When the Army is committed, the American people are committed; when the American people lose their commitment, it is futile to try to keep the Army committed."[2] After the Tet Offensive in South Vietnam, the American people lost their commitment to Vietnam. Through the demonstrations, media criticism, and congressional indecision, President Nixon was obliged to withdraw U.S. combat forces from Vietnam. However, abandoning South Vietnam immediately would mean betraying an ally and surrendering unreasonably to the communists of North Vietnam. The new leader of the free world would not do it. Nevertheless, some suggested the war in Vietnam be solved in such a way.

Secretary of defense Clark Clifford, in a meeting with Kissinger during the transition period, persuaded the new National Security Council to advise the president to abandon the United States effort in Vietnam hastily. Secretary of state Dean Rusk had the same opinion.

Though the American people were impatient of the war in Vietnam and the polls in January 1969 showed that 52 percent opposed it, the role of the United States as the strongest super-power of the free world obliged President Nixon to place the "defense of the national prestige" as the foremost priority in solving the war. His cogent policy toward Vietnam was to keep "maximum pressure" on the communists of North Vietnam while seeking a political solution. The withdrawal of U.S. forces from South Vietnam was certain, but it was to be done the "honorable" way instead of abandoning it unconditionally. Indeed, the president had a response; he said:

> Abandoning the South Vietnamese people ... would jeopardize more than lives in South Vietnam. It would threaten our long-term hopes for peace in the world. A great nation must be worthy of trust. When it comes to maintaining peace, "prestige" is not an empty word. I am not speaking of false pride or bravado — they should have no place in our policies. I speak rather of the respect that one nation has for another's integrity in defending its principles and meeting its obligations. If we simply abandoned our effort in Vietnam, the cause of peace might not survive the damage that would be done to other nations' confidence in our reliability."[3]

Melvin Laird, a chief military spokesman in Congress, was made secretary of defense at the same time William Rogers was secretary of state. Other notable politicians to the National Security Council helped carry out the administration's new policy in Vietnam, but the top Nixon aide was Henry Kissinger. As special assistant to the president for national security affairs, Kissinger, along with the president, would decide the fates of more than 540,000 American soldiers in South Vietnam and 18,000,000 South Vietnamese people. According to several historians, the U.S. Departments of Defense and State were only façades. President Nixon and political assistant Kissinger alone formulated the United States' new worldwide policy. Both of them possibly believed that the United States had to demonstrate that it had not been vulnerable before the eyes of the international communist leaders. In Vietnam, both Nixon and Kissinger wanted a "peaceful accord" with North Vietnam with "conditions" to quickly draw out U.S. forces from Vietnam in order to solve larger problems with China and the Soviet Union.

A week after his presidential inauguration, on January 27, 1969, a reporter in a news conference asked President Nixon his peace plan for Vietnam. His smooth reply was:

> We have been quite specific with regard to some steps that can be taken now on Vietnam. Rather than submitting a laundry list of various proposals, we have laid down these things which we believe the other side should agree to: the restoration of the demilitarized zone as set forth in the Geneva Conference of 1954; mutual withdrawal, guaranteed withdrawal of forces by both sides; the exchange of prisoners. All these are matters that we think can be precisely considered and on

which progress can be made. Now, where we go from here depends upon what the other side offers in turn.[4]

This news conference was related by journalist Tad Szulc in his book (1978). Szulc also noticed Kissenger's view on Vietnam:

In the beginning, Kissinger was telling everybody that we would be out in six months. You buy time and use that time, first of all, for the Vietnamization program. Second, to convey credible threats to the North Vietnamese — that you will destroy [them] if they engage in offensive operations after you withdraw; and, third, to build up political relations with China and Russia so that they have an incentive to try to deter the North Vietnamese from renewed escalations of war once the United States withdraws. That, I think, was the basic strategy: to buy time at home and carry out these policies overseas.[5]

By the time the White House's new political team formed and a U.S. new worldwide policy was drawn, including a policy on Vietnam, the peace talks in Paris had stagnated after several months discussing "the form of the negotiating table" for the delegations of the United States, North Vietnam, South Vietnam, and the Liberation Front. The South Vietnamese delegation considered the Southern Liberation Front a "political entity" but not a real government, and therefore avoided face-to-face recognition and discussion with its delegation. This would be a problem for the United States and especially for North Vietnam. Once again, the world would learn of Ho Chi Minh's cunning ability in politics. In June 1969, Ho summoned to Hanoi Nguyen Huu Tho, Huynh Tan Phat, Truong Nhu Tang, and Nguyen van Hieu of the Liberation Front to order them to form the "Provisional Revolutionary Government," or PRG. After their return to the South, they declared the newly formed PRG as the representative government of the South Vietnamese people. Hanoi promptly recognized the PRG and the PRG's delegation thereafter officially took part in the Paris peace talks. The formation of the PRG necessitated having two control zones, two administrations, and two armies in South Vietnam.

However, the peace talks were deferred because the North Vietnamese delegation posed two irrational premises to Henry Cabot Lodge, who again re-appeared as the United States chief delegate. The United States must first withdraw militarily from South Vietnam, then the two Vietnams would negotiate a political settlement between themselves. It would mean the Paris peace talks might proceed after these premises satisfied and only between the Vietnamese communists and nationalists. These prerequisites were unacceptable by the United States and became the main reason Nixon took hard military measures against Hanoi in all fronts in Indochina.

The communist 1968 General Offensive, which would eventually defeat President Johnson politically, could not bring about a "General Uprising" in the South and was a disaster militarily. The weighty losses suffered during this campaign, especially during the Tet Offensive, forced them to draw back from the war in South Vietnam. The morale of the communist forces was at an all-time low, especially after VC units were almost annihilated during the campaign and after tens of thousands of their cadres, soldiers, and guerrillas gradually rallied to the South Vietnamese side under the "Phoenix Program," or the Open-Arms Amnesty program which had been created by Ambassador Robert Komer, the deputy commander of MACV for pacification, who was replaced by William E. Colby in November 1968.

William Colby, the former CIA chief in Saigon, successfully conducted the U.S. Civil Operation and Rural Development Support (CORDS) Program coordinating U.S. military and civilian intelligence efforts to support, assist, and advise the South Vietnamese Phuong-Hoang Program, which sought to reduce the influence and effectiveness of the Viet Cong Infrastructure (VCI) in South Vietnam. These joint operations were set up in 44 provinces and

242 districts both to recruit VC units and organizations' military and political personnel to the side of the government (Chiêu-hồi, or Open-Arms Amnesty) but also to neutralize the VC infrastructure using local forces and special groups called Provisional Reconnaissance Units (PRUs) which were formed, trained, paid for, and operated by the CIA. Colby named this joint program "Phoenix." The program was very effective: in two and one-half years, from January 1969 to June 1971, the efforts of Phoenix resulted in the defection of 17,000 VC cadres and guerrillas, the capture of 28,000 VC infrastructure personnel, and the death of 20,000 others, according to the Colby's testimony to the U.S. Senate Foreign Relations Committee in late 1971. Nguyen Co Thach, North Vietnam's foreign minister, later admitted that the Phoenix efforts had wiped out many of their bases in South Vietnam and forced the rest of the VC units and the NVA to retreat to sanctuaries in Cambodia.

South Vietnam President Nguyen van Thieu fostered the return of village elections and land reform with the slogan "the farmers own the cultivated land" (Chủ-trương "Người cày có ruộng"), encouraging the villagers to secure their lands for themselves. At the suggestion of Colby, President Thieu agreed to arm with U.S. M-16 rifles local forces at the district and village levels, such as the People's Self-Defense Forces (PSDFs, or Nhân-dân Tự vệ) and the Popular Forces (PFs, or Dân-vệ). Many Phoenix operations were executed at these levels and with these forces. The total strength of PSDFs and PFs around the country rose from several thousand to four hundred-thousand men armed with rifles. The security of the countryside improved drastically with these infrastructure reforms. By June of 1970, the Hamlet Evaluation System (HES) rated 91 percent of the total 10,954 hamlets as "secured or relatively secured," 7.2 percent as "contested," and only 1.4 percent as "VC controlled." By early 1971, MACV's Deputy commander for pacification William Colby said that he could drive through the countryside at night without any concern for his safety. South Vietnamese Senator Tran Ngoc Nhuan and U.S. Army Colonel Harry G. Summer, Jr., the notable editor of *Vietnam Magazine*, echoed this truth.

At the central level, President Thieu ameliorated his regime's political stability after the 1968 Tet Offensive thanks to the continuous support of the Armed Forces Council, the Congress, the Nationalist parties and sects, and the populace. South Vietnamese people throughout the country had shown their faith toward the regime and the ARVN during and after the defeat of this communist offensive campaign. This advantageous situation favored the anticommunist efforts of the South Vietnamese government. Unfortunately, the war in Vietnam was decided in Washington, which fought a different war, the social and psychological war, that lasted several years and politically divided the nation. The obvious final result of this war was the defeat of the Nixon administration. However, before that was to occur several phenomena appeared: "Vietnamization," whereby the withdrawal of U.S. forces from South Vietnam would be viewed as the "finality," Paris "peace talks" as the "means," and military measures in Indochina as the "procedures," but time was really the "determinant."

Hanoi leaders precisely assessed the American domestic pressures which obliged President Nixon to withdraw U.S. forces from South Vietnam and end the war. What could not be done militarily by the 1968 Offensive campaign was almost realized politically: "To push the Americans from South Vietnam." However, their optimistic estimate underestimated the mentality and philosophy of the new president of the United States, Richard Milhouse Nixon. President Nixon was tough, and despite the intense demands for peace by a majority of Americans and by the media, he decided not to give up on the war so easily. The war intensified and the leaders in Hanoi gravely suffered as they tried to negotiate an advantageous political solution in Vietnam.

These communist leaders believed that even the peace talks failed, they could win the war and re-unify Vietnam by military means. Therefore, keeping regular forces in South Vietnam and continuing to fight was imperative. President Johnson's decisions to halt all air strikes on North Vietnam and the Ho Chi Minh Trail on October 31, 1968, had given them the precious time and opportunity to send more troops, equipment, and supplies to replace and replenish their units in sanctuaries in Laotian and Cambodian territories along the borders between South Vietnam.

Development along the Ho Chi Minh Trail continued and secret sanctuaries in these borderline areas were created. Truck traffic moving on the trail increased considerably. The Soviet Union continued to support Hanoi with three billion dollars a year in industrial and military aid of materiel and equipment including surface-to-air missiles (SAMs) and MIG-21 fighters. Supplies of war goods came from Hanoi via the important Hai-Phong Seaport. China's economic and military aid also rose to one billion dollars a year from 1970. War goods came to Hanoi via the Kunming-Hanoi and Nanning-Hanoi railway lines. Supplies from North Vietnam to the NVA and VC units in Cambodian sanctuaries were sent not only through the Ho Chi Minh Trail but also via the Sihanoukville (or Ream) Seaport, which Prince Norodom Sihanouk, Cambodia chief of state, was secretly afforded for Hanoi's use.

Washington feared that NVA regular divisions in these sanctuaries would severely harm South Vietnamese armed forces and the American "Vietnamization" plan. In other words, if the withdrawal of U.S. forces proceeded to quickly, the ARVN could not defend South Vietnam from attack by these NVA units coming from their sanctuaries in Laos and Cambodia.

In February 1969, General Creighton Abrams, MACV commander sent a briefing team to Washington to report on the presence of COSVN and several NVA regiments at secret Base Area 353 in Fish Hook, a corner of Cambodia jutting into South Vietnam 80 miles northwest of Saigon. General Abrams proposed a single B-52 operation to eradicate this communist highest command in South Vietnam. His proposal was approved on March 17. The next day, forty-eight B-52 sorties of this air operation, code-named "Breakfast," were launched. Base Area 353 was one of the fifteen NVA sanctuaries along the border regions between the Long-Mountain Range and the Mekong River from the Laotian Tchépone area to the Parrot's Beak area on the border South Vietnamese Tay-Ninh Province. General Earle G. Weeler, chairman of the Joint Chiefs of Staff, proposed to President Nixon a list of six to nine of these sanctuaries to be demolished by airstrikes. An air-operation plan was approved by the president under the code name "Operation Menu." It was a secret air war in Cambodia which followed a replica of the clandestine air operation "Commando Hunt" in Laos years before that had been designed to interrupt the Ho Chi Minh Trail. Once "Operation Menu" was approved, night after night, from spring 1969 through summer 1973, continuous air-strikes of more than 15,500 strategic and tactic sorties were sent and more than 535,000 tons of bombs were dropped on these NVA & VC sanctuaries. These were code-named "Lunch," "Dinner," "Dessert," "Snack" and "Supper," in addition to the first target "Breakfast." (See Map #4.)

Meanwhile, the U.S. Seventh Air Force received orders to reopen the "Commando Hunt" air-campaign that had been halted in October 1968, under the Johnson administration. This time airstrikes composed 60 percent of strategic air sorties. Once again, the Ho Chi Minh Trail caused the war to widen, this time to Cambodia in addition to Laos. In mid–May of 1969, three months after the first bombing on "Breakfast" and the renewal of the air campaign in the Laotian panhandle, Kissinger took a positive step toward a political settlement with the North Vietnamese delegation in the Paris peace talks. He proposed a mutual troop withdrawal from South Vietnam within a twelve-month period, a release of prisoners, an international supervised cease-fire, and new elections in Vietnam on the basis of the 1954

Geneva Accords. Hanoi was unresponsive to Kissinger's proposal. However, Ho Chi Minh responded to a private letter from President Nixon in June, accepting the "secret peace-talks" between Kissinger and Hanoi senior negotiator Le Duc Tho, an important VWP Politburo member. The first meeting was scheduled for August 4, 1969, in Paris. In June, President Nixon announced that 25,000 American troops would begin to leave Vietnam in July. The Vietnamization began even before the secret peace talks occurred.

U.S. secretary of defense Melvin Laird had a "timetable worked out" for additional training of ARVN and the withdrawal of U.S. air, sea, and ground combat forces. The timetable for Vietnamization was four years. But Laird was not the man who decided even military affairs in Vietnam; Kissinger himself, the most powerful authority after President Nixon, determined all U.S. political, diplomatic, and military issues. President Nguyen van Thieu, his government, the RVNAF, and South Vietnamese people had to endure every decision made by Kissinger. Vietnamization created many critical problems for South Vietnam, such as:

- First, Vietnamization occurred over three years, from July 1969 to August 1972, which left South Vietnam too little time to prepare for prolonged fighting against the communists, especially the North Vietnamese Army, which was potentially stronger than the ARVN in manpower and firepower. The North Vietnamese Army consisted of twenty infantry divisions and twenty attached regiment-sized artillery units, one for each division. In 1973, there were just ten NVA and five VC divisions permanently fighting in South Vietnam.
- Second, to replace seven U.S. Army infantry divisions, two U.S. Marine divisions and nearly four allied divisions, all of which had fought in South Vietnam years before, the ARVN was authorized to organize only a new division, the 3rd Infantry Division. Comprised of new recruits, this Division was weak in formation and poor in training, but it was put along the DMZ to replace two experienced U.S. Marine divisions.
- Third, the inflation, lower production and unemployment that resulted from the American troops leaving were burdensome for the government to combat. The nation had to use up precious economic and human resources to fight a complicated war while the United States cut down its economic and military aid for South Vietnam.
- Finally, and most importantly, Kissinger engaged in secret peace talks with Le Duc Tho without any consultation with or regard for South Vietnamese leaders, including President Thieu. Kissinger later placed President Thieu and his government under the de facto "political settlement" which was unfair for South Vietnam to safeguard itself.

As the "Vietnamization" materialized, the Republic of Vietnam faced the most dangerous situation of any time during the Vietnam War. The "high-profile defensive war," previously fought by more than 550,000 U.S. troops and nearly 60,000 Asian allied troops, now solely relied on the RVNAF. At the time, nobody believed the RVNAF could stand firmly against the overwhelming enemy. Indeed, after the Communist 1968 Offensive campaign, from mid–March 1969 until the signing of the Paris Peace Accords in January 1973, the war in Vietnam was fought by North Vietnamese Army regular units with the disintegrated VC units playing no significant role.

In any case, Vietnamization proceeded at the same time the war escalated in this critical period 1969–1972. Vietnamization may have been a good intention of Nixon and Kissinger in their worldwide and long-range policy to prosper the United States, but it immediately proved to be the Nixon administration's worst solution for the war in Vietnam. This consequence surfaced both in the United States and in Southeast Asia.

In the high speed materialization of the U.S. troop withdrawal from Vietnam while facing North Vietnam's steadfast determination in the Paris peace talks, Nixon and Kissinger firmly decided to use any necessary force to drive Hanoi leaders to come back to the secret peace talks. Some strategic and tactical measures of the Nixon administration during the Vietnamization period included bombing North Vietnamese sanctuaries in 1969 and attacking their regular units in 1970 in Cambodian territories; re-opening airstrikes on Ho Chi Minh Trail in 1969 and launching ground operations in Laotian panhandle in 1971 to cut their supply activities on the Trail; re-opening the air campaign against North Vietnam in 1969; blockading Hai-Phong Harbor; and massively bombing Hanoi in 1972.

However, these military measures sharply divided American society. The anti-war movement grew in intensity across America to the point that 450 colleges closed in protest for a few weeks in May and several massive demonstrations were held. On November 15, 1969, more than 250,000 people demonstrated in Washington. The escalation of the war in Indochina generated repercussions against the Nixon administration and the president himself. A case in point: the secret Arc-Light, or "Operation Menu" was disclosed by the *New York Times* on May 9, 1969. The next day, President Nixon perceived that the source could have been a National Security Council (NSC) staff member and ordered the wiretapping of the 17 telephone lines of the NSC staff officials and members of the news media at the White House. This first wiretapping of staffers and newsmen spread the first ripples, to be followed by the "Watergate" scandal that forced Nixon to resign. The secret air campaign targeting NVA sanctuaries in a neutral country was investigated by the House Judiciary Committee. After several debates, the Committee voted on an article to bring an action against Nixon. It read:

> In his conduct of the office of President of the United States, Richard M. Nixon, in violation of his constitutional oath, authorized, ordered, and ratified the concealment from the Congress of the facts, and the submission to the Congress of false and misleading statements concerning the existence, scope, and nature of American bombing operations in Cambodia, in derogation of the power of the Congress to declare war; and by such conduct warrants impeachment, and trial, and removal from office.[6]

It was the first call for "impeachment" against President Nixon. But the full House concluded that the Congress could not prosecute the president for actions in the war. However, the direct result of the congressional hearing on the Operation Menu was a repeal of the "Gulf of Tonkin" Resolution, removing important warmaking powers from the president and returning them to Congress. Still, President Nixon and Kissinger continued on their path to resolve the war in Indochina.

In Southeast Asia, by withdrawing the U.S. and Asian Allies' forces from South Vietnam under Vietnamization, President Nixon unofficially broke with the continuous "containment" policy against international communist aggression formulated and maintained by his four consecutive predecessors since the end of the World War II in 1945. This was the real turning point of the United States' policy in Southeast Asia. Probably, after Nixon had made his historical visit to China in February and to the Soviet Union in May 1972, it was foreseen that a worldwide geopolitical settlement would shape important tacit arrangements to allow Nixon to neglect the previous U.S. policy and abandon Indochina for a farther political purpose. The South-East Asia Treaty Organization (SEATO) thus automatically died without a sound. Many South Vietnamese historians felt this explained Kissinger's excessive concession made during his secret peace talks in Paris with Le Duc Tho. The dissonantly military actions of the Nixon administration during the Vietnamization period in Indochina were also assumed merely to be Nixon and Kissinger's tricks to gain necessary time to negotiate with China (but primarily not with North Vietnam) for a final political settlement for Southeast Asia. Once such a solution was accomplished, the rest was less important. Such an explanation would also interpret the Nixon-Kissinger concept of Vietnam as a "sideshow."

Sideshow, in its proper meaning, is "any subordinate event or matter." The Nixon Administration's foreign policy toward Vietnam, by its logical elucidation, was a subordinate or partial policy of the United States in Southeast Asia. Certainly, with the Vietnamization policy, Nixon and Kissinger meant to disengage the American military commitment in Vietnam and let South Vietnam to stand or fall on its own merits. But, to this day, no one knows the absurd meaning of the "sideshow" of Vietnam in the grand design of Nixon's global context. Kissinger could have explained it but he did not, probably for reasons of secrecy. In addition, no one could know the conversations between President Nixon and his national security adviser, Kissinger, who was the prime mover in Vietnam. Indeed, in the opinion of U.S. ex–assistant secretary of defense Adam Yarmolinsky, the key player of the Vietnamese games, including the Vietnamization, was Henry Kissinger. Yarmolinsky said that Kissinger's conceptual view evolved from "a paranoid fear of the consequences of withdrawal [from Vietnam] in terms of right-wing reaction ... and he was not prepared to take what he saw as a serious risk to Americans. And he was prepared to sacrifice large numbers of Americans, even larger numbers of Vietnamese lives, to avoid what he saw was at risk."[7]

With Vietnamization, Kissinger merely feared the "theoretical" but serious risk of a "political division" in America and chose to ignore the result of it in Vietnam. South Vietnam President Nguyen van Thieu saw the "honorable withdrawal" of U.S. troops as a "factual risk" to the South Vietnamese people and paid it his highest attention. Later, Thieu recalled: "Vietnamization depended on the US heart and mind. I repeated many times to the Americans it must be honest Vietnamization — You must honestly like to help us fight. If it's fully done, continuous, it could be a way to prevent the collapse of South Vietnam."[8] At the time, Kissinger regarded President Thieu as a real obstacle to his "peace with honor" process in Paris. Thieu considered Kissinger a real enemy of the South Vietnamese regime because he clearly perceived Kissinger's dark intentions to abandon Vietnam, in a "legitimate" way, through Vietnamization and the Paris peace talks; even as the United States adroitly pretended to escalate and widen the war against North Vietnam and in the whole of Indochina. His revenge against Kissinger was later seen in April 1975; and, it was the "real risk" that Kissinger would not anticipate.

The American armed forces in Vietnam and the RVNAF were the most piteous victims of Kissinger's political dark side and military designs in Vietnam, and the triangular poker games between Kissinger, Thieu, and Hanoi leaders during the Vietnamization period. Fighters in the South Vietnamese armed forces were blamed for incompetence in their own war while the U.S. army, its officers, and soldiers, were equally embittered by the slander of critics. Several texts, themes, and magazine articles by U.S. media reporters including some by American Vietnam War veterans have addressed this. In their view, Nixon's policy of seeking a negotiated peace through pressure was heavily felt by the American troops in Vietnam and the divided nation at home. They claimed the U.S. forces fighting during the Vietnamization phase-out period, 1969–1972, experienced "overall demoralization" or "lost heart." Many went too far when accusing U.S. Army officers and soldiers of "fragging" or murdering of civilians. The accidental killing at My Lai, a village complex at Quang-Ngai Province, on March 16, 1968 was widely circulated while the communist massacre of civilians at Hue during the 1968 Tet Offensive, which was more horrible by tenfold, was silently neglected.

Criticizing Nixon's new policy in Vietnam may have been reasonable, but dishonoring U.S. armed forces, or the RVNAF, and American and South Vietnamese officers and enlisted personnel, who were fighting for the noble cause of safeguarding freedom and democracy during the Vietnam War, was simply cruel. General Creighton W. Abrams, MACV commander in the most critical period (1968–1972) of the Second Vietnam War, acknowledged the combative ability and heightened the role of the ARVN in the battlefield; he noted that during the last phase of the communist 1968 offensive "the ARVN killed more enemy than all other allied forces combined." He also emphasized that "the South Vietnamese get relatively less support, both quantitatively and qualitatively, than U.S. forces i.e. artillery, tactical air support, gunships, and helilift."[9] In addition to Abram's notes, many U.S. generals voiced the problem of the ARVN being "outgunned" by the NVA. Indeed, NVA soldiers had introduced the AK-47, a modern and highly effective automatic rifle into the war since 1964 while ARVN soldiers were still using single-shot Garants M-1s and carbines from World War II. Only in March (or April) 1968, were a limited number of M-16 rifles distributed to ARVN elite units. That was ironic.

A CONTROVERSIAL ESCALATION OF THE WAR IN INDOCHINA

Having formulated a policy to "disengage" the U.S. military commitment in South Vietnam through "withdrawal with honor," the Nixon administration simply needed a military pact to effectuate its aim. But such a pact was not forthcoming. Both Washington and Hanoi continued to seek military and psychological advantages at the Paris peace talks. Nixon, when he first began his presidency, believed that under military pressure the aging Hanoi leadership would become weary and seek a political settlement for Vietnam. The Hanoi leadership, on the contrary, with its rigid authoritarian structure, was very staunch in its communist ideology and was willing to endure the war. The goals for the members of the Communist Party's Politburo — the liberation of the nation and the people — never changed; their long-term objectives — "fighting while negotiating" in order to push the Americans out of South Vietnam, "liberating" South Vietnam, and re-unifying the country — remained unchanged. They continued to fight and so the war escalated and became bitter and more tragic. The simple reason was that Hanoi misinterpreted the de-escalation of American combat troops from South Vietnam, while Washington continued to underestimate the competence and endurance of North Vietnam, which continued even though it experienced unprecedented American bombing from April 1969 and lost one of its greatest leaders, Ho Chi Minh.

Before Ho Chi Minh died of a heart attack, on September 3, 1969, he had seen the U.S. air war not only intensify in North Vietnam and Laos but also widen to Cambodia. He had seen the impact of the Paris peace talks. His will to continue the war until the final victory, to expel the Americans out of Vietnam, and to re-unite the country was later materialized by his comrades and disciples.

Ton Duc Thang, Ho's oldest comrade, replaced him as president of the Democratic Republic of Vietnam. Far different than Ho, Ton was only the symbol of the regime, while the real powers of the party rested with Le Duan and ten other Politburo members. As first secretary of the VWP, Duan was the leading voice of the Politburo members and the first leader of the party. The number two man, Truong Chinh, held the National Assembly as chairman. Pham van Dong, number three, retained the premiership; Pham Hung, number four, was first vice-premier; Vo Nguyen Giap, number five, was vice-premier, minister of defense, and commander in chief of the People's Army; Le Duc Tho held the post of permanent secretary of the Politburo in charge of liaison, organization, and security. The five other members of the Politburo were less important, including General Van Tien Dung, the 58-year-old general chief of staff of the People's Army, who was the youngest of the "eleven equal powers."

Pham Van Dong stated that the new equal powers of North Vietnam were of one mind and united, and the North Vietnamese people continued to live, work, and fight. Le Duan, born in Quang-Tri Province, Central Vietnam, had spent seven years in French jails. He was the first organizer of guerrilla forces against the French in 1945 and the architect of the southern communist structure and strategy against the Saigon government in 1955. Returning to North Vietnam, he was assigned first secretary of the VWP by Ho Chi Minh in 1961. Washington knew nothing about Le Duan and other members of the VWP Politburo, except General Vo Nguyen Giap, and probably, premier Pham van Dong.

Ho Chi Minh's heir, Le Duan, was a pragmatist rather than a theorist. His personal visitations and stumping tours around the countryside excited the people to continue the war against the Americans. In a greater perspective of war and peace, Le Duan was ordered to concede nothing further at the Paris peace talks. He declared that a definite cease-fire would be honored only if the United States would consider a total withdrawal, leaving the Saigon government and the Southern Provisional Revolutionary Government to negotiate and settle a political solution for South Vietnam between themselves. With such a declaration, Duan sought to neutralize South Vietnam with a neutral government similar to that of Laos, which had been set up due to the 1962 Geneva Accords. This "solution" would be Hanoi's first success in its march to isolate the Saigon regime, annihilate it, and reunite Vietnam.

By January 1970, in the first year of Nixon's presidency, 60,000 U.S. troops had withdrawn from South Vietnam. Hanoi regarded this number as insufficient and the secret peace talks stalled after six months of bargaining and four secret meetings between Kissinger and Le Duc Tho. While Kissinger was frustrated with his tough counterpart and the unproductive negotiations, President Nixon still believed that a military victory would probably come soon. In February 1970, secretary of defense Melvin Laird was sent to Saigon to plan a new campaign to strike NVA and VC units and demolish their sanctuaries inside Cambodia. Ground operations were drawn, but the key player of both political and military games in Cambodia was probably Kissinger, as Laird implied; "Kissinger was a thoughtful foreign policy leader."[10]

On March 18, 1970, while traveling abroad, Cambodia's head of state, Prince Norodom Sihanouk, was subverted by his army chief of staff, General Lon Nol. The United States denied any connection with the coup. Lon Nol established a militarist regime in Phnom Penh while Sihanouk set up a government in exile. Within two weeks, after considering the new situation in Cambodia, Washington decided to support Lon Nol. Military aid in the amount of $500,000 was forthwith offered to the new Phnom Penh government. Later, an "American Military Equipment Delivery Team, Cambodia" (MEDTC) was formed and sent to Phnom Penh to assist, equip and train the Cambodian national armed forces, or the "Forces Armées Nationales Khmères" (FANK). The new reformed FANK of 100,000 troops faced not only five NVA and VC regular divisions commanded by the moving COSVN, but also the army of the Khmer Rouge's "Parti Communiste du Kampuchia." The Khmer Rouge's army, composed of 100,000 to 120,000 regular troops and guerrillas, was formed, equipped, and trained by North Vietnam and backed by China. By the end of 1970, the Khmer Rouge's army was strengthened and reorganized into regiment- and division-sized units. Many of these units were framed with NVA officers and political cadres. These NVA and Khmer Rouge units occupied virtually all the large eastern corridor of Cambodia between the Mekong River and the Vietnamese border stretching from the northern area of Kratie to the southern part of the Kompong Trach Province.

With the new Cambodian regime established, the war proceeded furiously, reaching its most extreme and tragic results in April 1975, when the Khmer Rouge "liberated" Phnom Penh and massacred more than 1,500,000 people around the country. Assuredly, Kissinger could not have imagined that his policy decisions toward Cambodia would led to such a disaster for the Cambodian people, the worst in their long history. His decisions about Cambodia had contemplated widening the war in South-East Asia to achieve his single desire of "peace with honor." When Kissinger began to formulate a "plan" for Cambodia, he and his own political aides engaged in stormy discussions at staff meetings. Four of the five aides who assisted with these mini-meetings resigned after the Cambodian decisions were made. These included Washington notables such as Anthony Lake and William Watts.

In particular, a plan of ground operation in Cambodian territory was approved by President Nixon on April 27, 1970. The primary objective was to strike the North Vietnamese high command headquarters in South Vietnam, COSVN, which was moving mostly in Cambodian territory, to attack NVA and VC large units, and to destroy their logistical base areas, or sanctuaries, along the Vietnamese-Cambodian border.

The operation was mainly carried on by 45,000 troops of the ARVN and supported by MACV forces. MACV was cooperating with the ARVN operational forces in deploying several large units in vulnerable areas along South Vietnamese border, providing helicopters for ARVN operational troop movements and medical evacuations, and affording air and long-range artillery support for the ARVN units during their course of action in Cambodia. The American units then deployed no further than 30 kilometers, or 21.7 miles, into Cambodian territory.

On April 29, 1970, a separate two-prong access proceeded across the Vietnamese Cambodian border. The first prong, composed of an infantry division, an armored brigade, and two ranger task forces (regimental size), commanded by Lieutenant General Do Cao Tri, III Corps commander, crossed the border at Parrot's Beak, or NVA and VC sanctuaries 367 and 706. The second prong, composed of an infantry division and three ranger task forces, commanded by Lieutenant General Nguyen Viet Thanh, IV Corps commander, advanced to the Bulge area, or sanctuary 704, fifty miles southeast of Cambodia Takeo Province. These "external operations" (Hành-quân ngoại-biên) were named "Toàn Thắng" (41, 42, 43, and 44). ARVN II Corps also launched Operation "Binh Tay" (1, 2, 3, and 4) from May 6 to June 26, in northeastern Cambodia.

These operations were completely successful. In the first three weeks of May, more than 4,500 NVA and VC troops were killed, more than two thousand tons of ammunition destroyed and thousands of weapons captured, and their secret base areas at the Bulge, Parrot's Beak, and Fisk Hook totally overwhelmed and flattened. By the end of June 1970, NVA and VC casualties were enormous: 11,890 killed, 2,230 captured. Weapons and ammunition (individual and crew-served) and stacks of rice captured or destroyed were fivefold greater than the first three weeks of the operation.

Within the ARVN III Corps operational zone in Cambodian territory, the NVA 7th Division, the VC 9th Division, and several COSVN's specialized units, such as sapper, reconnaissance, logistical and combat support battalions, were hit and crushed in pieces by ARVN operational units in these base areas and in Mimot, Dambee, and Chup rubber plantations along international Road 7, from the Vietnamese-Cambodian border to the Mekong River. The remaining of these communist units were forced to withdraw and disperse over the northern bank of the Chhlong River, a branch of the Mekong River, running eastward more than 120 miles from Chhlong area in Kompong-Cham Province to the southern part of Kratie Province.

General Tri's forces advanced deeply into Cambodian soil and linked up with the Cambodian units of Colonel Dap Duon, governor of Sway-Rieng Province, on international Road 1, two miles from Sway-Rieng City, and the Cambodian 1st Military Region's units of Brigadier General Fan Muong at Tonle-Bet, across Kompong-Cham, the terminus of the international Road 7 on the east bank of the Mekong River. General Tri had fair relations with both Colonel Dap Duon and General Fan-Muong, Commander of Cambodian 1st Military Region. This writer was the III Corps' first liaison officer to General Fan-Muong's headquarters at Kompong-Cham to coordinate RVNAF's air, artillery, and ground supports for the Cambodian 1st Military Region's forces in their fighting against the Khmer Rouge Army and the NVA. My missions included arranging with Cambodian authorities for the repatriation of two hundred thousand Vietnamese people from Cambodia.

General Do Cao Tri had planned to keep his forces along Road 7 and at Tonle-Bet as long as possible for the protection of this humanitarian mission and to block the NVA re-infiltration into Vietnamese III Corps & Region. He liked fighting the NVA on Cambodian instead of Vietnamese soil. Within the IV Corps operational zone, General Nguyen Viet Thanh, IV Corps commander, did the same.

Unfortunately, by the end of April 1970 General Nguyen Viet Thanh was killed during the operational process when his command helicopter collided mid-air with an American Cobra some ten miles from the Vietnamese border. On February 23, 1971, General Do Cao Tri, III Corps commander, suffered the same fate. His command helicopter exploded above the capital city Tay-Ninh a minute after taking off, killing him, his three main staff officers and the notable French press reporter François Sully. Four decades later, no one knows the true reasons for their deaths. Who killed them, and why? These generals were the most clever and brilliant commanders in the South Vietnamese Army.

In the first week of May 1970, while Operation "Toan Thang" was in process, President Nixon announced in the United States that 150,000 American troops would withdraw from South Vietnam over the next twelve months. His decision did not satisfy the internal dissidents. A Gallup poll showed that while 38 percent of the public wanted an immediate withdrawal of U.S. forces from Vietnam, 31 percent supported the withdrawal over as long period as necessary, and another 31 percent favored an increase in troop levels to finish off the war in a shorter time. Politically, America was evenly divided. Meanwhile, anti-war demonstrations emerged across the country; some were bloody. President Nixon also faced the congressional repeal of the Gulf of Tonkin Resolution and the issuance of an amendment prohibiting further U.S. troops or air support for the ARVN in Cambodia, and forbidding any further escalation of war in Southeast Asia without congressional approval.

In May of 1970, Le Duc Tho cut off the secret Paris peace talks with Kissinger after demanding the complete withdrawal of South Vietnamese troops from Cambodia and the removal of South Vietnamese president Nguyen van Thieu from office as conditions of any further discussions. Hanoi, meanwhile, regained its ability to fight both in Cambodia and in South Vietnam by moving thousands of tons of ammunition, supplies, and troops to the battlefronts. Trucks traveling southward along the Ho Chi Minh Trail continuously increased during the last six months of 1970, despite massive day and night U.S. bombing along the trail.

President Nixon was resolved to act firmly with Hanoi, but Hanoi's tenacious stance on the war had intensified the fighting in Indochina on all fronts. Casualties soared day after day for U.S. forces, the RVNAF, and the NVA and VC forces. The war escalated and became more tense and tragic. The Ho Chi Minh Trail created problems for yet another president of the United States. President Kennedy had allowed the trail to build up by the 1962 Geneva Accords;

President Johnson had refused Westmoreland's plan to cut the trail by ground forces in deploying a corps-sized U.S. unit along international Road 9. Now, President Nixon planned to cut the trail by a single operation effected by a couple of ARVN divisions traveling across the Long-Mountain Range into the Laotian panhandle.

Such a rough plan would raise the eyebrows of any ordinary tactician. Was it a calculated mistake? Or, was it a White House plan to test the ability of the ARVN prior to total "Vietnamization"? It seemed unlikely that a force of 17,000 South Vietnamese troops could perform this deadly mission when General Westmoreland and the Pentagon previously planned to accomplish it using 60,000 U.S. troops.

Ignoring the obvious risk, President Nixon approved the "invasion" plan of Laos on January 18, 1971. The Operation "Lam-Son" was set for February 8. The main objective of the operation was to destroy NVA sanctuaries 604, 641, and their logistical base area at Tchépone town, twenty-five miles inside Laos on international Road 9, or thirty miles from the abandoned U.S. outpost at Khe-Sanh. At least three NVA divisions were permanently stationed in these vast mountainous highlands. It was a tiger den. The "Lam-Son" Operation was an illogically massive sacrifice of ARVN forces, but the best of them: the Airborne, Marine, and 1st Infantry Divisions.

Starting from February 8, the main ARVN operational forces advanced slowly on the axis of movement along Route 9, while other infantry and artillery units were airlifted by American helicopters to build up several hilltop support firebases. It took them a month of hard fighting to reach Tchépone and destroy these NVA's sanctuaries. The NVA forcibly responded. All ARVN operational units at Tchépone and along Route 9, including any hilltop firebases, were continuously under NVA heavy artillery attacks and infantry assaults, day and night, for a week. It took the ARVN operational forces another three weeks fighting in retreat with huge losses. In sum, on April 9, the end of the Lam-Son 719 Operation, ARVN losses were 1,146 dead and more than 4,200 wounded; U.S. helicopter aircrew losses were 176 dead and more than a thousand wounded. It was not a surprise.

Anyone who recalled the Khe-Sanh battle in 1968 could have foreseen the bad outcome of this crucial operation. The ARVN operational forces were, indeed, proud. On their march to Tchépone they had destroyed at least a thousand tons of enemy supplies and ammunition and eliminated more than three NVA regiments. However, a "fierce tiger could not fight a herd of foxes," as a Vietnamese proverb says. In Washington, the effect of the Lam-Son Operation was more somber for President Nixon and Kissinger. The president faced a series of critics by Senators such as Edward Kennedy, George McGovern and William Fulbright. All had opposed President Johnson's war policy in Vietnam; now they began to obstruct Nixon's war policy in Indochina. The House Democrats voted to cease U.S. involvement in Vietnam by the end of 1972.

A most serious event then occurred that created a chain of reactions against the president: an important Pentagon official, Daniel Ellsberg, stole secret documents from the Pentagon concerning U.S. decision-making by five previous presidents of the United States on military strategies in Vietnam from 1945 to 1968. He copied these 7,100-pages of documents and turned them over, first, to Senator Fulbright, and after the invasion of Laos, passed the "Pentagon Papers" to a columnist of the *New York Times*. Several weeks later, on June 13, 1971, the *New York Times* began publishing excerpts of the "Pentagon Papers." President Nixon immediately obtained an injunction to stop the publication. The *New York Times* pleaded to the Supreme Court, which ruled in favor of it. The *Washington Post* also began to publish excerpts of these secret Pentagon documents. Newspapers across the country began to defy the president. The White House, after using secret methods to gather Ellsberg's personal

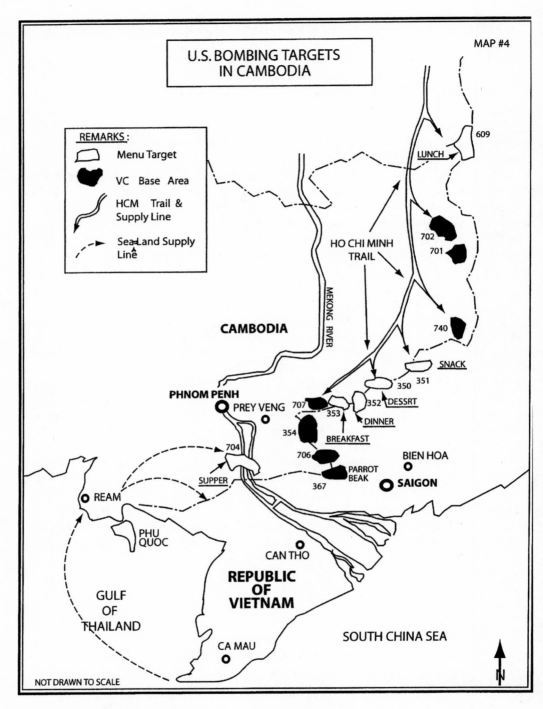

information, indicted him on charges of stealing and disclosing secret documents related to national security. Because of the administration's violation of his personal rights, all charges against Ellsberg that might have resulted in a sentence of 115 years were dismissed. Further, the secret methods used by the White House to investigate and gather information would later became evidence during the Watergate scandal.

The result of these events was to turn the Congress, the media and the public against Nixon's war in Indochina. Kissinger was sensitive to this critical situation. External demarches on even bigger problems would be the only remediable solution to alleviate internal displeasure. While the Strategic Arms Limitation Talks (SALT) were underway, Kissinger went to Moscow and Beijing to arrange for President Nixon's future visits to the Soviet Union and China. He also met Chinese Prime Minister Chou En-lai to discuss other political and diplomatic relations between the United States and China. American foreign policy proceeded effectively on all fronts except Vietnam. In Paris, in a secret meeting with Le Duc Tho, Kissinger proposed to drop demands for the withdrawal of North Vietnamese troops from South Vietnam. This was unknown to Saigon. Le Duc Tho did not respond to Kissinger's concession.

In short, during the last six months of 1971, Hanoi gained advantages on both the political and military fronts. In Cambodia, ARVN operational forces of the new III Corps commander, Lieutenant General Nguyen van Minh, were forced to withdraw back to the Vietnamese border under fierce NVA counter-attacks from June to September of 1971. In Laos, after Operation Lam-Son ended in April, only U.S. air bombing along the Ho Chi Minh Trail remained, although with fewer bomber and fighter sorties.

11

The RVNAF in the "Red Summer," 1972

By spring of 1972, all battlefronts were quiet. Both sides, the NVA and the ARVN, were exhausted after almost two years of fighting in Cambodia and in Laos. On the American side, the Vietnamization had proceeded and all seven U.S. Army infantry divisions and two Marine divisions were withdrawn. Only the 1st Brigade of the 1st Cavalry Division and two battalions of the 196 Light Infantry Brigade remained in South Vietnam. These last U.S. combat units were scheduled to leave before May 1972. The United States' "withdrawal with honor" was nearly complete while the "peace with honor" had yet to come. This was the reality.

North Vietnam took this opportunity to again test the ability of the South Vietnamese Armed Forces, then fighting alone, to obtain a definite victory on the battlefield and enhance its position at the negotiating table in Paris. Hanoi leaders saw the withdrawal of American combat troops as a sign that the United States had lost its will to retaliate against the North and re-intervene in the South. They, however, failed to evaluate correctly President Nixon's aptitude and reaction during this period when the Vietnamization was not fully complete. They planned and executed the so-called "Eastertide Offensive" campaign against South Vietnam, which was the NVA's largest conventional offensive to date across the DMZ and into South Vietnam.

Before the campaign, the VWP Military Committee had ordered the NVA command system in the South to be adjusted. The communist 5th Military Region, or MR5 — an army-sized field command, was assigned to directly command all NVA forces to attack South Vietnam's I Corps and the B3-Front field command in charge of those attacking the II Corps, while the COSVN would solely direct NVA and VC forces to attack the III Corps.

On March 30, 1972, more than 180,000 troops from 14 NVA divisions and 26 specialized regiments, totaling 22 division-equivalents, armed with Soviet tanks, surface-to-air missiles, 130mm artillery field guns, and new Chinese equipment, swept across the Partition line deep into South Vietnam's I Corps & Region and flanked the western borders into the II Corps and III Corps & Regions.

This North Vietnam offensive campaign was a surprise. The MACV and the RVNAF Joint General Staff (JGS) had estimated in February that an enormous enemy offensive campaign would occur in the dry season of 1972, but the exact date was unclear. In addition, until the first week of the campaign, MACV and RVNAF's JGS did not realize the true objectives of these three frontal attacks. Would the NVA attempt to attack Quang-Tri through the DMZ and Thua-Thien through the A-Shau Valley, seizing these two northernmost provinces of South Vietnam, or would they attack Kontum throughout Binh-Dinh Province in the II Corps & Region to cut South Vietnam in two as they had attempted (and failed) in 1968? Or would the NVA attack Loc-Ninh and An-Loc to capture Binh-Long Province in the III

Corps & Region to officially present the puppet Southern Provisional Revolutionary Government? Allied intelligence deficiencies regarding the true objectives of the NVA meant the ARVN field commanders were confused about how to react to these enemy attacks.

Fortunately, once the enemy's Eastertide Offensive began, President Nixon's reaction was firm. He said: "The bastards have never been bombed like they're going to be this time."[1] The president authorized the massive use of U.S. Air Force and Navy fire power to support the ARVN defensive forces on all fronts. U.S. Air Force and Navy tactical fighter-bombers and Air Force strategic B-52 bombers prepared to pound enemy targets. U.S. Army helicopters with TOW (tube-launch, optical tracked, wire-guided) anti-tank missiles were used for the first time in Vietnam. TOW missiles for infantry units and M-72 anti-tank missiles were also given in great numbers to the ARVN units in their fighting. In the first month of the overwhelming NVA attacks, the ARVN suffered a number of losses. In the second month, it began to respond to the fighting with ability and competence.

IN I CORPS AND REGION

In I Corps & Region, Lieutenant General Hoang Xuan Lam, commander, and his adviser, Major General Frederick J. Kroesen, commander of the U.S. First Regional Assistance Command (FRAC), believed that Hanoi would not launch a frontal attack across the DMZ into Quang-Tri Province but would conduct an attack on Hue City through the A-Shau Valley as it had done in the 1968 Tet Offensive. These two generals concentrated their attention on defending Thua Thien and Hue City. General Lam kept the elite ARVN's 1st Infantry Division to face the NVA 324B Division, which was strengthened by two independent infantry regiments, the 5th and the 6th Regiments, plus an armored regiment and an artillery regiment. He, otherwise, committed the newly formed 3rd Infantry Division to the defense of the DMZ and deployed two detached ARVN Marine units, the 147th and 258th Marine Brigades, to the outskirts of Quang-Tri City. The 147th Marine Brigade camped at base-camp Mai-Loc, 25 miles west of Quang-Tri City and the 258th Brigade was at base-camp Dong-Ha and along Highway 1. Farther to the north of Highway 9, a series of firebases were established from Gio-Linh in the east to the old U.S. firebase Rockpile in the west. This loose arc of tiny firebases just south of the DMZ was known as the "Ring of Steel."

As a result, when the enemy's new offensive campaign exploded on April 30, 1972, three regiments of the green ARVN 3rd Infantry Division — the 2nd, 56th, and 57th — had to face the first prong of attack of the NVA forces, comprised of three regiments of the 308th Division, plus several separate infantry and sapper regiments and a tank regiment along the DMZ from firebases Fuller and Cam Lo in the west to Gio Linh District in the coastal area. In the western side of Quang-Tri, the ARVN's 147th Marine Brigade had to stand against three regiments of the NVA 304th Division plus a tank and an artillery regiments. All of these NVA units were placed under the command of the Communist MR-5, or NVA B-5. Hanoi also kept two infantry divisions, the 320B and 325th in the northern bank of the DMZ as reserves. The veteran NVA 312th Division was in the borderline area to support the 304th in the northern front and the 324B Division in the Southern front, in A-Luoi area, west of Hue. The latter was reinforced with two separate infantry regiments, the 5th and the 6th. The ARVN defensive forces on the DMZ also sustained the ferocious shelling of six NVA long-range 130 mm artillery regiments, which were dispersed along the northern bank of the Ben-Hai River, not including sixteen SA.2 surface-to-air missile emplacements, which would negate allied air support to ARVN defensive forces along the DMZ. In sum, I Corps & Region's defensive forces were out-manned and outgunned by the massive NVA attacking forces of six to eight division-equivalents, all of which were armed with the most modern Soviet and Chinese weapons, tanks, and anti-tank and anti-air missiles.

On the northernmost front-line, the ARVN 3rd Infantry Division's troop rotation was half completed on March 30 when the NVA artillery strikes opened. Unfortunately for their commander, Brigadier General Vu van Giai, the fatally destructive shelling of his firebases along the DMZ and the enemy ground attacks led to severe losses. On the third day of the attack, April 2, under the enormous artillery shelling of the NVA expending more than 11,000 rounds from 122mm, 130mm, and 152mm artillery guns, and through the consecutive fierce assaults of infantry and tank units, eight tiny firebases of the "Ring of Steel" had fallen; in the afternoon, the weak 56th Regiment of the ARVN 3rd Division surrendered to the NVA at base-camp Cam Lo. General Giai had to regroup his units and form a new line of defense along the Cua-Viet River. The 3rd Battalion of the 258th Marine Brigade at Dong-Ha, on Highway 1, was still holding its defensive line after blowing the Dong-Ha Bridge to halt NVA tank assaults. On the west side of Quang-Tri City, under the furious attacks of more than five NVA regiments, including a tank regiment, the ARVN 147th Marine Brigade's commander, Colonel Nguyen Nang Bao, decided to abandon base-camp Mai-Loc and fight in retreat to regroup with the Marine defenders at base-camps Pedro and Ai-Tu, 3rd Division's operational command headquarters.

On April 4, the 369th Brigade of the ARVN Marine Division was sent to Quang-Tri. The next day, the 147th Marine Brigade moved to Hue to be replenished. By April 5, reinforced by some Ranger, tank and artillery units, General Giai was ordered by General Lam to retake ARVN lost positions on the DMZ. Although he had under his command two infantry regiments (of his 3rd Division), two Marine brigades, four Ranger battle-groups, one armored brigade, and eight artillery battalions, the task proved impossible. On the contrary, he sustained forceful attacks by the NVA forces comprised of the 304th, 308th, 312th, 320B, 324th and 325th Divisions with ten attached independent regiments, or nine division-equivalents, plus two tanks regiments and at least an army-sized artillery unit on the DMZ and around Quang-Tri. Under such circumstances, no general could have done much better then General Giai had done. After three more weeks of bloody and heroic fighting and an unsuccessful counter-attack, General Giai's forces had to abandon Quang-Tri City, the old Citadel, and the whole Quang-Tri Province, and withdraw to My-Chanh River, the natural border between Quang-Tri and Thua-Thien Provinces.

As a consequence of these actions, General Giai was bitterly prosecuted before a court martial for losing Quang-Tri, stripped of his rank and thrown in prison. General Hoang Xuan Lam, I Corps & Region commander, was relieved of his command and replaced by the young Lieutenant General Ngo Quang Truong, a real troop leader and an ARVN hero.

With the diligent strategic air support of the US Air Force, US Navy tactical air and artillery assist, and Vietnamese Air Force (VNAF) tactical air cover, General Truong was able to halt the NVA attacks at all fronts of the I Corps & Region. Later, from June, he successfully conducted several counter-attacks against the NVA forces, retook Quang-Tri Province and pushed them back over the Thach-Han River.

IN II CORPS AND REGION

In early February of 1972, Colonel Trinh Tieu, Chief Staff G-2 (intelligence) of II Corps headquarters was fully informed about the move of the elite NVA 320th Division from North

Vietnam to Ben-Het in the Three-Frontier borderline area between Laos, Vietnam, and Cambodia. Colonel Tieu reported to Lieutenant General Ngo Du, II Corps commander, and estimated that the NVA would open a new campaign in the dry season; the main target would be Kontum Province.

General Ngo Du had under his commander two infantry divisions, the 22nd and 23rd· to defend the 12 provinces of his military region. It was not enough and impossible for any commander to assure the security of this crucial central part of South Vietnam. Prior to 1969, General Westmoreland had placed five allied divisions (one American, two South Korean, and two Vietnamese) in the II Corps & Region for a fair territorial defense.

The weakest zone of this military region was the west Central Highlands stretching 450 miles from north to south, on which lay the Kontum, Pleiku, Phu Bon, Darlac, Quang-Duc, Tuyen-Duc, and Lam-Dong Provinces. Five provinces comprised the coastal zone, but the most important was Binh-Dinh, which connects Pleiku by strategic Highway 19. Many times during the war, Hanoi tried to cut South Vietnam in two along this critical line.

The NVA forces could attack any of the Central Highlands provinces through four main accesses: Ben-Het in the north; Duc-Co, in the center; and Ban-Don and Duc-Lap in the South. Ben-Het in the Three-Frontier was the NVA's important sanctuary 609 and the base camp headquarters of General Hoang Minh Thao, commander of the communist B3-Front, or the 3rd Military Region of the communists in South Vietnam. In the summer of 1967, the U.S. 173rd Airborne Brigade suffered 257 dead and more than 1,000 wounded when attacking this enemy base camp.

Colonel Trinh Tien believed in March of 1972 that General Hoang Minh Thao, communist B3-Front commander, likely regrouped his NVA forces comprised of three infantry divisions, an armor and two artillery regiments in the Ben Het area, or Sanctuary 609, before launching an attack on ARVN II Corps & Region, first at Dakto and then at Kontum. In the summer of 1967, during the testing campaign of General Vo Nguyen Giap, Dak-To had been an area of intense fighting between the NVA forces and the American 4th Infantry Division, the 173rd Brigade Airborne and a brigade of the 1st Calvary Division. By February 1972, Dak-To was defended solely by the 42nd Regiment of the ARVN 22nd Infantry Division.

Based on current information concerning the presence of the NVA 320th Division at Ben-Het, and on the estimate of his staff intelligence officer, II Corps commander General Ngo Du decided to move the field command headquarters of the ARVN 22nd Infantry Division, its 47th Regiment and 14th Armored Regiment from Binh-Dinh to Dak-To. Colonel Le Duc Dat, 22nd Division Commander, camped his field command headquarters with the 42nd Regiment at Tan-Canh, an old base camp of the U.S. 4th Infantry Division, and deployed the 47th Regiment and the 14th Armored Regiment to the west of Dak-To, on provincial Road 512, to bar enemy access from Ben-Het. The disposition was completed at the end of February.

General Du also asked Saigon for troop reinforcements for his military region. The 2nd Brigade of the ARVN Airborne Division, with five battalions, was sent to Vo-Dinh, on Highway 14, seven miles south of Dak-To. Under the command of the young and competent Colonel Tran Quoc Lich, the 2nd Airborne Brigade deployed to the west bank of the Poko River and established a series of outposts and firebases on several mountain peaks of the strategic "Rocket Ridge," five to twelve miles southwest of Dak-To. These outposts and firebases were named by capital letters A, C, D, H and Y, or Alpha, Charlie, Delta, Hotel and Yankee. The most important of these were Delta and Charlie. Especially at Charlie, the 11th Airborne Battalion could hear NVA's trucks moving on the Ho Chi Minh Trail around Three-Frontier.

These outposts and firebases of the 2nd Airborne Brigade on the "Rocket Ridge" range along the west side of the Poko River and at Vo Dinh, on Highway 14, would all protect the ARVN supply-line from Kontum to Dak-To and cover the southwest flank of Dak-To and the northwest flank of Kontum City. NVA B3-Front commander General Hoang Minh Thao would neutralize the ARVN 2nd Airborne Brigade in this crucial area if he were to primarily attack Dak-To or Kontum.

On March 20, five days after the ARVN Airbornes were in position, NVA General Thao launched a test attack against Airborne outpost Delta with the 3rd Regiment of the NVA 320th Division. After three days of bloody fighting, the 2nd Airborne Battalion and the 2nd Airborne Recon Company crushed the NVA 3rd Regiment in pieces, killing hundreds and capturing 12 NVA troops, including the commander of the NVA 1st Battalion of the 3rd Regiment. The attack was a huge defeat. In the last week of March, General Thao then hastened two other NVA 320th Division regiments to the Rocket Ridge range in order to detain the 2nd Airborne Brigade in place, by intense shelling and harassing attacks, as other NVA large units moved into the outskirts of Dak-To.

The clear intention of NVA General Thao was to detain the 2nd Airborne Brigade at the "Rocket Ridge" range to attack the ARVN 22nd Division at Dak-To. If the NVA had defeated the ARVN 22nd Division and seized Dak-To, they would have obtained more political and psychological effect than defeating the Airbornes. However, in order to cut off the Airbornes' possibility of reinforcing Dak-To, the NVA had to attack again the 2nd Airborne Brigade. The NVA B3-Front commander needed three more weeks, from April 1 to April 22, and the NVA units suffered huge losses of weapons and personnel in isolating the Airbornes. The ARVN 11th Airborne Battalion at outpost Charlie lost its heroic commander, Lt Colonel Nguyen Dinh Bao, on April 14. The outpost was overrun and retaken two days later. In sum, under the brilliant and wise command of Colonel Tran Quoc Lich, the Airborne hero (later, in September 1972, promoted to Brigadier General and Commander of ARVN 5th Infantry Division), the 2nd Airborne Brigade was able to firmly stand on its positions.

A careful study of the case reveals that the fierce fighting of the 2nd Airborne Brigade on the Rocket Ridge gave the ARVN II Corps & Region commander enough time to move the ARVN 23rd Infantry Division from Ban-Me-Thuot to Kontum for a fair defense of its capital city. And, by consequence, this valiant resistance of the Airbornes also retarded the NVA attacks on Dak-To and Kontum. This resulted in a delay of the whole B3-Front's attack plan in ARVN II Corps & Region during the Eastertide offensive campaign and deprived NVA forces in the highlands of the precious time necessary to link-up with the NVA 3rd Division at Binh-Dinh, in order to cut South Vietnam in two as they had plotted. Thus, this NVA offensive campaign in the Central Highlands failed even though they did realize some temporary successes.

In the three consecutive days from 20 to 22 of April, Colonel Trinh Tieu, II Corps' chief of staff intelligence officer, gave detailed reports to General Du on the positions of NVA 10th and 968th Divisions that surrounded the ARVN 22nd Infantry Division field command headquarters and its two regiments at Tan-Canh and Dak-To. Colonel Tieu proposed to use strategic B-52 bombing to eradicate these NVA units. His proposition was refused by ambassador John Paul Vann, the only civilian official who was assigned to the job of U.S. general as adviser to the II Corps & Region commander. J.P. Vann did not believe that the NVA had the ability to use tanks and 130mm long-range artillery guns in the Central Highlands, especially at Tan-Canh and Dak-To, and refused to use B-52 bombing. As a result, on April 23, at 10:00 P.M., the field command headquarters of the ARVN 22nd Division was attacked by overwhelming NVA forces, including destructive artillery shelling and tanks assaults. On April 24, at 10:00 A.M., Tan-Canh base camp was overrun. Colonel Le Duc Dat, 22nd Division commander, was unheard of since then and most of his staff officers were killed or captured by the NVA forces. The Dak-To District was seized.

In the coastal area, from the beginning of April, the NVA 3rd Division continuously attacked the 40th and 41st Regiments of the ARVN 22nd Division at the three northernmost districts of Binh-Dinh Province along Highway 1, from Hoai-An to Tam-Quang. Without U.S. air support, Colonel Tran Hieu Duc, the ARVN commander of the area, had to abandon Hoai-An District to concentrate his units on the defense of the two Districts, Bong-Son and Tam-Quang. The loss of the ARVN 22nd Division at Tan-Canh and Dak-To in Kontum and at Hoai-An in Binh-Dinh Province was out of the control of General Ngo Du, II Corps commander, but was resulted from his adviser's decision. Ambassador John Paul Vann decided not to support Colonel Le Duc Dat. Vann's disgraceful behavior of a "modern super-regional governor," would kill one Vietnamese commander and make a grudging hero of another. Clear to the eyes of any high ranking officer was that Vann refused to afford U.S. strategic B-52 bombing to save the 22nd Division at Tan-Canh or at Hoai-An because Colonel Dat was not the man he had preferred to be assigned as commander of this division. A month later, he saved the ARVN 23rd Division at Kontum City, by affording maximum B-52 sorties to Colonel Ly Tong Ba, because Ba was his chosen man for the command of the 23rd Division.

In early May 1972, Lieutenant General Ngo Du, II Corps & Region commander, resigned. He was replaced by Lt. General Nguyen van Toan. Within a week, General Toan was ordered to move the 23rd Division from Ban-Me-Thuot to Kontum for the defense of the city. He also reinforced Kontum by an armored brigade and two Ranger battlegroups. The defenders of Kontum heroically sustained ferocious attacks by the communist B3-Front's forces, including enormous artillery 130mm round shelling and tank and infantry assaults over all their positions for almost two more months until they were able to lead counter-attacks and totally defeat the NVA 2nd, 320th and 968th Divisions. More than ten thousand NVA troops were killed, thirty tanks destroyed and ten others captured. The bulk of NVA casualties resulted from U.S. strategic B-52 bombings and U.S. and VNAF tactical air strikes. Colonel Ly Tong Ba, ARVN 22nd Division commander, was promoted to Brigadier General.

General Ba would later claim that his great victory at Kontum went unnoticed by the foreign media and was barely mentioned by the Vietnamese press. If he understood that most will despise those who seek honor from the devoted protection of an arrogant figure, such as the "modern governor" John Paul Vann, he would know the true reason why his victory was left behind. Vann was criticized by Americans after the victory of the ARVN at Kontum, when he gushed: "This race, the women are fantastic lovers, the men can not be heroic soldiers, but they are the people of good use and able to bring us victory we wish for, if we take the trouble to teach them."[2] Possessed of such an attitude of ethnocentrism, this brave soldier but stupid diplomat, John Paul Vann, was naturally censured by American opinion; likewise, General Ly Tong Ba, Vann's protégé, was not appreciated by Vietnamese opinion.

IN III CORPS AND REGION

From early February 1972, intelligence had gathered information from contacts between ARVN units and regular NVA reconnaissance force elements in III Corps & Region concerning a huge new communist offensive campaign. Captured documents revealed that all NVA units under the command of COSVN were studying the option of a "combined attack of tank, artillery and infantry" into cities and towns. Lieutenant Colonel Tran van Binh, III Corps

Chief of Staff G-2, briefed the III Corps commander and all ARVN regional commanders regarding this intelligence information and estimates. The information suggested the communists would conduct a massive attack into Tay-Ninh or Binh-Long Province, to seize one of these provinces for the presentation of their Southern Provisional Revolutionary Government. Binh-Long would possibly be the NVA main target.

The attacking NVA forces would be the VC 5th and 9th Divisions, the newly formed 320C and 7th Divisions, and the COSVN's 69th Artillery Division, which was transformed into the 70th Artillery Division, reinforced by an anti-air artillery regiment and an armored regiment from North Vietnam. There were two elements that III Corps staff intelligence could not predict: first, the exact starting date of the communist campaign and second, the ability of the NVA to move tanks from far away into the III Region for a "combined attack."

General Nguyen van Minh, III Corps & Region commander, had under his command the ARVN 5th, 18th and 25th Infantry Divisions, an armored brigade, and three Ranger battlegroups to defend his military region, which included the Capital Military Special Zone. The 18th Division, camped at Xuan Loc, assured the security of Long-Khanh, Phuoc-Tuy and Binh-Tuy Provinces; the 5th Division, camped at Lai-Khe plantation on Route 13, was in charge of Phuoc Long, Binh-Long and Binh-Duong Provinces; the 25th Division, with its base camp headquarters at Cu-Chi, operated in Tay-Ninh, Hau-Nghia and Long-An Provinces. Brigadier General Le van Hung, 5th Infantry Division commander, established his field command headquarters at An-Loc, the capital city of Binh-Long Province.

Contrary to the general opinion saying that General Minh, III Corps commander, neglected the defense of Binh-Long, he believed in the estimate of his staff intelligence and perceived the COSVN intention to attack Binh-Long instead of Tay-Ninh. First, he sent Colonel Le Nguyen Vy, his operational assistant, to Binh-Long to prepare to shift his field command headquarters from Tay-Ninh City to An-Loc, and then reinforced the 5th Division with the 52nd Task Force of the 18th Division at Can-Le Firebase on the northern bank of the Can-Le River, six miles north of An-Loc. He also requested Saigon to reinforce the 5th Division with an Airborne brigade. In mid–March, the 1st Airborne Brigade was dispatched to Chon-Thanh, a district of Binh-Long Province, 18 miles south of An-Loc. The defense of Binh-Long was almost completed.

As chief of staff G-2 of the 5th Infantry Division, during February and March, I sent continuous long-range reconnaissance teams and covert intelligence agents across the Binh-Long and Phuoc-Long borders into Cambodia Kratie's southern forested areas to collect any evidence of NVA tanks in the region. Air observations were also used but in vain. No traces of NVA tanks were found. Later, during the fighting at An-Loc, a captured NVA officer from the 203rd Tank Regiment confessed that 60 tanks, including PT-76 and T-54, were carried into the III Region. This shifting of NVA tanks through their long and difficult itinerary must be regarded as an incredible feat. However, when these tanks came into the fighting, they became the prey for the An-Loc defenders. Nobody could have imagined that the battle at An-Loc would be the largest and most ferocious of the Vietnam War. It was bigger than Dien-Bien-Phu in 1954 and Khe-Sanh in 1968. It was more brutal because An-Loc was a city but not a strongly defensive outpost like Dien-Bien-Phu and Khe-Sanh. NVA units did not hesitate to shell the city and kill thousands of its residents. Such was the true nature of the Vietnam communists who wanted to "liberate the people."

On March 30, at 2:00 A.M., NVA units suddenly attacked all positions of the ARVN 49th Regiment along Road 22 in Tay-Ninh Province. The next morning, they ambushed this ARVN unit on this route, at 3 kilometers South of Thien Ngon base camp, when it was on the move in retreat to Tay Ninh City. All ARVN base camps and firebases from Thien Ngon to Xa Mat were completely overrun after twelve hours of fighting. The most important was firebase Lac-Long, 20 miles north of Tay-Ninh City. General Minh, III Corps commander immediately moved the 1st Airborne Brigade from Chon-Thanh to Tay-Ninh and committed two other regiments of the 25th Division and a Ranger battlegroup to the battlefield. But when these units arrived, the enemy units had disappeared. They left without collecting equipment, weapons, and artillery (105mm and 155mm guns) left by the ARVN 49th Regiment at Lac-Long firebase and others, and even without gathering the bodies of their comrades dispersed all over Route 22 from Trang-Lon Airfield to Xa Mat on the frontier. Captured documents on these NVA troop bodies revealed that they belonged to the newly formed 320C Division, or the Binh-Long Division of the COSVN. On April 2, order in the northern area of Tay-Ninh Province was secured. It was clear that the NVA attack on ARVN positions at Tay-Ninh was a deception. COSVN had reserved its main forces, the 5th, 7th, 9th Infantry Divisions, the 70th Artillery Division and other reinforced units from North Vietnam, the 203rd Tank Regiment and the 271th Anti-Air Regiment, for its nearby offense against Binh-Long Province, its prime target.

Three days passed with an eerie silence in all corners of III Region. Then the communists began their brutal attack into Binh-Long, starting with the Loc-Ninh District. On April 5, at 3:00 A.M., Colonel Nguyen Cong Vinh, commander of the 9th Regiment, reported to his direct superior, General Le van Hung, commander of the ARVN 5th Infantry Division, that his base-camp headquarters and the Loc-Ninh District headquarters were under ferocious enemy shelling. Two battalions of his regiment, the 2/9 and the 3/9, operating in the southwest and northeast of the city, were engaged with overwhelming NVA forces. The 1st Armored Regiment and its attached 4/9 Battalion at base-camp Loc-Tan, a frontier-guard Ranger battalion at outpost Alpha on the frontier, two miles west of Loc-Tan, and the 1/9 Battalion at Bo-Duc, a district of Phuoc-Long Province on Route 14, 12 miles northeast of Loc-Tan, were also under heavy enemy shelling. All of these units would be assaulted within hours. General Hung immediately reported the situation to General Minh, III Corps & Region commander, and requested air support for his units in Loc-Ninh and ground troop intervention for Binh-Long.

In mid–March, Lieutenant Nguyen Hong Quan of the NVA 70th Artillery Division's Reconnaissance Battalion was arrested in an area one-and-one-half miles north of Loc-Ninh. He confessed that his battalion was charged with studying the terrain for the 70th Artillery Division to place artillery guns for a combined attack against both the ARVN 9th Regiment at Loc-Ninh and the 1st Armored Regiment at Loc-Tan. He knew only that a huge offensive campaign imminent and that the target was Binh-Long; but not the detailed allotment of NVA large units in each phase of the campaign.

As chief of staff for intelligence of the ARVN 5th Infantry Division, I presented to General Hung my estimate concerning the two possible COSVN actions. First, it might simultaneously attack An-Loc and Loc-Ninh with divisional-sized units, plus tank and artillery units, and freeze our reinforcements on Route 13, somewhere north of Chon-Thanh District. Second, COSVN might first attack the 9th Regiment at Loc-Ninh and the 1st Armored Regiment at Loc-Tan, and ambush our reinforcements on Route 13, north of Can-Le Bridge and somewhere on Route 14, between Loc-Tan and Bo-Duc, and then concentrate its forces to attack An-Loc, the capital city of Binh-Long Province.

In the early morning of April 5 at the Lai-Khe base-camp, before General Hung took his command helicopter to the air of An-Loc and Loc-Ninh to directly command his units, which were under enemy fire, he told me:

Fortunately, the NVA has performed the second estimated possibility by attacking the 9th Regiment at Loc-Ninh and the 1st Armored Regiment at Loc-Tan. This will give me enough time to defend An-Loc. If they had followed the first option, we would have lost both Loc-Ninh and An-Loc, because our two units at Loc-Ninh could not move and the sole 7th Regiment at An-Loc could not safeguard the city without a defense system. However, in such a critical situation, under the enemy attacks of four divisions, we are at risk of losing Loc-Ninh and our 9th Infantry and 1st Armored Regiments. If Colonel Vinh and Lt. Colonel Duong can resist and slow them for at least three days, they will be heroes. Anyhow, I will try to do my best to save them.

General Hung could not save Loc-Ninh and his units, despite Vietnamese Air Force (VNAF) fighters and bombers that were called in to support the 9th Regiment base camp and cover the itinerary for the 1st Armored Regiment and its attached artillery and infantry units as they withdrew from Loc-Tan in order to join the 9th Regiment at Loc-Ninh. These ARVN 5th Division units were overwhelmed by superior enemy forces numbering ten to one and were totally defeated after two days of fighting, except the 1/9 Battalion at Bo Duc District which was commanded by the brave and competent Major Vo Trung Thu, who had graduated 1st in the National Military Academy's Class of 1961 (15th Promotion).

General Hung lost contact with Lt. Colonel Nguyen Duc Duong, 1st Armored Regiment commander, on April 6 at 10:00 P.M., and with the 2/9 and 3/9 Battalions on April 7, at 06:00 A.M. At 10:00 A.M., the 9th Regiment base camp and the Loc-Ninh District headquarters were overrun. Colonel Nguyen Cong Vinh, commander of the 9th Regiment, was arrested by the NVA but his deputy commander, Major Tran Dang Khoa, took his own life while the communists were pouring into his command post after requesting General Hung bomb the base camp. On the morning of April 7, in the command helicopter in the air above Loc-Ninh, I saw General Hung shed tears for the death of a hero. It was the first and last time I witnessed one hero weeping silently for another. Later, on April 30, 1975, the last day of the Republic of Vietnam, as deputy commander of IV Corps & Region, General Hung also took his own life after President Duong van Minh announced the surrender to the communists.

Loc-Ninh had fallen completely. The communist COSVN leaders had mustered more than 40,000 troops to the battlefield at this small northernmost district of Binh-Long Province; but by doing so, they had lost the opportunity to capture An-Loc. This was their biggest strategic mistake in III Corps & Region. They had even launched into the battle Soviet tanks and various Soviet and Chinese modern weaponry, including artillery long-range 130mm guns with piercing and delayed detonator shells, and anti-aircraft 23mm, 37mm guns and surface-to-air SA-7 missiles.

From April 5, General Nguyen van Minh decided to reinforce An-Loc City with the 3rd Ranger Battle-Group and the 8th Regiment, which was an organic unit of the ARVN 5th Infantry Division. He moved back the 1st Airborne Brigade from Tay Ninh to Chon-Thanh and requested from Saigon reinforcement ground troops and the U.S. II Field Forces for strategic and tactical air support. Within two days, from April 5 to April 7, General Hung had 4,000 troops, including 200 local guards of Binh-Long Province, to organize the defense of An-Loc. As field commander of all ARVN units, General Le van Hung displayed his strength of will, energy and leadership in defending An-Loc, even at the sacrifice his own life.

On April 7, after the last contact with Major Tran Dang Khoa of the 9th Regiment, General Hung, flying in his command helicopter back to An-Loc, observed the NVA tanks and troops hastily moving southward on Route 13. He ordered Lieutenant Colonel Nguyen van Hoa, commander of two infantry companies and an artillery company (six 105mm guns) at Can-Le Bridge Firebase, to discharge all artillery shells on the enemy before destroying his guns and blow up the Can-Le Bridge. Meanwhile, he ordered the commander of the 52nd Regiment at Can-Le base camp to engage two of his battalions to block the enemy forces on Route 13, one mile north of Can-Le Bridge. He also requested an immediate VNAF airstrike on NVA units moving along the road and the Be River.

At noon, a strategic U.S. B-52 sortie performed the first bombing box on the advanced command headquarters of the VC 5th Division at three miles northeast of Can-Le Bridge on the west bank of Be River. (A B-52 box was a target consisting of an area measuring 2.5 by 1 kilometers. In one shot a B-52 bomber might drop 20,000 mini-bombs on the box.) From noon to midnight, at the request of General Hung, ten more B-52 boxes were realized on NVA suspect concentration positions in the vicinity of An-Loc and along Route 13 north of Can-Le River.

At 6:00 P.M., the 52nd Regiment at Can-Le Firebase was overrun and its two battalions blocking on Route 13 were also overwhelmed. The remainder of this ARVN unit, more than five hundred, withdrew to An-Loc. Enemy losses along Route 13 were enormous, estimated at more than eight hundred killed by U.S. B-52 bombing, VNAF airstrikes, and fighting with the ARVN 52nd Regiment. Several NVA tanks were also destroyed, according to reports of ARVN troops retreating from Loc-Ninh on April 8 and the following days.

General Hung's quick and vigorous decisions and the U.S. B-52 intervention had slowed the NVA attack on An-Loc for almost a week. His decisive reactions were the main factors that saved An-Loc from the early days of the communist offensive campaign against the city. If General Hung had not demolished the Can-Le Bridge, stopped the enemy march by the 52nd Regiment, and annihilated the VC 5th Division advanced command headquarters, An-Loc would have been attacked and taken in the afternoon of April 7 by tanks and the VC 5th Divisions. Indeed, the NVA 7th Division had pulled out from its previous positions on Route 13, north of Can-Le River on the night of April 6 and, in the afternoon of April 7, it cut the Route 13, south of An-Loc, from Sa-Cat Plantation to Tau-O Stream, 4 miles north of Chon-Thanh District. An-Loc was not hit on that day, but it was isolated after that. Anyhow, General Hung had enough time to reorganize the defense of the city even if four thousand troops and almost ten thousand civilian residents were provided food and supplies only by helicopters of the VNAF 237th Helicopter Squadron on U.S. Huey and CH-47 Chinooks via Dong-Long Airfield, north of the city.

From April 7 to April 13, the two kilometer long and one kilometer wide city was shelled with a hundred artillery rounds a day. General Hung had to move his field command headquarters to another place in order to avoid the enemy's concentrated shelling. His wise decision would avoid the devastation of his staff headquarters throughout a hundred days of brutal enemy shelling. Within the first three days more than a hundred civilians were dead and three hundred wounded. Two groups of refugees, led by a Catholic priest and a Buddhist monk, tried to escape southward along Route 13. They were shelled and fired upon by the NVA 7th Division. Hundreds were killed along the road, the majority being women and children.

From April 8, General Minh, III Corps commander, ordered the 1st Airborne Brigade to dislodge the enemy blockade at Tau-O Stream and clear Route 13. But when Saigon decided to reinforce Binh-Long the 21st Infantry Division from IV Corps & Region, the 1st Airborne Brigade of Colonel Le Quang Luong was ordered to pull out from the action zone for the next move. The 21st Division had been fighting to clear Route 13 since April 12. Its field command headquarters was at Chon-Thanh.

In the meantime, in An-Loc, General Hung ordered all units to consolidate their defensive positions and prepare for a big battle. Every defender was to have his own fighting foxhole and shelter strength. I was ordered to prepare targets for B-52 bombing to cut enemy supply lines, tank and troop accesses, and suspect concentrated positions. During one hundred days under enemy siege and attack, I had proposed 196 boxes for B-52s. Later, after the city was released and the enemy defeated, I learned that 90 percent of these proposed boxes had been approved and performed by U.S. Strategic Air Command (SAC).

On April 9, three war reporters of the *Song Than* newspaper, Nguyen Tien, Duong Phuc, and Thu-Thuy, flew into An-Loc to interview General Hung. Occupied at this moment with operational concerns, General Hung directed me to receive them, saying: "Convey to the reporters my excuses and tell them 'I will defend An-Loc to the death, I will never come out of the city alive, if I lose it.'" His words were instructions for his troops that roused them in the fighting. In the morning, when the *Song Than* newspaper appeared, the whole nation learned that An-Loc would be a battle to the death, and it would not be ended until the last defensive unit was sacrificed.

This small city of two square kilometers, 60 miles north of Saigon, came under the main communist attack on April 13. The old NVA tactics involved heavily destructive shelling followed by forceful continuous assaults with overwhelming forces. From 3:00 A.M., to 6:00 A.M., the COSVN's 70th Artillery Division shelled more than 8,000 rounds of 130mm and 122mm into the city. Immediately after the last wave of concentrated fire stopped, the VC 9th Division units, the main striking force, accompanied by T-54 tanks, assaulted the ARVN 8th Regiment in the northwest and the ARVN 7th Regiment in the west and southwest, while the VC 5th Division units assaulted the ARVN 52nd Regiment in the north, the ARVN 3rd Ranger Battle-Group in the northeast and the east, and the Binh-Long Sub-sector headquarters, which was protected by a Civil Guard battalion, in the southeast of the defensive line. In the afternoon, under the enemy's fourth fierce assault wave, the front line of the 8th Regiment, the 52nd Regiment, and the 3rd Battle Group from the west to the east of the city and at Dong-Long Airfield was pierced. These units had to withdraw to the second defensive line, south of the main avenue that cut the city in two from east to west. A Civil Guard company at Doi Gio (the Windy Hill, 176m) and Hill 169 (169m), three to five kilometers southeast of An-Loc, was brutally attacked and annihilated.

In the early morning, VNAF fighters were called in to support the defenders. During the day, U.S. strategic B-52 bombers dropped more than 30 boxes on enemy positions around the city and along their access points and supply lines. Enemy casualties from the U.S. and VNAF air strikes were enormous, with 400 killed on the attacking lines and countless others around the city.

Four NVA tanks, oddly unaccompanied by infantry troops, strayed around the streets and seemed lost. One such tank coming across the defense line of the ARVN 5th Division field command headquarters was shot by Colonel Le Nguyen Vy, and was soon burning and exploding. ARVN troops shouted out with joy and jumped from their bunkers to the streets with their M-72 anti-tank guns to hunt the other NVA tanks, which were also shot and demolished. On the night of April 13, a U.S. Gunship AC-130 Specter that was covering the air over An-Loc shot down two more NVA T-54 tanks and four PT-76 armored carriers. The morale of the defenders was extremely high. After that, they did not lose one more inch of city ground to the enemy. On April 14, NVA units tried to attack again the ARVN 8th Regiment and the 3rd Ranger Battle-Group new defensive lines, but failed and were pushed back to the northern part of the city. The 52nd Regiment thereafter was ordered to move to the southwest defensive line.

However, the loss of the half city in the north and the Dong-Long Airfield put General Hung's troops under daily enemy pressure and pushed the general himself into the impossibility of evacuating wounded soldiers and transporting ammunition and provisions for his troops. An-Loc was completely besieged. Serious problems began surfacing. The city hospital was hit by NVA shelling that destroyed it and put it out of operation. More than 400 civilians were wounded and two hundred others killed by NVA shelling. Colonel Bui Duc Diem, 5th Division operational chief of staff, personally directed the digging of several of collective graves on the large hospital's frontal court to bury the dead. ARVN unit commanders had to bury their dead soldiers on the spot within their defensive positions. Troop replacements were cut off. Wounded soldiers continued fighting in place. Two hundred were on the defensive lines. The communists continued shelling the city with nearly two thousand rounds a day, killing and wounding hundreds more defenders and civilians. Reinforcement of troops and supply of ammunition and food for An-Loc were the most imperative decision for General Minh, III Corps commander. Shortage of strength and supplies would place An-Loc on the verge of collapse, despite the iron will of General Hung and his troops to defend it.

With the loss of Dong-Long Airfield on April 13, the unique landing zone (LZ) for additional troops and supplies by CH-47 Chinooks and helicopters was cut off. VNAF promptly received orders to airlift by fixed-wing airdrops, using Fairchild C-123s and C-119s. At An-Loc, the NVA had modern anti-aircraft weapons, including 37mm and 57mm canons, and began using hand launched surface to air SA-7 Strela guided missiles. Vietnamese C-123 and C-119 airlifters found themselves facing the deadliest concentration of fire ever seen in South Vietnam. In three days, two C-123s were shot down and after 27 missions, only 10 percent of the 135 tons of ammunition and supplies were recovered by the defenders.

The most important problem that happened in these days was the disagreement on tactical matters between General Hung and his U.S. advisor, Colonel William H. Miller. Colonel Miller many times tried to push General Hung to take positive action to retake the northern part of the city and more than once threatened to request TRAC (U.S. Third Regional Assistance Command) to "rescue" his Advisory Team from An-Loc. Sometimes Hung responded nicely but many times he kept his silence and left the operational bunker (a long, underground shelter-trench used as a TOC, or tactical operational center). Once, General Hung told me: "I respect him as an experienced soldier, but he does not know much about the enemy in this war compared to me. How could I execute a counter-attack? As you know, we had just a small force without ammunition and supplies. I just need him for air support and supplies, not for his knowledge and tactics." Colonel Miller also told me: "Your 'young' General is good for keeping his silence rather than for speaking and acting." I politely replied: "Yes, Sir; his 'silence' means he would stand firm to fight and his soldiers would look at him to stand firm for the fight. He is young but he is the best and a very experienced combatant of our army." Later, I knew they became "enemies" on the sly. They underestimated each other.

An-Loc was becoming more and more like Dien-Bien-Phu or Khe-Sanh as the NVA artillery anti-aircraft units, attached to infantry divisions, managed to thwart the airlifters' efforts at resupplying the besieged defenders. The next step was to decisively destroy them by ground assaults. Every Vietnamese and American leader knew that if An-Loc were lost, Saigon would be shaken and the Vietnamization would fail. Saving An-Loc was a question of vital importance for Saigon.

President Thieu immediately ordered the 2nd Airborne Brigade to move back from II Corps to reinforce III Corps, plus the 15th Regiment of the 9th Infantry Division of IV Corps & Region. MACV commander General Abrams also instantaneously ordered the U.S. 374th Tactical Airlift Wing (U.S. 374th TAW) to commence airdrop supplies for An-Loc since the VNAF C-123 and C-119 airlifters' efforts had proved so ineffective under the intense enemy ground-fire around the besieged city. After two weeks of risky airlifts and the loss of three

C-130s, a new dropping method to keep An-Loc supplied had been discovered. Flying at high-altitudes of over 10,000 feet, U.S. C-130s were out of range of NVA SA-7 missiles that made their appearance in the vicinity of An-Loc. The high-velocity and delayed-opening parachute droppings would guarantee 98 percent of the special bundles of supplies and ammunition would be recovered by the defenders. The U.S. 374th TAW C-130 crews were the first saviors of General Hung's troops after the U.S. B-52 bombers' crews. Their supply missions continued successfully until the enemy siege was released and the defenders totally defeated their enemy. But the real saviors of An-Loc were the ARVN 1st Airborne Brigade and the 81st Special Airborne Battlegroup commanders and troops. General Minh, III Corps commander, undertook to save An-Loc by reinforcing General Hung with these elite units.

Colonel Le Quang Luong, commander of the 1st Airborne Brigade, was the great tactical commander of the Republic of Vietnam Armed Forces (RVNAF) after General Do Cao Tri and General Nguyen Khanh. On April 14, he flew into An-Loc to meet General Hung before engaging his troops into the battlefield.

The initial plan of III Corps commander was to airlift the 1st Airborne Brigade by VNAF helicopters and drop them on a landing zone (LZ), the vast, dry rice-field between the Can-Le River and the Dong-Long Airfield, five kilometers north of An-Loc. From there, the airbornes would move southward to attack the NVA units occupying the Dong-Long Airfield and the northern part of the city on April 13. In combination, General Hung's units would attack the enemy from the south in order to recapture these lost targets. This III Corps' operational plan sounded good, but it was far from perfect. In a meeting with General Hung, Colonel Luong explained that if the 1st Airborne Brigade landed in this flat and exposed rice-field, they would have become live targets to be destroyed by the NVA artillery. He foresaw more than half of his troops would be lost by this feasting of the cruel vultures on airborne flesh. The remainder would be unable to successfully fight as they would be pinned down and destroyed under direct enemy fire. Colonel Luong proposed that instead of attacking the enemy to retake the lost portion of the city and the Dong-Long Airfield, consolidating the morale of the defenders would be the better course. Giving them provisions and ammunition to fight and evacuating the wounded soldiers in each ARVN unit while providing thousands of additional troops should precede any counter-attack measures.

Colonel Luong proposed airlifting 1st Airborne Brigade troops by VNAF helicopters and dropping them on a secret LZ near Hill 169, four to five kilometers southeast of An-Loc. From there, one of his battalions would advance and attack enemy elements on Hill 169 and the "Windy Hill," retake these highest points in the vicinity of An-Loc and set up a strong support firebase. They would protect the two other battalions, which would proceed into the city and establish a temporary landing path for VNAF helicopters and U.S. C-47 Chinooks on a spacious portion of Route 13, abutting the Binh-Long Sub-Sector headquarters compound in the southern part of the city. His units would protect this landing path of three kilometers in length and 800 meters in width for the resupply of An-Loc defenders until they could regain their strength for a future counter-attack. General Hung saw the wisdom of Colonel Luong's operational plan to rescue An-Loc and backed it. General Minh also approved this clear-sighted design which became the key factor that led the ARVN units at An-Loc to final victory.

Colonel Luong's officers and troops resolutely followed this master plan. At sunset on April 15, the 6th Airborne Battalion was dropped at the designed LZ. They promptly moved forward and suddenly attacked elements of the VC 5th Division at Doi-Gio (the Windy Hill) and Hill 169. After two hours of fighting, the Airbornes broke the enemy unit to pieces and reoccupied these highest strategic points to set up their firebases. Before daybreak on April

16, the two other battalions of the 1st Airborne Brigade and Colonel Luong's command head-quarters were on the assigned defensive line in the city. The 8th Airborne Battalion was charged with managing and securing the landing path for helicopters and chinooks as planned while the 5th Battalion was established near General Hung's headquarters as his reserve. Colonel Luong's headquarters encamped within the Binh-Long Sub-Sector's compound of Colonel Tran van Nhut, Sub-Sector commander and province-chief.

On April 17, the ARVN 81st Special Airborne Battle-Group, commanded by Lieutenant Colonel Phan van Huan, entered the city at sunset and immediately launched a night attack against the VC 9th Division's units in the northern part of the city. At daybreak of April 18, ninety percent of this commercial section was recaptured. From then on, fighting continued day and night from street to street for several weeks (see Map 5).

The 1st Airborne Brigade and the 81st Special Airborne Battle-Group at An-Loc caused NVA troops great consternation by their flexible tactics, determined action, and competence of nightly movements and attacks. In addition, the establishment of the new landing path for helicopters to resupply and refresh the city's defenders surprised the COSVN to the point that it could not react adequately to the new situation on the battlefield. General Hung took advantage of this opportunity to evacuate wounded soldiers and receive two thousand fresh troops within a single week, by VNAF helicopters and U.S. CH-47 Chinooks via the new landing path. Allied supply activities in this landing path continued and lasted to the end of the An-Loc battle. Provisions and ammunition for the defenders and food for the residents, about thirty percent of the total sum needed, came through this arterial supply path. The greater part of supplies remained in the hands of the U.S. 374th TAW C-130 airlifters.

On the ground were about twenty American advisers to the ARVN 5th Infantry Division, the Binh-Long Subsector, and the 81st Special Battle-Group. These small groups of people greatly helped the ARVN defenders through strategic and tactical air support and supply. Their heroic work contributed to the victory of An-Loc.

In sum, the marvelous presence of the ARVN 1st Airborne Brigade and the 81st Special Airborne Battle Group on the ground and U.S. Air Force B-52 bombers, AC-130 Specter Gunships, and C-130 Airlifters plus VNAF fighters and helicopters in the air, had brought with them a new, fresh wind for the An-Loc defenders and changed the complexion of the battle. The presence of these brave saviors of An-Loc also revealed the unworkable tactics of the communist COSVN and the inefficiency of their anti-air activities. The communists missed all opportunities to defeat General Hung's forces at An-Loc. The defenders, their morale extremely high, were ready to forcefully greet any new enemy attacks or wait for a general counter-attack if Route 13 were cleaned by the ARVN 21st Infantry Division and its attached units, the 2nd Airborne Brigade, the 5th Armored Regiment, and the 15th Regiment of the 9th Infantry Division.

The COSVN leaders were forced to change their offensive plans. Over the following two months they launched several violent combined attacks against General Hung's forces, including the Airborne and Ranger units, but all of their efforts ended in failure.

On April 19, COSVN launched the second phase of the offensive against An-Loc. In the early hours of the morning, after attacking the city for two hours with concentrated artillery fire of more than five thousand rounds, ten thousand troops of the VC 9th and 5th Divisions, plus twenty T-54 and PT-76 tanks, attacked ARVN units positions at all frontlines. At the same time, the 275th Regiment of the VC 5th Division and the 141st Regiment of the NVA 7th Division struck the ARVN 6th Airborne Battalion's firebases at Hill 169 and the Windy Hill. After twelve hours of fighting, supported by the VNAF fighters, the airbornes still firmly held the fight against several waves of enemy assaults. But at night, outnumbered by the enemy, two airborne companies at the Windy Hill had to cut the siege and withdraw to rejoin the 1st Airborne Brigade. Two other companies of the 6th Airborne Battalion, commanded by Lt. Colonel Nguyen van Dinh, had to destroy six artillery 105mm guns before abandoning Hill 169 and fighting in retreat to the Be River. From there, in the next morning, these two airborne companies were rescued by VNAF helicopters to Lai-Khe to be replenished. The 6th Airborne Battalion had lost more than a hundred troops killed or missing in action.

Fighting in the city continued the next day, April 20. Communist attacking forces were unable to advance one inch, except several T-54 tanks that again erred and were destroyed. Enemy casualties numbered more than 800 killed. A dozen T-54 and PT-76 tanks were demolished. Communist forces suffered further casualties around the city because of VNAF fighters, U.S. AC-130 Specter gunships, and U.S. strategic B-52 bombers. In two days, April 19 and 20, twelve B-52 bombing-boxes were dropped on their positions.

After recapturing the Windy Hill and Hill 169, COSVN leaders believed they could dominate the city and neutralize the new landing path, south of Binh-Long Subsector's compound, by attacking the 1st Airborne Brigade. On April 21, they ordered two other regiments of the VC 5th Division, the E6 and 174th, to move and join the 275th Regiment at Sa-Cam rubber plantation, four kilometers south of An-Loc, in order to attack the 5th and 8th Airborne Battalions and the 2/7 Battalion. But, at night, a U.S. AC-130 Specter gunship, providing air coverage for the city, detected five moving NVA tanks and destroyed them. In addition, these communist units were hit by two B-52 bombing-boxes at midnight. COSVN's attempt to attack An-Loc from the south failed.

In the first three days of their second-phase attack on An-Loc the communists would lose possibly two thousand troops killed and twenty tanks destroyed. After this defeat, COSVN had to delay its next offensive phase against An-Loc for almost three weeks, despite the announcement on April 18 by Hanoi's Broadcasting Station that the city would be presented by the North Communist Party to honor its puppet government in the South, the Southern Provisional Revolutionary Government, at An-Loc on April 20. The 70th Artillery Division would continue firing into the city nearly 2,000 rounds a day from heavy artillery guns, causing more damage to the city, its defenders, and its civilian residents. But evacuation of wounded soldiers, replacement of troops, and supply of provisions and ammunition continued to proceed successfully by VNAF helicopters via the new landing path, although, on Route 13, the ARVN 21st Division had not yet dislodged the NVA 7th Division at Tau-O Stream. An-Loc remained under enemy siege.

On May 11, the COSVN launched the third phase of its attack on An-Loc. In this phase, the VC 5th Division, after replenishing its strength, undertook the main effort with the assistance of the VC 9th Division, plus tanks and artillery anti-aircraft of the 271st Regiment. The communist tactics were unchanged. From midnight to 5 A.M., the 70th Artillery Division concentrated ferocious firing into the city of more than 11,000 rounds by heavy 150mm and 130mm guns, 122mm rockets, and 120mm mortars. This was the most devastating concentrated NVA artillery shelling seen throughout the Vietnam War. An-Loc City almost collapsed except for the iron morale of the defenders. Immediately after the artillery firing stopped, communist attacking units assaulted the defenders at all frontlines. Again, their troops were killed and tanks destroyed by M-72 personal anti-tank guns of the defenders.

This enemy plan of attack was anticipated. An NVA officer who had been rallied to an ARVN unit at An-Loc on May 8 had disclosed it. Therefore, when the attack started, U.S. B-52 bombers and VNAF A-37 fighters urgently interfered on the battlefield. In twenty-four hours, thirty B-52 sorties dropped several tons of bombs on enemy positions and their accessible itineraries in the vicinity of An-Loc. To avoid the danger of mass-killing, enemy forces closely approached ARVN defensive lines before fiercely attacking. The fighting occurred hand-to-hand, or removed only by a wall, a small yard, a building, or a street.

The battle's most critical event happened on the morning of May 11, when a regiment of the VC 9th Division, after piercing the ARVN 3/7 Battalion's positions, advanced and assailed General Hung's headquarters command post (CP), which was defended by the 5th Reconnaissance Company. General Hung instantly ordered the 5th Airborne Battalion to move from the southern defense line to reinforce his CP. Since dawn that day, Captain Chanh, 5th Reconnaissance Company commander, and 43 remainders, despite the loss of two-third of the troops, had heroically fought and successfully safeguarded General Hung's CP before all of his staff officers and NCOs, including Colonel Le Nguyen Vy, Colonel Bui Duc Diem, and U.S. Divisional Advisory Team chief, Colonel W. F. Ulmer (who replaced Colonel Miller in early May), came up to the defensive line. General Hung himself, with a signal team, stood in his CP's front courtyard without a combat helmet, like a simple company commander, but with a black star added to his combat uniform's collar. For more than an hour he gave orders to ARVN commanders at all city fronts and directly communicated with two VNAF A-37 fighter crews to guide their firing on the nearest enemy attack positions, until the 5th Airborne Battalion appeared on the battleground. This elite unit, commanded by Lieutenant Colonel Nguyen Chi Hieu, intensely attacked the enemy troops from their flank in front of General Hung's headquarters CP, and crushed them completely before noon.

The communist offensive continued until May 13. However, after a huge loss of troops and tanks inside the city, and unable to reinforce troops from the outside for a continuous attack, the communist units' offensive efforts hourly withered as their assaulting strength faded and diminished. Finally, all enemy attacking forces were broken to pieces and disappeared. The third phase of the offensive against An-Loc was entirely defeated by the afternoon of May 14.

Four days on the offensive resulted in communist casualties so enormous that COSVN could not launch another attack against An-Loc, despite their ultimate ambition of seizing it for political gain. Inside the city more than a thousand had been killed and two dozen tanks destroyed. On the outskirts an even greater number of manpower, firepower, and tanks were annihilated by allied strategic and tactical airstrikes. In total, ¾ of their artillery field guns and ⅘ of their tanks were estimated demolished and more than four thousand troops were killed.

The month after this last enemy offensive phase, General Hung and his adviser, Colonel Ulmer, proceeded with their plans to attack the enemy by U.S. strategic and VNAF tactical air raids against their supply lines along Saigon and Be Rivers. The air raids, especially by the U.S. B-52 bombings, targeted farther enemy sanctuaries 708, 350, 352, and 353 in Perrot's Beak and along the border of Cambodia and Binh-Long Province.

Inside Binh Long Province the communist units were not totally destroyed for one reason. Lieutenant Colonel Tran van Binh, III Corps Staff G-2, and this writer, as General Hung's Staff G-2, knew that these communist units could not hide in their secret-zones, such as Duong-Minh-Chau, Long-Nguyen, or Ben-Than, but would instead go to Loc-Ninh Rubber Plantation or several others around An-Loc such as Quan-Loi in the east, Sa-Cam, Sa-Cat, and Sa-Trach in the south along Route 13, and Dau-Tieng in the west along the Saigon River. We proposed a number of B-52 bombing-boxes to eradicate them, especially aimed at the communist COSVN and the Southern Provisional Revolutionary Government (SPRG) at Loc-Ninh, and the NVA 7th Division at Sa-Trach Rubber Plantation. However, General Minh, III Corps commander, would not sow more terror or death on innocent people, tens of thousands of whom had been unable to escape from these rubber plantations since the communist offensive campaign occurred. Another explanation was that General Minh would not devastate these plantations, which were all owned by Frenchmen, because it would cause complicated political problems for the U.S. and South Vietnamese governments with France. While I had to respect General Minh's humane and political motives to refuse our proposal, these untouchable plantations became the last but solid bastions for the communist units to shelter as their base-camps. This prolonged the battle in Binh-Long.

The difference between the Vietnamese communists and Vietnamese nationalists was made clear on Binh-Long battlefield in the summer of 1972. The communists would do anything to achieve their goals, even the most savage and cruel of measures, such as pushing the women and children refugees from Quan-Loi in front of their troops as shields, to cover them, on the first day of their attack on An-Loc; firing on the masses of refugees from the city on Route 13, killing thousands of them and leaving their exposed bodies on the ground to decay; and randomly shelling the commercial areas and the hospital of the city, killing thousands of others. The Vietnamese nationalists refused to act without consideration for human beings, their lives, their feelings, and their property. For this reason, ARVN units had to sacrifice more soldiers' lives in fighting against the communists to save innocent people. General Minh knew that, when he refused to allow U.S. B-52 bombing against the communist COSVN in Loc-Ninh and the NVA 7th Division in Sa-Trach and Sa-Cat Rubber Plantations. He had to change his operational plans to dislodge the NVA 7th Division units at Tau-O Stream and along Route 13 to release An-Loc from the enemy siege, although the city had been stable since May 15.

General Minh organized a special task force, comprised of the 15th Infantry Regiment, the 5th Armored Regiment, and the 6th Airborne Battalion, and moved the latter by helicopter to Tan-Khai in the west of Route 13, four kilometers north of Tau-O Stream. From there, this task force would attack the NVA 7th Division from its east flank and advance to An-Loc. The ARVN 21st Division was ordered to push its 31st Regiment to attack the enemy at Tau-O Stream while two other regiments, the 32nd and 33rd, were carried by helicopters to an LZ, west of Sa-Cat and Sa-Cam Plantations, to attack the enemy on their west flank. The 1st Airborne Brigade at An-Loc was also ordered to attack the enemy at Sa-Cam Plantation from the north. General Minh's new operational plan was successfully carried out by all ARVN units under his command.

On June 11, the 6th Airborne Battalion of Lieutenant Colonel Nguyen van Dinh fiercely attacked the NVA 141st Regiment, in revenge, broke it into fragments, and linked-up with the 8th Airborne Battalion of Lieutenant Colonel Van Ba Ninh on Route 13 four kilometers south of An-Loc. On the same day, the 32nd Regiment of the ARVN 21st Division, after dislodging the enemy from positions at Sa-Cam Plantation, also coupled with these two Airborne units.

Inside An-Loc, from May 18, ARVN units had counter-attacked and eliminated all the remainders of the enemy 5th and 9th Divisions in the northern portion of the city. On June 12, the 81st Special Airborne Battle Group recaptured the Dong-Long Airfield and eradicated the last enemy unit at Dong-Long Hill, two kilometers northeast of the airfield.

The national flag flying on the top of Dong-Long Hill in the afternoon of June 12 marked the final victory of all ARVN units at An-Loc.

On July 7, President Nguyen van Thieu flew into An-Loc to honor the ARVN heroes who had fought the biggest battle of the Vietnam War. The city had been completely devastated by the unimaginable communist shelling. Eighty-five percent of the city's structures were collapsed. Every wall and tree, if still standing, was traced with numerous shell-splinters. Only the 15-foot-tall statue of Jesus Christ on the west end of "Sunset Avenue" remained in

Top: **While An-Loc City collapsed under the thousands of artillery rounds launched by the communists, the fighting spirit of the defenders did not. ARVN soldiers held their ground in a life-or-death battle. Courtesy Nguyen Cau and Sao Bien.** *Bottom:* **ARVN 5th Infantry Division troops at their defensive line. Courtesy Nguyen Cau and Sao Bien.**

an untouchable mighty state under the sunlight when President Thieu came to pray before Him. Thousands of ARVN soldiers who had sacrificed their lives to defend this small city of God against the army of Satan, would live eternally with Jesus Christ in this glorious ground.

Communist casualties, during the three months of their Summer 1972 Offensive Campaign in III Corps & Region, especially at An-Loc, were fivefold greater than those of the

Soldiers of the ARVN 3rd Ranger Battle Group in a counter-attack in the northern part of An-Loc City (June 1972). Courtesy Nguyen Cau and Sao Bien.

ARVN. It was estimated that half of their attacking forces, twenty-five to thirty thousand infantry troops were killed, eighty percent of their artillery and anti-aircraft guns destroyed, and ninety five percent of their tanks demolished. The majority of these casualties were caused by U.S. strategic bombing and U.S. and VNAF airstrikes.

The South Vietnamese commanders who achieved victory for the ARVN forces at An-Loc in summer of 1972 were Lieutenant General Nguyen van Minh, III Corps & Region commander, Brigadier General Le van Hung, ARVN 5th Infantry Division commander and An-Loc field commander, and Colonel Le Quang Luong, 1st Airborne Brigade commander (later, in December 1972, promoted to Brigadier General and Commander of the Airborne Division). Certainly, in this grand battle, all ARVN commanders of smaller units, officers, NCOs, and soldiers at An-Loc and on Route 13, were heroes. Among them, the most glorious would be Colonel Le Nguyen Vy (later, in 1973, promoted to Brigadier General and Commander of the ARVN 5th Infantry Division), Colonel Tran Van Nhut (later, in September 1972, promoted to Brigadier General and Commander of the ARVN 2nd Infantry Division), Colonel Truong Huu Duc, commander of the 5th Armored Regiment (killed in action); Colonel Bui Duc Diem, 5th Infantry Division operational chief of staff; Lieutenant Colonel Phan van Huan, 81st Special Airborne Battle-Group commander, Lieutenant Colonel Nguyen van Biet, 3rd Ranger Battle-Group commander, Lieutenant Colonel Nguyen Viet Can, 32nd Regiment commander (killed in action), Lieutenant Colonels Le van Ngoc, Nguyen Chi Hieu, Nguyen van Dinh, and Van Ba Ninh, four heroes of the 1st Airborne Brigade. The list would include Lt. Colonel Ly Duc Quan the 7th Regiment Commander, Major Huynh van Tam, deputy commander of the 8th Infantry Regiment, Captain Pham Chau Tai of the 81st Special Airborne Battle-Group and Captain Le van Chanh, commander of the 5th Reconnaissance Company.

On July 11, the ARVN 18th Infantry Division of Brigadier General Le Minh Dao, replaced the ARVN 5th Infantry Division at An-Loc and the ARVN 25th Infantry Division replaced the ARVN 21st Infantry Division at Chon-Thanh. On July 20, the 25th Division finally dislodged the NVA 7th Division's blockades at Tau-O Stream and along Route 13 to An-Loc.

The battle of An-Loc ended and the communist Summer 1972 Offensive Campaign against ARVN III Corps & Region was completely defeated. The victory of An-Loc in III Corps and Kontum in II Corps permitted the Joint General Staff of the RVNAF to move the Airborne Division and the 81st Special Airborne Battle-Group to reinforce I Corps & Region for a counter-attack campaign against the communists to recapture Quang-Tri Province.

On July 28, General Ngo Quang Truong, I Corps & Region commander, launched the Lam-Son 72 counter-attack campaign against the communist forces, which had increased to six infantry divisions and two other division-sized armored, artillery and anti-aircraft units in the northern part of his military region. His plan was to recapture Quang-Tri Province's territory north of My-Chanh River, the capital city, and the Old Citadel with two ARVN elite Airborne and Marine Divisions, while keeping the 1st, 2nd, and 3rd Infantry

Brigadier General Le van Hung, ARVN 5th Infantry Division and An-Loc Field Commander. The General declared he would fight to the death; he would never leave the city if he lost An-Loc. On April 30, 1975, after President Duong van Minh surrendered to the Communists and disbanded the Republic of Vietnam Armed Forces, this hero took his own life. Courtesy Brigadier General Le Quang Luong.

Divisions for the search-and-destroy operations in Thua-Thien, Quang-Tin, Quang-Nam, and Quang-Ngai Provinces to secure his rear side.

The ARVN units' competence at fighting was again proved in this unbalanced battleground, particularly in Quang-Tri Province. Even though outnumbered by the communist forces, the Airborne and Marine Divisions, plus some additional armored and artillery regiments, under the direct command of General Truong, advanced along both sides of Highway 1 and successively crushed the communist small and large units on their march to the Quang-Tri capital city. After three months of proceeding with the decisively powerful support of U.S. Air Force strategic B-52 bombers, U.S. Navy warships' firepower along the coast, and U.S. and VNAF tactical bombers-fighters, these ARVN Airborne and Marine Divisions, and their attached units, finally recaptured Quang-Tri City and the Old Citadel on September 16, 1972, and pushed the NVA forces over the Thach-Han River. This latter victory marked the disastrous end of the communist Summer 1972 Offensive Campaign in South Vietnam. South Vietnamese writer Captain Phan Nhat Nam named this communist campaign "Red Summer 1972."

The total communist losses in the battles were assuredly enormous. It was estimated that sixty percent of their troops and eighty percent of their war materiel, including tanks, artillery fields guns, and anti-aircraft guns and missiles that had poured into South Vietnam battlefields in this audacious Summer 1972 Offensive Campaign, were destroyed. In the third week of

September, when President Thieu and COMUS-
MAVC General Abrams visited the ARVN Airborne Division's field command headquarters at
Hiep-Khanh, Quang-Tri, they saw abundant
NVA war materiel captured, tanks (T-54, PT-76,
and BTR 85); field artillery guns (75mm, 122mm
and 130mm); anti-aircraft missiles and guns (SA-
7, AT-3, 12.8mm, 37mm, and 57mm) plus three
dozen transport vehicles (Zi and Molotova) and
thousands of personal weapons of all kinds. The
Soviet-made war equipment had been carried
from the Soviet Union to North Vietnam via the
Hai-Phong Seaport.

During this communist offensive campaign,
the ARVN troops had proved their bravery, ability and competence. They would have assured the
success of the Vietnamization if the United States
had continued to strongly support them with air-
power and firepower. In addition, the South Vietnamese Army should have been strengthened with

Top: Brigadier General Le Quang Luong, Commander of the Airborne Division, a prominent tactician
and RVNAF hero. He commanded the 1st Airborne Brigade that saved An-Loc in May and June of
1972. Courtesy Brigadier General Le Quang Luong. *Bottom:* Lieutenant General Nguyen Van Minh
(center), Commander of ARVN III Corps and Region. Brigadier General Le Van Hung (right), Commander of ARVN 5th Infantry division and An-Loc's Field Commander. Colonel Le Quang Luong
(Left), commander of ARVN 1st Airborne Brigade (in December 1972, he was promoted to Brigadier
General and Commander of ARVN Airborne division). Courtesy General Le Quang Luong.

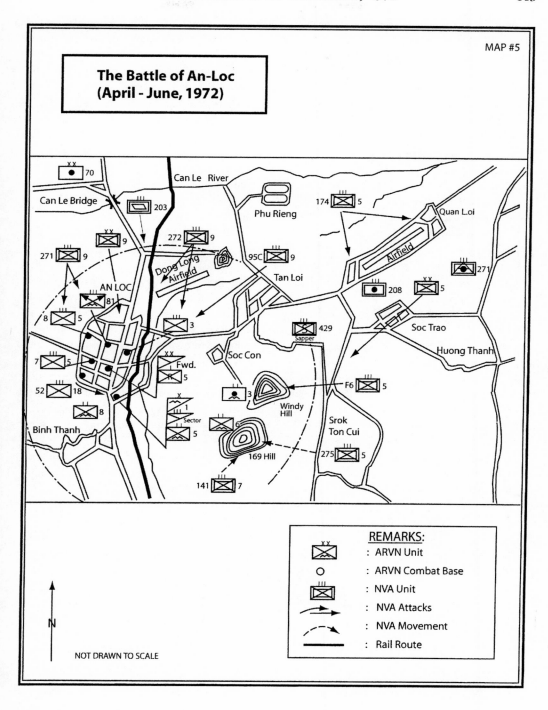

MAP #5

The Battle of An-Loc
(April - June, 1972)

REMARKS:

: ARVN Unit

O : ARVN Combat Base

: NVA Unit

: NVA Attacks

: NVA Movement

: Rail Route

N

NOT DRAWN TO SCALE

at least four or five more divisions to replace the eleven U.S. and Allied large units that had left South Vietnam in the previous months. This crucial augmentation of ARVN combat units should have been realized prior to any political solution to preserve the existence of the South Vietnamese regime. If the United States had never engaged combat troops in this "testing ground," the question of the life and death of South Vietnam would have depended on its own government. But now, after ten years of directly engaging, leading and escalating this complicated war to the point that it puzzled even the most clever brains of the world, the United States had the responsibility to do its best for the ARVN before transferring the heaviest burden of the war to the shoulders of its commanders and troops. President Nixon and his adviser Kissinger should know these problems, especially after the communist 1972 Summer Offensive Campaign, where ARVN units everywhere had been outnumbered and outgunned by the NVA units.

On their side, South Vietnam's leaders should have learned from the Red Summer that without the strong support of US Air strategic and tactical firepower, ARVN units, through with determined morale, bravery and fighting capacity, could not fight and defend their assigned grounds. Thus, had the Vietnamization been completed, the U.S. Air Force would have gone and the equation "ARVN + U.S. Air Powers = NVA + Inter-Com Weaponry" would have been deficient and become "ARVN < NVA + Inter-Com Weaponry." Further, the balance of firepower in the battlefield would tilt to the enemy side and South Vietnam would be in danger.

In this situation, the most imperative needs for the RVNAF to continue safeguarding democracy were firepower from the air force and the navy and more troops for the army. Undeniably, President Thieu had vision concerning these important matters. However, he lacked the determination to deal with the Nixon administration. The period prior to the U.S. 1972 presidential election was very sensitive to President Nixon. Every political or military event in South Vietnam could seriously affect his second-term presidential candidacy. If President Thieu exposed his desire to give up his power in South Vietnam, then that might have changed Nixon's decisions to transform the RVNAF into a really modern armed force. Or, at the very least Thieu could have called for a nationwide "Committee for Reforms" with selected and elite politicians, economists, and strategists to carefully study measures for South Vietnam in a longer-standing struggle against North Vietnam while the United States had clear intentions to disengage from Vietnam.

President Thieu took several political and military actions to strengthen his administration after the Red Summer, but these moves were not clear enough, not efficacious enough, and less known to visionaries. On the contrary, everybody knew that he shared power with a few feckless and corrupt generals who, instead of contributing their knowledge to heal a fragmented society after the Vietnamization and a wounded armed force after the Red Summer directed contraband and black markets or spread corruption for their own greed and prosperity. They ruined both the administration and the armed forces by selling important posts to mediocre officers and collecting monthly bribes from them. Corruption at the highest levels of South Vietnam wreaked the greatest havoc to the regime and most discouraged its supporters in Washington and around the world. South Vietnam in the 1970s was different from South Korea in the 1950s. How would the United States solve the problem of Vietnam reasonably?

12

"Washing Their Hands"

The crucial problem of modernizing the South Vietnamese Armed forces was not considered by American leaders, who instead looked to "wash their hands" by effectuating a single political solution with North Vietnam. Knowledgeable opinion said that if the RVNAF were suitably modernized, the South Vietnamese leaders could handle the war by themselves and the war would intensify to an extent beyond the control of the United States. Then, there would be no more peace talks nor would Nixon's policy of Peace with Honor be realized. American leaders would probably perceive any issues of Vietnam at that time, from Hanoi leaders' political and military aims for the South and Saigon leaders' aspiration to defend their regime, but they would just solve the superficial problems and let the imperative ones to be naturally ignored and buried in silence. Otherwise, Washington would see only the issue to immediately use its military powers to force Hanoi to accept its will at the Paris peace talks. Kissinger was the author and director of this dramatic but dynamic war-game involving American actors.

THE LAST WAR GAMES

President Nixon reacted in retaliation to the communist Summer Offensive Campaign by ordering the massive Linebacker I bombing offensive against North Vietnam. Unlike the Rolling Thunder air campaign under Johnson's presidency, this air campaign was a no-limited-targets offensive. Almost every strategic and tactical objective in the North, including the Hanoi Capital and Hai-Phong Harbor, was targeted. At the time, North Vietnam's air-defense network was extremely strong, composed of more than 2,000 surface-to-air SAM-7 Sparrow missiles, 4,000-plus heavy anti-aircraft batteries, and more than two hundred Soviet MIG fighters. U.S. strategic B-52 bombers and tactical fighter crews that flew over North Vietnam faced a higher threat from the air-defenses than they could imagine.

The U.S. Navy received orders from the White House to mine North Vietnam's Hai-Phong Harbor. The mining operation, "Pocket Money," began at 08:30 A.M. on May 8, 1972. From the decks of aircraft carrier U.S.S. *Coral Sea*, U.S. Navy and Marine mine-laying aircraft carried and laid three dozen one-ton anti-shipping magnetic-acoustic sea mines into the channel that links the port of Hai-Phong to the Gulf of Tonkin. Protected by two cruisers, the U.S.S. *Chicago* and U.S.S. *Long Beach*, these U.S. Navy and Marine mine-laying aircraft completed the mining in only a few minutes. Four North Vietnamese MIGs tried to intercept and one was shot down by surface-to-air missiles from the U.S.S. *Chicago*.

The blockade of Hai-Phong Harbor was supposed to have been achieved many years earlier. As a poor country lacking any industrial or economic means of production, North Vietnam could not make war without the communist bloc's continuous and abundant economic and military aid. Concerning military aid, a U.S. intelligence estimate disclosed that of all war equipment and materials supplied to North Vietnam, 65 percent came from the Soviet Union, 25 percent from China, and the other 10 percent from other Eastern European communist countries. When conflicts occurred between the Soviet Union and China, the Soviets cut back their land shipment of war goods through Chinese railroads and shifted to sea transport into North Vietnam.

The Soviet Union assured the war goods would arrive in North Vietnam through two naval transport fleets. The first fleet, comprised of 125 vessels, ran consecutively 7,500 miles from Odessa to Hai-Phong Harbor. The second fleet of 25 vessels ran from Vladivostok to the same North Vietnamese seaport. Hai-Phong Harbor, day after day, became the artery port for all Soviet warships pouring war equipment and materiel into North Vietnam, including MiG-17 and MiG-21 combat aircraft; SAM-7 anti-aircraft missiles; 130mm heavy artillery guns; T-54, PT-76, and BTR-85 tanks; and all kinds of small guns and ammunition. Had Hai-Phong been neutralized in 1965, as proposed by U.S. Navy Admiral Thomas Moorer, commander-in-chief of Pacific Command, the ability of the communists of North Vietnam to wage war would have faded even before the 1968 Tet Offensive and the 1972 Summer Offensive campaigns in South Vietnam; the United States would not have lost a great number of its air force and navy warplanes and air crews in North Vietnam during the Rolling Thunder and the Linebacker I air campaigns; and the war would have ended earlier.

Perhaps the prime reasons the previous administrations of the United States delayed blockading Hai-Phong Harbor were that such an American military measure might lead to a widened war with China, a reconciliation between China and the Soviet Union, and more political conflict between the United States and the Soviet Union, especially if a Soviet cargo ship were hit by American sea mines. Now, under the magical wand of Kissinger, two weeks after mining this important North Vietnamese seaport, on May 22, 1972, President Nixon visited Moscow. The next day, many of the largest newspapers in the world carried photos of the president of the United States shaking hands with the prime minister of the Soviet Union. Several agreements between the United States and the Soviet Union, including the strategic arms agreement, followed. China, also, kept its secret silence about this new American military measure against North Vietnam. The long-feared violent Soviet and Chinese reactions to the mining never happened.

The super-powers had played the biggest and most risky games. However, the losers of the games would be the Vietnamese people, both in the North and in the South. Even today, nobody knows the curious games of these giants. No one would fathom the secret agreements to shape the "world order" between the leaders of the United States, the Soviet Union, and China that would determine the fate of Vietnam. But everybody would come to know that South Vietnam was sacrificed during the course of these games.

In Vietnam, by mid–September 1972, the North Vietnamese communists were exhausted and had come to the end of their tether about continuing the war. Their invasions of the South by conventional attacks to capture Quang-Tri, Kontum, and An-Loc had failed with heavy losses of manpower and firepower. The remainders of their regular units were dispersed and speckled in forested and mountainous buffer zones and in the border areas. These units were unable to concentrate again for any frontal attacks on any ARVN positions but passively sheltered themselves to avoid U.S. bombings and ARVN counter-attacks. We might conclude that the North Vietnamese war potential had gradually been drained, not only by the continuous U.S. bombings, but also by the serious losses in Laos, on the Ho Chi Minh Trail, in Cambodia, and in South Vietnam. The U.S. blockade of Hai-Phong Harbor aggravated the shortage of their economic and military potential.

In particular, there was a manpower shortage. The Vietnamese Communist Party had to draft children aged 15 and 16 years for its People's Army. Tens of thousands of these kids were sent to the battlefields in the South and thousands of them were killed during the 1972 Summer Offensive Campaign. Suffering from this disastrous offensive campaign and facing the Linebacker I bombing and the mining of Hai-Phong Harbor, the most vital need of the communists of North Vietnam was for a détente of at least two to four years, to reconstitute and replenish their People's Army, both in the North and in the South, in order to continue their long-term military goals. Had Communist Party leaders been so foolish as to continue the war during this critical period, the People's Army would doubtlessly have been destroyed and North Vietnam would have collapsed. This absolute necessity of "a time for détente" was the main reason that the VWP's Politburo ordered Le Duc Tho, its member and chief negotiator, to request a meeting with Kissinger on October 1, 1972, at Paris, to continue the secret peace talks.

Le Duc Tho, this time, came to Paris as a negotiator in a bad position who "implored" rather than "imposed" merciful conditions. Ironically, Kissinger, the assistant professor of a notable university of the United States and a very honorable international politician, was less skillful in negotiations in Paris than Le Duc Tho, a graduate from a Vietnamese high school. The great magician of the modern civilized world was not equal to the dark and savage sorcerer of the wild jungles.

THE LAST "POLITICAL SETTLEMENT" WITH A PROMISE

Le Duc Tho met with Kissinger in a secret meeting on October 8, 1972. He passed to Kissinger North Vietnam's proposal for "Ending the War and Restoring Peace" in Vietnam. Some historians have named this proposal a "military settlement." In reality, the proposal was North Vietnam's complete package for peace, which included both military and political solutions for Vietnam. The "military settlement" portion consisted of articles concerning a cease-fire in-place in return for the complete withdrawal of all U.S. forces from South Vietnam, the stopping of all U.S. military activities in North Vietnam, including the clearing of all US sea mines from North Vietnam's waters, and an exchange of war prisoners.

The "political settlement" was composed of articles concerning the establishment of a "National Council of Reconciliation" and a general election to settle a new political regime for South Vietnam. This political solution was a little different from that of Le Duc Tho in 1971. With the new proposal, Hanoi leaders took a step back in from their previous extreme demands for a "coalition government" in the South and the "removal" of President Thieu from power. Thieu would remain in his position and the official government of South Vietnam would continue until the new "National Council of Reconciliation" could organize and complete the general election for a new regime and leadership for the South.

The most important article of the North Vietnam peace package was the "cease-fire in place," which would permit the North to leave an estimated of 150,000 NVA regular troops in-place in South Vietnam or on its borders. Although the U.S. forces were required to totally withdraw from South Vietnam, the NVA forces could stay as organic units of the South Liberation Government Army.

The other importance of this peace proposal was that the communists of North Vietnam bore no responsibility for the war in Indochina and implied that the United States was the source of all hostilities that devastated Vietnam, Laos, and Cambodia. The U.S was an invader that had the obligation to compensate war-costs, to heal the wounds of the war, and to reconstruct North Vietnam and Indochina. In other words, the communists' proposal implied that the United States was the loser. Le Duc Tho, himself, and Hanoi leaders, who had been in the verge of collapse in the previous months, must have jumped for joy and convulsed with laughter when every article of their proposed military and political settlement was completely accepted by Kissinger.

Hanoi leaders set the trap and baited Kissinger to walk into it by bestowing on the United States the great face-saving device of letting South Vietnamese President Thieu remain in power; and by regulating the "honorable withdrawal" of the American combat troops, which had been completed in August 1972, the "peace with honor" that would satisfy the American public could be gained. In addition, the timing of this peace proposal would help President Nixon gain maximum votes in his second term presidential candidacy in the November election.

Perhaps these reasons explain why Kissinger grabbed Le Duc Tho's peace package and considered it his personal victory. Otherwise, explaining Kissinger's conduct in acting like a loser is difficult. Although the American public had turned against the war, the Americans would not want to be the losers. President Nixon obviously needed "peace with honor" and a second term presidency, but he would not want to be a loser and he would not want to make any concessions to Hanoi leaders. Then, should Kissinger's inclination for bestowing South Vietnam to the communists be interpreted as intentional? Or, did President Nixon himself, the greatest political designer of the time, perhaps plan the long-term foreign policy for the United States in Southeast Asia to include giving up South Vietnam to gain peace for the region? Nobody knows.

In ten lively days after the secret meeting between Tho and Kissinger on October 8, a complete peace treaty was drafted in detail by Washington and Hanoi. President Nixon and North Vietnamese prime minister Pham van Dong also exchanged letters concerning arms replacement after the cease-fire and the schedule for releasing the 566 American pilots held captive in North Vietnam.

The signing of the peace agreements was set for October 31, 1972. President Thieu and his delegation at the Paris conference were kept in the dark about the secret peace talks between Le Duc Tho and Kissinger and the peace agreement between the United States and North Vietnam until Kissinger came to inform Saigon of the results, suggesting that President Thieu accept the agreements and sign the peace treaty. On October 18, President Thieu received Kissinger in a cold and frigid manner, in the presence of U.S. Ambassador to Saigon, Ellsworth Bunker, and Kissinger's military adviser, General Alexander Haig.

Doctor Kissinger might have thought that by keeping Thieu in power, Thieu would be content the peace agreements designed by Hanoi and Washington. Perhaps this intellectual immigrant from a European country to the United States underestimated Thieu's patriotism. Later, Thieu was obliged to emigrate to the United States, but bearing the spirit of Asian culture, he never lost his love for his country. Perhaps the difference between Doctor Kissinger and President Thieu was related in this essential point: Kissinger miscalculated Thieu's notion of "country, quality, and dignity." There are many ambitious men who want the so-called "carrot," but there are others who do not want it. This is the essential point that distinguishes honest men from small-minded ones.

Later, President Thieu recalled his confrontation with Kissinger: "They said I am an unreasonable man. I acted as a patriot, as a Vietnamese, and as a President who is responsible for the fate of our country." And, he clarified:

> I said that the life or death of South Vietnam relied on two points. One, the North Vietnamese troops had been allowed to stay forever; secondly, there's a coalition government camouflaged under the form of a National Council. Mr. Kissinger had negotiated over our heads with the com-

munists. At that point the Americans wanted to end the war as fast as possible to wash their hands, to quit Vietnam because of the domestic problem in the United States. It was not an error in politics. It was a deliberate wrong political choice.[1]

Both Ambassador Bunker and General Haig, who were present at the meeting, were sympathetic to President Thieu. However, these two wise American authorities were later ordered by Washington to persuade President Thieu to accept the peace agreements that Thieu had rejected on October 22. On the plane flying back to Washington, Kissinger told one of his aides that he would take a very brutal way to end the war and not let it continue for another four years under President Nixon's second term.

On October 25, President Nixon asked Hanoi for a delay in the signing of the peace treaty, reflecting Saigon's dissidence. The next day, Hanoi Radio made an announcement of the full terms of the peace treaty and the pre-agreed October 31 signing date. The same day, Kissinger responded by asserting that "peace is at hand." In late October, President Nixon ordered a halt to the Linebacker I air campaign against North Vietnam. A week later, on November 7, President Nixon was reelected with 60.7 percent of the votes.

Two weeks later, on November 20, Kissinger flew back to Paris and continued secret peace talks with Le Duc Tho. This time, the United States introduced a list of sixty changes and clarifications on the terms of the peace treaty to comply with President Thieu's requests. All of these proposed changes were minor except for the requirement of the withdrawal of North Vietnamese troops from South Vietnam. In the meantime, Washington promised a significant increase in military and economic aid for Saigon. President Nixon also sent messages through Ambassador Bunker to reassure the president of South Vietnam that the United States would not accede to a peace treaty with North Vietnam without the consent of Saigon. On the contrary, Nixon asked Thieu to comply with the United States' peace policy and not widen the discord between Washington and Saigon while there was in the United States such tremendous pressure on the administration, from Congress and the public, to stop the war.

In Paris, no one would know the exact details of discussions between Henry Kissinger and Le Duc Tho behind closed doors. However, the Hanoi counter-demands were stiffened so that Kissinger cabled Ambassador Bunker on November 25 to suggest President Thieu deploy his armed forces to control South Vietnamese territory as much as possible to prepare for a cease-fire in place. Hanoi agreed to make a few minor changes in the terms of the peace conditions but would firmly retain its armed forces in place in South Vietnam. This life or death problem for the South was the one that President Thieu constantly struggled against during those days.

General Haig, between mid–November and mid–December 1972, was a lively shuttle between Washington and Saigon. Several times he persuaded President Thieu, in the worst case scenario, to accept the risks of the peace treaty rather than lose all U.S. military and economic aid. He also carried a little hope for President Thieu, which was an assurance letter written by President Nixon, dated November 15, 1972, and addressed to President Thieu. A portion of the letter read: "You have my absolute assurance that if Hanoi fails to abide the terms of this agreement, it is my intention to take swift and severe retaliatory reaction."[2]

On November 26, President Thieu sent two special envoys to Washington to present to President Nixon a letter concerning the two points of the preliminary peace treaty to which the United States had agreed that would sink South Vietnam: (1) allowing the North Vietnamese Army to stay in the South; and (2) creating a National Council comprised of "three fragments." President Thieu explained that the destiny of the South Vietnamese people and their chosen regime would depend on these military and political conditions that Hanoi had imposed to usurp the government of the South in the near future. Accepting such a peace treaty would mean admitting to the demolition of the South Vietnamese democracy.

President Thieu's concerns sounded acceptable in the White House but not at the negotiating table in Paris. Indeed, Le Duc Tho, Hanoi's chief negotiator, rejected all requests by the U.S. to reverse on these issues, which were at the core of their plan.

In the beginning of December 1972, an aide to Kissinger remarked that North Vietnamese negotiators were sliding away from an agreement. They were dragging their counter-demands as "stalling technicalities." The United States had no choice but to break off the negotiations and the secret peace talks with North Vietnam. On December 13, the North Vietnamese delegates walked out of the Paris peace-talks. The talks came to a complete breakdown. This led to the "brutal way," as Kissinger foretold. Five days later, the last act of Kissinger's war game was performed by the U.S. Strategic Air Command (SAC) and Tactical Air Command (TAC) in the massive air campaign Linebacker II against North Vietnam.

During October and November, Hanoi leaders were using the suspension of the post–Linebacker I air campaign to rebuild the strength of their People's Army, both in the North and in the South. In the North, they used up their last anti-aircraft guns and surface-to-air missiles to strengthen their air-defense networks, especially in Hanoi and Hai-Phong. In the South, NVA large units were replenished and strengthened by new recruits infiltrated from the North. These units regained their activities to widen their occupied zones and encroach on new areas, which were mostly in the buffer zones and mountainous and desert areas along the borders and the Mekong Delta in ARVN IV Corps & Region. By mid–December, the NVA strength reached 180,000 men, not including 90,000 from the local VC units. These NVA units in the future would become the seeds of misfortune for the South Vietnamese regime, but in December 1972, were the source of disagreement between the United States and both North Vietnam and South Vietnam.

Prior to the complete breakdown of the secret peace talks on December 13, 1972, Kissinger had warned Le Duc Tho that a breakdown in negotiations would result in a resumption of massive military means to solve the war. In the meantime, South Vietnamese president Nguyen van Thieu was also informed that there would be a total cut off of all American military and economic aid for South Vietnam if he did not consent to the military and political settlements for a "peace with honor."

On December 15, President Thieu notified Ambassador Bunker that he would accept the North Vietnamese Army troops "staying in place" in the South and place his trust in the United States, particularly in President Nixon's assurance.

The Linebacker II air campaign began in the afternoon of December 18. The Americans sought to show their tough and serious intentions in order to convince the communists of North Vietnam of the benefits of returning to the negotiating table. The campaign would also strangle the communist war effort and their ability to sustain a major offensive within South Vietnam. The Americans aimed to extinguish their war potential, by massively bombing pinpoint targets, such as the Hanoi Capital, Hai-Phong Harbor, railroad networks, arterial roads and bridges, power facilities, equipment and supplies storage facilities, troops installations, airfields, and surface-to-air missiles sites and facilities. In all, 59 strategic targets in North Vietnam were chosen by U.S. planners.

This huge Linebacker II air offensive "provided for continuous around-the-clock" attack, as a U.S. Air Force colonel described it, by using tactical air strikes by day and massive B-52 strategic bombing raids by night, to keep "constant" pressure on North Vietnam.

Phase 1 of the Linebacker II ran from December 18 to December 20. The first night more than 120 B-52s attacked Hanoi Capital in three separate waves. Communist air-defense units fired more than 270 SAMs at the U.S. strategic attacking bombers and shot down three. On December 19, and 20, they fired more than 380 SAMs and shot down seven others. Phase 2 of the U.S. air campaign began on December 21 and lasted until December 24. The communist anti-aircraft network at Hanoi and Hai-Phong fired fewer SAMs than the three previous days, only 110, and shot down two B-52s.

After the 36 hour Christmas stand-down, U.S. SAC and TAC reopened Phase 3 on December 26, the last phase of Linebacker II, with paramount destructive bombing by 120 B-52 bombers, in ten waves over all chosen targets in North Vietnam. This intensive bombing lasted for two more days, December 27 and 28. In this last phase of attack, only three B-52s were shot down and the communists fired only 70 SAMs. This showed the ruin of their war potential.

President Nixon warned Hanoi leaders that the bombing would not stop unless they agreed to come back to the negotiating table in Paris and accept the terms of the peace agreements previously discussed in October and November 1972. Finally, on December 28, North Vietnam asked for a return to the Paris peace conference and the resumption of the secret peace-talks between Le Duc Tho and Kissinger.

On December 29, President Nixon ordered a halt to the Linebacker II air-campaign against North Vietnam. This marked the last act of U.S. direct military involvement in Vietnam and Indochina. In the eleven days of the Linebacker II air campaign against North Vietnam, the United States lost 23 aircraft, including 15 B-52s, with thirty-three pilots killed and another thirty-three captured. However, North Vietnam was on the verge of collapse. In eleven days and nights of this air campaign of "terrifying destruction," the United States dropped 100,000 bombs on Hanoi and Hai-Phong. This quantity is equivalent to five of the atomic bombs dropped on Hiroshima.

U.S. Air Force General William W. Momyer, the former Seventh Air Force commander, noted: "The 11-day [Linebacker II] campaign came to a close on the 29th of December 1972, when North Vietnamese responded to the potential threat of continued air attacks to the economic, political, social and military life of their country. It was apparent that air power was the decisive factor leading to the peace agreement of 27 January 1973."[3]

There were several contradictory comments on the last air-campaign against North Vietnam, but the most notable one came from Winston Lord, one of Kissinger's aides. Lord related the precise motives of the campaign: "The President felt that he had to demonstrate that he couldn't be trifled with — and, frankly, *to demonstrate our toughness to Thieu* — this was the rationale for the bombing."[4] In this comment, Lord himself put a phrase in italics. According to Lord's judgment of the "rationale," the Linebacker II air campaign against North Vietnam was a military feint that smothered Washington's intent to politically attack South Vietnam. And if the word "toughness" means Kissinger's "brutal way," or brutality, everybody would conclude that Washington's act of seeding the military brutality in Hanoi was synonymous with the dissemination of political brutality in Saigon in order to collect a certain harvest, "peace with honor."

Indeed, if Washington were able to draw the Hanoi leaders back to the Paris peace talks through this war game, the Saigon leaders would be forced to accept the peace treaty. However, the difference between the North and the South was that the North endured eleven days of forceful bombing and was compensated by the United States with every favorable condition for peace. The South, on the other hand, suffered from every oppressive condition of the peace treaty. Certainly both Nixon and Kissinger knew that. The only thing President Nixon could do for South Vietnam was make honorable promises to South Vietnamese President Nguyen van Thieu that in case North Vietnam violated the peace treaty, the United States would respond with military means. Meanwhile, Congress clearly reneged on America's pledge to South Vietnam, which had been ensured in the South-East Asia Resolution of August 7, 1964.

On January 5, 1973, three days prior to the resumption of the Paris Peace Conference and Kissinger-Tho's secret peace talks, following the suggestion of Ambassador Bunker, President Nixon wrote another letter to reassure President Thieu that the United States would strongly support South Vietnam before the signing of the Paris peace agreement, agreeing to rush one billion dollars of war equipment for the RVNAF and promising to react vigorously to any communist violation of the peace agreement.

On January 20, 1973, in the inaugural address of his second presidential term, President Nixon declared the change in United States' foreign policy; he said: "We shall do our share in defending peace and freedom in the world, but we shall expect others to do their share. The time has passed when America will make every other nation's conflict its own, or make every nation's future our responsibility, or presume to tell other nations how to manage their own affairs."[5] Thus, the fate of South Vietnam was sealed.

On January 23, the final settlements for the peace of Vietnam were initiated in Paris by Henry Kissinger and Le Duc Tho. All proposed North Vietnamese conditions for the peace treaty were blindly agreed to by Kissinger. Many historians comment that Kissinger himself gave in but not President Nixon. Indeed, the president and the American people were taken in by this master politician. But there was not enough evidence to examine the case. Anyway, South Vietnam was sold out. The signing of the Paris Accords was scheduled on January 27, 1973. The accords would go into effect on the same day at 24:00 Greenwich Mean Time.

In these days, General Alexander Haig was present in Saigon. He submitted to President Thieu a letter from President Nixon, dated January 18, suggesting the South Vietnamese president sign the Paris Accords. Otherwise, any opposition by Thieu would result in a sudden and total cessation of all American military and economic aid for South Vietnam by the U.S. Congress. Facing the immediate "death sentence" of South Vietnam, President Thieu had to accept the Paris Accords. He had to believe in Nixon's promises assuring him that the United States would "react very strongly and rapidly" and "with full force" if Hanoi seriously violated the truce. Later, in March 1975, when North Vietnam conducted its final campaign against South Vietnam, the two letters of President Nixon, dated November 14, 1972, and January 5, 1973, respectively, became waste papers.

THE SURRENDER: PARIS "PEACE ACCORDS"

For the Paris accords, the two "secret peace negotiators," Le Duc Tho and Henry Kissinger, were jointly awarded the 1973 Nobel Peace Prize. The latter accepted the award; the former, who was more honest, declined, saying there was still no peace in Vietnam. Tho's "modest manner" in refusing this honorable award, in reality, was a warning of further North Vietnamese offensives against South Vietnam and, at the same time, an expression of disdain toward the United States and the other nations that signed the Paris Peace Accords. Tho's attitude was clearly foolish and eccentric. However, he was a dominant adversary to the honorable Professor Kissinger.

Indeed, what the communists of North Vietnam were unable to gain in the battlefield over the previous 18 years, since 1955 — to oust the Americans from Vietnam and defeat the South Vietnamese by military means, and to establish a so-called coalition government in

South Vietnam as the prime step of their goal "to liberate the South"— Le Duc Tho had won, in principle, by political and diplomatic means from Kissinger in Paris.

Actually, the Paris Peace Accords were seen by many military and political observers as a defeat for the United States. Retired U.S. Colonel Eugene H. Grayson had a clear view of the peace treaty after its implementation; he wrote: "The Paris Peace Accords, which ended U.S. involvement in Southeast Asia, were a year old, and there was no doubt in the eyes of the North [and anyone else with a reasonable degree of intelligence] that those agreements represented a major victory of Hanoi and a costly defeat for the United States."[6] A political observer, John Negroponte, one of Kissinger's negotiators, stated: "The peace treaty did nothing for Saigon. We got our prisoners back; we were able to end our direct military involvement. But there were no ostensible benefits for Saigon to justify all of the enormous effort and bloodshed of the previous years."[7]

The comments of these American military and political observers were precise, impartial, and accurate. The content of the treaty proved that the United States was a victim of the North Vietnamese communists' foul play. The nine Chapters of 23 Articles of the so-called Agreement on Ending the War and Restoring Peace in Vietnam, or the Paris accords, was the kind of "unconditional surrender" proclamation of a vanquished nation. If there were conditions in the agreements, they were the ones imposed by the winners and enforced on the losers.

- Article 2, Chapter II, the most significant issue of the Paris Peace Accords, read: A cease-fire shall be observed throughout South Vietnam as of 24:00 hours G.M.T. on January 27, 1973.

At the same hour, the United States will stop all its military activities against the territory of the Democratic Republic of Vietnam by ground, air and naval forces, wherever they may be based, and end the mining of the territorial waters, ports, harbors, and waterways of North Vietnam as soon as this Agreement goes into effect.

The complete cessation of hostilities mentioned in this Article shall be durable and without limit of time.

This article may be read to imply that the United States was an "invader" that had attacked North Vietnam but now would have to stop all military activities — ground, air and naval — against this country.

Many other articles of the Paris Treaty may be elucidated in the same sense: the United States and its allied forces were "invaders" forced to withdraw not only from South Vietnam but also from Laos and Cambodia, dismantling their military bases under the control of international and local commissions. Other articles in the Paris Peace Accords read as follows:

- Article 3(a), Chapter II: "Within sixty days of the signing of this Agreement, there will be a total withdrawal from South Vietnam of troops, military advisers, and military personnel, including technical military personnel and military personnel associated with the pacification program, armaments, munitions, and war material of the United States and those of other foreign countries mentioned in Article 3(a). Advisers from the above-mentioned countries to all paramilitary organizations and the police force will also be withdrawn within the same period of time."
- Article 6, Chapter II: "The dismantlement of all military bases in South Vietnam of the United States and of the other foreign countries mentioned in Article 3a shall be completed within sixty days of the signing of this Agreement."
- Articles 16, 17, and 18 of Chapter VI prescribe the formation of joint military commissions of "two parties," "four parties," and an "international commission" to control and super-

vise the implementation of the Paris Peace Accords. In fact, the mission of these "commissions" was to survey and enforce the United States' troop "withdrawal and military" dismantlement.

Meanwhile, the Republic of Vietnam (South Vietnam) was the real loser in the Paris Peace Talks Treaty, as revealed in its articles:

- Article 3(b), Chapter II: "The armed forces of two South Vietnamese parties shall remain in-place. The Two-Party Joint Commission described in Article 17 shall determine the areas controlled by each party and the modalities of stationing." Based on this Article, the North Vietnamese Army, described as the Southern Provisional Revolutionary Government's Army, would stay in several areas in South Vietnam (see Map 6). These NVA forces were the seeds of misfortune for the South Vietnam in the very near future.
- Article 12(a), Chapter IV, determines the establishment of a "National Council of National Reconciliation and Concord" of "three equal fragments" and Article 12(b) fixes its functions.
- Article 12(b): "The National Council of National Reconciliation and Concord shall have the task of promoting the two South Vietnamese parties' implementation of this Agreement, achievement of national reconciliation and concord and endurance democrat-liberties. The National Council of Reconciliation and Concord will organize the free and democratic general elections provided for in Article 9(b) and decide the procedures and modalities of these general elections. The institutions for which the general elections are to be held will be agreed upon through consultations between the two South Vietnamese parties. The National Council of Reconciliation and Concord will also decide the procedures and modalities of such local elections as the two South Vietnamese parties agree upon." This political solution was opposed by President Thieu, who had argued that the National Council of Reconciliation and Concord was a disguised "coalition government" in the South imposed by North Vietnam.

These articles not only illustrate the irony of the Peace Treaty, they also were to engender agony for South Vietnam, Laos and Cambodia. North Vietnam, the real invader of South Vietnam and the source of all hostilities in Laos and Cambodia, was not charged by the Paris treaty. On the contrary, this peace treaty offered the North Vietnamese leaders every fortunate condition to "liberate" South Vietnam and occupy Laos and Cambodia. Whatever articles of the treaty enforced restrictions against a foreign nation's military activities in Laos and Cambodia were applicable only to the United States and not to North Vietnam.

For example, Article 20(a), Chapter II, sets forth that "all parties participating in the Paris Conference on Vietnam shall strictly respect the 1954 Geneva Accords on Cambodia and the 1962 Geneva Agreements on Laos"; Article 20(b) asserts that "foreign countries shall put an end to all military activities in Cambodia and Laos, totally withdraw from and refrain from reintroducing into these two countries troops, military advisers and military personnel, armaments, munitions and war materiel"; but North Vietnam did not stop developing the Ho Chi Minh Trail nor withdrawing its armed forces from Laos and Cambodia. On the contrary, again and again, NVA forces continued to violate the neutrality of these countries and used these territories as their accesses and advanced bases to invade South Vietnam.

For the communists of North Vietnam the terms "restriction" and "violation" were meaningless. They had violated the 1954 Geneva Accords on Indochina and the 1962 Geneva Agreements on Laos without any restriction; surely they would violate the Paris Peace Agreements to "liberate" South Vietnam and occupy Laos and Cambodia. The only question was when.

An American historian observed: "Clearly, intelligent men such as Kissinger had to know that this [peace treaty] was a band-aid, knowing perfectly well it was a question of time, a relative short time, before that structure we were leaving behind would collapse."[8]

Washington certainly knew that, because Kissinger had allowed the communists of North Vietnam to keep their armed forces in South Vietnam. In addition, Article 21, the second to last article, obligates the United States to "contribute to healing the wounds of the war and to postwar reconstruction of the Democratic Republic of Vietnam [North Vietnam]." After signing the Treaty, President Nixon sent a secret letter to North Vietnam prime minister Pham van Dong, promising $4.75 billion in postwar reconstruction aid "without any political conditions."[9] In addition, Kissinger and a group of aides went to Hanoi from February 11 to 13 to meet Le Duc Tho and Pham van Dong. After the trip he announced the formation of a United States–North Vietnam Joint Economic Commission. This was ironic. The conquerors were compensated and the defenders were punished.

All American concessions and recompenses to North Vietnam were the sole price for a "peace with honor" and a return of American prisoners of war (POWs), some 566 U.S. Air Force and Navy pilots. In the end, American politicians listened to the American people, and the American people decided that Vietnam was not a war they wanted to continue. The decision was one they had the right to make. Yes, the Americans were right to end the longest war in their history. The logic behind the decision was to stop their government from continuing a hopeless and bloody war. Unfortunately, their right desires were carried out by the wrong politicians who dumped them and American history by a one-sided treaty that resembled surrender. If these American politicians and diplomats had patiently performed at the Paris peace talks the duties entrusted to them by the American people, they would have won an honest peace treaty similar to the 1953 Korean Armistice Agreements. The Americans would not have been the losers and South Vietnam would be secured as South Korea.

The article that most seriously compromised South Vietnam in the Paris Peace Treaty — the cream of the advantageous edges that Henry Kissinger offered to North Vietnam — was Article 7 concerning the reception and replacement of war equipment, armaments, and munitions. This article forbade South Vietnam from receiving war equipment, armaments, and munitions from the outside except for the periodic replacement on a piece-for-piece basis of that destroyed, damaged, worn out or used up after the cease-fire. The provisions, however, did not interdict North Vietnam on the same matters. In other words, North Vietnam could obtain war materiel, equipment, armaments, and munitions of any kind and quantity desired from the Soviet Union, China, and the Eastern Europe's communist countries. Imagine a fighter introduced into an ancient stadium with his hands tied in the back, struggling heroically, defending himself despairingly, and killed cruelly by another with unfettered use of weapons. This was the situation of South Vietnam when fighting against the North Vietnamese communists after the implementation of the Paris Treaty.

In sum, the Paris Peace Agreements were unequal, absurd, and illogical. Many American historians consider this peace treaty to be a "written act" of betrayal by the United States toward its long-standing ally, South Vietnam. All in all, the Paris Peace Treaty was a means for the Americans to wash their hands of South Vietnam, a "necessary détente" for the communists of North Vietnam to replenish, refresh and strengthen their armed forces both in the North and in the South for a further invasion of South Vietnam, and a "death sentence" for South Vietnam, Laos, and Cambodia. The tragedy of Indochina was about to begin.

The Nixon administration secured peace for America with the Paris Peace Agreements, but not for Indochina. After undertaking long and hard military, political and diplomatic

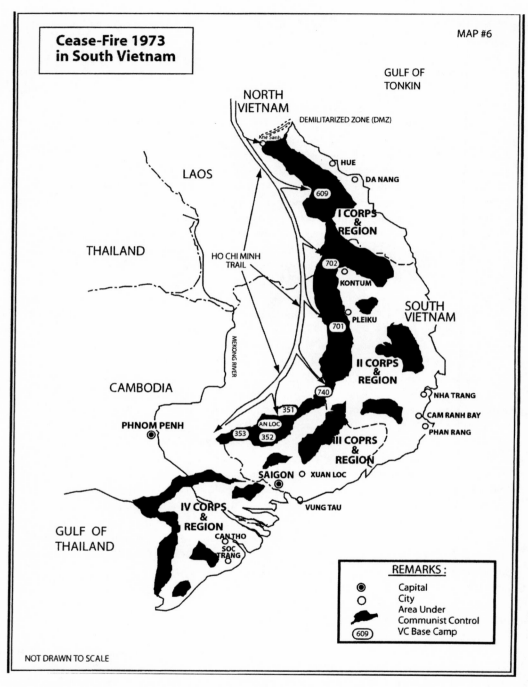

Cease-Fire 1973 in South Vietnam

MAP #6

NORTH VIETNAM

GULF OF TONKIN

DEMILITARIZED ZONE (DMZ)

Khe Sanh

LAOS

HUE

DA NANG

609

I CORPS & REGION

THAILAND

HO CHI MINH TRAIL

702

KONTUM

SOUTH VIETNAM

MEKONG RIVER

701

PLEIKU

II CORPS & REGION

NHA TRANG

CAM RANH BAY

PHAN RANG

CAMBODIA

740

351

PHNOM PENH

353

AN LOC

352

III COPRS & REGION

SAIGON

XUAN LOC

VUNG TAU

IV CORPS & REGION

GULF OF THAILAND

CAN THO

SOC TRANG

REMARKS :

◉ Capital
○ City
⬛ Area Under Communist Control
609 VC Base Camp

NOT DRAWN TO SCALE

measures, the Nixon administration completed its new foreign policy in Southeast Asia. John Ehrlichman, domestic affairs adviser to President Nixon, commented about this peace and the new U.S. policy. He remarked that President Nixon had "won a prize in opening China and in forging some kind of alliance with China vs Russia — and if the price of that was a cynical peace in Vietnam, then historians are going to have to weigh the morality and the pragmatism and all these other things that historians like to weigh."[10] Ehrlichman's conclusion would open new issues for the researches of the United States long-term policy toward Southeast Asia.

In my own opinion, what the United States leaders consider in Southeast Asia was communist China's aggression in other countries of the region but not that of the communist North Vietnam; anyhow, Vietnam was a small country. To bring about diplomatic relations with China was a superficial measure to temporarily hold its ambition to make the region communist, but to use the whole of Vietnam as a permanent fortress to deter the southward aggression of the Chinese communists was the deep design of the Nixon administration.

With this undisclosed purpose, the United States would satisfy North Vietnamese communist leaders not only to give them South Vietnam in the first half of 1970s but also would give them more tangible importance so long as the expansionist Maoism exists in mainland China. And if this hypothesis is correct, Vietnamese nationalist political groups in America nowadays that try to persuade American leaders to subvert the communist regime in Vietnam will have little chance of succeeding.

Because the United States purposely abandoned South Vietnam for political reasons, the 1973 Paris Peace Treaty could not be a reproduction of the 1953 Armistice Agreements in Korea. Morality and pragmatism depend on a nation's interests. In politics, "morality" is usually a superfluous word or a term of trifling importance. Vietnam in 1973 met the test of pragmatism but not of morality. But the American politicians of that time, particularly Kissinger, refused to hear the unpractical term "morality."

Ironically, Thieu still believed in Nixon. Indeed, three months after the 1973 Paris Accords went into effect, in early April, he went to America to ask for American military support and economic aid. He was welcomed by President Nixon at San Clemente (but not in Washington) and was given a few more promises by the latter. Thieu should have known he should firmly demand from the Nixon administration everything he needed for South Vietnam in its standing fight against North Vietnam after the cease-fire, prior to the 1972 general election in the United States, which meant after the "1972 Red Summer." Everything after that was too late, null, invalid, or deceptive. He had a blinded entourage that let him go to America begging for help. Why did he not go there in July or August of 1972?

13

"Betrayal"!

The first goal the communists of North Vietnam brought with them to the Paris Conference on May 12, 1968, was for "the United States [to] first withdraw military forces from South Vietnam." After four years of negotiations, they achieved this and other demands, through the Paris Peace Accords. All American forces were to leave Vietnam no more than sixty days after the peace treaty went into effect. Hanoi leaders knew that once the American ground combat troops, air fighters and bombers, and naval warships were completely out of Vietnam, they would never again return.

On March 29, 1973, one month after implementing the treaty, the last American troops left South Vietnam. Only 8,500 civilian technicians remained in the country, plus a small number of U.S. Embassy personnel, fifty military members of the Defense Attaché Office (DAO), and a small U.S. delegation of the Four-Party Joint Military Team (FPJMT). General Frederick C. Weyand, the last MACV commander, who had replaced General Creighton W. Abrams on June 28, 1972, left Vietnam. MACV dissolved and DAO prime attaché Major General John Murray assisted U.S. Ambassador Bunker in military affairs and coordinated U.S. military assistance to the Republic of Vietnam Armed Forces (RVNAF).

By March 29, a total of 587 American POWs were released by North Vietnam. Another 1,913 American military personnel were listed as missing in action in Vietnam, not including several hundred missing in Laos and Cambodia. Three and half months later, on June 14, 1973, U.S. Senators Frank Church and Clifford Case introduced to the Congress a bill to ban the use of any past or future appropriations for U.S. combat activities in any part of Indochina without the specific authorization of Congress. Passing this so-called "Case-Church Amendment" impeded the U.S. administration from becoming involved again in Indochina and effectively prevented it from enforcing the terms of the Paris accords the U.S. had pledged to uphold. President Nixon's solemn promises to South Vietnamese President Thieu were obstructed by this amendment.

Hanoi leaders were aware of President Nixon's written guarantee to President Thieu that any serious violation of the peace treaty would meet with fierce retaliation by the United States. They surely must have known of the "Case-Church Amendment" forbidding the U.S. administration from using military forces again in Indochina. However, they were unsure of how the United States would respond to a violation, if it happened, until President Nixon resigned from the presidency on August 9, 1974, after a congressional investigation of the Watergate break-in.

The uncertainty among Hanoi leaders of the U.S. reaction, combined with their losses in the recent American Christmas bombing and in the 1972 offensive campaign in South Vietnam, were the main reasons the NVA acted with restraint in the South from March 1973 to mid–August 1974. One might say that the war never stopped after the cease-fire, but it was limited to skirmishes of regiment-sized units in the hinterlands between the ARVN and the NVA forces, which were allowed to remain in South Vietnam according to the absurd terms of the Paris Peace Accords. Significantly, after the truce more than 210,000 people from the communist-controlled areas in the countryside fled to the towns and cities — the highest refugee rate since the end of the 1972 Red Summer. This new burden on the South Vietnamese government gave the impression to foreign reporters that the war was being stepped up and was more ferocious during that period.

GENERAL PERSPECTIVE OF THE REGION AFTER THE CEASE-FIRE OF 1973

Republican leader of the U.S. House of Representatives Gerald R. Ford, who had been appointed to replace vice president Spiro Agnew who resigned in 1973, became president of the United States after the resignation of President Nixon in August 1974. President Ford's policy toward Indochina, in general, continued Nixon's foreign policy of refusing to intervene militarily again in the region, despite the promise of the former president to renew military actions to enforce the peace treaty if it were broken by the North Vietnamese. According to some American historians, President Ford refocused the containment of the international communist expansion in other parts of the world but not in Southeast Asia. Thus, Indochina became a free ground for the communists of North Vietnam to ravish. The Paris Peace Accords had become wastepaper.

After the 1973 January Cease-Fire, the hostilities in Laos continued between the Pathet-Lao Army — in joint operations with the North Vietnamese People's Army — and the rightist forces of General Phoumi Nosavan, to the point that an additional agreement, the "Renewed Cease-Fire Agreement" of September 14, 1973, was signed to temporarily hold them for a short time. However, the North Vietnamese Army continued to freely develop the Ho Chi Minh Trail and extend a series of strong sanctuaries in southern Laos and along the borders until the war ended in April 1975.

In Cambodia, the military situation grew more serious after the cease-fire. Fighting continued between the Khmer-Rouge forces, which were supported by NVA large units, and the national armed forces of President Lon-Nol. The Cambodian president declared a state of emergency beginning March 17, 1973. A month later, Phnom-Penh was virtually under siege. The North Vietnam communist forces not only used the Cambodian borders between South Vietnam to develop their sanctuaries but also to deeply invade Cambodian territory on the west bank of the Mekong River to join with Khmer-Rouge units in their offensive attacks against Lon-Nol's forces. The war lasted throughout the 1973–1975 "Cease-Fire Period."

In South Vietnam, President Thieu began to worry that the United States' assurance to retaliate against North Vietnam, in the event it violated the Paris Accords, had gone with Nixon. Henry Kissinger, unfortunately for Saigon, was given the influential post of secretary of state. According to President Thieu, Kissinger believed that six months after the peace treaty signing South Vietnam would have collapsed. Thieu implied that Kissinger was the first and highest-ranked American politicians who wanted to abandon South Vietnam; to be done as soon as possible, like excising a tumor that had created suffering.

President Thieu's anxiety about the future of South Vietnam was not baseless, and his criticism of the dismantling of Saigon's war potential was not a denunciation against Kissinger and American politicians but a bitter reality. Major General Homer D. Smith, who replaced Major General John Murray in September 1974 as U.S. defense attaché in Saigon, later recalled: "Logistics was to be my primary focus, overseeing the $1 billion in U.S. military assistance authorized by the Defense Assistance Vietnam program. But the decision of U.S. Congress to appropriate $700 million of that billion-dollar authorization was a sure sign that American support for its South Vietnamese ally was waning."[1]

The new U.S. ambassador to Saigon, Graham Martin, who had replaced ambassador Ellsworth Bunker in May 1973, may have thought that the United States had the obligation to back South Vietnam as long as needed once American military involvement ended and the South Vietnamese armed forces were on their own in fighting against the communists. In the eyes of Saigon leaders, ambassador Graham Martin was the last possible hope to speak for South Vietnam. Perhaps the ambassador would persuade Washington to keep its promises, officially and according to the terms of the Paris Peace Accords, and honor the guarantee of a U.S. president to a small allied country's president.

Ambassador Martin did what he was expected to do, but in vain. From mid–1973 to December 1974 he sent various cables to Kissinger with the same purpose: to remind him of "South Vietnam's trust" and "America's honor." Most of his calls went unanswered by Washington. Concerning American military aid for South Vietnam, Ambassador Martin noted that the war in the Middle East in 1973 was a disaster for South Vietnam, because American military aid was diverted to Israel, placing South Vietnam as a "lower priority." Also, because of escalating prices due to the Arab oil embargo, the American military budget for South Vietnam was worth only a quarter of its face value. Later, President Thieu recalled: "The economic aid was cut, the military aid was cut — and we had no means to fight," and he added:

> our potential had been reduced by sixty percent. Meanwhile, the war potential of the North had been increased by the overwhelming help of Russia. I can tell you, during those two years since the signing of the Paris Agreement, the war was more cruel than before the signing. Every week of every month I sent delegates to Washington — military men, political men, Vietnamese senators, to explain. I wrote to the American President and I explained the danger to the Ambassador in Saigon — and nothing happened.[2]

President Thieu's complaints reflected the realities in the 1973–1974 Cease-Fire Period in Vietnam. For instance, after the signing of the Paris Peace Accords, the Soviet Union continued the promises of Soviet President Nicolai Podgony, who had visited Hanoi in 1972 and pledged to modernize the North Vietnamese People's Army with new waves of war equipment and armaments. Military aid was abundantly endowed for years. Particularly, after the completion of the U.S. Navy's "End Sweep Operation" clearing U.S. sea mines from North Vietnamese waters, in two years (1973 and 1974) Soviet military aid quadrupled, and the transport of war goods from Soviet seaports to Hanoi via Hai-Phong Harbor was considerably increased month after month. With the modern Soviet war equipment and with the general mobilization of male children age sixteen and women, the People's Army became the fourth largest and strongest army in the world.

Sixty percent of this army's strength and equipment were sent to Laos and Cambodia, and the majority was sent to South Vietnam. With the Ho Chi Minh Trail freely developing as a highway network, including the newly built Corridor 613, the units of the People's Army in the South were fully replenished and strengthened. According to U.S. and South Vietnam intelligence information, from 1973 to March 1975, the communists sent South somewhere between 200,000 to 250,000 troops and about 1,349,000 tons of supplies, equipments, and ammunition.

The most controversial problem frequently discussed by the U.S. CIA and DIA during the length of the Second Vietnam War was the communist strength in South Vietnam. Neither of the highest intelligence organizations in the United States could provide the White House accurate numbers of the communist troops fighting in each period of the war. However, the estimated number of 150,000 NVA troops left in the South after the 1973 Cease-Fire was acceptable. This number may have doubled by the end of 1974.

Retired U.S. Army Colonel Eugene H. Grayson, Jr., made a logical discernment of the communist strength threatening South Vietnam in those days, writing:

> Intelligence agencies estimated that the NVA left between 10 to 12 divisions in South Vietnam in 1973 following the Paris Peace Accords, plus upward of 300,000 Viet-Cong main force, local force and guerrilla members. By late 1974, in another clear violation of the peace agreement, some 100,000 additional NVA soldiers — with a full complement of equipment and logistical support — had infiltrated south into base camps along the Laotian and Cambodian borders, and some had even gone into "liberated" areas inside South Vietnam.[3]

Thus, according to Grayson, by the end of 1974, the communists had an army of 550,000 troops along the borders and inside South Vietnam. Seventy percent of the VC regular force strength was North Vietnamese who infiltrated to the South from 1968 on to replace these VC units' casualties. This replacement of North Vietnamese troops for the VC regular units became a general rule. But after the 1973 cease-fire, it would be considered a grave violation of the peace treaty.

The International Commission was incompetent in controlling the increase of NVA troops and armaments infiltrating the Ho Chi Minh Trail and pouring into base camps along the borders and inside South Vietnam. This incompetence had an ironic cause. On April 7, 1973, an International Commission helicopter carrying nine of its members, who had attempted to investigate one of the numerous and serious violations of the communists throughout the South, was shot down by an NVA missile in the northern region of Quang-Tri Province. All were killed. After that, the International Commission sought to avoid any similar event that might kill more of its members by controlling the army in towns rather than in the jungle. Thus, the ARVN was subjected to the control but not the NVA.

On the whole, the curtailment of U.S. military aid, the increase of NVA troops and modern war equipment, and the ineffectiveness of the peacekeeping commissions created serious problems for South Vietnam's attempts to fight an extended war by itself during the Cease-Fire Period, after all U.S. ground, air, and naval forces had completely withdrawn. The only hope of the Saigon government was the competent fighting of the ARVN, which needed to be built up at least to 20 regular divisions for a fair defense of South Vietnam. The withdrawal of 11 U.S. and allied large units had left several big gaps in its defense system. Lacking forces, the ARVN, which at the time had thirteen regular divisions stretched over more than a thousand miles from the north to the south, on a geographically rugged terrain, could not cover all the gaps, especially in the Central Highlands of II Corps & Region.

This military region composed of seven provinces in the Central Highlands and five others in the coastal area should have been protected by at least four divisions. However, only two divisions assured the territorial defense of both areas and maintained the security for the major road networks that connect these widely separated areas. This was the prime weakness for which Saigon's leaders were responsible. After the signing of the peace treaty and the withdrawal of U.S. ground forces, President Thieu did not change the strategic disposition of the ARVN. He continued to maintain three divisions at each military region, but only two in II Corps & Region.

Though Thieu understood this critical disposition of the ARVN in South Vietnam, he would not do anything because he had missed the golden opportunity to strengthen the ARVN prior to the signing of the 1973 Paris Accords, precisely during the six-month period prior to the 1972 general election in the United States. In my opinion, instead of opposing the staying in place of 150,000 NVA troops in South Vietnam, President Thieu might have accepted it in exchange (with Washington) for the formation of six more infantry divisions for the ARVN and fighters and bombers for the VNAF (A-4 and A-7 fighters plus CBV-24, CBV-55, and Daisy Cutter Blu-82 bombs.)

He had to maintain the airborne and marine divisions in I Corps Region. First, President Thieu believed that in case the communists flagrantly violated the peace treaty by a major attack, Danang — with its large airfield and seaport — would be used again by the American forces, for a large-scale retaliation; so he kept these two general reserve units in I Corps & Region to protect this strategic city. Second, under the pressure of six NVA divisions in the region, Saigon had to maintain these elite units at I Corps & Region to protect the two northernmost provinces of South Vietnam, Quang-Tri and Thua Thien. In addition, with the U.S. curtailment of economic aid, Saigon had to keep the present divisions at IV Corps & Region in place to protect the vast and rich rice fields of the Mekong Delta for its long-term economic and military purposes. In any case, stationing only two divisions in II Corps & Region was illogical. Certainly, the weakness of Saigon in the Central Highlands was clear in the eyes of Hanoi leaders. And what was to happen, happened in the spring of 1975.

THE COMMUNIST TESTING CAMPAIGN IN SOUTH VIETNAM

After issuing the "Case-Church" amendment to prevent the U.S. executive branch from using military forces in Indochina and curtailing the military assistance budget for fiscal 1974 for South Vietnam, the U.S. Congress next refused to approve all military aid funds that had been appropriated for this small ally for fiscal 1975. The House of Representatives first cut down the proposed $1.45 billion in military aid to $1 billion, and then to $700 million. When it reached the Senate, this amount was cut to $500 million. A majority of the U.S. Congress, it seemed, wanted to abandon their long-time ally. The U.S. "abandonment syndrome" then surfaced and emerged among the upper class intellectuals, politicians, and generals in Saigon.

President Thieu, however, in late 1974 still believed that the United States, despite the opposition from Congress, would continue to support South Vietnam were North Vietnam to flagrantly violate the peace treaty by a large-scale attack on the South. Hanoi leaders may have regarded the United States as did President Thieu, even though they had many times violated the peace treaty to some degree and observed that the will of the Ford administration had clearly weakened to commit aid and troops again to Vietnam. But a general offensive against South Vietnam would be a serious violation that might provoke a rigid enforcement, or a perilous retaliation by American forces. For this reason, before launching a total offense, they had to test the American reaction with some weighty attacks against South Vietnamese territory.

The first testing offensive campaign began in the first week of August 1974, with the attempt to cut South Vietnam in two along National Road 14 from the Laotian border to the coastal area, south of the 16th parallel, or possibly to isolate I Corps & Region, particularly Danang, the most important strategic port of Vietnam, whereon camped the I Corps & Region headquarters.

If the communists captured Thuong-Duc and Dai-Loc Districts on Road 14, situated respectively 25 miles and 14 miles southwest of Danang, they could advance to attack Hoi-An City, 15 miles south of this seaport. Then the I Corps & Region of General Ngo Quang Truong would be isolated from the south, or in danger; but Danang would primarily be under siege. These possibilities were predicted by U.S. and ARVN intelligence services. However, in my own estimate, I would say that, after the Vietnamese Workers' Party's convention held on February 11, 1974, the prime purpose of Hanoi was to relieve ARVN's control over the western bank of South Vietnam's territory from Cam-Lo in Quang Tri Province to Quang Duc Province in II Corps & Region in order to continue building up and developing the Eastern Truong Son Route, or Corridor 613, on the eastern side of the Long Mountain Range for their further final campaign to "liberate" South Vietnam. This corridor would be the shortest way for NVA units moving southward. Thuong Duc, Duc Duc and Nong Son Districts in I Corps & Region were the closest ARVN locations that would impede their construction plans for the corridor, with the center stage consisting of the 559th special groups located at Ben Giang, 15 miles southwest of Thuong Duc District. This communist convention was a continuation of a previous one which was held by Le Duan and 10 other members of the Vietnamese Workers' Party Politburo on October 1st, 1973 (Convention 21) that decided to change political means into military means to "liberate" South Vietnam. Therefore, they ordered the People's Army to continue developing and consolidating the construction of the Eastern Truong Son Route to realize their aim in the future.

Hanoi first launched two infantry divisions, the 304th and 324B, plus an artillery regiment and a tank regiment into the attack beginning July 18, 1974. Thuong-Duc District, defended by the ARVN 79th Ranger Battalion and several Regional Force companies, was captured after a month of fighting. However, the NVA attacking forces were stopped right there by two regiments of the ARVN 3rd Infantry Division and a Ranger task force and could not advance to attack Dai-Loc District.

General Truong decided to move the Airborne Division from the north of Hai-Van Col to Dai-Loc for a counter-attack. The hero of An-Loc, Brigadier General Le Quang Luong, commander of the Airborne Division, once again, proved his outstanding command acumen in this battlefield. His division had three brigades and an extra force of twelve "versatile companies," which were organized by using a majority of his staff, logistic, and administrative service troops, without any additional expense and armaments provided by the ARVN. The general utilized his men and transformed them into excellent fighters. The Airborne Division was the only ARVN unit that self-strengthened its capacity of fighting after the implementation of the Paris Peace Accords.

Although the Airborne Division did not recapture Thuong Duc District headquarters, it was successfully held back the enemy corps-sized unit in this mountainous area. The fights were violent and lasted for three months; the most ferocious occurred around the 1062 Hill in the area. Finally, General Luong's units pushed away all NVA units from the region, creating serious losses for them, and smashed their attempt to cut I Corps & Region from the South.

Now, if we deem the U.S. and ARVN intelligence services' estimates to be the most accurate, we must conclude that this test by Hanoi of Washington's reaction was in vain, because the battle was solved solely by ARVN units before it could become a matter of much importance requiring the attention of the United States, despite being a momentous violation of the Paris Peace Accords. The battle of Thuong-Duc from August to December 1974 was a great victory for the ARVN, especially the Airborne Division, despite limitations of firepower and air support. Otherwise, we have to admit that Hanoi realized their purpose of controlling the left flank of South Vietnam I Corps & Region after the Thuong Duc battle to continue building their Eastern Truong Son Route and the RVNAF had enough means to recapture lost territories.

Hanoi leaders were aware of the difficulties of South Vietnam. In December 1974, they shifted their testing offensive campaign to another objective in III Corps & Region, Phuoc-

Long Province. Phuoc-Long Province, with its capital city Phuoc-Binh, 75 miles north of Saigon, was located in the southern mountainous area of the Central Highlands along the last portion of Road 14. At an altitude of more than 850m (2800 feet) above sea level, Phuoc-Long was relatively isolated and favorable for the communists to attack and to hold.

The province was defended primarily by four ARVN Regional Force battalions, a number of Popular Force platoons, plus four 155mm and sixteen 105mm artillery howitzers. The total strength numbered about 1350 men. On December 13, 1974, the communists launched a testing attack on Phuoc-Long with an outmatching force of the newly formed NVA 301st Corps, consisting of the 3rd Division, the 7th Division, an artillery regiment, an anti-aircraft regiment, a tank regiment, and several sapper and local units. All of the provincial outposts around Phuoc-Binh were picked off by attacking the NVA forces in two days, and the city itself went under siege. All accessible communication axes were shutdown and the NVA shelling began to concentrate into the city.

The garrison of Phuoc-Binh was reinforced by two battalions of the ARVN 5th Infantry Division, a Ranger battalion, and six 105mm howitzers. Defenders numbered fewer than 3,600 men, in comparison to the 20,000 attacking NVA forces.

Starting on December 20, NVA artillery fire increased to 3,000 rounds per day. Infantry and tank assaults were ferocious and the resistance was fierce. The garrison was completely cut-off from any intervention, reinforcement or re-supply. Saigon had no more reserves and the ARVN III Corps & Region's commander was incapable of saving Phuoc-Binh City. Finally, after four weeks of heroic but hopeless fighting, enduring day and night attacks, and suffering the loss of all artillery guns and two thirds of the troops, the province's chief, Colonel Thanh, who was seriously wounded by NVA tank direct fire, decided to abandon the city on January 6, 1975. Colonel Thanh, his staff and the defenders tried to breach the NVA siege and fought in retreat along the Be River, but he was captured by the NVA. Phuoc-Binh City fell on that day. Some 850 ARVN troops and 3,000 out of 32,000 civilians escaped from the city. Many province, district, village and hamlet officials were captured by the communists and savagely executed.

The communists' attack and capture of Phuoc-Long Province was the most alarming violation of the Paris Peace Accords. But the United States reaction was ineffective. Only a Marine division on Okinawa was placed on alert and the U.S.S. *Enterprise* carrier and its accompanying taskforce received orders to get out of the Philippines and move closer to Vietnam. U.S. defense secretary James Schlesinger, however, made the irresponsive statement that this serious violation by the communists was "not yet an all-out offensive." Was the United States waiting for the communist "all-out offensive" in order to react? History provided the answer to this question.

Hanoi leaders were thoroughly delighted with the results of this offensive campaign, not only by capturing a province of South Vietnam, but also by learning the answer to their pressing question about the "American reaction." Military historian retired U.S. Colonel Harry G. Summers, Jr., commented that the disaster of Phuoc-Long could only mean a failure of U.S. political will and the weak character of President Ford, writing:

Tragic as those losses were, however, the battle had far grimmer consequences. The little-known battle for Phuoc-Long was one of the most decisive battles of the war, for it marked the U.S. abandonment of its erstwhile ally to its fate. Le-Duan's "resolution" had been all too correct. In the face of this blatant violation of the Paris Accords — and it was deliberately designed to be flagrant so as to clearly test U.S. resolve — President Gerald Ford pusillanimously limited his response to diplomatic notes. North Vietnam had received the green light for the conquest of South Vietnam."[4]

Indeed, Hanoi leaders received the "green light" to conquer South Vietnam not only from the United States but also from the Soviet Union. During the first week of their offensive campaign against Phuoc-Long, Hanoi leaders gave a warm welcome to Soviet Union Deputy Defense Minister, General Viktor Kulikow. After the U.S. Congress vetoed Secretary of State Kissinger's request to designate the Soviet Union as a "most favored nation" for trade purpose, Kulikow carried to Hanoi this bad news and suggested Hanoi leaders conquer South Vietnam with the pledges to fully support them with any war equipment and armaments needed during to do so.

THE COMMUNIST FINAL RESOLUTION AND THE BATTLE OF BAN ME THUOT

On December 19, 1974 — five days after the attack on Phuoc-Long — the Vietnamese Workers' Party's Politburo convened to decide plans for the final offensive in the South. The convention lasted until January 19, 1975. At this VWP war convention, all eleven members of the Politburo unanimously decided to "liberate" South Vietnam and reunite the country through a final offensive campaign. Important senior military commanders and political cadres of the VWP in the South were also summoned together with their leaders to present their own viewpoints. However, the top leader's decisions always became final.

General Vo Nguyen Giap stated that the final offensive would be successful but it would take years, at least two or three, and everything would depend on the response of the United States. General Van Tien Dung, now commander in chief of the People's Army, was provident about the U.S. B-52 re-intervention in the battlefield because the United States' reaction was not clear in Phuoc Long battle. Political leaders such as Pham van Dong and Le Duc Tho believed that the United States had lost its will to defend South Vietnam and the South Vietnamese army was demoralized by the uncertainty of U.S. support. To conclude, Le Duan, the party's first secretary, told them not to worry about B-52s or the U.S. will to re-enter the war because the Watergate scandal and the resignation of Nixon had turned the Americans inward.

Le Duan's statement became the VWP's "resolution" to invade South Vietnam. The essential part of this resolution, which was later related by Colonel Summers, resumed: "Having already withdrawn from the South, the United States could hardly jump back in, and no matter how it might intervene it would be unable to save the Saigon administration from collapse."[5] After the Phuoc-Long battle, Pham van Dong had assessed President Gerald Ford's attitude toward Vietnam similarly in this arrogant statement, "He's the weakest president in U.S. history; the people didn't elect him; even if you gave him candy he wouldn't dare to intervene in Vietnam again."[6]

Finally, before leaving Hanoi, General Viktor Kulikow of the Soviet Union not only endorsed the Vietnamese VWP's plans to conquer South Vietnam but also incited Hanoi leaders to carry them out as soon as possible. Two months after taking Phuoc-Long Province, the communists threw the Paris Peace Accords into the garbage by launching their largest invasion of South Vietnam with all the strength of their military forces.

General Van Tien Dung later described another war conference of the VWP's Politburo, which had been held on January 8, 1975, writing: "It was obvious that the United States ... would hardly return.... To fully exploit this great opportunity we had to conduct large-scale annihilating battles to destroy and disintegrate the enemy on a large scale."[7]

With Hai-Phong Harbor open and the railroad networks from the Chinese borders to

Hanoi operating freely, war equipment from the Soviet Union and China was poured into North Vietnam massively for months. Contrary to the common opinion, Hanoi benefited from the rift between these two largest of communist countries. Both the Soviets and the Chinese tried to outdo each other to fulfill their promises of war support for Hanoi. However, the Soviets surpassed the Chinese, believing that they could reassert their leadership of the international communist movement and restore their prestige in Third World countries. Therefore, the enormous military aid provided by the Soviet leaders to North Vietnam was the outcome of their strategy to counteract the refusal of the US Congress to consider "most favored nation" status for their country.

After the return of General Kulikow to Moscow, Soviet ships bearing war goods began arriving at Hai-Phong Harbor day after day. The quantity of war equipment coming to Hanoi quadrupled over the previous months. According to Van Tien Dung, massive numbers of tanks, armored cars, rockets, and long-range artillery guns were unloaded in Hai-Phong Harbor. Most of these war goods were sent to NVA units in South Vietnam through the Ho Chi Minh Trail network which was then composed of two systems of routes: The Western Trường Sơn Route, or the old Ho Chi Minh Trail, and the Eastern Trường Sơn Route, or Corridor 613.

Corridor 613 appeared to be the most important route for the NVA to take. This corridor was a newly built strategic route running from Cam Lo, in Quang Tri Province, along the left flank of ARVN I Corps & Region to Ben Giang, 15 miles southwest of Thuong Duc District. This route was the new-repaired network of the abandoned Route 14 connecting International Route 9 to A-Luoi, A-Shau Valley in Quang Nam Province and prolonged to Kham Duc, Ta Ngot in Quang Tin Province; Dak Pek, Dak-To in Kontum, Duc Co in Pleiku, and Duc Lap in Quang Duc Province. The portion of Corridor 613 from Duc Co to Duc Lap was a short-cut to evade the ARVN II Corps & Region's units which were positioned strongly along Route 14 from Kontum to Ban Me Thuot. After the capture of Phuoc Long, the NVA 559th Special Group continued to repair two separate routes from Don Luan up to Duc Lap, but the construction was stuck outside this strategic point. Visibly, Duc-Lap District of Quang-Duc Province and Ban-me-Thuot — capital city of Darlac Province and base-camp of the ARVN 23rd Division — stood as the nearest NVA targets that might be struck. Indeed, Pham Hung, who was then the highest VWP authority in South Vietnam, went to Hanoi and received orders from the VWP Politburo (Bộ Chính-trị Đảng Lao-Động) to "clear" the Duc-Lap's corridor (the portion of Corridor 613 at Duc-Lap) prior to the start of any decisive North Vietnamese campaign to "liberate" South Vietnam. Therefore, the communist "Tây Nguyên Campaign," or "Campaign 275," at the Central Highlands of ARVN II Corps & Region in the spring of 1975 was merely a large-scale military operation of the NVA to "pave the way" for the construction completion of the Eastern Truong-Son Route before their final invasion of South Vietnam. Unfortunately, the highest authorities of South Vietnam did not know the purpose of the communist campaign, or wrongly estimated the intention and scheme of Hanoi leaders.

Indeed, the preparation of such a campaign had begun. In addition to preparing logistical system along the Western Truong Son Route, the NVA also established many secret logistical bases along the new Corridor 613. In the south of the DMZ, Dong Ha became an important logistical center. The river port Cua Viet was organized as a major off-loading port for North Vietnamese Navy vessels. A fuel pipeline was extended to the outskirts of Phuoc Long. Khe-Sanh on the borderland northwest of Quang-Tri, Ban-Het on the Three-Frontier, Duc-Co on Highway 19, and Duc-Lap on Route 14 northeast of Phuoc-Long, were transformed by the NVA into their major logistical centers. Farther in the southeast, Loc-Ninh Rubber Plantation served as the North Vietnam center of politico-military high command in the South. The fuel pipeline was extended to the area north of Phuoc-Long. Two abandoned airfields, one in Tchepone and one in Khe-Sanh, were repaired. Phuoc-Long seemed the departure point for the NVA units to suddenly attack Saigon in their final campaign.

An accurate assessment would reveal that with the control of the DMZ, the free movement on the Ho Chi Minh Trail network, which included the Eastern Truong Son Route, and the capture of Phuoc Long Province, North Vietnam was able to invade South Vietnam at any time after the beginning of 1975. Their shortest itinerary to approach South Vietnam's capital would be the Eastern Truong Son Route. The NVA would use 550,000 troops for that final stage with 80 percent of them maneuvering along this corridor instead of fighting ARVN units along Route 1 from the north of I Corps & Region to the South of III Corps & Region before entering Saigon. Thus, the Central Highlands of ARVN II Corps & Region would be the prime battlefield for this final NVA campaign. However, Hanoi leaders planned such a final campaign to "liberate" South Vietnam in two or three years starting from the spring of 1976.

On the other side, after losing Phuoc-Long Province, South Vietnamese nationalist forces led by President Thieu had to face the life and death fact that, obviously abandoned by the United States, they must fight alone against their forceful enemy without suitable weapons and ammunition. Indeed, when the Soviet and Chinese military aid to Hanoi was drastically increased, the American aid to Saigon was decreased to the minimum. The shortage of ammunition was particularly critical; for example, artillery 155mm and 105mm guns were allowed to consume only three rounds per day per tube. Moreover, the shortfall of spare parts for VNAF fighters and helicopters curbed air supports for the ARVN and handicapped its mobility on the battlefields. Faced with such a situation, it came as no surprise that the ARVN had no mobility and not enough firepower when the communists began their final offensive,

In early February, three weeks after the loss of Phuoc-Long in ARVN III Corps & Region, NVA activities in II Corps & Region had increased considerably. Communist regiment-sized units attacked many ARVN outposts and fire support bases to cut strategic highways 14, 19, and 21, so as to isolate the Central Highlands from the north, the south, and the coastal areas. These activities gave preliminary signs of an impending NVA large-scale attack on one or two provinces in the Central Highlands, possibly Quang-Duc and Darlac in the south or Pleiku and Kontum in the north.

Colonel Trinh-Tieu, chief of II Corps & Region's Staff G-2 (intelligence), after a careful analysis of all information concerning enemy activities, reported to Major General Pham van Phu, II Corps & Region commander, that the NVA would launch a large-scale attack on the Central Highlands in early March 1975, and Ban-Me-Thuot, the capital city of Darlac Province, would be the NVA's first and foremost main target. However, Duc Lap District, 95 miles South of Ban Me Thuot would be the primer. Capturing this strategic point meant completing the construction of this strategic route to Saigon.

Unfortunately, on March 4, Highway 19, which connected Binh-Dinh Province to Pleiku and Kontum, was cut between Mang-Yang and An-Khe. The Phu-Cat Airfield, north of Qui-Nhon City, came under heavy NVA shelling. At the same time, numerous ARVN outposts and fire support bases north and west of Pleiku and Kontum came under serious NVA attack. This series of events convinced General Phu that the main enemy attack would be directed at Kontum and Pleiku, in which his headquarters base camp was housed. Thus, Colonel Tieu's estimate was disregarded by his boss. General Phu concentrated his forces for the defense of these two provinces. As a result, he fell into the communists' trap. Their main target was Ban-Me-Thuot as it was assumed by Colonel Tieu. On March 6, Highway 14, which connected Ban-Me-Thuot to Pleiku, and Highway 21 connected Ban-Me-Thuot to the coast, were cut.

The Central Highlands was then isolated. Duc Lap District fell to the NVA the night of March 9, 1975.

Within 48 hours, most ARVN outposts west of Ban-Me-Thuot were overrun. Once again, Colonel Tieu urged General Phu to move back two regiments of the 23rd Infantry Division to Ban-Me-Thuot to defend the city, because there were indications which showed that the NVA 10th and 320th Divisions in the Three-Frontier, west of Kontum, were moving southward to strengthen the NVA forces in the west of Ban-Me-Thuot purposefully for a combined attack against the city. Once again, his proposal was rejected.

On March 10, before dawn, a devastating artillery attack fell on Ban-Me-Thuot City, mostly concentrated on Phung-Duc Airfield. The city and the airfield were defended by the ARVN 23rd Division's 53rd Regiment, a 21st Ranger Battle-Group's battalion, and some Regional Force battalions, with a total strength of fewer than 4,000 troops. After hours of artillery firing, two NVA divisions and tanks assaulted all ARVN positions and installations inside the city and the airfield. Although NVA losses were extremely heavy, by noon on March 11, Ban-Me-Thuot City fell. The remnants of the ARVN and hundreds of retreating local forces' Montagnards escaped from the city and joined the defense of Phung-Duc Airfield, three miles southeast of the city. The defenders of the airfield magnificently continued the fighting for several days, and destroyed a major portion of the NVA 316th Division and a great number of NVA tanks. The communists had to reinforce their attacking forces at Phung-Duc with the 320thth Division and the 10th Division.

The fighting was fierce. VNAF F-5 fighters had intercepted several NVA assault waves on ARVN positions and inflicted serious losses for NVA troops and tanks. However, without relief or reinforcement, and outnumbered by the attacking enemy, the ARVN defenders of Phung-Duc Airfield had to abandon their positions on March 12. They fought in retreat along Highway 21 to Khanh-Duong or Phuoc-An District, 35 miles southeast of Ban-Me-Thuot, but the majority were dispersed by NVA forces; less than a thousand men attained Phuoc-An with tens of thousands of refugees from Ban-Me-Thuot (see Map 7).

The ARVN 23rd Division's 44th and 45th Regiments were ordered to helilift from Pleiku to Phuoc-An to prepare a counter-attack to recapture Ban-Me-Thuot. However, many troops of these regiments simply broke ranks, fled to search for their families and disappeared into the streaming flow of refugees. Four days later, ARVN forces at Phuoc-An were overrun by the NVA 10th Division. On March 18, a new defense line was formed by the ARVN 3rd Airborne Brigade which was moved in from Danang.

The outcome of the Ban-Me-Thuot battle was purely the problem of unbalanced forces between the NVA and ARVN. The NVA outnumbered and outgunned the ARVN at this battlefield by a ratio of 5.5-to-1 in personnel, 2.5-to-1 in tanks, and 3.5-to-1 in artillery. The loss of Ban-Me-Thuot to the NVA was literally inescapable. However, the effect of this battle was awfully unexpected. First, the United States again refused to enforce the terms of the Paris treaty and ignored the promises of former President Nixon to respond with military force if North Vietnam violated that agreement. The United States showed its clear intention to abandon South Vietnam. Second, President Thieu suddenly ordered his senior commanders to abandon one half of the South Vietnamese territory.

These two veracities were the true factors that perished the RVNAF, in addition to the South Vietnamese democracy, before the communists of North Vietnam could resolve the leftovers by their "Great Spring Offensive Campaign."

The RVNAF had endured several severe communist offensive campaigns in the past, such as the 1968 Tet Offensive and the 1972 Eastertide Offensive, but it did not lose its fighting spirit and its latent vigor in the battlefield. The collapse of the RVNAF will to fight within

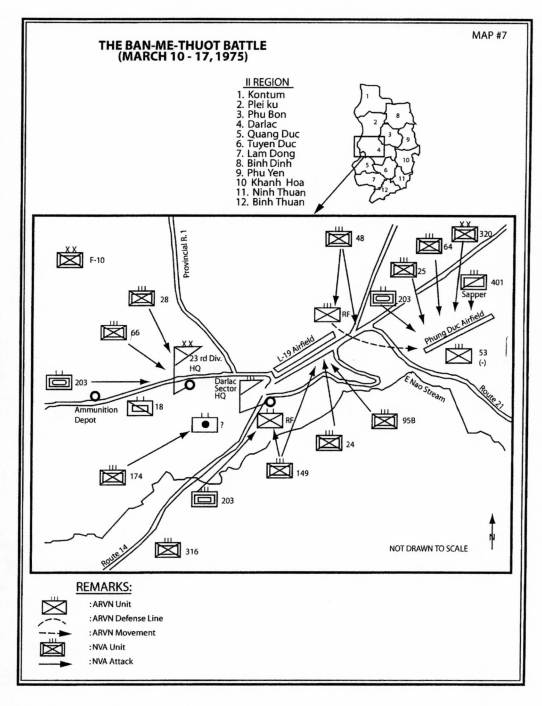

THE BAN-ME-THUOT BATTLE
(MARCH 10 - 17, 1975)

MAP #7

II REGION
1. Kontum
2. Plei ku
3. Phu Bon
4. Darlac
5. Quang Duc
6. Tuyen Duc
7. Lam Dong
8. Binh Dinh
9. Phu Yen
10. Khanh Hoa
11. Ninh Thuan
12. Binh Thuan

NOT DRAWN TO SCALE

REMARKS:

: ARVN Unit
: ARVN Defense Line
: ARVN Movement
: NVA Unit
: NVA Attack

a single week should raise questions among honest observers and historians. The conclusion that the North Vietnamese communists merely defeated the South Vietnamese armed forces to "liberate" South Vietnam by the so-called Great Spring Offensive is not adequate without a careful examination of the critical situations in March 1975, when the RVNAF was abandoned by everyone.

The communist offensive campaign in the Central Highlands in March 1975 was not a final campaign against South Vietnam, but just a limited corps level campaign to remove obstructions and clear the transit on the secret strategic Eastern Truong Son Route for their further decisive campaign that would begin in spring 1976. Had President Thieu and his top advisors known this they would have not ordered the abandonment of the Central Highlands and I Corps & Region that fatally devastated our armed forces and ruined our democracy. Had President Thieu shown an iron will to retake Ban Me Thuot or had ordered ARVN units to fight in place for a more few months, this communist offensive campaign would have withered with the coming rainy season. Hanoi leaders planned to liberate South Vietnam in two years but President Thieu had given them the easiest and shortest route to Saigon. No one knew the importance of the Eastern Truong Son Route and the true nature of the communist offensive campaign in the Central Highlands in March 1975.

14

The Communists' Final Campaign

Some American historians comment reasonably that the South Vietnamese soldiers lost their fighting spirit due to the "family syndrome" (changing their focus to take care of their own family) in the last period of the war. The prime cause, however, was actually the "abandonment syndrome" rather than the family syndrome, which followed the latter in the last fleeting days. The "abandonment syndrome" started from Washington, moved to Saigon and spread among the leaders, politicians, intellectuals, and senior generals after the Nixon administration forced South Vietnam to sign the Paris Peace Accords. By the time the communists attacked and captured Ban-Me-Thuot, the contagion spread from Saigon to Pleiku and Da Nang, infecting all South Vietnamese cities, towns, units, officers, soldiers and the population, specially in I and II Corps & Regions. This contagion destroyed the fighting spirit of South Vietnamese armed forces.

The abandonment syndrome was a psychological illness rooted in the discouraged state of mind of Washington leaders, who sought to straddle internal difficulties and renounce the American policy of interference in Indochina, particularly in South Vietnam. Nixon and Kissinger realized this policy by giving North Vietnam many opportunities to freely act in South Vietnam through the Paris Treaty. Ford kept Kissinger in order to keep Nixon's strategic plan under the control of the U.S. Congress, of which the majority wanted to abandon South Vietnam by severely cutting off military aid for its armed forces. President Nguyen van Thieu considered these American political facts as "betrayal." The abandonment syndrome was, in effect, a chain of betrayal resulting in a series of catastrophes for the RVNAF and the South Vietnamese people. They were victims of American and Vietnamese political games.

It is necessary to take a backward step to reexamine the case. After the communist capture of Phuoc-Long in January 1975, Ambassador Graham Martin went back to Washington and persuaded President Ford to stand behind Richard Nixon's promises, as President Thieu requested, and provide additional military aid for the RVNAF. President Ford asked Congress for $300 million in supplemental aid for Saigon, but could not guarantee any future retaliation against the communist's open invasion of South Vietnam. Washington's response to Saigon was vague until the North Vietnamese Army attacked Ban-Me-Thuot on March 10, 1975.

When the NVA began to isolate the Central Highlands by attacking ARVN outposts and fire support bases along Highways 19 and 21, President Thieu alerted Ambassador Martin of what was a repeat of Phuoc-Long. He anticipated a new North Vietnamese total offensive with forces invading across the borders and the DMZ. Through the ambassador, he suggested Washington react appropriately. However, once the attack on Ban-Me-Thuot appeared to be a truly large-scale offense, Washington maintained its willful silence. Thieu became desperate after a week of continuously but hopelessly appealing for firm U.S. support. No favorable response was received.

Instead, in those days, ambassador Graham Martin let President Thieu know the deterioration of the climate in Washington, particularly in Congress, and the possibility that all military aid to South Vietnam would be cut off. President Thieu learned that not only was it highly unlikely that South Vietnam would receive any supplemental aid, it was unlikely that they would receive any aid at all in the next fiscal year, beginning in June. The RVNAF would face within a few months an abrupt halt of any means of continuing the war. This was a deathblow for Saigon's leaders and the RVNAF. As a result, Ban-Me-Thuot was quietly lost.

The fall of Ban-Me-Thuot, from a military viewpoint, would not amount to serious damage for South Vietnam because the ARVN might be able to retake it, had they the means to fight. Even if they could not recapture this lost city, the communists could not easily defeat the RVNAF and "liberate" South Vietnam without undergoing years of terrible fighting, as General Vo Nguyen Giap estimated — two or three years — and only after suffering heavy damage to their armed forces.

By contrast, from a political viewpoint Ban-Me-Thuot may be considered a final conclusion, or a clear exposition of the will of the American powers to betray their honor by ignoring the U.S. signature on an international treaty, by neglecting the promises of a U.S. president, by betraying a longtime U.S. ally, and by betraying tens of thousands of U.S. soldiers who had sacrificed their lives to defend the freedom for this small country.

South Vietnamese President Nguyen van Thieu would conclude that the United States betrayed him, his regime, and the RVNAF, saying: "It's better to let the Americans speak for themselves — and I have heard many very important men, who had a great responsibility in Vietnam, say that we have no other word than 'betrayal.' 'Betrayal.'"[1] Thus, because of this perception, Thieu made the fatal decision to abandon South Vietnamese I Corps and Region and the Central Highlands of and II Corps & Regions, which led to the collapse of RVNAF fighting spirit in these military regions. The abandonment syndrome began to spread widely and the tragedy of South Vietnam continued after Thieu's decision.

ABANDON THE CENTRAL HIGHLANDS

President Thieu's abandonment concept could be clearly seen just 24 hours after Ban Ma Thout was attacked. On March 11, 1975, he called a meeting with key figures such as prime minister Tran Thien Khiem, General Cao van Vien, and Lt. General Dang van Quang to decide the fate of I Corps & Region and the Central Highlands. Thieu concluded, "Given our present strength and capacities we certainly cannot hold and defend all the territory we want."[2] He meant that he would save his armed forces to hold populous and flourishing areas, including several coastal provinces of II Corps & Region, territories of III and IV Corps & Regions, and the continental shelf, rich with newly discovered oil.

On March 13, 1975, President Thieu, in the presence of prime minister General Tran Thien Khiem, summoned Lieutenant General Ngo Quang Truong, I Corps & Region commander, to Saigon and ordered him to abandon I Corps & Region. General Truong hesitated to execute this tragic order until March 19, 1975, when he was summoned again to Saigon.

On March 14, 1975, Major General Pham van Phu, II Corps & Region commander, was summoned to Cam-Ranh Bay for a meeting with President Thieu and his Military Council members: General Tran Thien Khiem, prime minister; General Cao Van Vien, chief of the RVNAF Joint General Staff; and Lt. General Dang Van Quang, Thieu's military adviser. President Thieu ordered General Phu to withdraw his armed forces from Pleiku, Kontum, and the Central Highlands to the coastal provinces to provide additional forces for the defense of these vital areas. Thieu explained: "We had to take troops from the isolate areas, gather our forces to defend the more vital areas, because we judged that the United States would not help us again. If they wanted to help us they would have done so by then and we could not wait until it became too late. We had to take the calculated risk because withdrawal without mobility and great firepower is a risk. But it was a must for us."[3]

Despite the above explication, Thieu's decision to abandon the Central Highlands, remains one of the biggest secrets of the Vietnam War. When General Phu implemented this disastrous decision on March 16, 1975, the move shocked the American authorities in South Vietnam, South Vietnamese intellectuals, and RVNAF generals and middle-ranking officers. However, the surprise of the communist leaders would rise to the highest degree. Thieu had given them the generous opportunity to win the war two years earlier than they had expected.

If Thieu's reasons for the withdrawal were as he stated, then his decision may be perceived as one of the most foolishly strategic maneuvers in the history of war. But a general like Thieu surely must have known better. Perhaps there were other reasons. One of these might be that Thieu took this fatal decision as an act of revenge against the so-called "betrayal" by the United States. He knew that if the United States abandoned South Vietnam, the war would certainly be lost. He would not allow the United States to unweave itself from the defeat. The "tit for tat" behavior that Thieu displayed was very simple: if the United States wanted to abandon South Vietnam to the communists, he would push the process forward sooner than had been imagined.

A different explication finds expression in rumors saying that the plan to abandon the Central Highlands and I Corps & Region was a design of Lieutenant General Dang van Quang, Thieu's adviser, who had secret relations with American authorities in the background to quickly push the abandonment in exchange for American assurance of the fortune of Saigon leaders afterward. Rumors also spread among international observers and South Vietnamese intellectuals that a deal had been struck to give the North Vietnamese half of the country without resistance. Meanwhile, Ambassador Martin explained Thieu's order to be the only wise course of action to cut the military lines short and retain the great economic part of the country — the southern delta. In any case, the abandonment of the Central Highlands was an enormous mistake. (Before Thieu's death on September 29, 2001, until today, nobody has seen any of his "memoirs" on his political life or on the Vietnam War. Yet we have to respect his silence. Perhaps history will not reveal the secret of this last period of the Vietnam War.)

Major General Phu, ARVN II Corps commander, implemented President Thieu's orders to abandon the Central Highlands. Phu's staff had only 48 hours to prepare plans for the withdrawal of more than 55,000 troops of all ARVN units from these cities to Tuy Hoa Province in the coastal area. The first convoy that left the Central Highlands, on March 16, 1975, was the 20th Engineer Group which had the mission to repair the road and bridges along the way. When the main convoys began to move, more than 400,000 people joined them. The retreat of II Corps & Region troops became an enormous exodus. On its march, the massive exodus convoy, which included thousands of military and civilian cars of all kind, moved slowly along the unusual, mountainous and narrow Route #7B from the Highlands to Phu-Bon Province, an 80 mile saga. How could ARVN units move quickly while protecting the mass composed of 80 percent women, old people, and children, riding on minor means of transportation or trudging on foot? How could they organize a safe convoy to react when the enemy attacked? How could they feed tens of thousands of people who hastily left their homeland without any provision? Anyone who has experience on the battlefield can imagine the thousand-and-one risks of a tactical retreat. Remember, the ARVN withdrawal from the Central Highlands in March 1975 was transformed into a massive exodus convoy of hundreds of thousands of civilians, who wanted to escape from the communist massacre and the cruelty of the communists as happened in Hue City in 1968. Thus, the withdrawal lost its characteristic as a purely tactical maneuver and assumed more risks.

NVA General Van Tien Dung initially seemed surprised by the retreat of ARVN II Corps & Region forces from the Central Highlands. But after safely acquiring the empty Pleiku and Kontum cities, he sent the 320th and 968th Divisions in pursuit of the exodus. The pursuit was a little late but was enough to kill more than two hundred thousand people of this exodus from the highlands.

On the ARVN side, the half-million people moved safely for two days on the abandoned Route 7B under the command of Brigadier General Pham Duy Tat. It reached Hau-Bon, the capital city of Phu Bon Province, as its first resting place. Five hundred thousand people — soldiers and civilians, men and women, elderly and children — jammed into every corner of the city. Unfortunately, on the morning of March 18, 1975, the 7th Ranger Battle Group, in a search operation south of the city, was wrongly hit by VNAF bombers and fighters that caused the death of more than 150 and destroyed two tanks. That night the NVA 320th Division opened fire on the city with artillery. Thousands of innocents were killed under this ferocious shelling of more than a thousand shells. Flesh and blood scattered all over the city's market and many buildings and houses were burned down. An enormous number of tanks, gun-armored carriers and civilian buses exploded. A large column of flames and smoke billowed up to the darkened sky. Groans and cries resounded desperately throughout the night. Han Bon City, extending a kilometer each side, was completely in ruin. Seventy percent (70%) of ARVN II Corps & Region's heavy guns, equipment and tanks were destroyed. Thousands of innocents and soldiers were wounded and many soldiers, including officers and NCOs, broke rank to take care of their families. The family syndrome began to emerge.

On the morning of March 20, the exodus convoy continued moving along Route 7B to Phu Tuc District, 22 miles Southeast of Hau Bon where it had to stop at the bridge "Le Bac" on the Ba river (600 m long) and the newly built up pontoon bridge west of Phu Tuc to gradually pass over. General Dung's units moved up and launched an enormous number of shells on the retreating mass that stretched several miles along the route. After one hour of artillery fire, the NVA 320th Division assaulted this large convoy and cut the mass into fragments. Thousands of civilians jumped into the river to evade the firing, only to drown. Other thousands stampeded in all directions to be killed by crushing themselves, by direct enemy fire, and mostly by enemy shelling. Countless children and women were killed. Their bodies dispersed all over this five-mile portion of the highway and around the two long bridges or in the waters of the Ba River. Anyway, the exodus convoy passed through the enemy ambush that day.

ARVN troops reacted fiercely and close combat occurred everywhere. The most intense was the resistance of the ARVN 21st Armored Battalion, the 203rd Artillery Battalion, and the Ranger troops. On March 21, the ARVN 7th Ranger Group attacked a unit of the NVA 320th that had captured Phu Tuc and retook this small city for the exodus to repose. On March 22, the convoy moved out again to the next destination, Cung Son, 40 miles west of Tuy Hoa City. Again, the column was ambushed by the 60th Regiment of the NVA 320th Division. Again, tens of thousands of innocents were killed at the pontoon Dong Cam, 6 miles west of Cung Son. Fortunately, two ARVN Ranger battalions, the 35th and the 51st, that covered the last portion of the column broke forth to inflict heavy casualties on the 60th Regiment of the NVA 320th Division while other ARVN units fought their way through enemy road blocks. Finally, the exodus convoy arrived at Tuy Hoa on March 27, 1975.

Of those who took part in the exodus, only one in four of the troops reached the coastal province. Sixty percent of civilians, women and children were killed by NVA troops and the rest were captured. In other words, only 20,000 of the 55,000 troops made it through and only 700 rangers survived among the 7,000. And only 100,000 of the 400,000 civilians reached Tuy Hoa City.

Tens of thousands of ARVN soldiers cried for this tragic withdrawal from the Central Highlands. They cried for the fatal orders that forced them to abandon their lovely fortified lands without fighting; they cried for their family members, loved ones and fellows who were cruelly killed before their eyes while they were unable to protect them; and they cried for the heart-rending sorrow of seeing innocent people dying hour after hour of hunger, thirst, and disease while enduring another 80-mile journey from Phu-Bon Province to the coast, after March 18. The massive exodus of a half million people fled from the Central Highlands on Route 7B was remembered as the "Convoy of Blood and Tears."

South Vietnamese soldiers and innocent inhabitants of the Central Highlands were, first and foremost, pitiful people defeated by both the Saigon leaders' strategically unrealistic decisions and Hanoi leaders' strategically real ambitions. Other RVNAF soldiers and people in other parts of South Vietnam would follow their fates in the very near future. But Van Tien Dung's victory on Route 7B amounted to the collective killing of unfortunate people, a great slaughter but not really the excellent combat of a great captain. He was no better than any barbarous general in ancient times.

Everywhere, the communists were feared by the South Vietnamese population who wanted to follow the ARVN soldiers anywhere, even to the death, rather than stay with the communists. The so-called General Uprising never happened in South Vietnam after the communists began their "General Offensive." The communists of North Vietnam could occupy South Vietnamese towns and cities but not South Vietnamese hearts and minds. Ironically, the bloody terror that the communists had previously sowed in South Vietnam, such as the collective massacre of innocents at Hue in their 1968 Tet Offensive, was the main factor that created such panic among the population and the family syndrome among ARVN soldiers in I Corps & Region in late March, in addition to President Thieu's decision to abandon Quang-Tri and Thua-Thien Provinces.

ABANDONING THE TWO NORTHERNMOST PROVINCES OF I CORPS AND REGION

While Major General Pham van Phu, II Corps commander, was trying to establish a new command headquarters at Nha-Trang and relocate his units to form a new defense line in the coastal areas, Lieutenant General Ngo Quang Truong, I Corps commander, was stuck with President Thieu's order to abandon Quang Tri and Thua Thien, the two northernmost provinces of his military region on March 13. As previously mentioned, until the third week of March, General Truong still hesitated to implement President Thieu's order, because he had under his command more than 250,000 troops of ground, sea, and air forces in excellent dispositions and all were willing to fight even though the military situation everywhere in his military region was under trouble, including Quang-Tri and Thua-Thien. During the week, from March 13 to March 17, many times General Truong called the prime minister, General Tran Thien Khiem, to report the situation and suggest he ask President Thieu to annul the order to abandon I Corps & Region.

On March 14, President Thieu decided to move the Airborne Division from the south and west of Da Nang back to Saigon as his strategic reserve, minus a brigade which would be put down to the defense line at Khanh Duong District on Highway 19, fifty miles northwest of Nha-Trang, to block the NVA units access to the coast. With this move, Thieu showed his intention of shortening the north-south defense line down to the 12th parallel, at somewhere north of Nha-Trang. General Truong persuaded President Thieu that the withdrawal of the Airborne Division from Da Nang would enable him to move the Marine Division from Quang-Tri to defend this crucial port. In doing so, he would probably give up Quang-Tri and Thua-Thien Provinces to the communists. On the same day, General Truong called Lieutenant General Lam Quang Thi, his deputy and I Corps Advanced Command Headquarters' commander at Hue, to order him to move the two Marine Brigades 258th and 369th from Quang Tri Province to Da Nang by March 17. In the meantime General Truong insisted President Thieu reconsider his order to abandon Hue.

On March 18, under the request of the two highest commanders of I Corps & Region, General Tran Thien Khiem, the prime minister, visited Da Nang to review the situation. He left Da Nang in the afternoon without any special recommendations. On March 19, General Truong flew to Saigon to submit the new defense plan of the I Corps & Region to President Thieu and suggested again he keep the two northernmost provinces of his military region. President Thieu's decision was probably not clear. Thus, when he went back to Da Nang on March 20, General Truong told General Thi that Hue would be defended; however, he ordered General Thi to draw a "contingency plan" to evacuate the last 147th Marine Brigade and the 1st Infantry Division from Thua Thien Province to Da Nang. The plan was drawn but no one knew exactly for what reason all of ARVN forces under General Thi's command moved out of Quang Tri and Hue by March 24. Quang-Tri and Thua-Thien Provinces were completely vacated by ARVN regular forces. They were abandoned.

Within hours, residents of these provinces, especially Hue, were struck by dread at their fate. The withdrawal of the ARVN Marine Division from Quang-Tri and the I Corps Advanced Command from Hue was like an atomic bomb exploding on their heads. The dread of a communist mass-killing and the panic of the real ARVN abandonment generated the family syndrome, which began to spread widely in every separate ARVN unit and among local forces. Commanders, officers and soldiers of these units, relinquished by their senior commanders, could not do anything but manage to save their families and their own lives. By all means they sought to evade the communist bloodbath before the arrival of the barbarous troops.

Every corner of the land, town, district, and village was transformed into a chaotic state. People sought to leave their native lands before it was too late. Masses of people began to pour onto Highway 1 using whatever means of transportation they had, with their most necessary provisions, and unintentionally formed into a colossal exodus of more than a million refugees, moving southward for several days. Others took the sea route on every kind of boat floating along the coastal water to indefinite destinations in the southern provinces.

Quang-Tri was occupied by the communists on March 24. Only a day later they captured Hue. North Vietnamese General Van Tien Dung then reorganized his forces in the region into a new corps-sized unit to pursue the mass-exodus, which was moving slowly on a sixty-mile escape road from Hue to Da Nang. It was too late, despite Dung's spurring on his units with the slogan "lightning speed, daring and daring" to attack the innocent refugees. What a militarily talented maneuver to capture the empty cities and pursue a disorderly exodus of mostly women and children on this lengthy itinerary! A million people reached Da Nang City.

Da Nang then doubled its population to three million. Refugees from Quang-Tri and Hue, however, created serious problems for the I Corps & Region commander and the American Consul. In the first instant, when the mass of refugees came into the city, an enormous number of soldiers from the ARVN 1st and 3rd Divisions deserted and joined them. The family syndrome, which followed the abandonment syndrome, then became a psychological contagion that gravely affected these ARVN divisions and other units.

THE LOSS OF I AND II CORPS AND REGIONS

Most soldiers and officers of ARVN units in I Corps & Region had families in Quang-Tri, Thua Thien, and Quang-Nam Provinces. Therefore, not only those of the 1st and 3rd Infantry Divisions but also others of all combatant and specialized units such as ranger, armor, artillery, logistics and supply units, were in a state of disquietude. The majority wanted to abandon their units to look out for the welfare of their families. Many deserted to search for their families among the mass of refugees from Quang-Tri and Hue, or joined them throughout Da Nang City to prepare for another evacuation to the south. Commanders of these units were at the point of doing nothing.

As a result, all military activities in Da Nang stagnated and the fighting spirit of all ARVN officers and soldiers in the region was destroyed. General Ngo Quang Truong suddenly lost the major part of his fighting strength. He knew that, with the downfall of troop morale, he could no longer defend Da Nang and maintain his military region. His only hope was to keep fighting as long as possible to draw the bulk of war materiel out of Da Nang. But the situation became hopeless when the Marine Division was ordered by Saigon to retreat from Da Nang and move to Vung Tau in III Corps & Region.

After March 26, the defense lines of the 1st and 3rd Infantry Divisions in the northwest, west and southwest of Da Nang practically ceased to exist. On the next day, Highway 1 in the south was cut off and several NVA units approached in the vicinity of the city. The chance for refugees to escape from Da Nang lessened except by air and sea transport. But Vietnamese Air Force (VNAF) aircraft and Vietnamese Navy (VNN) transport ships were limited.

After March 26, the American Consulate at Da Nang began to evacuate staff, American officials and technicians, and Vietnamese officials and their families by Air America's aircraft. Vietnamese Navy transport ships and cargo boats could not approach any dock or beach to put on board the hundreds of thousands of people, but only to rescue those who swam toward them. Hundreds were drowned in the sea evacuation. Disorder and bedlam inside the city, at the airport and along the beach was inevitable as millions of refugees and thousands of ARNV soldiers were not under the control of any official body. In addition, from March 27, the communists began to shell the city and the airport causing more problems for the evacuation and intensifying the panic among the masses.

Finally, on the morning of March 29, after thousands of soldiers began to mob the airfield runways, wresting their way on-board the first of three World Air Boeing 727s of American billionaire Ed Daly, any further air evacuation from Da Nang was canceled. General Truong's staff, some 4,000 troops of the 1st and 3rd Divisions, and 6,000 marines left Da Nang on the same day by transport ships moving south for the defense of Saigon. Da Nang was abandoned. On the next day, March 30, the communists occupied the city. In sum, only ten percent of the 3,000,000 refugees had been able to escape from Da Nang.

During the preceding week, on March 24, the ARVN 12th Ranger Battle Group and the 2nd Infantry Division at Tam-Ky had abandoned Quang-Tin and Quang-Ngai Provinces. Some 5,000 or 6,000 troops of the 2nd Division pulled out from their defense line and moved to the port of Chu-Lai to be drawn out by VNN ships, first to Cu-lao Re, a small island 20 miles offshore, then to Binh-Tuy Province in III Corps & Region. These two provinces were captured by the communists several days later. The whole of I Corps & Region was lost to the communists in less than two weeks without serious fighting anywhere. Lieutenant General Ngo Quang Truong, an elite commander of the ARVN, was unable to make any moves under the fickle Saigon leadership. The RVNAF just abandoned one city after another. The communist forces just moved in and occupied the five northern provinces of South Vietnam one by one without losing even a minor fraction of their armed forces.

President Thieu's strategy to abandon the Central Highlands in II Corps & Region and Quang-Tri and Hue in I Corps & Region was a disaster for the RVNAF. Abandoning the "isolated areas" to keep the ARVN's strength for the defense of the "richer parts" of South Vietnam did not work. On the contrary, two corps-sized units of more than 400,000, including other combatant and support units, were merely disbanded by these fatal decisions. But, the most important factor was the fall of the RVNAF's fighting spirit — due to the abandonment syndrome and the family syndrome. In reality, these two psychological foes defeated South Vietnamese troops, not the real communist army.

As these events unfolded, General Van Tien Dung had the great opportunity to quickly push two corps-sized units, one from the Central Highlands and another from the north, to other coastal provinces of II Corps & Region. President Thieu ordered the withdrawal of the ARVN 22nd Infantry Division from Qui-Nhon on March 31. Binh-Dinh Province was abandoned. Afterward, even if he wanted to organize a new defense line north of Nha-Trang to protect the other coastal provinces, Khanh-Hoa, Ninh-Thuan, and Binh-Thuan, he would not be able to do so because of the increased pressure of the enemy and the impossibility of replenishing or reforming ARVN units which had been withdrawn from the forsaken territories.

On the same day, Hanoi announced that it was ready to talk with Saigon about a new political settlement for South Vietnam, but not with Thieu. Meanwhile, the communist leaders devised new offensive plans to promptly and totally occupy South Vietnam. Frank Snepp, CIA's chief strategy analyst in Saigon, outlined in a report to his superior that the North Vietnamese Communist Party's Politburo had reconvened and made a new decision — they would go for total victory in 1975, instead of following the two-year timetable they had previously planned, because they had stumbled on unforeseen victory.

Indeed, the situation drastically changed after President Thieu abandoned the "isolated areas" that led to the destruction of almost half of his armed forces. Hanoi diplomat Ha van Lau's statement proved the accuracy of Frank Snepp's assessment; Lau said: "After the fall of Hue and Danang, our leadership decided to intensify the preparations to end the war before the rainy season. This is to say, in the month of April 1975."[4]

In the preceding weeks, when President Thieu abandoned the Central Highlands, Hanoi leaders were surprised and believed that Thieu would lay some dreadful traps for them. After acquiring Pleiku, Kontum, Da Nang and Binh-Dinh, they discerned that, instead, Thieu had simply given them the most precious opportunity to "liberate" the South, more than they could conceive in their grandest dreams. They had opened the Ho Chi Minh Trail for their "long march" to the South to take possession of the land for the creation on a communist regime without success. But now, Thieu suddenly allowed their armed forces to march down the largest avenues to Saigon, to come for the final victory, and to make history, faster, shorter, and easier. Why not take this opportunity to realize their dreams? Dreams became reality for the communists on April 30, 1975. However, these realities then crushed the dreams of the other Vietnamese people who hoped for a reunited country of freedom, prosperity, and happiness. Under the communist regime they shall never acquire such desires. For how long will this bitter situation last?

15

The Bitter End of South Vietnam

Hanoi's goals set forward in the VWP-Politburo's approved offensive plans for the NVA forces in South Vietnam were to totally defeat the RVNAF and promptly occupy Saigon. There was no political matter in these new plans as they now clearly sought to solve the war by military force. First, all communist forces in South Vietnam, NVA and VC divisions, separate regiments and specialized units, were incorporated into corps-sized units. Each corps was commanded by a two- or three-star general and carried out a special battle plan for each front line as an attacking spearhead. Second, almost all combatant units, reserve troops, new war equipment, and additional supplies were sent to the South through the Ho Chi Minh Trail and Highway 1, across the Ben-Hai River, to reinforce or replenish each corps. Tens of thousands of vehicles, carrying full troops, weapons, ammunition, and supplies, continuously rolled down these accesses day and night to their destinations in the South. Finally, all NVA forces of 20-division equivalents were directed toward Saigon in a final campaign named "Ho Chi Minh," to "liberate" South Vietnam. This offensive campaign was directed by the VWP's Politburo with three of its eleven members, such as Le Duc Tho, Pham Hung, and Van Tien Dung, commanding all forces in South Vietnam.

A New Defense Line

In the first week of April, Phu-Yen and Khanh-Hoa Provinces and Cam-Ranh Bay, one of the finest and most important harbors in the Pacific, were consecutively occupied by NVA forces. The ARVN line of defense held by the ARVN 3rd Airborne Brigade at Khanh-Duong had been overrun by the overwhelming NVA I Corps forces and the ARVN Marine Division at Cam-Ranh was ordered to move to Vung-Tau Harbor in ARVN III Corps & Region.

President Thieu then decided to establish a new defense line north of Ninh-Thuan, his native province, to defend the last portion of ARVN II Corps & Region in the coastal areas. He placed Ninh-Thuan and Binh-Thuan Provinces under the command of ARVN III Corps & Region commander, Lieutenant General Nguyen van Toan, and ordered him to organize the III Corps Advanced Command Headquarters at the military airfield, five miles northwest of Phan-Rang, the capital city of Ninh-Thuan Province. Lieutenant General Nguyen Vinh Nghi was assigned as field commander to direct all RVNAF units in the region, including several Regional Force battalions, some fighter and helicopter squadrons of the VNAF 6th Division that had been withdrawn from strategic Phu-Cat Airfield, and the ARVN 2nd Airborne Brigade moving from Saigon to the region on April 8. He also reinforced the defense line with the ARVN 2nd Infantry Division from Ham-Tan and the 3rd Ranger Battle-Group from Bien-Hoa.

These actions came too late, since the communists had two corps of six to seven divisions in front of Ninh-Thuan and three others that began to attack ARVN units in III Corps

& Region. However, ARVN troops at the Ninh-Thuan defense line and farther in the south were willing to fight, even to the death, to protect their native lands and their families, if their leaders were determined to steadfastly stand and fight. With them the abandonment syndrome stopped and the family syndrome no longer ravaged the RVNAF's will to fight. They would possibly lose to the overwhelming communists forces which had definitely gained leverage after the disappearance of ARVN I and II Corps & Regions. Unfortunately, after the communist "Ho Chi Minh Campaign" went into effect on April 9, 1975, the political climate between Saigon and Washington worsened, which damaged again the RVNAF's fighting spirit.

After South Vietnam lost Phuoc-Long in early January, the Ford administration had proposed an additional $300 million in military aid for the RVNAF. Before approving Ford's proposal, the U.S. Congress sent a delegation to South Vietnam (and Cambodia) for a fact-finding mission in the last week of February. This congressional delegation was comprised of seven representatives and a senator, led by Representative John Flynt, Jr. Among them were anti–Saigon-regime activists Peter McCloskey, Donald Fraser, Millicent Fenwick, and Bella Abzug, who behaved rudely and attempted to humiliate Saigon leaders and U.S. Embassy and American officials anytime they could.

Upon returning to Washington on March 2, these activists vocally exaggerated the nature of the situation in South Vietnam and the mistakes of Saigon leaders in order to agitate anti-war feelings among the American people. In Congress, they canvassed congressmen to vote down Ford's proposed additional military aid for Saigon. One activist, Pete McCloskey, when answering an interview question by Professor Larry Engelmann, charged South Vietnam with human rights violations for beating some urban communist prisoners, but closed his eyes to the extreme cruelty of the communists when they captured Phuoc-Long and executed hundreds of South Vietnamese provincial officials and innocent people. He did not see the deadly wound the South Vietnamese people and their army suffered from the "stab-in-the-back" by an ally when facing a ferocious enemy that continued to be strongly supported by its communist allies. The cut back of military aid and the broken promise to our army and people were acts of betrayal.

In the beginning of the war between the communists and nationalists, our leaders and intellectuals had no illusions about leaning on the United States to fight against our foes. But, the war itself had become something else, an international conflict between the communist bloc and the free world, and the United States had transformed South Vietnam into a "testing-ground" for their new worldwide strategy. The nationalists were pushed toward an "absolute necessity" of fighting in alliance with and under the support of the United States, until one day this powerful ally withdrew its 550,000 troops "with honor" from our country. McCloskey blamed the South Vietnamese Army of being unable to "make the war" against the communists, conveniently forgetting that the United States itself, in its ten years of direct commitment in the country using potent fire power, full troop strength, and every strategy did not achieve victory. Shifting the war burden to the RVNAF while cutting all support was shockingly cruel for such a nation. Could U.S. Congressman McCloskey and his peers comprehend these realities? Could they all know they would be the real creators of South Vietnam's tragedy in April 1975?

The South Vietnamese were not the only people who blamed McCloskey. Many American politicians and generals, officers, and enlisted personnel who had fought in Vietnam, also did, because they shared with the RVNAF feelings of defeat. One of them, the wise U.S. senator Daniel Patrick Moynihan, observed about the betrayal, "to be an enemy of the United States could be unpleasant, but to be a friend of the United States could be fatal."[1] I am thankful that American political conscience always exists in the hearts of many congressmen in Washington, so that the United States can continue its leadership of the free world. With dignity, numerous American congressmen represent a people who like freedom, justice, and truth.

Unfortunately, there were few such in the U.S. Congress in 1974–1975. Ambassador Martin went back to Washington on April 2, with the fact-finding congressional delegation, to present the situation and request Congress' approval of the additional military aid for Saigon; his voice fell on the deaf ears of the majority of the congressmen. When he returned to Saigon, four weeks after disappearing to some paradise in America, he would see South Vietnam going to hell. The Central Highlands in ARVN II Corps, Quang-Tri and Hue in I Corps had fallen, and Da Nang was under communist siege.

That same day, General Frederic C. Weyand, then U.S. Army chief of staff, came to Saigon with Ambassador Martin, as President Ford's special envoy, to review the situation in South Vietnam. He was the last hope for Saigon to get the $300 million of additional military aid. Returning to Washington after Da Nang, Qui-Nhon, Nha Trang, and Cam-Ranh Bay had fallen to the communists, General Weyand testified before Congress asking for this urgent aid for Saigon. But his demand was also rejected. U.S. assistant secretary of state for East Asian and Pacific affairs Philip Habib, who was up on Capitol Hill waiting for the good news from the congressmen, later wrote, "you know they wanted to wash their hands of Vietnam. They wanted to forget it. That kind of mood was prevalent in Congress in 1974–1975."[2]

Meanwhile, in South Vietnam, the political and military situation was worsening day by day. Ambassador Martin returned to Saigon with Kissinger's clear message to abandon South Vietnam. Martin was told: "You gotta get back out there because the American people have gotta have somebody to blame."[3] According to Martin, Kissinger and Brezhnev, the Soviet Union's top leader, had an arrangement on the last day for the Americans to leave Saigon; it was May 3.

EVACUATION PLANS

Ambassador Martin, who said that he would personally come to Da Nang to lead the ARVN troops to fight against the communists, instead ordered his deputy, Wolf Lehmann, and Major General Homer D. Smith, defense attaché in Saigon, to prepare plans for the evacuation of all Americans and South Vietnamese officials, RVNAF high-ranking officers' families, and those who were considered to be in danger of execution if captured by the communists.

The Defense Attaché Office's overall evacuation plan called for: first priority, using commercial flights; second priority, using fixed-wing U.S. C-130 aircraft, from Tan-Son-Nhut Airport to Clark Air Force Base in the Philippines and Andersen Air Force Base in Guam; third priority, possibly using transport ships from Vung-Tau to Subic Naval Base in the Philippines; and the last option, or "Option Four," using a frequent-wing or helicopter lift, in case of emergency. Originally, the U.S. Embassy in Saigon was authorized to evacuate only 35,000 Vietnamese into the United States. But in reality, said Lehmann, the categories of Vietnamese at risk were countless.

According to General Smith, the evacuation began on April 1 with the "Evacuation Control Center" (of his attaché office) operating 12 hours per day. From April 3, this center was functioning 24 hours a day, primarily to "assist with refugee operations." But according to Lehmann, the evacuation began in the end of March. Certainly, the evacuation by commercial flights and U.S. C-130s was secretly commenced at the beginning of April to prevent chaos in Saigon. However, after the crash of the C-5A Galaxy in "Operation Babylift," which removed hundreds of Vietnamese orphans from Saigon, secrecy could no longer be maintained, because the crash sadly had killed hundreds of children and several female U.S. personnel who volunteered to take care of them on the plane back to the United States. The story of children's bodies dispersed from Hoc-Mon to Tan-Son-Nhut drew tears from everyone who heard it.

After this crash everyone knew that the United States was conducting an evacuation. Every Vietnamese family in Saigon tried to find a way to get out the country. The abandonment syndrome then reappeared among South Vietnamese politicians, generals, and high-ranking officials. In reality, at least 25,000 people had fled the country by commercial flights and U.S. C-130s in the previous week. All of them were upper-class rich people or U.S. direct employees. The evacuation continued during the following weeks.

COMMUNIST POLITICAL TRAPS AND MILITARY PUNCHES

During those days, rumors widely spread that former Vice-President, Major General Nguyen Cao Ky, would plan a coup against President Thieu to seize power and lead the RVNAF in the fighting against the communists, while other "third force" politicians and some generals would arrange a peaceful transfer of power to General Duong van Minh for a possible negotiation with Hanoi on the "coalition government" in South Vietnam. This political solution was perhaps proposed by French Ambassador to Saigon, J. M. Merillon, based on the rumors that "Big Minh" was accepted by Hanoi. On March 24, North Vietnamese Prime Minister Pham van Dong suggested to French Ambassador to Hanoi, Philippe Richer, that the French might successfully achieve such a solution in the South. Accordingly, the Frenchmen entered the games. Later, all of them, the French, those in the Vietnamese "third-force," and Duong van Minh himself, realized they had been taken in by a deceitful trap. Actually, North Vietnamese leaders had the solution of defeating South Vietnam and taking Saigon by force, through the "Ho Chi Minh Campaign," as they had newly planned. Indeed, five days after capturing Cam Ranh Bay on April 8,1975, Le Duc Tho called a meeting at Loc Ninh of all commanders and political cadres of COSVN, military regions, and all high-ranking officers newly coming from the North to study the March 25 Resolution of the VWP's Politburo which decided to "liberate" South Vietnam by military means. Tho made known the Politburo's decision to form a command Headquarters of the "Ho Chi Minh Campaign" which consisted of:

1. Field commander: General Van Tien Dung
2. Field political supervisor: Pham Hung
3. Deputy commanders:
     a. Lieutenant General Tran Van Tra
     b. Major General Le Duc Anh
     c. Major General Le Trong Tan

4. Deputy commanders of logistics:
     a. Major General Dinh Duc Thien
     b. Brigadier General Bui Phung

5. Deputy political supervisor: Brigadier General Le Quang Hoa
6. Chief of staff: Brigadier General Le Ngoc Hien

After the meeting, the communists launched their final attacks on ARVN III Corps' defense lines around Saigon from April 9.

The NVA II Corps of Major General Nguyen Huu An, composed of the 304th, 324B, and 325th Divisions, began to attack at Ninh-Thuan, on Route 1 and inter-provincial Route 11. The ARVN defense line was defended by the ARVN 2nd Division, the 2nd Airborne Brigade, and the 3rd Ranger Battle-Group. The NVA IV Corps of Major General Hoang Cam, comprised the 341st, 6th, and 7th Divisions plus an artillery regiment and an armored regiment assailed the ARVN 18th Division along inter-provincial Route 20 and at Xuan-Loc, the capital city of Long-Khanh Province, 45 miles northeast of Saigon. The NVA I Corps of Major General Nguyen Hoa was comprised of the 308th, 312th, and 320B Divisions. It was moving a long way from Quang-Tri and Thua-Thien to attack the ARVN 5th Division, which defended Binh-Duong Province, 25 miles north of Saigon. The NVA III Corps of Major General Vu-Lang, with three divisions, 320th, 316th, and 10th, began to attack the ARVN 25th Division along Route 1, northwest of Saigon. Finally, the corps-level Tactical Force 232nd of Major General Le Duc Anh, with four divisions, the 3rd, 5th, 9th infantry, and the 27th sapper, cut Route 4, south of Saigon to block reinforcements from ARVN IV Corps & Region. (See Map 9.)

After the war, the communists said they had only used 280,000 troops, 400 tanks and 420 artillery pieces in this 1975 spring campaign. This claim is not true. The actual figure is likely double that, because to serve the 280,000 combat troops would require at least an equivalent number of troops in supportive and logistical services. By mid–April, on every front, ARVN units were outnumbered by NVA forces 1-to-5 in manpower and 1-to-4 in firepower.

On April 15, the NVA II Corps of General Nguyen Huu An forcefully attacked all over the Ninh-Thuan defense line and the Phan-Rang Airfield, at which was quartered the ARVN III Corps Advanced Command Headquarters of Lieutenant General Nguyen Vinh Nghi. Despite the fierce resistance of the ARVN 2nd Airborne Brigade (minus one of its battalions that had helilifted to Bien-Hoa on the previous day as part of a move back to Saigon), the airfield was overrun by overwhelming NVA forces after two days of fighting. Lieutenant General Nghi, Brigadier General Pham Ngoc Sang, VNAF 6th Division commander, and Colonel Nguyen Thu Luong, 2nd Airborne Brigade commander, were captured by the communists on April 17, while fighting in retreat to Binh-Thuan. The only ARVN commander who escaped from Ninh-Thuan was the one-star general, 2nd Division commander, who fled on the command helicopter of General Nghi at the beginning of the NVA attack. This unit was fighting without its commander and dispersed. The ARVN 3rd Ranger Battle Group was also overrun. The Ninh-Thuan defense line disappeared on April 18. Binh-Thuan and Binh-Tuy Provinces also fell to the NVA II Corps in the following days. This NVA large unit advanced to Phuoc-Tuy on Highway 1.

The last and largest battle between the RVNAF and the NVA occurred at Xuan Loc, the capital city of Long Khanh Province, 40 miles northeast of Saigon. The ARVN 18th Division and Attachéd Airborne and Ranger units, and several Regional Force battalions, supported by VNAF fighters and bombers, heroically devastated the overwhelming NVA force comprised of four infantry divisions, an armor brigade, and two mechanized ground and anti-aircraft artillery brigades in twelve days of fierce resistance against them from April 9 to 20, 1975.

Located at the intersection of Route 1 and Route 20, Xuan Loc City was the home base of the ARVN 18th Division and the strategic point that blocked NVA access to ARVN III Corps & Region and Saigon from the Highlands and the northeast coastal area. General Van Tien Dung, commander of the Communist Ho Chi Minh Campaign, launched the NVA II

Corps' attack on the ARVN III Corps' new defense line at Ninh Thuan. To effectuate his tactics of "lightning speed, more lightning; boldness, more boldness," he ordered NVA IV Corps, led by Major General Hoang Cam, to neutralize the ARVN 18th Division of Brigadier General Le Minh Dao at Xuan Loc. This was an effort to secure the way for his main army to have a prompt approach to Saigon for the final stage of South Vietnam's "liberation."

On the morning of April 9, after several hours and 4,000 shells of destructive artillery fire into Xuan Loc, the NVA IV Corps launched a three-pronged attack on ARVN defensive positions around the city's perimeter. The attackers were the 266th Regiment of the NVA 341st Division plus tanks from the northwest, the 165th Regiment of the NVA 7th Division plus tanks from the north, and the 209th Regiment of this division plus tanks from the northeast and east. After the first wave of shelling into the city, the Forward Command Headquarters of the ARVN 18th Division led by Colonel Nguyen Xuan Mai, deputy commander, wisely moved to a new base in a plantation at Tan Phong, 6.5 miles south of Xuan Loc, while General Dao was still at his Long Binh base camp. Evidently, the real commander who directed the defense of the 18th Division at the city was the young and brilliant Colonel Le Xuan Hieu, then commander of the ARVN's 43rd Task Force, which consisted of the 1/43 and 3/43 Battalions, the 5th Armor Regiment minus, and the 82nd Ranger Battalion of the ranger hero, Major Vuong Mong Long. There were also two Regional Force battalions in the city commanded by Colonel Pham van Phuc, province chief of Long Khanh. Under the command of these elite commanders, the defenders of Xuan Loc fiercely and successfully neutralized all enemy assaults on their positions. Hundreds of NVA troops were killed and a dozen tanks were destroyed. However, some ARVN positions were lost.

In two days, Colonel Hieu conducted several counter-attacks and recaptured lost territory, causing serious losses for the NVA 7th Division and the 266th Regiment of the NVA 341st Division. General Le Minh Dao had come to the new Forward Command Post at Tan Phong in the morning of April 9. On April 10 he ordered the 2/52 Battalion of the 52nd Task Force moving from Nguyen Thai Hoc Hamlet back to the city to reinforce the 43rd Task Force. On the way back to the city, this elite battalion of Captain Huynh van Ut encountered an NVA unit and killed more than 60 of its troops and captured several dozen guns, including 37 mm anti-aircraft guns. On the eastern side of the perimeter, the 82nd Ranger Battalion of Major Long also nullified the assaults of the NVA 209th Regiment. The remains of NVA troops and tanks were dispersed all around the L-19 Airfield.

Units of the 52nd Task Force of the ARVN 18th Division, commanded by Colonel Ngo Ky Dung, were also violently attacked by two regiments of the NVA 341st Division along Route 20, from Dau Giay Crossroads to Horseshoe Hill. The 1/52 Battalion at Dau Giay was especially steadfast in withstanding for days the ferocious attacks of the 33rd Regiment of the NVA 6th Division. The ARVN 18th Division's 48th Task Force of Lieutenant Colonel Tran Minh Cong, which was along Route 1 from Tan Phong to Suoi Cat, southwest of Chua Chan Hill, had contact with elements of the 141st Regiment of the NVA 7th division in a plantation north of the Route. Before noon on April 9, ARVN III Corps commander, Lieutenant General Nguyen van Toan sent a combined force composed of the 3rd Armor Brigade of Brigadier General Tran Quang Khoi, the 8th Regiment of the ARVN 5th division of Lieutenant Colonel Nguyen Ba Manh Hung, and three Ranger battalions, to reinforce Xuan Loc. This combined force formed into three task forces: the 315th, the 318th, and the 322nd Task Forces moving along Route 1 from Bien Hoa to Xuan Loc. The first column, or the 315th Task Force, was first stopped by the enemy at Hung Nghia Hamlet and then at Hung Loc Hamlet, several miles west of Dau Giay Crossroads. Large skirmishes continued for days and the NVA III Corps had to reinforce the roadblocks of the NVA 6th Division's 33rd Regiment by the 274th Regiment of this division and a Regiment from the NVA 341st Division. Although these task forces of ARVN III Corps could not reach Dau Giay to link up with the 1/52 Battalion of the ARVN 52nd Task Force, they did attract half of NVA IV Corps' force fighting in a different direction and this really impeded the plans of NVA General Van Tien Dung's to neutralize the ARVN 18th Division and capture Xuan Loc City.

On the other hand, ARVN III Corps commander, General Toan also asked the RVNAF-JGS to reinforce Xuan Loc with the 1st Airborne Brigade. On April 12, this elite unit of Lieutenant Colonel Nguyen van Dinh was helilifted west of Tan Phong Rubber Plantation. Immediately, it's five battalions, which included an artillery Battalion, moved up to Route 1 and Suoi Cat, several miles southwest of Chua Chan Hill, to replace the 48th Task Force which was ordered to move to the south and west of Tan Phong as reserves for the ARVN 18th Division. The Airbornes pushed back the 209th and 141st Regiments of the NVA 7th Division to Chua Chan Hill and decimated at least a battalion of the latter. With the reinforcement of the Airbornes, the ARVN's defense at Xuan Loc was strengthened.

By the evening of April 12, the fights turned to the ARVN's favor at all Xuan Loc fronts. The NVA IV Corps' losses were serious, with more than 3,000 troops killed and more than two dozen tanks destroyed. General Van Tien Dung ordered the NVA IV Corps to cancel its attack plans and repulse its units from Xuan Loc City. He called the ARVN's heroic and successful defense of Xuan Loc "the enemy's stubbornness." Communist Command Headquarters of the Ho Chi Minh Campaign sent Lieutenant General Tran van Tra to Xuan Loc Front on April 13 to take over the command of all NVA units for a new phase attack on the ARVN units at Xuan Loc. The NVA IV Corps of Major General Hoang Cam was reinforced by the separate 95B Regiment from the Central Highlands and the 325th Division of the NVA II Corps from Ninh Thuan. General Tran van Tra changed offensive plans against the ARVN units at Xuan Loc Front in this new phase. (See map #8.)

After April 13, Xuan Loc City was not hit by further NVA infantry and tank assaults but only by artillery fire of some three to four thousand shells per day. In the meantime, the NVA 7th Division sent back its 209th and 141st Regiments to Route 1, fighting with the purpose of pinning down in position the ARVN 1st Airborne Brigade. Meanwhile, two other NVA IV Corps' divisions and the 95B Regiment strove to wipe out the ARVN 52nd Task Force along Route 20 and push back the ARVN III Corps' task forces on Route 1, west of Dau Giay. NVA main efforts clearly shifted to the west side of the Xuan Loc Front. In three consecutive days, from April 13–15, the 270th and 273rd Regiments of the NVA 341st Division and the 95B Regiment, supported by an armored Regiment and two mechanized artillery regiments, strongly attacked all ARVN positions along Route 20, from Dau Giay Crossroads to Nguyen Thai Hoc Hamlet and Horseshoe Hill. The fights were extremely fierce, especially at Horseshoe Hill. The 1st Company of the ARVN 3/52 Battalion had to resist the overwhelming assaults by the NVA 95 B Regiment and the deadly artillery fire of the NVA 55th Artillery Regiment from Nui Ma (or Phantom Hill). No one could have imagined the result, that "everything around us was destroyed and the slope of the hill in every side appeared changing its altitude with NVA troop bodies mingled with uprooted brushes and trees' branches, piling up layers and layers," as reported by first Lieutenant Nguyen Thanh Truong, the company commander, to his battalion commander, Major Phan Tan My.[4]

Major My sent a company from Nguyen Thai Hoc Hamlet to reinforce the defenders of Horseshoe Hill. The fight at Crossroads Dau Giay was at the same intensity between the ARVN 1/52 Battalion and the 33rd Regiment of the NVA 6th division. The losses on both sides were too high. 200 ARVN troops were killed and the NVA casualties were innumerable. On the night of April 13, the 3/52 Battalion withdrew to rejoin the 52nd Task Force at Nguyen Thai

Hoc Hamlet. Dau Giay was lost to the NVA, but fighting on Route 20 continued for two more days. In the meantime, three ARVN III Corps task forces, under the command of Brigadier General Tran Quang Khoi, were striving to linkup with the 52nd Task Force. They were unable, however, to cross the NVA roadblocks and barrages from an infantry division and an artillery Regiment in the area north of Hung Loc Hamlet on Route 12 Soc Lu Hill. The ARVN 52nd Task Force was then isolated and fought alone, but bravely. However, outnumbered by the enemy ten to one, and under continuous enemy attack, the 700 remaining members of this besieged task force could not resist any longer. On the night of April 15, Colonel Ngo Ky Dung decided to abandon Route 20 and led his troops in a fighting retreat to Trang Bom on Route 1, west of Dau Giay Crossroads.

On the morning of April 16, considering the request of General Toan, III Corps' commander, General Cao van Vien, Chairman of the RVNAF-JGS, ordered the VNAF to drop two Daisy Cutter Blu-82 bombs on the NVA troop concentrations at Xuan Loc. One was dropped at Dau Giay Crossroads that blew up the command headquarters of the NVA 341st Division and killed hundreds of its troops; another was dropped on the command headquarters of the NVA IV Corps at some area northeast of Xuan Loc City. Later in the day, captured telecommunication reports from this NVA Corps revealed that 75 percent of its staff personnel and hundreds of other troops were killed. After April 17, there were no more strong NVA attacks on ARVN units at Xuan Loc. NVA General Van Tien Dung ordered a drop of any offensive plans against the ARVN 18th Division. The NVA II Corps, after seizing Ninh Thuan and Binh Tuy, made a detour to the east of Saigon, on Route 25, instead of joining the NVA IV Corps at Xuan Loc as planned. The latter was also ordered to withdraw from Xuan Loc and move to Bien Hoa for a new offensive phase. Only two regiments of the NVA 7th Division remained around Chua Chan Hill. The battle of Xuan Loc was over three days later. General Van Tien Dung could not have imagined that 8,000 ARVN troops in this small city could stop and defeat 40,000 of his troops in 12 days of fierce resistance, killing more than 5,000 of his troops and destroying more than three dozen of his tanks. He judged that attacking the ARVN 18th Division again was unnecessary. On the ARVN side, General Nguyen Toan, III Corps commander, felt that Bien Hoa, his rear base, would be in danger if he did not have enough forces to defend it. He ordered General Khoi's Task Forces at Hung Nghia Hamlet to get back to Bien Hoa and the 18th Division and its attached units to withdraw from Xuan Loc and move along Route 22 to Long Binh on April 20. Only the 1st Airborne Brigade of Lieutenant Colonel Nguyen van Dinh was ordered to remain at Phuoc Tuy to defend Vung Tau Port. Thus the heroic victory of ARVN units at Xuan Loc would pass into worldwide military history as a glorious defense of a city.

There were several factors that contributed to this victory: (1) the determined will to fight by commanders and troops at Xuan Loc; (2) the displacement of the ARVN 18th Division Forward Command Headquarters to a secret underground base, which secured the safety of General Dao to command his units; (3) the creation of ingenious underground emplacements for dozens of artillery batteries secured a continuous counter-fire throughout the resistance; (4) the VNAF air support, which was adequate; especially, two Daisy Cutter Blu-82 bombs dropped at Dau Giay and northeast of Xuan Loc City that caused thousands of casualties for the NVA and forced them to change their operational plans.

US Army Lt. General Philip B. Davidson, once chief of staff J2-MACV, admitted, "The battle for Xuan Loc produced one of the epic battles of any of the Indochina wars, certainly the most heroic stand in Indochina War III.... In this final epic stand the ARVN demonstrated for the last time that, when properly led, it had the 'right stuff.'"[5] Also, Major General Homer Smith, then U.S. defense attaché in Saigon, reported to General George Brown, the chairman of the Joint Chiefs of Staff in Washington, that "the valor and aggressiveness of GVN [Government of Vietnam] troops appears to settle for the time being the question, 'Will ARVN fight?'"[6] Yet, once again, the voices of American generals fell upon deaf ears in the U.S. Congress.

Indeed, on April 17 (April 18 in Saigon) the U.S. Congress voted down $300 million in additional military aid and $722 million in emergency aid to Saigon, which had been proposed by President Ford on April 10; but authorized $200 million for the evacuation American personnel. This proved to be the decisive "washing hands" of South Vietnam by the congressmen, about which President Ford commented: "Those bastards." President Thieu sent a delegation to Washington in an effort to persuade the U.S. Congress not to announce publicly its decisions. This was to prevent the demoralization of ARVN troops and keep them fighting. But it was too late.

On April 19, the U.S. Embassy in Saigon received orders to complete most evacuations of Americans and sympathetic Vietnamese as previously planned, while secretary of state Henry Kissinger and others, including ambassador Graham Martin, were still hoping they might be able to persuade Hanoi to negotiate a truce or a "coalition government" for South Vietnam. However, Hanoi refused to negotiate with Thieu. Ambassador Martin suggested President Thieu resign, after he persuaded Major General Nguyen Cao Ky to suppress the coup against Thieu. He also sent U.S. Army Lieutenant Colonel Harry G. Summers, Jr., who was then chief of a U.S. delegation of the Four-Party Joint Military Team (FPJMT), to Hanoi with all members of the FPJMT. Colonel Summers had no purpose except to receive from Hanoi the terms of the U.S. withdrawal. Colonel Summers did not disclose the exact date, but it was expected that the last day of all U.S. personnel leaving South Vietnam would be May 1, 1975, except those who would remain to negotiate with Hanoi on compensation for war damage in return for information about American POWs and MIAs.

Colonel Summers' delegation was the last U.S. diplomatic envoy to officially have discussions with Hanoi, but nothing concerning a temporary truce or a coalition government was noted or mentioned. The "coalition government" problem would be managed by Ambassador Martin himself, or by Thomas Polgar, then CIA Saigon station chief, who had a relationship with a certain Hungarian peacekeeper of the International Commission in Saigon. Later, Ambassador Martin blamed Polgar of such a contact. The ambassador himself said that he did not believe in a coalition transition, but he did explain the situation to Thieu and said that Saigon's generals could not do anything to solve the South's problems with Thieu in power. Thieu also said Martin never asked him to resign. However, the transition of Thieu's power to someone else for a possible negotiation with Hanoi was a clear necessity. In due course, South Vietnamese Lieutenant General Tran van Don, the last defense minister of the Saigon regime, later said:

In the last days, the French Ambassador told me that if you would like to save Saigon from long-range artillery, if you would like to have a compromise solution to keep South Vietnam neutral, the only man who could do it was Big Minh. I asked the French Ambassador "Why Big Minh?" He said because Big Minh is the only one the other side would like to recognize as the new leader in South Vietnam. When I asked the American Ambassador, Graham Martin, he told me the same thing — maybe he got it from the French Ambassador.[7]

The last ten days of April 1975 were a time of tremendous confusion in Saigon. On the morning of April 20, President Thieu held a long meeting with Ambassador Martin. After that, Lieutenant General Nguyen van Toan, III Corps & Region commander, was summoned to meet the president at the Presidential Palace. No one knew exactly what matters the president and the ambassador discussed and what orders the general received from his commander in chief. On the same day, Brigadier General Le Minh Dao, ARVN 18th Division commander, received orders from General Toan to withdraw his forces from the defense line at Xuan-Loc. Abandoning Xuan-Loc would mean giving easier access for the NVA II and IV Corps to promptly advance to Saigon.

The next day, April 21, the communists occupied Xuan-Loc. In the evening, president Nguyen van Thieu announced his resignation before the National Assembly. In a long televised speech, Thieu accused the United States of being unfair, irresponsible, and inhumane, and of all manner of "betrayal." In an inspired moment, he pledged that he would stay with the armed forces to fight the communists as a soldier. Instead of yielding power to Big Minh, President Thieu chose to follow the South Vietnamese Constitution and turned over the presidency to vice-president Tran van Huong, an old but respectable politician in South Vietnam.

Two days later, the U.S. completely abandoned South Vietnam. The declaration was made by U.S. president Gerald Ford himself. On April 23, in a speech at Tulane University in New Orleans, Ford announced: "Today America can regain the sense of pride that existed before Vietnam. But it cannot be achieved by re-fighting a war that is finished as far as America is concerned."[8] According to Robert Hartman, Ford's councilor, the president of the United States was delighted and highly elated by the success of this trip to New Orleans after his speech was loudly applauded by the students at this university. Ford would, however, ignore the tragic effects of this fatal intentional declaration. Disaster immediately came to Saigon through a rising terror of "American abandonment" and "communist massacre." After that, every person and every family tried to find a way to escape from the country. Panic and desperation spread to all corners of the South Vietnamese capital.

Within 24 hours, former president Nguyen van Thieu was secretly escorted by Thomas Polgar and his CIA team to Tan-Son-Nhut Airfield. Along with prime minister Tran Thien Khiem, he fled Saigon on a U.S. DC-6 plane to Taiwan. Their families had gone before them. In the following days, sooner or later, almost all of Thieu administration's ministers, generals, and senior officers quietly abandoned their posts and fled by whatever means. Among those who fled were General Cao van Vien, chairman of the RVNAF Joint General Staff (JGS), Lieutenant General Nguyen van Toan, III Corps & Region commander, and Lieutenant General Nguyen van Minh, Capital Military Special Zone commander, who were first and foremost responsible for the defense of Saigon. With the top commanders disappearing, their senior staff officers also vanished in the following days.

By midnight on April 28, the RVNAF Joint General Staff and other central arms, branches, and services were almost abandoned by their bosses and could not properly function to direct, support and supply combat units in III Corps & Region. Commanders of ARVN divisions around Saigon were left with no specific plans to defend it. Consequently, these divisions and smaller separated units had to fight the stronger enemy forces in their previously assigned defense lines without top ARVN command orders, support, and coordination.

In such a situation, President Tran van Huong could do nothing, as commander in chief, to continue the fighting to save Saigon. Five of General Van Tien Dung's communist corps were approaching and Saigon's political dreamers still believed in negotiating with Hanoi on the "coalition government." Finally, under the pressure of these dreamers, President Huong stepped down on April 27. The same day, the National Assembly immediately elected Duong van Minh as President. Big Minh took office on the afternoon of April 28.

On the American side, after President Ford's declaration at Tulane University, there was discord between the State Department and the Defense Department on the evacuation of

Americans from South Vietnam. According to some American observers, the evacuation proceeded too late because Henry Kissinger was still playing at diplomacy with the communists while James Schlesinger, who viewed abandoning South Vietnam as a serious error and the failure of American policy, had ordered his men to hurry the evacuation from Saigon of American military personnel and all Americans. In addition, according to Ambassador Martin, Kissinger had an arrangement to leave U.S. war equipment, which was used by the RVNAF, for the communists while Schlesinger sent people to South Vietnam for the secret recuperation of these heavy war equipment.

In Saigon, the mess created by this difference between U.S. departments was clearer. In the critical days of late April 1975, Ambassador Martin hoped that Hanoi would respect the Kissinger-Brezhnev verbal agreement to give him enough time to organize a timely and safe departure for all Americans. For this purpose, he tried to keep his men from doing things that would provoke the NVA to attack sooner or would excite the ARVN troops' opposition, repercussion, or retaliation against the Americans. To be sure, Martin contended that he could not pull out many ARVN senior officers because it would keep them from leading their units and maintaining their troops' fighting capability to protect the safe withdrawal of the Americans. Similarly, Martin tried to slow the evacuation of 5,000 Americans, believing in a temporary truce or a coalition government, which would be arranged by the intermediation of French Ambassador Merillon, or at least to use the appearance of this as a psychological screen to deceive the South Vietnamese people that the Americans did not abandon them. All of Martin's plays were concealed in deception intended to once again beguile South Vietnamese people, ARVN officers and troops in the late days of Saigon.

In the meantime, honest and pragmatic U.S. senior officers like Defense Attaché Major General Smith, Colonels LeGro, John Madison, Jr., and Harry Summers, Jr., were trying to progressively push forward the evacuation plan of Americans, ARVN senior officers' families and South Vietnamese collaborators by U.S. fixed-wing C-130s. More than 5,000 people left the country every day from April 24. Before that, in mid–April, U.S. defense secretary James Schlesinger sent his delegate, assistant secretary of defense Erich von Marbod, to Saigon with the mission to recuperate U.S. heavy war equipment, which had been offered to the RVNAF during the Vietnamization period.

After Phan-Rang Airfield fell on April 18 and the communists seized several F-5s and A-37s, Marbod secretly persuaded Lieutenant General Tran van Minh, South Vietnamese Air Force (VNAF) commander, to evacuate all war planes at Bien-Hoa and Tan-Son-Nhut Airfields to Thailand. All in all, by April 28, VNAF pilots flew more than 130 war planes to U-Tapao Royal Thai Air Force Base.

Marbod also sent U.S. Navy Lieutenant Commander Richard Lee Armitage, who had spent nearly six years on active duty in South Vietnam, back to Saigon to privately meet his old friend, Captain Do Kiem, South Vietnamese Navy's (VNN) deputy chief of staff, and ask him for help in planning the evacuation of the South Vietnamese fleet to the Philippines. Captain Do Kiem presented the idea to Vice Admiral Chung Tan Cang, South Vietnamese Chief of Naval Operations (CNO), and persuaded him to approve the plan of evacuation.

Vice Admiral Cang first hesitated, but after meeting with president Duong van Minh hours after his presidential inauguration, Cang decided to move his fleet as Captain Kiem and Amitage proposed. Admiral Cang later recalled: "He [Minh] said that if we were going to fight there would be loss of life and bloodshed with no purpose because the situation was hopeless. So in this case everyone had their own solution. I went back to headquarters and called for a staff meeting, and we decided that now was the time to move out."[9] The evacuation of the South Vietnamese fleet began in the evening on April 29. The operation was finally completed after the fall of Saigon with 34 transoceanic warships, which carried 30,000 Viet-namese refugees, reaching Subic Naval Base in the Philippines. In addition, about a dozen small patrol boats were abandoned at large after transferring their passengers and crews to other vessels, since these boats were not seaworthy.

In general, the plans to recuperate this expensive war equipment from South Vietnam were successfully done by U.S. assistant secretary of defense Erich Marbod. However, Ambassador Martin would later blame these activities for creating problems for his timely and orderly evacuation plans, because the communists had rocketed Tan-Son-Nhut Airfield on April 28, thinking that the United States had broken their word to them in removing the heavy war equipment they supposedly had agreed to leave in place for them. And, because enemy shelling of the airport prevented the fixed-wing operation from functioning, he had to order the last frequent-wing option: the helicopter lift.

Certainly, the head representative of the United States in Saigon, Ambassador Martin, would do everything he could to evacuate the Americans and avoid any possible disaster. U.S. assistant secretary of defense Erich von Marbod also did what was in the interests of the United States. They should not be blamed for their actions.

Because these American authorities had carefully planned for the final act of "washing their hands" of South Vietnam, especially after the United States arranged with Hanoi for a fixed-date departure for the Americans, Saigon could no longer stand. Thus, whatever Ambassador Martin did to keep the ARVN fighting, it was done intending to protect the safe withdrawal of the Americans but not for the life and death of South Vietnam. Fighting to survive was hopeless. A great number of South Vietnamese generals and senior officers stayed with their units to face their stronger foes in these most critical days of South Vietnam. Later many of them sacrificed their lives for the honor of their armed forces.

THE BITTER END

The mass of people in Saigon did not know just how bad the situation was when General Duong van Minh took office on April 28. They did not know that all ARVN combat units in III Corps & Region and in the Capital Military Special Zone (CMSZ) had been left behind by their top commanders since the early morning, and now, these units were separately fighting without any coordinated plan to defend Saigon while five NVA corps-sized units approached and surrounded it at a 30 to 40 kilometer (20 to 25 miles) perimeter. These NVA units could attack Saigon at any time.

Believing in the protection of the ARVN, which had been able twice to push back the communist attacks in 1968, people in the capital went about their daily activities. The face of Saigon appeared peaceful and quiet. Markets, stores, and restaurants were open as usual and traffic was normal. Streets were filled with pedestrians, bicycles, and cars. Schools around the city were not yet closed; kids were still playing in schoolyards or studying in classes. Everything appeared in it's habitual state. But there was an eerie silence throughout the city, mixed with occasional sounds of gunfire or explosions echoing from the outskirts. Everyone felt that something very important was going to happen soon.

While the families of high-ranking government officials and RVNAF senior officers were being successfully evacuated by U.S. fixed-wing C-130s from Tan-Son-Nhut Airfield, the majority of the Saigon population, especially the middle class, thought a temporary peace with a coalition government, which had been widely rumored days before, would occur; or there would be a withdrawal of all ARVN forces in III Corps & Region and in Saigon to the

Mekong Delta, the richest part of South Vietnam, for the formation of a new defense line along the Tien-Giang River, as was previously planned by former President Thieu. They patiently waited for news, good or bad. If the first possibility were realized, the people in Saigon and in the Mekong Delta would have had at least a short period to decide their futures. If a new defense line were formed to protect the Mekong Delta, the war would continue with more intensive bloodshed, because all RVNAF units at IV Corps & Region were at full strength and led by elite generals, such as Major General Nguyen Khoa Nam, an airborne commander, and Brigadier General Le van Hung, the hero of An-Loc. Commanders, officers and troops in this military region were willing to fight. No one was thinking of a third solution in those days: surrender to the communists. Nevertheless, all possibilities were illusions except the third one, which materialized promptly beyond anyone's imagination. I was one of Saigon's witnesses during its final days.

At the time, I was RVNAF-JGS-J2's liaison officer to the IV Corps & Region Staff-G2 at Can-Tho, the capital of the Mekong Delta. I was living at General Hung's residence. This ARVN hero had been my best friend since we were cadets of the Thu-duc Reserve Officer School's 5th Class in 1954. He was my platoon-mate and roommate then; later, in the first three years of the 1970s, he was my boss, when he commanded the ARVN 5th Infantry Division. Now, at IV Corps & Region, after almost twenty years in the army, General Hung still considered me as his closest friend despite my rank of Lieutenant Colonel.

On the morning of April 28, General Hung sent me back to RVNAF Joint General Staff-J2 (JGS-J2, the highest military intelligence staff-service of the South Vietnamese armed forces) to gather accurate information on the political and military situation. I flew back to Saigon on General Hung's command-helicopter. The helicopter had to take a detour to the sea to fly along the coast to Saigon, instead of following the routine itinerary along Highway 4, afraid of being hit by an enemy SA-7 personal anti-aircraft missile. An NVA division had cut this important road at Tan-Tru in Long-An Province, some twenty kilometers south of Saigon, isolating it from ARVN IV Corps & Region. On the plane approaching Saigon from the east, I watched the city as it peacefully went about its normal activities.

The helicopter crew dropped me off at the RVNAF-JGS compound and flew the plane back to Can-Tho. At JGS-J2 Office, I met the colonel deputy chief-of-staff J2 and some officers who were in charge of the intelligence and operation branches. I learned that an hour before noon, almost all top commanders and senior officers of the JGS were gone. Officers and personnel of this highest command headquarters of the Republic of Vietnam Armed Forces were left behind by their bosses. However, everyone remained in place, believing in new President Big Minh, who would negotiate with the communists about the "coalition government." They waited for new orders. Consequently, activity at the staff service loosely continued as a matter of form.

JGS-J2 provided me a jeep with a driver. I went home, which was located on Tran Hung Dao Street, 5th District, passing over the Presidential Palace, the Saigon Market, and the Saigon Police Department headquarters. Nothing had changed anywhere. In the afternoon I returned to J2. I was able to use the hotline to call General Hung and report the general situation — something like a weather forecast. I told him that at this hour, 3:30 P.M., Saigon was very calm but "very hot." A "big hurricane" seemed to be coming soon, because west of the capital we already heard the echoes of thunder. The north, the east, and the south remained quiet but the "high wind" was poised to rise quickly into an alarming cyclone. I also pointed out that people said in the last several nights that Saigon was very cloudy, so that all the "big stars" had disappeared. General Hung was very astute in comprehending the situation. He asked me if Saigon had prepared for the hurricane. I told him they had not. Hung asked again:

"Tell me, if you know, what they are doing or what they are going to do, especially the new 'Sun'?" I answered: "I don't exactly know. There would possibly be a 'mixed drink' prepared soon, but I'm not sure." He replied: "Impossible! Now, tell me would you return to Can-Tho or not?" I answered him: "I don't know. I'm waiting; I will call you again." After we hung up, I was unable to make any further contact with him or see him again. (The new "Sun" meant the new president; the "mixed drink" meant the coalition solution).

In my heart, I wanted to join General Hung at IV Corps & Region to help him in the future fighting against the communists. That was why I did not try to flee the country but instead searched for a way to return to Can-Tho. However, the road was blocked and everything happened very fast. When I left the JGS compound about 5:00 P.M. that day, April 28, I saw two warplanes, A-37 fighters, in the air of Tan-Son-Nhut, bombarding the airfield. I wondered why at this time two A-37 fighters of the VNAF were attacking their headquarters base camp. I did not think Major General Nguyen Cao Ky would order VNAF pilots to do it even if he conducted a coup d'état (rumors of this had circulated), because Tan-Son-Nhut was his residence and principal base. Later, I learned that these A-37s were among those captured by the communists at Phan-Rang Airfield on April 18 and were being flown by two former VNAF pilots, who had defected to them that day.

Fifteen minutes later, I came to Kim-Son Restaurant on Le-Loi Avenue. There, I would meet the most knowledgeable people in the capital: journalists, writers, professors, politicians, and even senators and representatives. In Saigon, several restaurants had become "pocket information centers" for years and Kim-Son was one of these. I wanted to meet those intellectual people to learn about the political climate in Saigon after Duong van Minh seized power. Several were my friends and would let me know everything because they considered me to be a liberal poet rather than an army intelligence officer.

Indeed, I met some of them. They were discussing Big Minh's inauguration speech, the possible appointees to his new cabinet, his policy, and particularly his coalition government with the communists in the South. Based upon the recent political and military situation, they concluded that to save Saigon a certain bloodbath, Big Minh was inclined toward the coalition solution, of which Lieutenant General Tran van Don, then defense minister, appeared as a very smart activist. For days before Big Minh inaugurated his presidency, General Don had run back and forth between French ambassador Merillon, American ambassador Martin, and Big Minh to push forward the demarche of this political solution. These intellectuals named Don a "cracked go-between" and considered Big Minh a "wavering coalitionist," a mediocre but lucky general and an illiterate politician. Therefore, their activities would not go anywhere and Saigon would fall soon. I was considerably saddened. I thought I had better rejoin General Hung in IV Corps & Region.

There was a curfew that night. Two hours before dawn, on April 29, the communists began to show their presence around Saigon by shelling Tan-Son-Nhut Airfield, DAO compound, and RVNAF-JGS headquarters. At DAO compound two U.S. Marines were killed. In the morning, Ambassador Martin arrived to observe the Tan-Son-Nhut Airfield and ordered a stop to the U.S. C-130s fixed-wing operation, thinking RVNAF's top command had pulled out, no one was left to command the defense of the airfield, and the evacuation was no longer protected by South Vietnamese troops. The evacuation of Americans and select Vietnamese was carried out by U.S. helicopters and was called the frequent-wing operation and held at the DAO compound.

At 9:00 A.M., I arrived at RVNAF-JGS. The guards allowed me to pass through the main gate. At J-2, I met a Lieutenant Colonel who was the Chief of the Internal Intelligence Branch. I knew that since the previous night there had been no further contact with the ARVN 25th

Infantry Division at Cu-Chi, on Highway 1, west of Saigon. It meant that this largest ARVN unit on the western defense line of Saigon had been overrun by the communist forces of the NVA III Corps.

In the North, the ARVN III Corps & Region command headquarters at Bien-Hoa disappeared and the ARVN 3rd Armored Brigade moved to Go-Vap, five kilometers north of Saigon. Farther in the northwest, the ARVN 5th Infantry Division had several small contacts with the NVA I Corps but still retained its command headquarters at Lai-Khe Plantation. In the northeast, the ARVN 18th Infantry Division, the 81st Special Airborne Brigade, and two Airborne Brigades still held their positions along the New Freeway from Long-Binh to Cat-Lai and the New Port, while a brigade of the ARVN Marine Division at Vung Tau was moving to its base-camp Song-Than at Thu-Duc. Possibly, the NVA IV Corps, which had attacked the ARVN 18th Division at Xuan-Loc, would carefully advance on this access. Meanwhile, the NVA II Corps, after attacking the ARVN 1st Airborne Brigade at Long-Thanh, would make a detour farther to the southeast, overlapping ARNV units in the northeast and advancing along interprovincial Road 25 to Nhon Trach, on the east bank of the Saigon River, ten miles southeast of Saigon. In the south and southeast, the newly formed ARVN 106th Ranger Division, composed of the 7th, 8th and 9th Battlegroups, had few contacts with the NVA 232nd Tactical Force.

In sum, by April 29, the ARVN had five divisions around Saigon and the NVA had sixteen divisions or more, according to JGS-J2's estimate. Saigon could not be held if the enemy attacked immediately that day.

Perhaps Lieutenant General Dong van Khuyen, JGS-Chief of Staff, was the last highest authority of the RVNAF who received this J-2's report. However, this general could do nothing but secretly leave his post on the morning of April 29 by the rear gate to DAO compound and flee to the U.S. Seventh Fleet, which was at some distance from the shore of Vung-Tau, on a U.S. helicopter.

At JGS, everyone could see U.S. helicopters landing and taking off at DAO compound carrying Americans and select Vietnamese to the fleet. I knew that on-board these planes important people — ministers, directors, and seniors officers — had started to become refugees in a foreign country with ambiguous destinies. But at least they were lucky enough to evade any communist reprisal if the ARVN could not hold Saigon. We, the anonymous officers, NCOs, and soldiers, stood there watching our bosses leave with endless feelings of sadness. By this time, an hour before noon, command at JGS, the highest headquarters of the RVNAF, had pulled out. All superior officers were gone. The numbers of personnel who were left behind were diminishing by the minute. How could ARVN combat units around Saigon fight without a head!

And the Americans who early on came into this country believing in a just cause were now leaving it in a hurry. What did they think of the situation? Was it a defeat? It was strange, this complicated Vietnam War. An officer at J-2 told me that Professor Vu van Mau, the former minister of foreign affairs who had resigned from his post to oppose President Diem's policy toward the Buddhists' riots in 1963, that morning had announced in an Armed Forces regular broadcast President Big Minh's decision to chase out the Americans. That also was strange. We really did not comprehend the complex politics of the parties involved.

I learned from another officer that on April 28, after the inauguration of his presidency, President Minh had sent a delegation composed of the Catholic priest Chan Tin, the Buddhist priest Chau Tam Luan, and Lawyer Tran Ngoc Lieng to Camp David at Tan-Son-Nhut to meet NVA Brigadier General Vo Dong Giang, Hanoi's highest representative at the Four-Party Joint Military Commission, to arrange a cease-fire.

I left JGS headquarters about 1:00 pm this afternoon after failing to make contact with General Hung in IV Corps & Region. At that time, only authorized people could enter and leave the gates. I wanted to go to VNAF headquarters at Tan-Son-Nhut Airport to find a means to go back to Can-Tho.

I spent almost forty minutes reaching the VNAF headquarters' main gate. It seemed that every vehicle in the city was carrying a full load of people and driving on Cong-Ly Avenue to the American Defense Attaché Office (DAO) compound and Tan-Son-Nhut Airport seeking a way out of the country. All kinds of cars and thousands of people massed at the airport gate, trying to get in. Of course, no one was permitted to enter the gate, not even VNAF officers. I told the jeep driver to take me back to JGS compound. But then the main gate was secured by the ARNV 81st Special Airborne Brigade's troops. Nobody was allowed to come in or get out. It was about 2:45 P.M.

I heard that Lieutenant General Vinh Loc was made chairman of the Joint General Staff and ex–Brigadier General Nguyen Huu Hanh, a suspected communist discharged from the army a long time before, was assigned by Big Minh as JGS chief of staff. I wondered how these newly assigned generals could run an empty JGS since almost all senior officers and key personnel at all joint-staff offices were fleeing or wandering throughout the city? Who would work for them when they did not allow people to come back to their offices?

I left the JGS gate while the sky of the DAO compound buzzed with U.S. helicopters were flying back and forth like birds over a burning forest. The evacuation of Americans and select Vietnamese continued. My family members supposedly would have been placed aboard one of these planes had I returned to Saigon three days earlier. They were supposed to be evacuated from the country on April 23 or 24, since U.S. Colonel William LeGro, DAO's senior officer in charge of military intelligence and RVNAF-JGS-J2's advisor, had close relations with Colonel Hoang Ngoc Lung, JGS' chief of staff J-2, and had established an evacuation list of family members of all J-2's senior officers. All of them had left for Guam days before by U.S. C-130s, except those of my family, whose names were not on that list or on any U.S. departure manifest, because during these days I was working at IV Corps & Region and none of the J-2 authorities could inform me of this secret evacuation. Now, I knew that I could do nothing to help my family leave the country. I, myself, wearing a uniform, could not even enter through the gates of any Vietnamese or U.S. installation for any reason. I thought to myself, "I will accept my destiny and will suggest my family do the same."

Desperate, I told the jeep's driver to take me to the Pagoda Restaurant, on Tu Do Avenue, another one of Saigon's "pocket of information centers." I met some friends and learned that all members of President Minh's delegation had been retained at Camp David in Tan son Nhut Air Base the night before by the communists, and NVA General Vo Dong Giang had informed them about Hanoi's ultimatum forcing of President Minh to surrender unconditionally.

At the Presidential Palace, President Duong van Minh was always surrounded by his new aides (who were called members of the "Third Force" Party), such as the notable jurist Professor Vu van Mau, Lawyer Ngo Ba Thanh, the Buddhist nun Huynh Lien, some political rookies such as Nguyen van Hao and Ly Qui Chung, and some pro-communist teachers and students such as Hoang Phu Ngoc Tuong and Huynh tan Nam. All had once been received by French ambassador Merillon, on April 22, but had been chased out from Camp David on April 24 by Phan Hien, the chief of all Hanoi's delegates at the Joint Military Commissions in Saigon, when they accompanied General Duong van Minh for a precocious talk on political settlement prior to his seizure of power in South Vietnam. Now, it seemed the communists turned down any negotiation with President Minh but his surrender. I thought this could not be happening.

I left the Pagoda Restaurant about 4:00 P.M. By that time, U.S. CH-53 helicopters were flying back and forth over the city. Several landed on the roof of the U.S. Embassy building and others on Hai Ba Trung Street, taking off from there, fully loaded. The majority of these birds still came and left from the DAO compound in Tan-Son-Nhut.

I felt that the highest stage of the American evacuation had come. That the Americans were hastening to leave meant the communists were pressing to come. I wanted to go to the U.S. Embassy to take a look. Between the intersection of Hai Ba Trung Street and Thong Nhut Avenue and the embassy building were thousands of people. The embassy was surrounded by a huge crowd of Vietnamese, American, and third-country nationals who were trying to get in. The main gate was closed and numerous U.S. Marines had secured it. However, people were trying to climb over the walls. Some were taken in but many were pushed out. It was a complete mob scene, crazy and piteous.

Up to that point, I did not know how many Americans had already left and how many more were going to leave the country, but I surely knew that, contrary to the suspicion of some American authorities, the people of Saigon, even those who were left behind, did not hate the Americans. Hundreds of thousands of Vietnamese wanted to go with them but nobody tried to hurt them as they made their way out of the country. ARVN soldiers in Saigon, at all units, were under control. The majority were still awaiting orders to fight. Perhaps they did not know that all the big bosses had already left.

I told the driver to take me to the Vietnamese Navy (VNN) headquarters on Bach-Dang Quay, following Nguyen Hue Avenue. Thousands of people crowded the quay along the riverside, but the four large VNN battleships floated gently on the water at several piers along the naval camp's riverfront. The gates of these piers were closed and strictly guarded by numerous armed seamen. No one could pass through. The traffic was jammed with cars and motorbikes abandoned in the streets.

Because travel to the VNN headquarters had become impossible, I decided to go home. We returned to the center of Saigon. On Tu-Do and Le Loi Streets, people were still walking, shopping, or even waiting in line at some movie theaters. It was strange. I wondered if these people knew that not too far from there, at the U.S. Embassy and along the naval base's waterfront, thousands of others were trying to find a way to escape from the country. Probably they did not know that their lives would be forever changed when the communists came and took over the city.

A heavy thunderstorm moved over Saigon late in the evening of April 29. After taking a shower, I was going to bed when my nephew told me that he just heard Major General Nguyen Cao Ky announcing on the Armed Forces radio broadcast that he would stay to fight the communists to his last drop of blood, until his death. I said, "Yes, every ARVN soldier in Saigon wants to fight to the death rather than to live with the communists; but, you know, many generals are gone and I would appreciate it if General Ky would stay to fight." However, I did not trust our unpredictable leaders, who lacked steadiness and loyalty.

In the morning of April 30, the jeep came. The driver was First Sergeant Kim Nhi, who had been my longtime driver when I was deputy commander of the ARVN Military Intelligence Center (MIC) from 1966 to 1968. He and I went to have breakfast at a restaurant on Gia-Long Street. All the restaurants around Saigon Market were open. Sergeant Nhi told me that the night before there had been major fighting in the west outskirts, along Highway 1, and this morning when driving the jeep to my home he saw many refugees running from the Bay Hien area to Phu-Tho, where the MIC was located. Bay Hien was the base camp of the

Airborne Division. I knew that in this area and around Tan-Son-Nhut Airport, at that time, there were at least two airborne brigades, the Third of Lieutenant Colonel Tran Dang Khoi and the Fourth of Lt. Colonel Le Minh Ngoc. I believed in these airborne commanders' fighting competence and leadership. I thought they could hold the west defensive line for days and the communist attack against them would be bloody. I realized that the communists had finally come. Times would be hard for all of us and disastrous for Saigon's people. I never thought the end would be bitter. But it was.

After breakfast, about 8:30 A.M., we went to the Vietnamese Navy headquarters, on Bach Dang Quay. I saw no more battleships docked at the piers along the river. Back to Thong Nhat Avenue, at the US Embassy, the crowd had almost disappeared, but several looters mobbed in and carried out everything they could find. Certainly all the Americans were gone.

On the way to JGS headquarters, we were stopped at Cong-Ly Bridge; many cars were also stopped right there. People said that this morning several enemy rockets had fallen into and around this RVNAF highest headquarters compound and there had been fighting around Tan-Son-Nhut Airport. I decided to go to the Military Intelligence Center, my former unit, on To Hien Thanh Street in the Phu-Tho area. I met Lt. Colonel Nguyen van Nhon, deputy commander of the unit. Lt. Colonel Nhon told me that president Duong van Minh had announced on Saigon Broadcasting at 9:30 A.M. his policy of "reconciliation and concord" with the communists to save the people from carnage; he suggested all RVNAF soldiers stop fighting and stay in place, and declared his intention to meet the Provisional Revolutionary Government's official representatives to discuss the formalities of an orderly changeover of power to avoid unnecessary bloodshed. Brigadier General Nguyen Huu Hanh also ordered RVNAF generals, officers and soldiers to execute President Minh's commands.

In hearing Lt. Colonel Nhon summarize these orders, I felt a chill creep along my spine and spread to my brain. I wondered how this could be happening. The fighting that had erupted around Saigon from the night before lasted until that morning. I could not imagine whether the airbornes, the marines, the rangers and soldiers of other ARVN units would obey these orders, especially the troops at IV Corps & Region. By that time, in this military region there were more than three infantry divisions, 18 ranger battalions, 15 artillery battalions and 55 separated companies with almost 400 field howitzers, five to six armored regiments with 500 tanks, the 4th VNAF Division with a hundred fighters and bombers, and the 4th VNN Force with nearly 600 large and small battleships. How could generals, officers, and soldiers of these RVNAF units simply turn over their installations, materiel and equipment to the communists whenever they might come for an "orderly changeover"? Pausing for a moment, I then asked Lt. Colonel Nhon: "What do you think about General Minh's orders; are these a surrender declaration?" He said: "I don't know. It seems we lost the war in an unusually peaceful manner. But, we have to wait for clearer orders. I'm confused. I don't know whether our armed forces will continue to fight or not. We have to wait."

At 10:25 A.M., we heard President Minh broadcasting his second declaration. This was his unconditional surrender to the communists; something that would be remembered as: "As President of the Republic of Vietnam, I, General Duong van Minh, request all the armed forces give up their arms and unconditionally surrender to the Liberation Army. I declare all governmental bodies, from central to rural level, dissolved." We seemed to be paralyzed for a while as if we had swallowed something at a gulp. We knew it was the end, a tragic end that we had never imagined. Many of us were crying.

President Minh's declaration of surrender to the communists and his orders abolishing the regime and the armed forces were a death sentence for all of us, officers, NCOs and soldiers of the RVNAF, who had sworn to sacrifice our lives for years to defend our democracy and protect the people of the South. Our work and merits gained through sweat, tears and blood dried up within hours due to the actions of our incompetent and fickle leaders.

Colonel Nhon left the office with his personnel to burn classified documents and files. Upon returning, he exclaimed, "That's it! That's the end! What are we supposed to do now? You were my superior in this unit before so now you may give me good advice in this situation." I told him: "We certainly do not expect the communists will tolerate us when they come. It's better to tell our people to disperse, then we abandon the empty camp for them." It was the sole solution. Later, I learned the majority of RVNAF unit commanders did the same.

Colonel Nhon went out and said something to his personnel. Within fifteen minutes, I saw MIC's officers, NCOs, and enlisted men leaving from the main gate. Those who were living within the camp's barracks had changed their uniforms and left the camp with their wives and children. I did not know where they might go but I imagined they were en route to an indefinite and miserable path for their lives. The bitter end of my former unit and almost all others also happened like that. Heartbroken, lamenting, and resentful, we were soldiers of the RVNAF after that.

Sergeant Kim-Nhi, a trustworthy and loyal ethnic Cambodian driver, was still there waiting for me. I called him in, thanked him for his services, gave him a little money, and told him to take his family back to his natal village, somewhere in Vinh-Binh Province. He cried, held my hands for a while, and left. Now alone, Colonel Nhon and I shared the last tragic moment of the disintegration of our unit, our army, and our regime. We shook hands, said "adieu" to one another, and left MIC with tears quietly streaming over our cheeks. I drove the military jeep home still wearing my uniform.

At home, everybody was waiting for me. They had heard the bad news and were worried for me. All of my personal documents, photos, and uniforms were burned, including several intelligence certificates given by British and American intelligence schools. My eighty-year-old mother suggested that I change my uniform and go hide in my first cousin's house somewhere on the New Freeway. The jeep parked in the street had disappeared; I caught a taxi and went to my first cousin's house, a lacquer-painting factory, near the New Port. It was a quarter to noon. This afternoon I saw the communists coming into the city in their Soviet-made tanks and trucks. Along the freeway, people were watching them. Yes, it was not a bloodbath. It did not happen right away. But South Vietnamese blood would later pour out at all corners of the land, little by little, to the point that everyone wanted to leave the country.

At night, my first cousin told me she had heard from witnesses that the Presidential Palace's main gate had been hit by communist tanks before noon and the national flag on the top of the palace had been replaced by a Liberation Front flag. I asked her to stop talking. I did not want to hear things like that. Yes, we had lost the war and the winners could do anything they wanted. I suffered in silence the loss of our regime and the disbanding of our armed forces that we had built for twenty years. The flag, the eminent symbol of our regime power and the spirit of our armed forces, was replaced! Every one of my cousins words pierced my heart. This gentle and virtuous girl seemed to read my silent feelings. She began quietly crying.

General Duong van Minh had bet his dignity on the gamble of power. But power had not brought any honor or pleasure for him, first when plotting the coup to overthrown president Ngo Dinh Diem in 1963 and finally when haggling to seize the presidency in the last days of April 1975. On the one hand, power for him was only an illusion. On the other hand, it was a destructive tool that devastated his honor and destroyed the free regime of the South

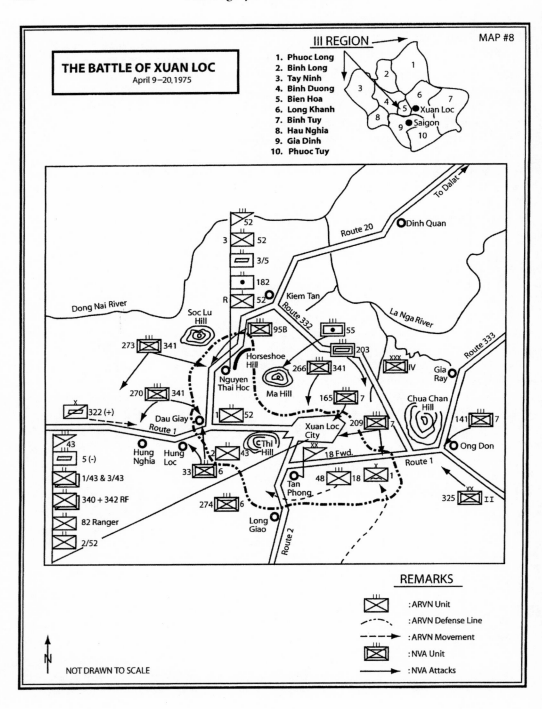

THE BATTLE OF XUAN LOC
April 9–20, 1975

III REGION — MAP #8

1. Phuoc Long
2. Binh Long
3. Tay Ninh
4. Binh Duong
5. Bien Hoa
6. Long Khanh
7. Binh Tuy
8. Hau Nghia
9. Gia Dinh
10. Phuoc Tuy

REMARKS

: ARVN Unit
: ARVN Defense Line
: ARVN Movement
: NVA Unit
: NVA Attacks

NOT DRAWN TO SCALE

Vietnamese people. Not only did General Minh terminate the First Republic, but he also abolished the Second Republic of the South and its armed forces. He was different than General Nguyen van Thieu. Thieu, at least, enjoyed the "pleasure of power" for ten years while Minh only suffered its sadness.

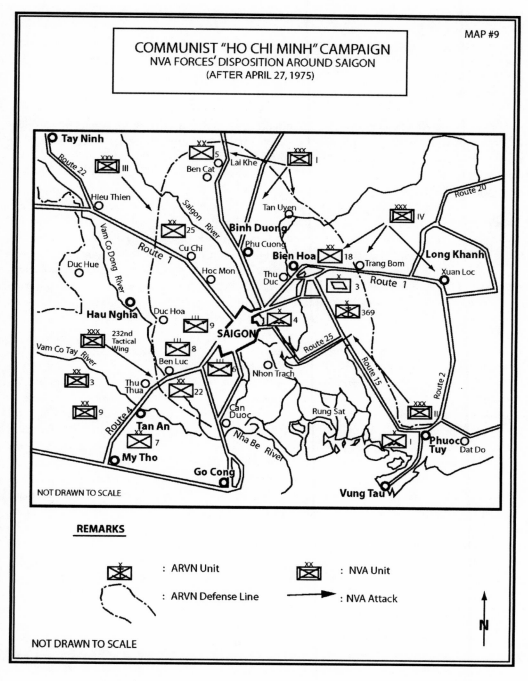

COMMUNIST "HO CHI MINH" CAMPAIGN
NVA FORCES' DISPOSITION AROUND SAIGON
(AFTER APRIL 27, 1975)

MAP #9

REMARKS

: ARVN Unit

: NVA Unit

: ARVN Defense Line

: NVA Attack

NOT DRAWN TO SCALE

However, both of them were unlucky stars in the southern sky — the vandalized rulers. Thieu, who had real power, had given up half of the South's territory to the communists without fighting, leading to the loss of half of its armed forces in a two-week margin. Minh, with his illusory power, had exterminated the body of the South Vietnamese political and social structure and eradicated the rest of its defensive forces in a brief margin of two hours. The shift of national power into the hands of the communists would lead to a long-lasting test of endurance for the Vietnamese people, both of the North and the South, who were overloaded by misfortune under the violent, brutal, and inhumane communist regime. Yet, to save millions of Saigon's residents from a bloodbath in the last minutes of South Vietnam, a responsible leader in the position of president "Big" Minh would do no differently than he did. His last dime bet in that complicated war could have been the last and greatest contribution of his life for his country.

Two days later, my wife came from the Mekong Delta and brought me the most sorrowful news. At ARVN IV Corps & Region, a few hours after hearing President Minh's declaration of surrender, Major General Nguyen Khoa Nam, commander; Brigadier General Le van Hung, his deputy; and Brigadier General Tran van Hai, ARVN 7th Infantry Division commander; committed suicide. All ARVN units in the delta were disbanded. On the same day, two more ARVN generals also took their own lives: Brigadier General Le Nguyen Vy, commander of the 5th Infantry Division, and Major General Pham van Phu, the former commander of II Corps & Region. Later, I learned that a great number of RVNAF unit officers, NCOs and soldiers had chosen the same honorable and valiant death. Among these heroes, there were two lieutenant colonels, three majors, and a captain of J2-JGS and its subordinated units. I cried for all of them, and particularly for my superior and close friend, General Le van Hung. The lofty sacrifice of these ARVN heroes mirrored the indomitable tradition of the armed forces of South Vietnam and the unyielding spirit of the young generation of South Vietnamese generals, officers and soldiers. With dignity, they sacrificed their lives for the honor of their land, regime, and army.

The end of our regime was bitter because the halo of the heroes was shaded by the cloud of shadow of our highest leaders. We lost the war because of bad leadership and not by the inefficiency of our armed forces. The RVNAF was an elite army in the world. We would have been able to confront the communist People's Army on the battlefield with competence if, after the Vietnamization, our ally and leaders did not tie our hands and turn our backs for the enemy to shoot at us. How could we defend the regime and the people of the South in such a wretched situation? We were formed, trained, and then sacrificed for the sake of others, including our leaders, in the course of the war.

I felt very ashamed of myself for hiding in my cousin Thanh-Lan's factory. She, a talented artist and a pretty woman, was trying in those gloomy days to teach me the art of making a lacquer painting. However, a few weeks later, I began to wander down the next phase of my life, which started in several communist concentration camps. One day, I received a letter from my wife saying that Lan had escaped from the country by boat and disappeared, with many others, into the depths of the Pacific. I felt the profound sense of the Taoist philosophy concerning human life and remembered two lines of an ancient Chinese poem:

From olden times, beautiful women like famous generals

Promise not, in this world, to see their hairs turning gray.

This was also the fate of the famous General Le van Hung and the beautiful artist Thanh Lan, two of my intimates, whom I will always hold in highest esteem and admiration.

16

The Vietnam War's Aftermath

The fall of Phnom-Penh to the Khmer-Rouge on April 17, Saigon to the communists of North Vietnam on April 30, and Vientiane to the Pathet-Lao on August 23, 1975, marked the end of the Indochina War — or the Second Vietnam War. The whole of Indochina was made communist under their total control, especially the communists of Vietnam. In America, some said that since the last American combat unit had left Vietnam almost three years prior to the fall of Saigon, the United States was not militarily defeated by the North Vietnamese Army. This was true. However, the war was lost and a majority of Americans felt that the United States had lost its pride and honor, especially after the last American ambassador to South Vietnam, Graham Martin, with all of his embassy personnel, left Saigon in a hurried evacuation in Operation Frequent Wing just a few hours before communist tanks and troops arrived to take over on April 30, 1975.

That ironic day marked a turning point in American war history. Researchers and historians in America have tried to understand the root causes of this fatal reality. Many media articles, comments, and analyses, and a large number of books, memories, and symposiums discussed the Vietnam War and its outcome, but it seemed that none completely satisfied public opinion. Thus, the "Vietnam trauma" or "Vietnam syndrome" lingered on for years with pains, sorrows and resentments among the American people, particularly among those who had fought in Vietnam. The search for the truths of the Vietnam War has continued.

In my research, I tried to retrace the realities and the superficial lost causes of the war, since I could not reveal the truths, which were deeply covered under many layers of political secrecy of the time. However, while engaging in this comprehensive work, it would have been too ambiguous if we had said that the United States lost the war. It is better for me to say that, for some reason, the American leaders of the time did not want militarily to defeat the communists of North Vietnam and win the war. A military victory would create more problems because the United States would then have to defend Vietnam and the other prosperous countries in Southeast Asia. Although South Vietnam was lost to the Vietnamese communists, the United States achieved its long-term goal of deterring Chinese aggression toward the other countries in the region.

Various important Americans attempted to explain these reasons for losing the war, including Walt W. Rostow, the Vietnam-era national security adviser; Admiral Elmo R. Zumwalt, Jr., the ex-chief of U.S. Naval Operations; and other U.S. generals and admirals. For example, in a symposium on Vietnam at Hampden-Sydney College in the fall of 1993, Rostow opined: "If you assume that the purpose was to keep Southeast Asia independent, then it can be argued that we accomplished our objective. Thailand, Malaysia and Singapore — all of which were absolutely up for grabs in 1965 — emerged with confidence, with strong economies. Do you think these countries could have kept their independence without help from us? No way." Then, he added, "It was not a narrow political crisis in Vietnam. It was a crisis in Asia."[1] Admiral Elmo R. Zumwalt, Jr., in a conference on McNamara's book *In Ret-*

rospect at the Army and Navy Club in Washington, on November 9, 1995, echoed this view: "In a strategic sense, we did win, because our commitment in Vietnam 'made it possible' for countries such as Thailand, Singapore and Malaysia not to go communist."[2] More specifically, as noted by Marc Leepson, a columnist for *Vietnam Magazine*: "The United States actually did win the war in Vietnam. That's because the eight-year American military effort in Vietnam gave other Asian nations time to build up their forces to fight communism. While the communists triumphed in Vietnam in 1975, except for Laos and Cambodia, no other Asian 'dominoes' fell."[3]

I completely agree with the conclusion of these distinguished American figures, that the United States actually did not lose the war in Vietnam. However those in America who assert this controversial position are like "a grain of sand in the desert," because the claim is not evidenced or proved by a U.S. military success, a concrete exploit, or a visible victory. In my mind, logically I see no sense of an American failure in Vietnam but rather, a successful defeat politically over the communists, both Chinese and Vietnamese. With a step back in Vietnam and the abandonment of South Vietnam in the first half of 1970s, American leaders solved several crucial problems, immediately and down the road.

In America, they instantly satisfied an American public that had ardently turned against the war in Vietnam, and saved the internal politics and economies, all of which were going to degenerate. In East and Southeast Asia, they temporarily appeased communist China and evaded a larger war that might lead to a nuclear war, and saved the peace for other Asian countries. Finally, in Indochina, with a long-term view of transforming the whole of Vietnam into a stronger fortress to permanently deter the Chinese communist aggression toward other Southeast Asian countries, they created more favorable conditions for the Vietnamese communists to unify the country. The latter solution would be the prime cause for the United States to abandon South Vietnam.

Acquiring a more solid fortress (than South Vietnam) with less expense constituted a perfect success by the United States in its long-term policy toward Southeast Asia. If the communists of Vietnam had established any political, diplomatic, or economic relations with the United States, they would have fallen into the American trap. This would be a potential political victory by the United States over the Vietnamese communists. The sooner the communists seek access to the wealthy American pockets through-economic aid, loans, investments, or commercial dealings the sooner they will become submissive to and dependent upon the United States in Southeast Asia. To defeat an enemy by a peaceful process is always better than by a military victory.

The above assumptions, however, are hypotheses. Practically, most American authorities, especially those in the armed forces who had fought in Vietnam, felt fully responsible for the loss of South Vietnam. The last message from the U.S. Embassy in Saigon on April 30, 1975, proved that bitter outcome: "It has been a long and hard fight. The battle is over.... We have lost. Let us hope we have learned our lessons."[4] The Vietnam War was one of the longest and costliest in the history of the United States. The unexpected loss of the war seriously affected the nation and the armed forces, both physically and spiritually. The war's costs afflicted the Americans on many issues for years after the war.

DEFEAT AND ITS EFFECTS
ON THE UNITED STATES

According to U.S. Marine Colonel James A. Donovan, American casualties during the war in Vietnam ranked fourth in number of battle deaths and the third costliest in number of servicemen wounded in action in American war history. From the death of the first American serviceman in action on December 22, 1961, to March 28, 1973, when the last U.S. combat unit left Vietnam, the United States had engaged directly in the war for 11 years and one month and suffered 211,318 in total casualties of servicemen, including 58,015 deaths, 153,303 wounded in action, 766 prisoners of war (POWs) officially listed, and another 1,913 considered as missing in action (MIA). Because of the short one-year term of duty, more than 3.74 million Americans served in Vietnam. At its height, the American force ceiling was 525,000 men in August 1967, under the command of General Westmoreland.[5] According to Colonel Donovan in an article in the April 1996 issue of *Vietnam Magazine*, "Assessing the War's Costs," the loss of U.S. equipment and supplies in Vietnam exceeded that of any previous war. Some of the costliest items were:

- High-cost equipment such as strategic and tactical aircraft were lost in large numbers. A total of 8,612 aircraft of all types were destroyed, including 3,744 fixed-wing jets. Of these, 1,646 were lost in action and 2,098 were due to accidents and other non-hostile causes; 4,868 helicopters were lost, of which 2,288 were destroyed in combat action and 2,588 by other causes. The total costs of all aircraft lost amounted to $12 billion or more.
- Consumable munitions for U.S. and Allied forces expended in the battlefield were some 15 million tons that cost between $30 and $35 billion. Particularly, during the seven years of air combat in Indochina, the U.S. Air Force dropped 7.35 million tons of bombs, twice the tonnage dropped in all theaters of World War II. The costs of the bombs were estimated to be $7 billion.
- Strategic and tactical jet fuel, gasoline, and naval fuel consumed by the U.S. Air Force, U.S. Navy and allied armed forces averaged a million barrels per day, which was an enormous drain on the United States and led to a "national fuel crisis" in 1973, especially after an oil embargo was declared by the Arab League of 11 Arab nations on June 5, 1973.
- Other heavy modern equipment lost in Vietnam, such as tanks and artillery howitzers were not mentioned in Colonel Donovan's assessment of war costs, but everyone would agree that the cost of this equipment would add up to several billion dollars.

In sum, the dollar costs to the United States for the war in Vietnam were difficult to total, as Colonel Donovan writes. However, he estimates that the U.S. military expenditures in Vietnam, Laos and Cambodia reached $97.9 billion, not including the considerable funds expended for military aid to South Vietnam, Laos, and Cambodia, which would amount to $10.7 billion. The war's total costs may be estimated at about $108.5 billion. On the other hand, Nixon's defense secretary Melvin Laird estimated the war's monetary costs in Vietnam to be $236 billion, or $100 billion greater than the official estimate and more than double the estimate of Colonel Donovan.

Donovan points out:

> The high cost of the Vietnam War forced the nation to postpone spending for many sorely needed domestic projects — hospitals, schools, roads, transportation systems and sewage plants. Also, while the nation focused its resources, skills and energies on the war, it experienced increasingly stiff business competition from abroad. At the same time, American productivity began to decline. But the greatest economic impact of the war may have been that it caused the nation to be less willing to commit military power and dollars to influence the world's stability and peace.[6]

According to Donovan, the costs of the war in Vietnam created serious problems for the United States, both internally and externally. However, the internal impact was clearer than its impact overseas. The bedrock of U.S. global policy at the time was to contain the international communist expansion and this prime purpose was indeed realized after the end of the Vietnam War. There was no room for blame regarding U.S. external affairs. Therefore, the effects of the war's losses on America itself became the major subject of study. In terms of "physical losses," the United States obviously lost tens of thousands of lives and a great deal of money during the Vietnam War. But the losses of the Vietnam war could not only be examined in terms of lives and money; but also the "spiritual losses." Any physical loss may lead to a psychological or spiritual loss that will more gravely affect a person, a community, or a nation for a certain period of time. The United States was no exception to this common rule during the second half of the 1970s.

In the political domain, most Americans felt a loss of national honor after South Vietnam was lost to the Vietnamese communists. Most American generals, officers, and soldiers, especially those who fought in Vietnam, felt a loss of pride for not defeating a small country's army. This heart-rending sorrow and resentment extended day after day and became the "Vietnam syndrome," which existed in the U.S. armed forces for years; the largest and longest psychological wound for the armed forces in America's history.

Second, American civilian leaders lost the respect and trust of the American people and the armed forces. Many U.S. generals, admirals, and officers complained that their civilian leaders lacked the will to win the war or applied flawed policies and indecisive strategies in Vietnam. The American public and the media blamed the government for concealing the realities while conducting an unnecessary war in a faraway country. As a result, many important political figures that were responsible for the loss of the war were "out" of the U.S. executive and legislative branches afterward.

Third, intellectuals expressed open suspicion about America's power. Some said that the United States should not be omnipotent and its power should be limited when resolving problems in remote countries of the world, because American dollars and guns are not the most effective weapons for winning the "hearts and minds" of other nations and achieving peace or freedom for them. Finally, the general public suspected that America's power was not used by American leaders to serve the interests of the American people during the Vietnam War. Regardless of whether or not this is true, this opinion appeared in the United States after the war.

In the social domain, assessing how deeply the war's losses affected American society was difficult. First, the enormous financial cost of the war spawned inflation and the devaluation of the dollar, which seriously agonized Americans both materially and mentally. Americans suffered the gradual siphoning off of America's wealth during the war. Second, the vast expenditures for the lost war created tension and disorder, corruption, and national guilt among the American people. Social unrest, confusion, contradiction, and discontent increased as Johnson's Great Society and other national plans to revitalize the growing social, ecological, and economic needs were undermined or canceled due to the war's vast cost.

Third, the war itself divided the nation. The ironic outcome aggravated the situation: difficulties between races, gaps between generations, disputes about responsibilities between the executive and legislative branches and between administrative organizations and media networks. American youth in particular were disrupted by the war. During the war most students accepted conscription but a significant number of university students avoided the draft by leaving the country to live abroad, or opposed the draft by engaging in anti-war movements and demonstrations. After the war, irrational, uncooperative, and illegitimate violence and riots on campus and in the streets, rooted in anti-war movements, surfaced in every corner of American society. The American social order drastically changed. The lost war and its aftereffects were the root causes of the growing counter-culture movement that turned away from the heroic traditions and courteous practices of the "World War II generation" and turned instead to bad manners, drugs, violence, free law and free love.

Finally, the national armed forces suffered the most from the lost war. The emotional feeling of "being defeated" haunted the armed forces' servicemen, particularly those who had fought in Vietnam. The failure in Vietnam seemed to damage everyone's psyche. Everyone felt a sense of loss to self-reliance, pride, and honor. The biggest wound of the armed forces was the sacrifice of soldier lives for nothing, neither for the interests of the United States nor for the freedom of South Vietnam, an allied country. The wound was serious. The Vietnam Veterans' Memorial Wall in Washington, D.C., with more than 58,000 names of the dead and 2,000 more of the missing were tragic marks or unforgettable blurs in the minds of the American soldiers for decades.

After the resonant victory of the U.S. armed forces in the Gulf War in 1991, president George Bush declared, "By God, we've kicked the Vietnam Syndrome once and for all."[7] We hope so. However, many U.S. generals, officers and soldiers did not think so, because Vietnam did not go away and remained an experience we must learn from for many more years. War is the disgusting outcome of political and diplomatic failure; but, should we decide to go to war, we must be determined to win it.

How Could the United States Have Won the Vietnam War?

After the war, many notable American politicians, military experts, and historians pointed out hundreds of reasons for the American failure in Vietnam. The main causes may be summarized as follows:

First, the U.S. foreign policy toward Vietnam formulated by five consecutive presidents was inconsistently followed from the beginning to the end (1954–1975). Objectives varied, not only by presidential philosophy, personality and conscience, but also due to the drastic changes to the domestic and worldwide situation during every period of the Cold War era. This inconsistency of U.S. policy in Vietnam was the prime cause of the failure.

Second, the United States did not want to win the war militarily; so, the White House and the Pentagon were unwillingly to formulate determined and convincing strategies with clear objectives to defeat North Vietnam. Had the United States wanted to defeat this small country it could have done so.

Although many military experts have described several different strategies the United States followed in Vietnam, including the "air offense" strategy against the North Vietnamese territory, American forces were solely attached to a "defensive war" strategy throughout the war in varying degrees, "low profile" to "high profile," to defend South Vietnam. That defensive strategy gave North Vietnam the necessary time and space to gain initiative to develop its revolutionary war. The United States only escalated the war in accordance with the increasing intensity of enemy strength and activities on the battlefield. The will to win the war was never mentioned by any U.S. administration.

Third, there was a lack of candor between the United States and South Vietnam at the high echelons on political, diplomatic, and military issues, all of which were necessary for any alliance to defeat the common enemy. The U.S. lacked confidence in the fighting competence of the RVNAF which hampered the combined efforts of the allied forces on the battlefield. This resulted in a huge credibility gap between the United States and South Vietnam in working to attain the goal of defending the advanced fortress of Southeast Asia. The loss of South Vietnam was the typical example of failure of alliance in any ideological war. Nowadays, the United States has faced the complicated war in Iraq which has similarities to the Vietnam

War from 1964 to 1966. I hope American leaders will learn from the above problems of the Vietnam War in order to: (1) consolidate the Iraqi government and its armed forces; (2) let them fight the war by themselves; (3) strongly support them, but withdraw U.S. forces from that land of different culture and life. These three important measure should be considered among dozens of others.

Fourth, according to U.S. Army Lt. General Phillip B. Davidson, once chief of American military intelligence in Vietnam, there were several reasons for the loss of the war. One of these was North Vietnam's "Superior Grand Strategy" which, from the beginning to the end of the war, harnessed all facets of national power to achieve the sole national objective: "the independence and unification of Vietnam, and eventually of all of French Indochina." Their most brilliant strategy was the "Strategy of Revolutionary War." American leaders did not grasp this important strategy. Instead of considering the communist revolutionary war as a total war and selecting appropriate strategies, the United States "reacted timidly by limited half measures." That was the "confusion of concept, counter-measures, organization, strategy, and above all, confusion of American people — this last by far the most critical," General Davidson wrote in his book *Secrets of the Vietnam War*.[8]

In the meantime, Norman B. Hannah, a former U.S. State Department officer, in his book, *The Key to Failure*, identified the United States' failure "to take decisive action on the ground to block North Vietnamese infiltration through Laos as the U.S. government's single greatest strategic error of the Vietnam War."[9] This observation of Norman is the most astute of all observations about the Vietnam War. I, myself, have thought that if the Ho Chi Minh Trail did not exist, there would not have been a Second Vietnam War.

The problem of cutting off the Ho Chi Minh Trail south of Laos was the main but most frustrating concern for General William C. Westmoreland in his military life. In June 1997, *American Legion* magazine asked the general, since he was retired, what had frustrated him the most about the war. He answered, "certainly the failure to follow my recommendations to cut off the flow of supplies down the Ho Chi Minh Trail was one of the biggest frustrations. I would have liked to see us able to go into Laos and Cambodia to get that job done more effectively with ground troops but politicians didn't want us to for a number of reasons they deemed sufficient."[10]

Fifth, the war could not be won because U.S. civilian leaders had no confidence in U.S. commanders and tied their hands while fighting the war with politicians and bureaucrats, expert or mediocre. Many feared the Chinese would intervene, which would widen the regional war to a world war. With such confused estimates provided by politicians and bureaucrats, American leaders would not permit the use of ground forces to invade and attack the communists in North Vietnam or to cut the Ho Chi Minh Trail in Laos. As a result, the cradle of the communist revolutionary war and the vein of subsistence for NVA forces fighting in the South were never destroyed. All measures proposed by U.S. Army, Air Force and Navy generals and admirals that might produce a tangible victory were rejected by American leaders, and thus the communists were not defeated in the North or the South.

Finally, because of the above factors, the war could not be ended sooner but was prolonged to the point it confused and demoralized the American people, and eroded their support for the (continuous) conflict in Vietnam. Consequently, by the time the American people decided not to pursue the war any longer, their civilian leaders had to listen to them. Thus, South Vietnam was abandoned and the war was lost. After the war, some knowledgeable Americans asked: "How could the United States have won the Vietnam War?"

Many U.S. political and military experts have articulated measures the United States might have taken to win the war. In my opinion, I believe that we lost the war because it lasted so long that it shocked and discouraged the American people. The communists of North Vietnam were able to prolong the war only after being heavily supported by the Soviet Union, China, and the communist bloc, with equipment and supplies. They then could conduct their revolutionary war in the South by exploiting the Ho Chi Minh Trail at full length to continuously supply their forces in this theater and in Cambodia.

Had the United States decided to win the war, they might not have needed to use ground forces in North Vietnam. Instead of approaching it as a limited war with a defensive strategy, after the Gulf of Tonkin Resolution, it should have been framed as a war of limited offensive strategy. In other words, the United States might have adopted a combination of U.S. commanders' measures. In the North, it might have applied Air Force General Curtis LeMay's proposition to conduct an air war without limited objectives and Navy Admiral Thomas Moorer's proposition to blockade the Hai-Phong Harbor. In Laos, it might have used Army General William Westmoreland's plan to block the Ho Chi Minh Trail by ground forces. In South Vietnam, it might have pushed firmly CIA expert William Colby's Phoenix Program, or the "Pacification Operations" to eliminate the communist infrastructure. These measures should have proceeded at the same time in a combined plan. Within two years, such a limited offensive strategy with combined actions would have made the North Vietnamese communists kneel in surrender. U.S. ground forces would not be used in the North and the Chinese would not be provoked to intervene in Indochina.

However, such an American victory would create burdens for the United States. General Phillip Davidson described these:

> But — as it was the case — the victory would have brought with it onerous problems. If the Korean experience furnishes an example — and it does — the United States would have to keep residual military force in South Vietnam for at least two decades. The American force would have been harassed by minor North Vietnamese forays over the DMZ and by small, but frustrating, ambushes and land mining operations carried out by communist guerrillas. The needs of the South Vietnamese government for economic and military aid would surely grow into significant fiscal burdens. To paraphrase the old adage — the price of liberty [for a Southeast Asian ally] is not only eternal vigilance, but the assumption of long-term and painful obligations as well.[11]

General Davidson's supposition was clear and concise. Based upon these realities and suppositions, the problems of the United States in resolving the war in Vietnam becomes clear. One final truth emerges from asking the question: "Did the United States lose the war or did it win the war politically over the communists of Vietnam?" We must affirm that "those who really lost the war were the South Vietnamese people." We suffered deeply from the effects of the loss because we were betrayed by our ally. That was the real fact of history.

THE SOCIAL REVOLUTION OF SOCIALISM IN VIETNAM

After the last president of South Vietnam, General Duong van Minh, declared the disbandment of the South Vietnamese regime and the surrender to the communists, the peace of all Indochina seemed promising. In America, most people thought the war in Southeast Asia had ended. The Pacific *Stars and Stripes* appeared on Thursday, May 1, 1975, with a sharp headline, that read, "IT'S OVER! The Saigon government surrendered unconditionally to the Viet-Cong Wednesday, ending 30 years of bloodshed."[12] Other newspapers carried the same image and pointed out that there was no bloodbath in Saigon. However, if the bloodbath did not happen in Saigon, it did in Phnom-Penh. And bloodshed continued all over Indochina for years after the war. More wars, more killings and more deaths were reported in the following years.

In comparison with the 20-year Indochina War, that ended in the deaths of 1.8 to 2 million people, the number of Indochinese killed in the post-war era—from 1975 to 1979—would reach 2,200,000. Pol Pot and his fellows were accused of inhumane manslaughter for the massacre of 1.5 million Cambodians. Vietnamese communist Party leaders should be considered as leading masters of the chaos in Indochina and the hideous creators of a massive exodus of three million South Vietnamese, who tried to flee their motherland during the two decades after the war. Among them, fewer than two million reached the free-world nations. The Vietnamese exodus was historically one of the largest and the most pitiful migrations of human beings since ancient times.

In addition, Vietnamese communist leaders proved themselves among the most ambitious, greedy and harsh dictators as they resolved post-war problems in Indochina and in South Vietnam. Several thousand-page books would be needed to report adequately their endless foolish, perilous, and venturesome attempts to solve these problems. The following provides but a few succinct glimpses of their "ideological revolutions" and their vindictive measures applied in South Vietnam, and their ambitions in Indochina, particularly in Cambodia.

After successfully violating the Paris Accords of 1973 by a full-scale attack on South Vietnam, seeing the last Americans leave Saigon, and accepting Duong van Minh's unconditional surrender, Vietnamese communist leaders might believe they accomplished their first and long-term strategic purpose of the "nation's liberation," or the liberation of the people from foreign domination to gain national independence. Their second strategic purpose was the "social class liberation," or the liberation of the proletariats and the peasants from the "domination" of the other social classes.

These "ideological purposes" were rooted in the communist dogma of Marx and Engels, which Lenin and Mao Tse-Tung had successfully applied as they struggled to establish communist regimes in their countries. Their disciples in Vietnam had carried out the "revolutionary war" for more than twenty years to realize these dreams. To establish a solid communist regime in Vietnam, the second objective "social class liberation" needed to be carried out, certainly in South Vietnam. The South had experimented with freedom and democracy for two decades. Therefore, it was not easy for the communists to achieve their goals. To destroy a free regime would not only mean demolishing its government and its armed forces, but also uprooting every source that nourished freedom for the people and their liberal perspective.

For these reasons, the Vietnamese communist leaders strictly applied the so-called "Social Revolution of Socialism" (Cách-Mạng Xã-hội Xã-hội Chủ-Nghĩa) all over South Vietnam only weeks after their victory celebration in early May 1975. This "revolution" that pretended to liberate poor people in reality was targeted to uproot all vestiges of the former society in all domains, both spiritually and physically. In other words, the communist leaders employed fierce measures to reform the society by targeting their revenge on all classes of people associated in any form with the old regime.

The "Social Revolution of Socialism" proceeded under several separate concurrent revolutions: ideological revolution, educational revolution, literary revolution, economical revolution, industrial revolution and agricultural revolution. Each revolution had prime objectives to be realized and subjective targets to be eradicated from their spheres. This social revolution was the most crucial scheme of the communists to completely degenerate a free society into a socialist society.

In the ideological revolution, the first and foremost targets to be eliminated or separated from the populace were RVNAF personnel, governmental officials, and those who had been

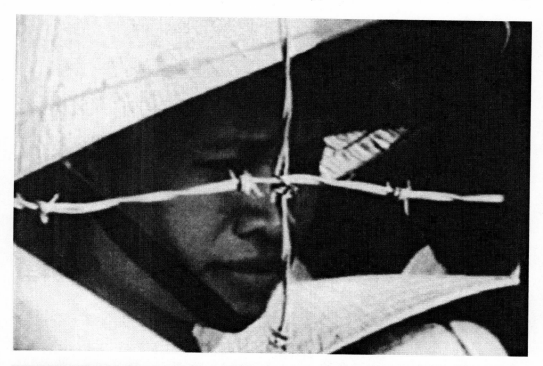

Top: After "liberating" Saigon on April 30, 1975, the Communists brainwashed most RVNAF officers in "re-education" camps around the country. Officers' wives were relocated to remote "new economic sites" and forced into hard labor. This photograph shows one of these unfortunate women at Le Minh Xuan Site. Courtesy Nguyen Cau and Sao Bien. *Bottom:* Children of RVNAF officers were forced into hard labor. This photograph shows children in Bien Hoa Province forced to smash rocks at Buu Long Mount for minimal food. Courtesy Nguyen Cau an Sao Bien.

associated with the former regime at all levels. All RVNAF officers with the rank of second-lieutenant to general, and high ranking officials, about 200,000 in number, were concentrated into "re-education camps" in remote areas around the country, from the peninsula of Camau to the northwest forests of North Vietnam to be brain-washed. Their families, were concentrated in different remote "new economic sites" (Khu Kinh-tế Mới) around South Vietnam to endure their new lives cultivating and developing the lands which had been devastated by the war. Millions of families were relocated from cities and towns to these new economic sites.

The second and most important targets were the leaders of Buddhist, Catholic, Christian, Cao-Dai and Hoa-Hao sects, and the leaders of nationalist parties. After the concentration of RVNAF officers, most of these sects and parties' leaders were soon being concentrated into re-education camps for different terms. All pagodas, temples and churches were closed to believers. Any public worship, celebration, or reunion at these religious places was forbidden. In a society of old traditions and customs based upon the teachings of Buddhism, Confucianism, Taoism, all western lifestyles were attacked by communist magazines, newspapers, and propaganda services day after day. All of these means were used to indoctrinate the people from cities to rural areas in "socialism" and "communism." A public fear emerged in every corner of South Vietnam: fear of doing, fear of saying, fear of being accused of being anti-regime, and so on.

In the educational and literary revolutions, the targets were intellectuals in the world of letters, writers, poets, novelists, university professors, theoreticians, philosophers, and, people of the press circles, owners, publishers, editors and journalists. Many were arrested put in jails, or concentrated in re-education camps. Establishments of production and publication such as printing-houses, publishing houses, editorial offices were seized. All spiritual works, old magazines, newspapers, novels, short stories, poems, books — including academic books — were confiscated and burned. All national libraries and all private bookstores were closed to the public. To be sure that the literary works of several liberal authors of the former regime could not be circulated and read, the communist government issued a first decree forbidding the people from reading or circulating under any literary form the writings of 56 authors (the name of this writer was on this fearsome decree).

A new and restrained educational system replaced the liberal one in school at all levels. The new system produced a mediocre standard of obedient, block-headed, and blind generations of youth. It also introduced many new, ridiculous, and funny words into the vocabulary of the Vietnamese language. There is a long list of these grotesque words that the communist Vietnamese lexicographers may not have the courage to put into their dictionaries.

After the re-unification of the country under the "Socialist Republic of Vietnam" (SRVN), Hanoi leaders immediately extended their revolutionary measures to their South Vietnamese comrades. The "Provisional Revolutionary Government of South Vietnam" (PRGVN) and the "Liberation Army," or Viet-Cong, were dissolved. Many PRGVN ministers and cadres were eliminated from all SRVN's organs. Some fled the country to exile abroad. Truong Nhu Tang, a PRGVN minister, fled to France and wrote a book criticizing the communist regime and its leaders for their cruelty, inhumanity, and lack of loyalty. Many Viet-Cong or southern-born military cadres, who were considered "little capitalists," were forced to retire. Some later wrote petitions, protestations, or books blaming the communist leaders for being narrow-minded, ambitious, and arrogant and the regime for being incompetent, rigid, corrupt and lawless. They implored "reforms."

In the economic, agricultural and industrial revolutions, Vietnamese communist leaders closely put into practice the theories of socialism, advocating that a country's land, transport, natural resources and chief industries should be owned and controlled by the whole community or by the State, and that wealth should be equally distributed. In reality, they confiscated all private lands, industrial factories, means of production, commercial establishments and stores, and properties of landowners, merchants, and rich people around South Vietnam, then transformed all of these into state properties and state factories to direct all production and manage all distribution. All smaller shops, stores, and factories were closed except those of the State. The monthly quantity of food or aliment was fixed for citizens, based upon each person's labor performance, new social class, and family members. People who were not associated with any government organization would purchase food at the lowest standard of quantity. Free market production and consumption ended only six months after the "liberation" of South Vietnam. The impoverishment of the South Vietnamese people peaked between 1976 and 1980. Tens of millions of people in more than twenty provinces did not have enough food and were at risk of starvation. Social activities seriously stagnated after millions of people lost their properties and tens of millions more lost their incomes, because of unemployment and the prohibition of practicing free commerce, business, and wholesale or retail trade. In some provinces the children were forced to hard labor.

In rural areas collective farms and in urban sectors state-enterprises were incapable of producing food and furnishing commodities enough for the people. The stagnation of the national economy was inevitable. In addition, the Communist Party's policy of eradicating the "capitalists" (Tư-sản) and "sellers" (Mại-bản), and especially the discrimination against indigenous Chinese created more problems for the regime. Rob Paschall, in an editorial letter in Vietnam Magazine, wrote: "Two years after the Saigon regime fell, rumors of border skirmishes between China and Vietnam emerged. Much of this armed dispute revolved around a Hanoi-inspired pogrom directed at its own 650,000 indigenous Chinese citizens. As accusations flew, some 263,000 Chinese began fleeing Vietnam. Then, a few months after Hanoi's victory in Cambodia, China invaded Vietnam."[13]

In short, the vindictive measures of the Vietnamese communist leaders in their "Social Revolution of Socialism" would result, in first, the exodus of nearly 3 million South Vietnamese, including the Chinese-Vietnamese. One-third of them lost their lives in the Pacific. Dictionaries of advanced nations became enriched with the term "boat people." Second, these measures resulted in the stagnation of the national economy and the poverty of the Vietnamese people, all of which would retard the development of the nation for decades.

Later, after 1986 and the transition from the "Socialist Economy to Market Economy," and after many changes in the Party's leadership, the Vietnamese communists believed that their "economic renovation" would bring modernization to the nation and prosperity to the people. On the contrary, after studying their "renovation," many international observers predicted that the Vietnamese economic reforms would only create a new class of rulers in Vietnam, who were "trying to consolidate the devastated communist regime in Vietnam while attempting to exploit its geographic position in Asia-Pacific and its human and natural resources for their own greed of wealth, property, and power. Their economic reforms have set up a new class of Red-Capitalists in Vietnam."[14]

THE VIETNAMESE COMMUNIST LEADERS' AMBITIONS IN INDOCHINA; THE INVASION OF CAMBODIA AND THE WAR WITH CHINA

From early 1952, during the First Vietnam War, the French Second Bureau in Indochina knew that the ultimate aim of the Vietnamese communist leaders was to install a communist regime not only in Vietnam, but also in Laos and Cambodia. To accomplish this, Ho Chi Minh and his disciples organized the Indochinese Communist Party (the forerunner of the Vietnamese Workers' Party), trained and encouraged several Laotian and Cambodian communist leaders, supported them, and led them in the struggle for the independence of their countries. The relations between these three countries' communist leaders were close throughout the long war.

After the Second Vietnam War ended, their relations changed little. In Laos, the Laotian communist leaders continued to answer to Hanoi and legitimized the presence of 40,000 Vietnamese troops already stationed in Laos by the "Friendship and Assistance Treaties" with Vietnam, signed July 18, 1977. In Cambodia, Pol Pot and other Khmer-Rouge leaders planned to slip out from the influence of Hanoi to determine their own path to rule the country. Unfortunately, this narrow path led them to destruction. In effect, after the seizure of Phnom-Penh and national power, Pol Pot and other Khmer-Rouge leaders immediately orchestrated a brutal, repressive and inhumane policy to eradicate the traces and subjects of the late regime. That policy resulted in the mass execution of more than 1,500,000 Cambodians and mass starvation in Cambodia.

Common opinion apparently says that Pol Pot's homicidal policy and the Khmer-Rouge's barbarity of slaughtering the Cambodian civilian population, including thousands of indigenous Vietnamese citizens, were the main reasons Hanoi invaded Cambodia. A closer examination reveals that the Khmer-Rouge's refusal to submit to Hanoi was the true cause. In addition, the Vietnamese communist leaders sought to dominate Cambodia in order to extract its wealth, exploit its natural resources and suck its cream to nourish the 1,500,000 men in the People's Army of Vietnam (PAVN), a task that could not be met by their national weak economy. With these Hanoi leaders' ambitions, war was inevitable.

The Vietnamese strategic plan to occupy Cambodia proceeded in several phases:

- From 1975 to 1977, PAVN units repeatedly conducted small attacks against the Khmer-Rouge along the borders to test their resistance and fighting ability.
- From November to December 1977, PAVN large units crushed a Khmer-Rouge division at Snoul on Road 13, twenty miles north of Loc-Ninh, then conducted an advance 70 miles deep into the eastern territory of Cambodia.
- On December 24, 1978, Hanoi leaders renewed their invasion of Cambodia. Several PAVN large units crossed the borders and quickly smashed Khmer-Rouge units in six eastern provinces of Cambodia. On January 7, 1979, these Vietnamese communist units captured Phnom-Penh and established a socialist "Puppet regime" led by Heng Samrin, a Khmer-Rouge division commander (later, he was replaced by Hun–Sen, the subject most loyal to Hanoi). Pol Pot's units were almost crushed by the PAVN force but they had enough force to resist the Vietnamese in several pockets in the countryside and in the borderline areas with Thailand.

During a visit to Singapore in November 1978, Chinese Communist Party leader Dang Xiao-ping had declared: "Those ungrateful people must be punished. We gave them $200 billion of aid, Chinese sweat and blood, and look what happened." He swore to "teach Vietnam a lesson."[15] On February 17, 1979, a Chinese force of 225,000 men, composed of infantry, artillery, and armored units, crossed the northern frontier of Vietnam and attacked Vietnamese positions at Lang-Son, occupied it, and advanced 15 to 20 miles deep into the Vietnamese territory. But the PAVN resistance was fierce. Both sides suffered serious casualties. The war lasted less than a month. In the first week of March, the war slowed. It was "unclear whether the Chinese slowed their offensive because of effective Vietnamese resistance or because of Chinese deliberately stopped their advances [as they claimed]."[16] The Chinese proclaimed that they had accomplished their mission and began to withdraw. The withdrawal was completed on March 15, 1979. After this, relations between these two communist countries were rocky for years. Later, Communist Vietnam had to pay a very high price to normalize relations with China.

The most serious offenses by the Vietnamese Communist Party's top leaders to their fatherland were the horrible crimes of selling lands and seas to Red China for secret reasons. Notable foreign media recently disclosed their acts of treason toward their country. According to these sources, on December 30, 1999, the VWP's leaders signed a secret agreement with the Chinese Communist Party (CCP) to cede China a vast portion of borderlands of about 789 square kilometers (305 square miles) along Cao Bang and Lang son Provinces. Historical heritages such as the Nam Quan frontier pass, the Ban-Doc Falls, and the Ho Dynasty's Citadel are now lost to China. Another top secret agreement was signed in December 2000 at Beijing in which Vietnam lost about 11,000 square kilometers (4,250 square miles) territorial waters to China in the Gulf of Tonkin and the South Sea. French journalist Sylviane Pasquier, in an article published by the prestigious weekly *L'Express* in France, describes these so-called top secret agreements to sell Vietnamese lands and seas by the VWP's leaders as "Marchandage Odieuse, Haute Trahison"— horrible haggling, high treason.[17]

THE AMERICANS MISSING IN ACTION (MIAS) AND THE DIPLOMATIC RELATIONS BETWEEN THE UNITED STATES AND VIETNAM

After the end of the Vietnam War, the most sensitive and emotional issue for the United States was the American personnel deemed missing in action (MIAs). More than 2590 Americans were MIAs in Indochina, of which 1,913 were believed to be in Vietnam, 567 in Laos, and 107 in Cambodia. During the late 1970s and the entire decade of the 1980s, although perceiving the seriousness of United States' concerns about this issue, Vietnamese communist leaders pretended to ignore the American proposition to talk on that subject until the early years of the 1990s.

In 1991, the Vietnamese communist leaders changed their opinion. Reconciliation with the United States might help save their national economy that was on the road to ruin. Indeed, the destruction caused by the war, the socialist economy, the American trade embargo, and particularly the cessation of Soviet economic aid in 1990 had blunted all efforts of the people to rebuild the country so that the communists could maintain their regime.

Looking back to the period that followed the Vietnamese communist force's withdrawal from Cambodia in November 1989, we can see several indicators of the grave deterioration of the Vietnamese economy, such as partial starvation in the northern and central provinces, poor crops production, a population increase, a high level of unemployment and underemployment, a high rate of inflation and deficits, a chaotic distribution system and short life expectancy, and the deterioration of national resources and potential. Among the basic issues facing Vietnam in that period, poverty was the most devastating.

In the previous years, the Vietnamese economy stood dependent upon the economic aid of the USSR and its allies in Eastern Europe. After the war with China, separately, Soviet economic aid to Vietnam was estimated about $1.5 billion a year. Although aid was provided by the USSR and Eastern European countries, Vietnam had to relinquish some of its sovereignty in exchange. The Vietnamese communist leaders agreed to the USSR setting up a naval base at Cam-Ranh Bay and were forced to "export labor" to these nations to repay debts which added up to $8.4 billion. In 1990, the Vietnamese economy verged on a total collapse when Soviet President Mikhail Gorbachev based upon his 1988 declaration of "Unilateral Convention Force Reduction," ordered the Soviet navy force to withdraw from Cam-Ranh and cut off 80 percent of the economic aid to Vietnam. Then, after the communist regime in Russia collapsed, Vietnam was nearly isolated and became one of the three poorest countries in the world.

The only hope of the Vietnamese communist leaders for the survival of their national economy and their regime was the crucial necessity of reconciling with the United States, so that it would lift its trade embargo, and normalizing diplomatic relations between the two countries. However, skillful negotiating meant approaching these issues indirectly. Instead, they turned to the issue of MIAs of both American and Vietnamese servicemen. They discussed with the American delegations this as the first and foremost issue among their "humanitarian concerns."

In 1991, at the Seventh Congress of the Vietnamese Communist Party, the problem of North Vietnamese troops missing in action was deliberated along with other important problems. There were about 300,000 NVA troops missing in action among more than 840,000 killed in action (KIAs). MIA issue became a crucial part of Vietnam's new policy to reconcile with the United States.

In mid–1992, basic agreements of mutual efforts to resolve the MIA issue for both sides were acknowledged at meetings of several middle-level delegates. At higher levels, in June of 1993, three very important persons of the SRVN government, prime minister Vo van Kiet, deputy prime minister Phan van Khai, and foreign minister Nguyen Manh Cam, at different places and on different occasions, raised the issue of the importance of U.S. government assistance to solve the problem of the missing Vietnamese service personnel in return for their efforts to find American MIAs. Specially, Nguyen Manh Cam appealed to Washington to "concretely pursue cooperation" with Vietnam to find its enormous number of MIAs. On the Vietnamese side, the MIA issue was only a "reason" or a first step to approach the United States for more political and economic purposes.

Assuredly, all of their proposals were joyfully received and appreciated by the United States.

During late 1993 and early 1994, Vietnamese communist leaders proved that the MIA issue was merely a vehicle for the two countries to "reconcile" when they began to ask for the release of the American trade embargo against them which had been in place since the end of the war. The process of lifting the embargo encountered a little difficulty in the United States, but it was finally done in March 1994. The second step of their strategy of "reconciliation" was satisfactorily accomplished.

After that, Hanoi leaders requested a normalization of diplomatic relations with the United States. This was also satisfied in August 1995. U.S. congressional representative Douglas "Pete" Peterson, a former air force pilot who had been imprisoned as a prisoner of war in

Hanoi for six and half years, was assigned by president Bill Clinton in September 1995 as U.S. Ambassador to Vietnam. His confirmation was delayed for almost two years; finally he arrived in Hanoi in late 1997 to do something "positive" as he said, "I have seen the negative, I look forward to the positive."[18] Following him were representatives of 400 business corporations, educationalists from 22 universities, and humanitarian people of 300 non-governmental organizations. All of these Americans came to every part of Vietnam to positively help the Vietnamese communist regime, its economy, and its people.

Billions of U.S. dollars poured in Vietnam from the U.S. government, private organizations and corporations, the World Bank and the International Monetary Fund (IMF). The "socialist economy" had not yet disappeared but the "market economy" had largely emerged from all corners of Vietnam. The Vietnamese economy was saved. The third step of the Vietnamese Communist Party's policy of "reconciliation" with the United States was perfectly accomplished. But, remember, any profit gained was at a price. The Vietnamese communist leaders had to ask themselves: What price would Vietnam have to pay to the United States? Had Vietnam become a U.S. satellite in Southeast Asia — like an advanced fortress deterring Chinese southward aggression? What would need to be done in this important region to pay its debts to its new benefactor? Money from the rich is a dangerous weapon.

More recently, sensitively perceiving they were "holding a double-sided knife," Hanoi leaders hesitated to accept proposals of U.S. "military relations" between Vietnam and the United States. The *Honolulu Advertiser*, on March 14, 2000, commented: "Leaders of the Vietnamese communist regime are wary that stronger ties with other foreign nations and the global economy could destabilize the country and loosen their grip on power. In addition, they are highly sensitive that any hint of U.S.— Vietnamese military alliance might arouse Chinese fears on encirclement."[19] Hanoi leaders would later reconsider the question of a "military alliance" with the United States. However, Red China would not let them do that.

Now, Vietnam surely is caught between the two strongest powers in the world, the United States and Communist China. Which path might Vietnam follow: continue on the communist trail or change in direction toward the free-world avenue?

17

The Laws of God

In our time, "war" means fighting a foe or an adverse alliance, not only by proper military means but also by political and economic means. In 1990, no military wars were fought between the Western Alliance (NATO) and the Eastern Communist Bloc (Warsaw Pact), but the collapse of the USSR foretold the disintegration of communist regimes in other Eastern European countries. These results came out of a long term "economic war" between the two opposite alliances. In addition, in a war fought merely by military forces, a battle and a front are less important than a theater of operation.

In my opinion, the United States, during its thirty years (1945–1975) of involvement in the war in Indochina, adopted the above notion, which meant that American leaders fought the war without using full American military powers but only the selected use of political and economic means. Moreover, Vietnam was a front in a greater theater of operation. American theaters of operation during that long period were the Asia-Pacific region and Southeast Asia. American objectives were to gain peace and security in these vast regions, even if the United States had to accept the loss of some fronts, such as South Vietnam, Laos and Cambodia.

For these reasons, contrary to common opinion, I would repeat that the United States under the seven consecutive presidents from Roosevelt to Ford, during these long decades of war in Indochina, did win the war in the Asia-Pacific region and Southeast Asia, since it was able to confine the wicked lion, Red China, to its den.

In addition, after the war, the United States had the opportunity to transform its old foe, the Socialist Republic of Vietnam, into one of its fortresses in Southeast Asia. I believe the people in these regional countries and the Americans should have enjoyed the outcome of the Vietnam War instead of sorrowing. Only the South Vietnamese people and their armed forces lost the war. They were all victims of an American policy toward the Asia-Pacific region and Southeast Asia.

We, the South Vietnamese people, have suffered and continue to suffer the effects of the Vietnam War. Sensitive to this problem, the United States and the other nations of the free world, for humanitarian reasons, saved more than two million South Vietnamese, including hundreds of thousands of former RVNAF personnel who were once prisoners of war in communist concentration camps, and their families. They settled the people in free and beautiful lands, and gave them opportunities to set up new lives and develop useful work and intellectual knowledge. We deeply thank the governments and the people of these nations.

However, there are more than 300,000 disabled veterans and more than 2,000,000 former soldiers of the RVNAF now enduring a miserable existence under the discriminatory and inhumane policies of the Vietnamese communist leaders. Moreover, the people of Vietnam live in extreme poverty. After three decades of communist rule, despite the Vietnamese Communist Party transforming from a rigid and party-controlled socialist economy into a more liberal market economy, Vietnam is still one of the ten poorest countries in the world.

As a Vietnamese, I deeply desire to see my country find independence, unification, freedom, and prosperity. But I will never see such a thing. I blame the Vietnamese communist leaders, led by the ruthless and hypocritical Ho Chi Minh, who carried communism into Vietnam and transformed the Vietnamese people into slaves. Younger Vietnamese intellectuals in exile assert that the partial renovation of the economic system in Vietnam only produces a new class of rulers, the "red capitalists," which creates more intensive forms of exploitation, corruption, alienation, enormous gaps between rich and poor, a deterioration of relations between the people and government, and the elimination of the notion of a nation-state. The bonds and trust necessary for normal societal functioning have evaporated. Consequently, the sense of community that once characterized Vietnamese society has faded away, replaced by selfish and short-sighted economic decisions. These red-capitalist leaders are neither able to solve the poverty of the masses in Vietnam nor able to assure the future will be one of national development and modernization, but may submerge Vietnam more deeply into the Pacific.

There must be an end to the communist monopoly of power and democracy must be restored as a right of everyone in Vietnam. Once the dictatorship is abolished, the new political spirit will allow a true national reconstruction, development, modernization and prosperity. Every Vietnamese has the right and is responsible for the reconstruction of the country. Every one of us learns the history of our nation not only to know its ups and downs but also to make it glorious and eternal.

However, we must also remember that eternity is something no different than the antagonism between the forces of creation and the forces of destruction. These two forces are frequently seen as opposing each other, but are also intrinsically hidden within any essential nature, any organic structure, or any bodily constitution, with the potential to raise it or to ruin it. Both forces are created by God and the processes of creation and destruction are also His laws. Were only one of these forces to emerge, then at some point, all things on the earth would be annihilated and this annihilation would be complete and definitive. Probably, the radical difference between these forces may be seen in the fact that, at all times, the force of creation performs its functions with a godlike spirit, while the force of destruction realizes its own functions with dazzling characters of cruelty and death.

Thus, so long as these forces exist on earth, anywhere and within anything at the same time, to some degree or extent, confrontations, struggles, conflicts and hostilities cannot be avoided. Occasionally, the force of destruction may triumph over the other for a period of time, and its blinded advance may eliminate all opposing components, good or bad, without difference. However, it shall ultimately be destroyed by the force of good or broken down by its own constituent factors, for the creation of a new cycle of antagonism that is necessary for nature to last and to regenerate.

Through seizing national power, eliminating the human rights of the people, and cruelly suppressing religions, the Vietnamese communists, the force of evil, cannot escape the laws of God, and their final perdition may not be avoided in the near future. While in the last half-century, several generations of Vietnamese could do nothing better for the country, I hope that the younger generations will learn from our experiences and rebuild Vietnam into an advanced nation with unity, solidarity, liberty, and democracy.

"A Sorrowful Existence
in a War Time"

I began to know my existence when I was ten.
By ten, I began to learn the history of my country.
My teacher usually harangued: "Love the white heron and the black buffalo in the rice field.
Love your mother, father, neighbors, old people, and newly born babies in the cradles.
Our ancestors bequeathed our land to us under the full sunlight.
Now, the sun has set. But why in the East?!"
Then, I began to imagine and to feel confused
When I look at the sun rising in the east and shining on the rice field.
There, scarecrows had been dressed and posted to ward birds away from crops
            for thousands of years.
There, buffaloes were still carrying plows and turning "right" and "left" on their furrows.
Poor peasants were still planting young rice plants with their hands.
There, the ground had traces of a millennium of Chinese occupation and eighty years of
            French domination.
Thus, with ten years of my childhood, I was living in the shadow of an aged foreign yoke.

I recognized better my existence when I was twelve,
By twelve, I began to miss the drum sounds calling for school daily
And began to suffer agony
When my family fled to the coastal site.
I felt so sad to leave my empty house behind.
Then, people arose for the independence fight
Leaving the rice field for wild weeds to overgrow.
There, I could not hear again charming lyrics and riddles on sunny days.
The scarecrows' rude garments were in rags and their straw bodies began to decay.
There, innocent people became scarecrows
Were disturbed at early dawn to keep watching for gunfire
And staggered at nightfall for deserted hallows or dense forests to be sheltered.
Since the colonists had come back to our ground
To kill and hound.
And the communists also made the same sounds.
Or, we were frightened by smelly corpses drifting along the waters
For hawks to lacerate and crows to peck.
Thus, since twelve years of age, I have seen my country covered
            with spreading flames in the air and blood on the ground.

At fourteen, I felt so sorrowful for my existence
When history changed its course
And society changed its face.
On every path many families began to return to their homes, in rags.
We also returned to our home village.
Our house with its red tiled roof had been perceived from afar
Now, I could not see it again.
The whole area was in ruins with an eerie emptiness.
Our once lovely abode disappeared without a trace.
Only some fruit trees remained with their smoking trunks and broken branches.
The garden was covered by thorny plants
And thick weeds overran its entrance.
This fertile soil had once flourished with beautiful flowers and sweet fruits.

All existed in my life as a happy paradise.
Now, it looked smaller and withered in my eyes.
After two years of wandering around
I had seen our immense country being set on fire.
Then, my life was growing with more sufferings and knowledge.
At fourteen, I felt older than I really was.

I committed to the war when I was twenty.
The war had long hung around to kill youths of my generation.
Abandoning lamp and books
I forgot my school life to wear a uniform.
With amazed emotions and eyes widely opened
I engaged into the battle and wondered:
"Do I need to handle a gun and shoot you, or let you target your guns to shoot at me?
Oh, men of the same skin shade and same mother tongues!"
Perhaps, the war would not hear the voice of anyone's heart.
Then, I was living a full life with my boots marching tirelessly around the country
From Thua Thien and Quang Tri
To Darlac and Kontumn,
From small cities and deserted towns
To gloomy hamlets and destitute villages.
Everywhere, there was war and sadness.
Everywhere, innocent people suffered malice
And were frightened by the gun sounds night after night.
Then came Dien Bien's violent fights and the resolute Geneva Treaty.
It divided my country,
The Ben Hai River was cut in the middle.
A million people migrated to the South,
And twenty-five million others beheld this calamity with anguished souls.
That was my existence when I was twenty.
At twenty, my miserable country was cut in two.

At thirty-two, I began to compose poetry to recount the existence of my self
And life of others in my generation
Who endured the war and had an age-long struggle for independence and freedom
                for the country.
My poems would cry for the people in the North
Who had been grasped by their souls and strangled in the red hell under the communist seizure
For a dozen years.
My poems would cry for the people in the South
Who had once touched on democracy and once made a revolution;
Still, their hearts were not content.
Opposing parties continued to march down streets with controversial demands.
My poetry, like a pitiful voice, was unheard at that age of disturbance
As it resonated from a desert at far distance.
How the Vietnamese younger generations could hear it and comprehend
The tragedy of our time.
In which, millions of people had once risen up and fallen down in order to safeguard
                peace and freedom for their motherland.
A land that was suffering misfortunes with tears and blood flowing full force.
That was my existence at thirty-two years of age
Since then, I have had a real image of my life.
                        Van Nguyen Duong (1966)

Appendix

The Eleven-Point Program Accords, January 1962

A SUMMARY

Facilities will be created for the training of village officials "so as to improve the administration where it has closest contacts with people."

Rural health and inoculation programs will be developed.

Primary schools will be created in every village.

Rural radio communications will be improved to enable the villagers both to listen to government broadcasts and to call for help when required.

New roads, particularly rural feeder roads, will be constructed.

The agricultural credit system will be extended.

A large-scale program on insect and cattle-disease eradication will be implemented.

A special effort will be made to have the mountaineer minorities share in "the progress of their (lowland) compatriots."

Increased help will be given the flooded Mekong regions.

An important public-works program will be launched to reduce unemployment.

The industrial-development effort of the past two years will be pursued.

Source: Agence France-Presse, January 4, 1962.

Chapter Notes

Chapter 1

The material in this chapter was drawn from the author's own experiences.

Chapter 2

1. John Dellinger, "The War Makers," *Vietnam Magazine*, April 1996, p. 35.
2. Georges Catroux, *Deux Actes du Drame Indochine* (Paris: Librairie Blon, 1959), p. 55.
3. Togo Shigenori, *The Cause of Japan* (New York: Simon and Schuster, 1956), p. 85.
4. Bernard B. Fall, *The Two Vietnams* (New York: Frederic A. Praeger, 1964), p. 46.
5. Samuel I. Roseman, *The Public Papers and Addresses of FDR* (New York: Harper and Brothers, 1950), p. 562.
6. Joseph B. Stilwell, *The Stilwell Papers* (New York: Sloane Associates, 1948), p. 115.
7. U.S. State Department, *Foreign Relations of the United States, Diplomatic Papers: The Conferences at Cairo and Teheran, 1943* (Washington, D.C.: U.S. Government Printing Office, 1943), pp. 485–509.
8. Roseman, p. 562.
9. Charles de Gaulle, *Memories de Guerre* (Paris: Librairie Plon, 1954), p. 167.
10. Claire L. Chennault, *Way of a Fighter* (New York: Putnam's Sons, 1949), p. 342.
11. De Gaulle, p. 165.
12. Cao The Dung, *Viet Nam Huyet Le Su* (n.p.: Dong Huong Publishers, 1996), p. 722.
13. Michael MacLlear, *The Ten Thousand Day War: Vietnam 1946–1975* (New York: Saint Martin's Press, 1981), p. 9.
14. *Ibid.*, p. 7.

Chapter 3

1. Harry G. Summers, Jr., *Historical Atlas of the Vietnam War* (Boston and New York: Houghton Mifflin Company), p. 45.
2. *Ibid.*, p. 46.
3. Nguyen Ky Phong, "Vũng Lầy của Bạch Ốc" *Người Mỹ và Chiến Tranh Việt Nam 1945–1975*. (Falls Church, Va.: Tủ Sách Quê Hương, 2006), pp. 57–58.
4. Summers, p. 46.
5. Nguyen, pp. 59–60.
6. *Ibid.*, pp. 61–62.

7. *The Pentagon Papers: Senator Gravel Edition* (Boston: Beacon Press, 1971), Volume 1, pp. 18–19.
8. Summers, p. 46.
9. Richard Holbrooke, "The Paradox of George Kennan," *Washington Post*, March 21, 2005, p. A19.
10. Ronnie I. Ford, "The Window of Opportunity," *Vietnam Magazine*, February 1995, p. 6.
11. Michael Maclear, *The Ten Thousand Day War: Vietnam 1946–1975* (New York: Saint Martin's Press, 1981), p. 23.
12. Qiang Zhai, *China and the Vietnam Wars, 1950–1975* (Durham, N.C.: University of North Carolina Press, 2000), pp. 11–28.
13. *Ibid.*
14. Zhai, pp. 28–32.
15. *The Pentagon Papers*, pp. 53–75.
16. *Ibid.*
17. *Ibid.*
18. Summers, p. 52.
19. Maclear, p. 27.
20. *Ibid.*, p. 28.
21. Summers, p. 41.

Chapter 4

1. *The Pentagon Papers: Senator Gravel Edition* (Boston: Beacon Press, 1971), Volume 1, pp. 1–52.
2. *Ibid.*, pp. 10–20.
3. Qiang Zhai, *China and the Vietnam Wars 1950–1975* (Durham, N.C.: University of North Carolina Press, 2000), p. 44. Nguyen Ky Phong, "Vũng Lầy của Bạch Ốc" *Người Mỹ và Chiến Tranh Việt Nam 1945–1975* (n.p.: Tủ Sách Quê Hương, 2006), p. 79.
4. Australian-American Alliance, "Vietnam Period 1847–1961." http://www.hotkey.net/au/marshalle/chon01chron01-htm.
5. Zhai, p. 44.
6. Michael Maclear, *The Ten Thousand Day War: Vietnam 1946–1975* (New York: Saint Martin's Press, 1981), p. 37.
7. *Ibid.*
8. Bernard B. Fall, *The Two Vietnams* (New York: Frederic A. Praeger, 1964), p. 227.
9. Zhai, pp. 63, 10–64.
10. Russell A. Fifield, *The Diplomacy of Southeast Asia: 1954–1958* (New York: Harper and Brothers, 1958), pp. 301–304; Fall, p. 233.
11. Phillip B. Davidson, *Secret of the Vietnam War* (Novato, Calif.: Presidio Press, 1990), p. 128.

12. *Ibid.*

13. *Ibid.*

14. Hoang Van Chi, *From Colonialism to Communism* (New Delhi: Allied Publications, 1964), p. 13.

15. John O'Daniel, "A Finger in the Dike Is Not Enough," *TVN Magazine,* April 29, 1962.

16. Stephen B. Young, "LBJ's Strategy for Disengagement," *Vietnam Magazine,* February 1998, p. 21.

17. Donald Lancaster, *The Emancipation of the French in Indochina* (New York: Oxford University Press, 1961), pp. 391–392.

18. Samuel L. Mayers, "Situation in Vietnam," *U.S. Senate Committee on Foreign Relations Records,* July 30–31, 1959, p. 171.

19. Harry G. Summers, Jr., quoted in Robert L. Hewitt, "Overemphasis on Counter-insurgency Led to the Misapplication of Limited War," *Vietnam Magazine,* June 1993, p. 58. 20. Nguyen Kien Giang, *Les Grandes Dates du Parti de la Classe Ouvriere du Vietnam* (Hanoi: Foreign Languages Publishing House, 1960), p. 53.

21. P.J. Honey, *Communisn in North Vietnam: Its Role in the Sino-Soviet Dispute* (Cambridge, Mass.: MIT Press, 1963), p. 168.

22. Fall, p. 146.

23. Chi, p. 55.

24. *Ibid.,* p. 193.

25. Thuy Khue, "Phong Trào Nhân văn và Giai Phẩm" [The Nhan van and Giai Pham Movement], *Hợp Lưu* (Vietnamese magazine from California), No. 81 (February-March 2005): 5–28.

26. The Democratic Republic of Vietnam (DRVN), The DRVN Constitution (1960), Preamble.

27. *Ibid.*

28. *Ibid.*

29. Sedgwick Tourison, Jr., quoted in Michael Lanning and Dan Cragg, *Inside the VC and the NVA* (New York: Faucett Columbine, 1993), pp. 231–235.

30. *Ibid.*

31. *Ibid.*

32. *Ibid.*

Chapter 5

1. John Dellinger, "The War Makers," *Vietnam Magazine,* April 1996, p. 36.

2. Hoang Van Chi, *From Colonialism to Communism* (New Delhi: Allied Publications, 1964), p. 33.

3. Vo Nguyen Giap, *People's War, People's Army* (Hanoi: Foreign Languages Publishing House, 1961), p. 55.

4. Phillip B. Davidson, *Secret of the Vietnam War* (Novato, Calif.: Presidio Press, 1990), pp. 17–20.

5. Giap, p. 56.

6. Michael Lanning and Dan Cragg, *Inside the VC and the NVA* (New York: Faucett Columbine, 1993), p. 187.

7. Stephen B. Young, "LBJ's Strategy for Disengagement," *Vietnam Magazine,* February 1998, p. 21.

8. Anonymous, "Le Sud-Est Asiatique en Danger," *Revue de Défense Nationale* (Paris), May 1961, p. 785.

9. Bernard B. Fall, *The Two Vietnams* (New York: Frederic A. Praeger, 1964), p. 279.

10. Quoted in Robert L. Hewitt, "Overemphasis on Counter-insurgency Led to the Misapplication of Limited War," *Vietnam Magazine,* June 1993, p. 58.

11. *Ibid.*

12. *Ibid.*

13. *Ibid.*

14. Norman B. Hannah, "History of Vietnam War: Continuity All the Way from JFK to LBJ," *Vietnam Magazine,* February 1995, p. 54.

15. Michael Maclear, *The Ten Thousand Day War: Vietnam 1946–1975* (New York: Saint Martin's Press, 1981), p. 61.

16. Maclear, p. 59.

17. Peter Brush, "The War's Constructive Component," *Vietnam Magazine,* February 1997, p. 70.

18. Jane Hamilton Meritt, "The Killing Field of Laos," *Vietnam Magazine,* December 1993, p. 49.

19. Meritt, "General Giap's Laotian Nemesis," *Vietnam Magazine,* February 1995, p. 27.

20. Norman B. Hannah, "The Harriman Line," *Vietnam Magazine,* August 1992, pp. 58–62.

21. *Ibid.*

22. *Ibid.*

23. Lanning and Cragg, pp. 73–74.

24. *Ibid.,* p.122.

25. Maclear, p. 172.

26. *Ibid.,* p. 182.

27. James Donovan, "Assessing the War's Costs," *Vietnam Magazine,* April 1996, p. 42.

28. Michael R. Conroy, "Trail along the Trail," *Vietnam Magazine,* October 1993, p. 32.

29. Hewitt, p. 60.

30. *Ibid.,* p. 62.

31. Harry G. Summers, Jr., quoted in ibid.

32. Emmanuel Mounter, *Le Personaliste* (Paris: Presses Universitaires de France, 1961), pp. 127–128.

33. *Ibid.*

34. Bernard B. Fall, *The Two Vietnams* (New York: Frederic A. Praeger, 1964), p. 285.

35. Maclear, p. 59.

36. Fall, p. 282.

37. David Nuttle, "The Boun Enao Project," *Vietnam Magazine,* October 1992, p. 24.

38. *Ibid.,* p. 27.

39. Wesley R. Fishel, *Problems of Freedom: South Vietnam since Independence* (New York: The Free Press of Glencoe, 1961), pp. 27–28.

40. Maclear, p. 62.

41. Charles F. Reske, "Operation Footboy," *Vietnam Magazine,* October 1995, p. 30.

42. William Wilson, "The Infamous Pentagon Papers Give Insights into the Johnson Administration's Thinking on the Vietnam War," *Vietnam Magazine,* February 1997, p. 62.

43. *Ibid.,* p. 63.

44. *Ibid.*

45. Reske, p. 33.

46. A.K. Davidson, "The Fatally Flawed OPLAN-34A Commando Raids on North Vietnam were a Disaster with Lasting Consequences," *Vietnam Magazine,* February 1997, p. 52.

47. J.T. Chapin, "An American in the War before 1964," *Vietnam Magazine,* October 1995, p. 52.

48. Rob Krott, "MACV-SOG Was One So Secret That the U.S. Government Denied Its Existence," *Vietnam Magazine,* October 1997, pp. 54–56.

49. Harry S. Summers, Jr., "Editorial Comments," *Vietnam Magazine,* February 1997, p. 6.

50. Maclear, p. 61.

51. Beverly, Deepe, "Saigon Telling Officers to Heed U.S. Advisers," *Washington Post,* January 20, 1963.

52. Quoted in Fall, p. 288

Chapter 6

1. Tran Trung Dung, "The American Hand and the Death of President Ngo Dinh Diem," *Phu Nu Dien Dan* (Vietnamese magazine from California), February 1994, p. 41.

2. *Ibid.*

3. Michael R. Fowler, "War within a War," *Vietnam Magazine,* February 1994, p. 41.

4. Michael Maclear, *The Ten Thousand Day War: Vietnam 1946–1975* (New York: Saint Martin's Press, 1981), p. 63.

5. William Wilson, "U.S. Complicity in the Overthrow of South Vietnam's President Made Impossible to Stay Uninvolved in the War," *Vietnam Magazine,* April 1997, p. 56.

6. *Ibid.,* p. 60.

7. *Ibid.*

8. Maclear, p. 75.

9. Richard Reeves, *President Kennedy* (New York: Simon and Schuster, 1993), p. 642.

10. *Ibid.,* p. 641.

11. *Ibid.*

12. *Ibid.,* p. 484.

13. *Ibid.,* p. 443.

14. Maclear, p. 78.

15. Reeves, p. 745.

16. *Ibid.*

17. *Ibid.*

18. *Ibid.,* p. 646.

19. *Ibid.*

20. *Ibid.,* p. 648.

21. *Ibid.*

22. *Ibid.,* p. 649.

23. Maclear, p. 81.

24. Reeves, p. 649.

25. Chu Ba Anh, "The American Hand and the Death of President Ngo Dinh Diem," *Phu-nu Dien-dan* (Vietnamese magazine), November 11, 1993, p. 39.

26. Reeves, p. 650.

27. *Ibid.,* p. 652.

28. Maclear, p. 82.

Chapter 7

1. Robert L. Hewitt, "Overemphasis on Counterinsurgency Led to the Misapplication of Limited War," *Vietnam Magazine,* June 1993, p. 61.

2. *Ibid.*

3. John Dellinger, "The War Makers," *Vietnam Magazine,* April 1996, p. 37.

4. Norman B. Hannah, "History of Vietnam War: Continuity All the Way from JFK to LBJ," *Vietnam Magazine,* February 1995, p. 60.

5. H.R. McMaster, "The Vietnam War Was Not Lost in the Field or by the Media. It Was Lost in Washington D.C., Even Before It Began," *Vietnam Magazine,* August 1997, p. 50.

6. Richard Reeves, *President Kennedy* (New York: Simon and Schuster, 1993), p. 379.

7. McMaster, p. 50.

8. *Ibid.,* p. 52.

9. Dellinger, p. 38.

10. McMaster, p. 52.

11. Hannah, pp. 54–58.

12. *Ibid.*

13. Dellinger, p. 37.

14. Bernard B. Fall, *The Two Vietnams* (New York: Frederic A. Praeger, 1964), p. 199.

15. Michael Maclear, *The Ten Thousand Day War: Vietnam 1946–1975* (New York: Saint Martin's Press, 1981), p. 112.

16. *Ibid.,* p. 120.

17. Lam Quang Thi, *The Twenty-Five Year Century* (Denton, Tex.: University of North Texas Press, 2002), p. 137.

Chapter 8

1. Phillip B. Davidson, *Secret of the Vietnam War* (Novato, Calif.: Presidio Press, 1990), p. 147.

2. Allan B. Calhamer, "It Took Nine Years to Decide to Block Hai-Phong," *Vietnam Magazine,* April 1998, p. 56.

3. Jacksel M. Broughton, "Wasted Air Power," *Vietnam Magazine,* August 1994, p. 19.

4. *Ibid.,* p. 23.

5. William Wilson, "The Rolling Thunder Strategic Air Campaign," *Vietnam Magazine,* April 1996, p. 16.

6. Michael R. Conroy, "Trail along the Trail," *Vietnam Magazine,* October 1993, p. 27.

7. Peter W. Brush, "The Story behind the McNamara Line," *Vietnam Magazine,* February 1996, p. 21.

8. *Ibid.,* pp. 21–22.

9. Michael Maclear, *The Ten Thousand Day War: Vietnam 1946–1975* (New York: Saint Martin's Press, 1981), p. 136.

Chapter 9

1. Ronnie I. Ford, "The Window of Opportunity," *Vietnam Magazine,* February 1995, pp. 40–41.

2. *Ibid.*

3. *Ibid.,* p. 44.

4. *Ibid.*

5. Robert Pisor, "Faking MACV Out of Position," *Vietnam Magazine,* February 1993, pp. 43–44.

6. William C. Westmoreland, "What Did North Vietnam Hope to Gain with Their 1968 Tet Offensive? Were They After the Cities, or More?" *Vietnam Magazine,* pp. 43–44.

7. Ford, p. 42.

8. *Ibid.,* p. 43.

9. Michael Maclear, *The Ten Thousand Day War:*

Vietnam 1946–1975 (New York: Saint Martin's Press, 1981), p. 199.

10. Pisor, p. 43.

11. Maclear, p. 203.

12. Zeb B. Bradford, "Firsthand Account with Creighton Abrams during Tet," *Vietnam Magazine*, February 1998, p. 47.

13. Westmoreland, p. 68.

14. Maclear, p. 197.

15. Harry G. Summers, Jr., "This Was a World War II Battlefield," *Vietnam Magazine*, February 1998, p. 47.

16. Doris Kearns, *Lyndon Johnson and the American Dream* (New York: Harper and Row Publishers, 1976), p. 349.

17. Frederic C. Weyand, "Troops to Equal Army," *Vietnam Magazine*, August 1998, p. 39.

Chapter 10

1. Michael Maclear, *The Ten Thousand Day War: Vietnam 1946–1975* (New York: St. Martin's Press, 1981) p. 282.

2. Frederic C. Weyand, "Troops to Equal Army," *Vietnam Magazine*, August 1998, p. 39.

3. Tad Szulc, *The Illusion of Peace* (New York: Viking Press, 1978), p. 65.

4. *Ibid.*, pp. 24–25.

5. *Ibid.*

6. Henry B. Crawford, "Operation Menu's Secret Bombing of Campuchia," *Vietnam Magazine,* December 1996, p. 27.

7. Maclear, p. 289.

8. *Ibid.*, p. 250.

9. Lewis Sorley, "South Vietnam: Worthy Ally?" (General Creighton W. Abrams Reassessing the ARVN), thehistorynet (3–15–03). Online at http://www.freerepublic.com/focus/news/866256/posts.

10. Harry G. Summers, Jr., "Snatching Victory from Defeat," *Vietnam Magazine*, April 1999, p. 38.

Chapter 11

1. Harry G. Summers, Jr., "Snatching Victory from Defeat," *Vietnam Magazine*, April 1999, p. 38.

2. Truong Duong, *Doi Chien Binh* (n.p.: Tu Quynh Publishers, April 1998), p. 35.

Chapter 12

1. Michael Maclear, *The Ten Thousand Day War: Vietnam 1946–1975* (New York: St. Martin's Press, 1981) p. 307.

2. Harry G. Summers, Jr., "The Bitter End," *Vietnam Magazine*, April 1995, p. 42.

3. Harry G. Summers, Jr., "Editorial Comments," *Vietnam Magazine*, November 1998, p. 6.

4. Maclear, p. 310.

5. James Donovan, "Assessing The War's Costs," *Vietnam Magazine*, April 1996, p. 44.

6. Eugene H. Grayson, "Fall of the Central Highlands," *Vietnam Magazine*, April 1994, p. 23.

7. Maclear, p. 310.

8. *Ibid.*, p. 311.

9. Tad Szulc, *The Illusion of Peace* (New York: Viking Press, 1978), p. 669.

10. Maclear, p. 311.

Chapter 13

1. Homer D. Smith, "The Final Forty-Five Days in Vietnam," *Vietnam Magazine*, April 1995, pp. 47–48.

2. Lam Quang Thi, *The Twenty-Five Year Century* (Denton, Tex.: University of North Texas Press, 2002), p. 318.

3. Eugene H. Grayson, "Fall of the Central Highlands," *Vietnam Magazine*, April 1994, p. 24.

4. Harry G. Summers, Jr., "The Bitter End," *Vietnam Magazine*, April 1995, pp. 42–43.

5. Harry G. Summers, Jr., *Historical Atlas of the Vietnam War* (Boston and New York: Houghton Mifflin Company, 1995), p. 192.

6. *Ibid.*

7. Summers, Jr., "The Bitter End," p. 43.

Chapter 14

1. Nguyen Van Thieu, "Presidential Last Address [Announcing Decision] to Resign," Saigon T.V., April 20, 1975.

2. Harry G. Summers, Jr., *Historical Atlas of the Vietnam War* (Boston and New York: Houghton Mifflin Company, 1995), p. 196.

3. Michael Maclear, *The Ten Thousand Day War: Vietnam 1946–1975* (New York: St. Martin's Press, 1981) p. 321.

4. *Ibid.*, p. 324.

Chapter 15

1. Harry G. Summers, Jr., *Historical Atlas of the Vietnam War* (Boston and New York: Houghton Mifflin Company, 1995), p. 190.

2. Phillip Habid, "Peace Envoy's Postscript," *Vietnam Magazine*, April 1993, p. 190.

3. Larry Engelmann, *Tears before the Rain* (New York: Da Capo Press, 1997), p. 53.

4. Phan Tan My, "Trận Đánh Trên Đồi Móng Ngựa" (The Fight on Horseshoe Hill). Special piece for "Thiên Anh Hùng Ca QLVNCH," *Mac Phong Dinh*, 2004.

5. Summers, p. 200.

6. *Ibid.*

7. Michael Maclear, *The Ten Thousand Day War: Vietnam 1946–1975* (New York: St. Martin's Press, 1981) p. 331.

8. Engelmann, p. 150.

9. Julie Kane, "Secret Evacuation of the VNN Fleet," *Vietnam Magazine*, April 1995, p. 33.

Chapter 16

1. Darrel Laurant, "Billed as a Symposium, the Hampden Sydney College Gathering Was More Like a Trial," *Vietnam Magazine*, April 1994, p. 62.

2. Marc Leepson, "At a Conference on McNamara's

Book 'In Retrospect,' Military Heavy Weights Lined Up to 'Knife The Mac,'" *Vietnam Magazine*, December 1996, p. 62.

3. *Ibid.*

4. James Donovan, "Assessing The War's Costs," *Vietnam Magazine*, April 1996, p. 42.

5. *Ibid.*, p. 45.

6. *Ibid.*, p. 48.

7. David H. Hackworth, "Perspectives," *Vietnam Magazine*, April 1995, p. 32.

8. Phillip B. Davidson, *Secret of the Vietnam War* (Novato, Calif.: Presidio Press, 1990), p. 144.

9. Merle L. Pribbenon, "North Vietnam's Master Plan," *Vietnam Magazine*, August 1999, p. 32.

10. "Vietnam the Domino That Fell," interview with General William C. Westmoreland, American Legion Magazine, June 1997, pp. 32–57.

11. Davidson, p. 165.

12. Rod Paschall, "Editorial Comments," *Vietnam Magazine*, April 2000, p. 6.

13. *Ibid.*

14. "Transition from Socialist Economy to Market Economy in Vietnam," *Hawaiian Advertiser* (Vietnamese biweekly newspaper in Honolulu), August 15, 1996, pp. 31–32.

15. Mehong Xu and Larry Engelmann, "Chinese Ordeal," *Vietnam Magazine*, October 1993, p. 19.

16. R. Ernest Dupuy and Trevor N. Dupuy, "Chinese Invasion of Vietnam," in *The Harper Encyclopedia of Military History*, 4th ed. (New York: Harper-Collins Publishers, 1993), p. 1525.

17. *Dong De Magazine* (Special edition # 3 by the former ARVN Officers), September 2002, pp. 11–19.

18. Cecil B. Curry and Patrick Barrentine, "A Former Prisoner of War Serves as America's Ambassador to the Socialist Republic of Vietnam," *Vietnam Magazine*, August 1998, p. 55.

19. "Shared Pain of Vietnam Is Recalled," *Honolulu Advertiser Newspaper*, March 14, 2000, p. A7.

Bibliography

English Language Sources

American Legion Magazine. "Vietnam: The Domino That Fell." Interview with General William C. Westmoreland. June 1997, pp. 32–57.

Australian-American Alliance. "Vietnam Period, 1847–1961." Online at *http://www.hotkey.net/au/marshalle/chon01chron01-htm.*

Bradford, Zeb B. "Firsthand Account with Creighton Abrams during Tet." *Vietnam Magazine,* February 1998, p. 47.

Broughton, Jacksel M. "Wasted Air Power." *Vietnam Magazine,* August 1994, pp. 19, 23.

Brush, Peter W. "The Story behind the McNamara Line." *Vietnam Magazine,* February 1996, pp. 21–22.

_____. "The War's Constructive Component." *Vietnam Magazine,* February 1997, p. 70.

Calhamer, Allan B. "It Took Nine Years to Decide to Block Hai-Phong," *Vietnam Magazine,* April 1998, p. 56.

Chapin, J.T. "An American in the War before 1964." *Vietnam Magazine,* October 1995, p. 52.

Chennault, Claire L. *Way of a Fighter.* New York: Putnam's Sons, 1949, p. 342.

Conroy, Michael R. "Trail along the Trail," *Vietnam Magazine,* October 1993, pp. 27, 32.

Crawford, Henry B. "Operation Menu's Secret Bombing of Campuchia." *Vietnam Magazine,* December 1996, p. 27.

Curry, Cecil B., and Patrick Barrentine. "A Former Prisoner of War Serves as America's Ambassador to the Socialist Republic of Vietnam." *Vietnam Magazine,* August 1998, p. 55.

Davidson, A.K. "The Fatally Flawed OPLAN-34A: Commando Raids on North Vietnam Were a Disaster with Lasting Consequences." *Vietnam Magazine,* February 1997, p. 52.

Davidson, Phillip B. *Secret of the Vietnam War.* Novato, Calif.: Presidio Press, 1990.

Deepe, Beverly. "Saigon Telling Officers to Heed U.S. Advisers." *Washington Post,* January 20, 1963.

Dellinger, John. "The War Makers." *Vietnam Magazine,* April 1996, pp. 35, 36, 37, 38.

Donovan, James. "Assessing the War's Costs." *Vietnam Magazine,* April 1996, pp. 42, 44, 45, 48.

Dupoy, R. Ernest, and Trevor N. Dupuy. "Chinese Invasion of Vietnam." In *The Harper Encyclopedia of Military History.* 4th ed. (New York: Harper-Collins Publishers, 1993), p. 1525.

Engelmann, Larry. *Tears before the Rain.* New York: Da Capo Press, 1997.

Fall, Bernard B. *The Two Vietnams.* New York: Frederic A. Praeger Publishers, 1964.

Fifield, Russell A. *The Diplomacy of Southeast Asia: 1954–1958.* New York: Harper and Brothers, 1958.

Fishel, Wesley R. *Problems of Freedom: South Vietnam since Independence.* New York: Free Press of Glencoe, 1961.

Ford, Ronnie I. "The Window of Opportunity." *Vietnam Magazine,* February 1995.

Fowler, Michael R. "War within a War." *Vietnam Magazine,* February 1994, p. 41.

Giap, Vo Nguyen. *People's War, People's Army.* Hanoi: Foreign Languages Publishing House, 1961.

Grayson, Eugene H. "Fall of The Central Highlands." *Vietnam Magazine,* April 1994, pp. 23, 24.

Habid, Phillip. "Peace Envoy's Postscript." *Vietnam Magazine,* April 1993, p. 190.

Hackworth,. David H. "Perspectives." *Vietnam Magazine,* April 1995, p. 32.

Hannah, Norman B. "The Harriman Line." *Vietnam Magazine,* August 1992, pp. 58–62.

_____. "History of Vietnam War: Continuity All the Way from JFK to LBJ." *Vietnam Magazine,* February 1995, pp. 54–58.

Hewitt, Robert L. "Overemphasis on Counter-insurgency Led to the Misapplication of Limited War." *Vietnam Magazine,* June 1993, pp. 58–60, 61, 62. [Hewitt related Harry G. Summers Jr.'s writing.]

Hoang Van Chi. *From Colonialism to Communism.* New Delhi: Allied Publication, 1964.

Holbrooke, Richard. "The Paradox of George Kennan." *Washington Post,* March 21, 2005, p. A19.

Honey, P.J. *Communism in North Vietnam: Its Role in the Sino-Soviet Dispute.* Cambridge, MA: MIT Press, 1963.

Kane, Julie. "Secret Evacuation of the VNN Fleet." *Vietnam Magazine,* April 1995, p. 33.

Kearns, Doris. *Lyndon Johnson and the American Dream.* New York: Harper and Row Publishers, 1976.

Krott, Rob. "MACV-SOG Was Once So Secret That the U.S. Government Denied Its Existence." *Vietnam Magazine*, October 1997, pp. 54–56.

Lam Quang Thi. *The Twenty-Five Year Century*. Denton, Tex.: University of North Texas Press, 2002.

Lancaster, Donald. *The Emancipation of the French in Indochina*. (New York: Oxford University Press, 1961.

Lanning, Michael, and Dan Cragg. *Inside the VC and the NVA*. New York: Faucett Columbine, 1993.

Laurant, Darrel. "Billed as a Symposium, the Hampden Sydney College Gathering Was More Like a Trial." *Vietnam Magazine*, April 1994, p. 62.

Leepson, Marc. "At a Conference on McNamara's Book 'In Retrospect,' Military Heavy-Weights Lined Up to 'Knife the Mac.'" *Vietnam Magazine*, December 1996, p. 62.

Maclear, Michael. *The Ten Thousand Day War: Vietnam 1946–1975*. (New York: Saint Martin's Press, 1981.

Mayers, Samuel L. "Situation in Vietnam." U.S. Senate Committee on Foreign Relations Records, July 30–31, 1959.

McMaster, H.R.: "The Vietnam War Was Not Lost in the Field or by the Media. It Was Lost in Washington D.C., Even before It Began." *Vietnam Magazine*, August 1997, pp. 50, 52.

Meritt, Jane Hamilton. "General Giap's Laotian Nemesis." *Vietnam Magazine*, February 1995, p. 27.

_____. "The Killing Field of Laos." *Vietnam Magazine*, December 1993, p. 49.

Nuttle, David. "The Boun Enao Project." *Vietnam Magazine*, October 1992, pp. 24, 27.

O'Daniel, John. "A Finger in the Dike Is Not Enough." *TVN Magazine*, April 29, 1962.

Paschall. Rod. "Editorial Comments." *Vietnam Magazine*, April 2000, p. 6.

The Pentagon Papers: Senator Gravel Edition, Vol. 1. Boston: Beacon Press, 1971.

Pisor, Robert. "Faking MACV Out of Position." *Vietnam Magazine*, February 1993, pp. 43–44.

Pribbenon, Merle L. "North Vietnam's Master Plan." *Vietnam Magazine*, August 1999, p. 32.

Reeves, Richard. *President Kennedy*. New York: Simon and Schuster, 1993.

Reske, Charles F. "Operation Footboy." *Vietnam Magazine*, October 1995, pp. 30, 33.

Roseman, Samuel I. *The Public Papers and Addresses of FDR*. New York: Harper and Brothers, 1950.

"Shared Pain of Vietnam Is Recalled." *Honolulu Advertiser*, March 14, 2000, p. A7.

Shigenori, Togo. *The Cause of Japan*. New York: Simon and Schuster, 1956.

Smith, Homer D. "The Final Forty-Five Days in Vietnam." *Vietnam Magazine*, April 1995, pp. 47–48.

Sorley, Lewis. "South Vietnam: Worthy Ally?" (General Creighton W. Abrams Reassessing the ARVN). thehistorynet (3–15–03). Online at http://www.freerepublic.com/focus/news/866256/posts.

Stilwell, Joseph B. *The Stilwell Papers*. New York: Sloane Associates, 1948.

Summers, Harry G., Jr. "The Bitter End." *Vietnam Magazine*, April 1995, pp. 42–43.

_____. "Editorial Comments." *Vietnam Magazine*, February 1997, p. 6.

_____. "Editorial Comments." *Vietnam Magazine*, November 1998, p. 6.

_____. *Historical Atlas of the Vietnam War*. Boston and New York: Houghton Mifflin Company, 1995.

_____. "Snatching Victory from Defeat." *Vietnam Magazine*, April 1999, p. 38.

_____. "This Was a World War II Battlefield." *Vietnam Magazine*, February 1998, p. 47.

Szulc, Tad. *The Illusion of Peace*. New York: Viking Press, 1978

"Transition from Socialist Economy to Market Economy in Vietnam." *Hawaiian News* (Vietnamese biweekly newspaper in Honolulu), August 15, 1996, pp. 31–32

Westmoreland, William C. "What Did North Vietnam Hope to Gain with Their 1968 Tet Offensive? Were They after the Cities, or More?" *Vietnam Magazine*, pp. 43–44, 68.

Weyand, Frederic C. "Troops to Equal Army." *Vietnam Magazine*, August 1998, p. 39.

Wilson, William. "The Infamous Pentagon Papers Give Insights into the Johnson Administration's Thinking on the Vietnam War." *Vietnam Magazine*, February 1997, pp. 62, 63.

_____. "The Rolling Thunder Strategic Air Campaign." *Vietnam Magazine*, April 1996, p. 16.

_____. "U.S. Complicity in the Overthrow of South Vietnam's President Made It Impossible to Stay Uninvolved in the War." *Vietnam Magazine*, April 1997, pp. 56, 60.

Xu, Mehong, and Larry Engelmann. "Chinese Ordeal." *Vietnam Magazine*, October 1993, p. 19.

Young, Stephen B. "LBJ's Strategy for Disengagement." *Vietnam Magazine*, February 1998, p. 21.

U.S. State Department, *Foreign Relations of the United States, Diplomatic Papers: The Conferences at Cairo and Teheran, 1943*. Washington, D.C.: U.S. Government Printing Office, 1943.

Zhai, Qiang. *China and The Vietnam Wars, 1950–1975*. Durham, N.C.: University of North Carolina Press, 2000.

French Language Sources

Catroux, Georges. *Deux Actes du Drame Indochine*. Paris: Librairie Blon, 1959.

De Gaulle, Charles. *Memoirs de Guerre*. Paris: Librairie Plon, 1954.

Mounter, Emmanuel. *Le Personaliste*. (Paris: Presses Universitaires de France, 1961.

Nguyen, Kien Giang. *Les Grandes Dates du Parti de la Classe Ouvrière du Vietnam.* Hanoi: Foreign Languages Publishing House, 1960.

"Le Sud-Est Asiatique en Danger." *Revue de Defense Nationale* (Paris), May 1961, p. 785.

Vietnamese Language Sources

Cao The Dung. N.p.: Dong Huong Publishers, 1996.

Chu Ba Anh. "The American Hand and the Death of President Ngo Dinh Diem." *Phụ-nữ Diễn-dãn* (Vietnamese magazine), November 11, 1993, p. 39.

Democratic Republic of Vietnam. *DRVN Constitution.* 1960. Preamble.

Dong De Magazine (Special edition # 3 by the former ARVN Officers), September 2002.

Nguyen Ky Phong, "Vũng Lầy của Bạch Ốc." *Người Mỹ và Chiến Tranh Việtnam 1945–1975.* Centreville, Va.: Tủ Sách Quê Hủỏng, 2006.

Nguyen Van Thieu. "Presidential Last Address [Announcing Decision] to Resign." Saigon T.V., April 20, 1975.

Phan Tan My. "Trận Đánh Trên Đồi Móng Ngựa" ("The fight on Horseshoe Hill"). Special Special piece for "Thiên Anh Hùng Ca QLVNCH." *Mac Phong Dinh,* 2004.

Thuy Khue. "Phong Trào Nhân văn and Giai Phẩm" (The Nhan Van and Giai Pham movement). *Hợp Lưu* (Vietnamese magazine in California), no. 81 (February-March 2005: 5–28.

Tran Trung Dung. "The American Hand and the Death of President Ngo Dinh Diem." *Phụ Nữ Diễn Đàn* (Vietnamese Magazine in California), February 1994, p. 41.

Truong Duong. *Đời Chiến Binh.* N.p.: Tú Quỳnh Publishers, April 1998.

Index